REGIONAL COURTS, DOMESTIC POLITICS, AND THE STRUGGLE FOR HUMAN RIGHTS

Despite substantial growth in past decades, international human rights law faces significant enforcement challenges and threats to legitimacy in many parts of the world. Regional human rights courts, like the European and Inter-American Courts of Human Rights, represent unique institutions that allow individuals to file formal complaints with an international legal body and render judgments against states. In this book, Jillienne Haglund focuses on regional human rights court deterrence, or the extent to which adverse judgments discourage the commission of future human rights abuses. She argues that regional court deterrence is more likely when the chief executive has the capacity and willingness to respond to adverse regional court judgments. Drawing comparisons across Europe and the Americas, this book uses quantitative data analyses, supplemented with qualitative evidence from many adverse judgments, to explain the conditions under which regional courts deter future rights abuses.

Jillienne Haglund is Assistant Professor of Political Science at the University of Kentucky. Her work has been published in *The Journal of Peace Research*, *International Studies Perspectives*, and *Conflict Management and Peace Science*. Haglund is also coauthor of *Violence against Women and the Law* (2015). Her current work has been funded by a three-year National Science Foundation grant.

Regional Courts, Domestic Politics, and the Struggle for Human Rights

JILLIENNE HAGLUND
University of Kentucky

CAMBRIDGE
UNIVERSITY PRESS

University Printing House, Cambridge CB2 8BS, United Kingdom

One Liberty Plaza, 20th Floor, New York, NY 10006, USA

477 Williamstown Road, Port Melbourne, VIC 3207, Australia

314–321, 3rd Floor, Plot 3, Splendor Forum, Jasola District Centre, New Delhi – 110025, India

79 Anson Road, #06–04/06, Singapore 079906

Cambridge University Press is part of the University of Cambridge.

It furthers the University's mission by disseminating knowledge in the pursuit of education, learning, and research at the highest international levels of excellence.

www.cambridge.org
Information on this title: www.cambridge.org/9781108489300
DOI: 10.1017/9781108776561

© Jillienne Haglund 2020

This publication is in copyright. Subject to statutory exception and to the provisions of relevant collective licensing agreements, no reproduction of any part may take place without the written permission of Cambridge University Press.

First published 2020

A catalogue record for this publication is available from the British Library.

Library of Congress Cataloging-in-Publication Data
NAMES: Haglund, Jillienne, author.
TITLE: Regional courts, domestic politics, and the struggle for human rights / by Jillienne Haglund, University of Kentucky.
DESCRIPTION: 1. | New York : Cambridge University Press, 2020. | Includes bibliographical references and index.
IDENTIFIERS: LCCN 2019042265 (print) | LCCN 2019042266 (ebook) | ISBN 9781108489300 (hardback) | ISBN 9781108702317 (paperback) | ISBN 9781108776561 (epub)
SUBJECTS: LCSH: International human rights courts. | International human rights courts–Europe. | International human rights courts–America. | European Court of Human Rights. | Inter-American Court of Human Rights.
CLASSIFICATION: LCC K3240.5 .H346 2020 (print) | LCC K3240.5 (ebook) | DDC 341.4/8–dc23
LC record available at https://lccn.loc.gov/2019042265
LC ebook record available at https://lccn.loc.gov/2019042266

ISBN 978-1-108-48930-0 Hardback

Cambridge University Press has no responsibility for the persistence or accuracy of URLs for external or third-party internet websites referred to in this publication and does not guarantee that any content on such websites is, or will remain, accurate or appropriate.

For Justin and Emerson.

Contents

List of Figures		*page* xi
List of Tables		xiii
Acknowledgments		xvii

1	**Introduction**		1
	1.1	Why Are Regional Human Rights Courts Important for Rights Protection?	8
	1.2	Comparing Regional Courts in Europe and the Americas	13
	1.3	Organization of the Book	20
2	**Explaining Regional Human Rights Court Deterrence**		24
	2.1	Introduction	24
	2.2	Explaining Regional Human Rights Court Deterrence	28
		2.2.1 Two Types of Deterrence	28
		2.2.2 The Deterrence Process	29
		2.2.3 Regional Human Rights Court Deterrence: General and Specific	31
		2.2.4 Regional Human Rights Court Deterrence: Prosecutorial and Social	35
	2.3	Regional Court Deterrence: The Role of the Executive	38
		2.3.1 Executive Implementation of Court Orders	38
		2.3.2 The Executive and Human Rights Policy	40
		2.3.3 The Executive's Trade-Off	43
	2.4	Executive Decision Making	47
		2.4.1 Executive Capacity and Human Rights Policy	48
		2.4.2 Executive Willingness and Human Rights Policy	54
		2.4.3 High Capacity, High Willingness, and Human Rights Policy	69
	2.5	Conclusion	71

3	**Examining Patterns of General Regional Court Deterrence**		76
	3.1 Practices and Procedures of Regional Courts		79
		3.1.1 The European Court of Human Rights	79
		3.1.2 The Inter-American Court of Human Rights	81
		3.1.3 Comparing Practices and Procedures across Regional Courts	82
	3.2 Regional Human Rights Court Effectiveness		85
		3.2.1 Effectiveness versus Compliance	87
	3.3 Examining General Deterrence		91
	3.4 Evidence of General Regional Court Deterrence		97
		3.4.1 General Deterrence through Regional Court Presence	97
		3.4.2 General Deterrence through Regional Court Activity	102
	3.5 Conclusion		107
4	**Does the Executive have the Capacity to Respond to Adverse Judgments?**		110
	4.1 The Role of Policy Change Feasibility		114
		4.1.1 Data and Methodology	115
		4.1.2 Evidence of Executive Capacity: Policy Change Feasibility	122
	4.2 The Role of Fiscal Flexibility		126
		4.2.1 Empirical Models	127
		4.2.2 Evidence of Executive Capacity: Fiscal Flexibility	128
	4.3 Conclusion		132
5	**Is the Executive Willing to Respond to Adverse Judgments? The Role of Mass Public Pressure**		133
	5.1 Data and Methodology		137
	5.2 Regional Court Deterrence Is Conditional on Mass Public Support		138
		5.2.1 The Role of Executive Job Security	138
		5.2.2 Evidence of Executive Willingness: Executive Job Security	140
		5.2.3 The Role of Threats to the Political and Social Order	152
		5.2.4 Evidence of Executive Willingness: Threats to the Political and Social Order	155
		5.2.5 Examining the Conflicting Effects of Mass Public Support	160
	5.3 Conclusion		164

6	\multicolumn{2}{l}{Is the Executive Willing to Respond to Adverse Judgments? The Role of Elite Pressure}	166

Contents

6 **Is the Executive Willing to Respond to Adverse Judgments? The Role of Elite Pressure** — 166
  6.1 Data and Methodology — 172
  6.2 Regional Court Deterrence Is Conditional on Economic Elite Support — 173
    6.2.1 The Role of Economic Elite Support — 173
    6.2.2 Evidence of Executive Willingness: Economic Elites — 175
  6.3 Regional Court Deterrence Is Conditional on Political Elite Support — 181
    6.3.1 The Role of National Judicial Support — 181
    6.3.2 Evidence of Executive Willingness: National Judiciaries — 184
    6.3.3 The Role of National Legislative Support — 191
    6.3.4 Evidence of Executive Willingness: National Legislatures — 193
  6.4 Conclusion — 203

7 **Amplified Regional Court Deterrence: High Executive Capacity and High Executive Willingness** — 207
  7.1 Evidence of High Executive Capacity and Willingness — 215
    7.1.1 Regional Court Deterrence: The Effect of Executive Capacity in the Presence of High/Low Willingness (Hypothesis 8a) — 218
    7.1.2 Regional Court Deterrence: The Effect of Executive Willingness in the Presence of High/Low Capacity (Hypothesis 8b) — 221
    7.1.3 Robustness Tests: Examining Change in Respect for Rights — 224
  7.2 Conclusion — 226

8 **Conclusion** — 228
  8.1 Main Argument and Findings: Summary — 229
  8.2 Comparing Regional Courts in Europe and the Americas — 232
  8.3 Policy Implications: An Effective International Human Rights Regime — 240
    8.3.1 Designing an Effective International Human Rights Regime — 240
    8.3.2 Designing Effective Regional Human Rights Arrangements — 244
  8.4 A Path Forward: Future Research — 246

	8.4.1 General Deterrence and Regional Human Rights Courts	247
	8.4.2 Strategic Regional Court Judges	249
	8.4.3 Complementary or Competing: International and Regional Human Rights Bodies	251
	8.4.4 Backlash in the International Human Rights Regime	252
8.5	Concluding Comments	253
Appendix A	**Chapter 3 Appendix**	254
A.1	Control Variables	254
A.2	Full Model Results	257
Appendix B	**Chapter 4 Appendix**	260
B.1	Control Variables	260
B.2	Full Model Results	264
Appendix C	**Chapter 5 Appendix**	273
C.1	Control Variables	273
C.2	Full Model Results	274
Appendix D	**Chapter 6 Appendix**	292
D.1	Control Variables	292
D.2	Full Model Results	293
Appendix E	**Chapter 7 Appendix**	306
E.1	Control Variables	306
E.2	Full Model Results	307
References		311
Index		323

Figures

1.1	Average respect for physical integrity rights before and after adverse Inter-American Court judgments	*page* 4
1.2	European Court of Human Rights applications and judgments	14
1.3	Adverse European Court judgments by country (1999–2016)	16
1.4	Inter-American Court of Human Rights applications and judgments	17
1.5	Adverse Inter-American Court judgments by country (1997–2016)	18
2.1	Theoretical framework and empirical implications	72
3.1	European Court general deterrence in Poland	77
3.2	Mean physical integrity rights over time in Europe and the Americas	88
3.3	Number of adverse physical integrity rights judgments in Europe and the Americas over time	93
3.4	Number of adverse European Court physical integrity rights judgments (1980–2012)	95
3.5	Number of adverse Inter-American Court physical integrity judgments (1989–2012)	96
3.6	Level of respect for rights in Europe and Americas	98
3.7	Level of respect for rights in Europe by country	99
3.8	Level of respect for rights in the Americas by country	101
3.9	Predicted influence of adverse regional court activity on respect for rights	106
4.1	Number of adverse Civil/Political and Physical Integrity rights judgments in Europe and the Americas over time	118
4.2	Predicted influence of adverse European Court judgments on respect for rights	122

4.3	Predicted influence of adverse Inter-American Court judgments on respect for rights	125
4.4	Predicted influence of adverse European Court judgments on respect for rights across fiscal flexibility	130
4.5	Predicted influence of adverse Inter-American Court judgments on respect for rights across fiscal flexibility	131
5.1	Predicted influence of adverse European Court judgments on respect for rights before election	143
5.2	Predicted influence of adverse Inter-American Court judgments on respect for rights before election	144
5.3	Predicted influence of adverse Inter-American Court judgments on respect for rights two years prior to election / non-election year	146
5.4	Predicted influence of adverse European Court judgments on respect for rights across electoral competitiveness	148
5.5	Predicted influence of adverse Inter-American Court judgments on respect for rights across electoral competitiveness	149
5.6	Predicted influence of adverse European Court judgments across political stability	157
5.7	Predicted influence of adverse Inter-American Court judgments across political stability	159
6.1	Predicted influence of adverse European Court judgments on respect for rights across FDI	177
6.2	Predicted influence of adverse Inter-American Court judgments on respect for rights across FDI	179
6.3	Predicted influence of adverse European Court judgments across judicial power	185
6.4	Predicted influence of adverse Inter-American Court judgments across judicial power	189
6.5	Predicted influence of adverse European Court judgments across legislative opposition	195
6.6	Predicted influence of adverse Inter-American Court judgments across legislative opposition	198
7.1	Testing Hypothesis 8a: Predicted influence of adverse regional court judgments across executive capacity for high and low levels of executive willingness	219
7.2	Testing Hypothesis 8b: Predicted influence of adverse regional court judgments across executive willingness for high and low levels of executive capacity	222

Tables

3.1	Strength of association between compliance and effectiveness	*page* 89
3.2	Mechanisms through which State A is deterred by regional court	92
5.1	Predicted human rights scores in the presence of adverse European Court judgment at different combinations of electoral competitiveness and political stability	161
5.2	Predicted human rights scores in the presence of adverse Inter-American Court judgment, the presence/absence of election, and high/low political stability	163
6.1	Predicted probability of torture following adverse European Court judgments (Article 3 – Freedom from torture) across judicial power	188
6.2	Predicted probability of torture following adverse European Court judgments (Article 3 – Freedom from torture) across size of the legislative opposition	197
6.3	Predicted probability of political imprisonment following adverse Inter-American Court judgments (Article 7 – Freedom from political imprisonment) across size of the legislative opposition	201
8.1	Summary of findings in Europe and Americas	233
A.1	Control variables	255
A.2	The European Court of Human Rights and general deterrence	257
A.3	The Inter-American Court of Human Rights and general deterrence	258
B.1	Control variables	261
B.2	Hypothesis 1: Effect of adverse European Court judgments on civil and political rights and physical integrity rights	264

B.3	Hypothesis 1: Effect of adverse Inter-American Court judgments on civil and political rights and physical integrity rights	265
B.4	Hypothesis 1: Effect of adverse regional court judgments on *change* in respect for civil/political rights and physical integrity rights (3 years postjudgment)	266
B.5	Hypothesis 2: Effect of adverse regional court judgments and fiscal flexibility on respect for rights (1 year postjudgment)	268
B.6	Hypothesis 2: Effect of adverse regional court judgments and fiscal flexibility on respect for rights (3 years postjudgment)	269
B.7	Hypothesis 2: Effect of adverse regional court judgments and fiscal flexibility on respect for rights (5 years postjudgment)	270
C.1	Control variables	274
C.2	Hypothesis 3: Effect of adverse regional court judgments and electoral incentives on respect for rights (judgment 1 year before election)	274
C.3	Hypothesis 3: Effect of adverse regional court judgments and electoral incentives on respect for rights (judgment 2 years before election)	275
C.4	Hypothesis 3: Effect of adverse regional court judgments and electoral incentives on respect for rights (judgment 3 years before election)	276
C.5	Hypothesis 3: Effect of adverse European Court judgments and electoral incentives on respect for rights (interaction term models)	278
C.6	Hypothesis 3: Effect of adverse Inter-American Court judgments and electoral incentives on respect for rights (interaction term models)	279
C.7	Hypothesis 3: Effect of adverse Inter-American Court judgments and electoral incentives on respect for rights using change in respect for physical integrity rights dependent variable	280
C.8	Hypothesis 3: Effect of adverse regional court judgments (1 year before election) and electoral incentives on respect for rights	282
C.9	Hypothesis 3: Effect of adverse regional court judgments (2 years before election) and electoral incentives on respect for rights	283
C.10	Hypothesis 3: Effect of adverse regional court judgments (3 years before election) and electoral incentives on respect for rights	284
C.11	Hypothesis 3: Effect of adverse regional court judgments and electoral incentives on change in respect for rights	285

C.12	Hypothesis 4: Effect of adverse regional court judgments and political stability on respect for rights (1 year postjudgment)	286
C.13	Hypothesis 4: Effect of adverse regional court judgments and political stability on respect for rights (3 years postjudgment)	287
C.14	Hypothesis 4: Effect of adverse regional court judgments and political stability on respect for rights (5 years postjudgment)	288
C.15	Hypothesis 4: Effect of adverse regional court judgments and political stability on change in respect for rights	289
C.16	Hypotheses 3 and 4: Effect of adverse regional court judgments, political stability, and electoral incentives on respect for rights (1 year postjudgment)	290
D.1	Control variables	292
D.2	Hypothesis 5: Effect of adverse regional court judgments and foreign direct investment on respect for rights (1 year postjudgment)	294
D.3	Hypothesis 5: Effect of adverse regional court judgments and foreign direct investment on respect for rights (3 years postjudgment)	295
D.4	Hypothesis 5: Effect of adverse regional court judgments and foreign direct investment on respect for rights (5 years postjudgment)	296
D.5	Hypothesis 5: Effect of adverse regional court judgments and foreign direct investment on change in respect for rights	297
D.6	Hypothesis 6: Effect of adverse regional court judgments and judicial power on respect for rights (1 year postjudgment)	298
D.7	Hypothesis 6: Effect of adverse regional court judgments and judicial power on respect for rights (3 years postjudgment)	299
D.8	Hypothesis 6: Effect of adverse regional court judgments and judicial power on respect for rights (5 years postjudgment)	300
D.9	Hypothesis 6: Effect of adverse regional court judgments and judicial power on change in respect for rights	301
D.10	Hypothesis 7: Effect of adverse regional court judgments and legislative opposition on respect for rights (1 year postjudgment)	302
D.11	H7: Effect of adverse regional court judgments and legislative opposition on respect for rights (3 years postjudgment)	303
D.12	Hypothesis 7: Effect of adverse regional court judgments and legislative opposition on respect for rights (5 years postjudgment)	304
D.13	Hypothesis 7: Effect of adverse regional court judgments and legislative opposition on change in respect for rights	305

E.1	Control variables	306
E.2	Triple interaction model results (1 year postjudgment)	307
E.3	Predicted influence of adverse regional court judgments across capacity and willingness on three-year change in respect for physical integrity rights	309

Acknowledgments

This project represents the culmination of many years of research on the European and Inter-American Courts of Human Rights. I am heavily indebted to my mentors, colleagues, family, and friends for their support throughout the completion of this research. Although there are too many to name here, and I will likely omit someone, I want to extend my gratitude to several individuals who deserve my appreciation and recognition.

I want to begin by thanking my graduate school advisor, Will H. Moore. Will's guidance, direction, and support made the pursuit and completion of this project possible. He spent countless hours not only training me to think like a political scientist, but also helping me develop my ideas, reading countless paper and chapter drafts, and continually challenging me to improve my work. Although Will left this world too soon, his influence on my development as a scholar has been profound, and I would not be where I am without his patience, dedication, and investment in me, both personally and professionally. Thank you, Will, your passionate intellectual pursuits will continue to have a deep influence on my life for many years to come.

I would also like to thank Ashley Leeds, Jeff Staton, and Yonatan Lupu for their participation in a book workshop at the University of Kentucky in the spring of 2018. Their feedback was invaluable in the development of this book. I am so fortunate to have had the opportunity to bring together this group of brilliant scholars to read and comment on the book manuscript. Their ideas and suggestions helped me produce a much improved book manuscript, and I am incredibly grateful.

Further, the research in this book benefited tremendously from the help of many smart and talented colleagues at the University of Kentucky. I am so thankful to Tiffany Barnes for reading every page of my book at various stages, helping me to frame and shape my ideas for a wider audience, and offering me guidance from the early stages of the project to publication. Her guidance, mentorship, and friendship have been invaluable to me as I've worked to complete this book manuscript. I remain greatly indebted for not only her support in the completion of this project, but also her investment in my growth as a scholar. I also owe a big thank-you to Justin Wedeking for reading drafts of all of my book chapters at various stages, offering me guidance and direction, organizing departmental workshops for various chapters, and serving as my formal mentor. Justin's service has not gone unrecognized, and I consider myself fortunate to have such a dedicated faculty mentor in my department. I am also thankful to Jesse Johnson for reading through my chapters and offering me critical feedback at various stages. Opportunities to talk through ideas and discuss challenging issues with colleagues are not always common, and I am so grateful for Jesse dedicating the time to do so over the past several years. I also want to extend my appreciation to Clayton Thyne for participating in workshops of my book chapters over the past several years and offering incredible institutional support as I completed this book. The time you all dedicated to the project has been incredibly valuable in helping me to produce my first book manuscript.

Other colleagues at the University of Kentucky have also been so supportive, and I am grateful for their encouragement and advice: Emily Beaulieu Bacchus, Horace Bartilow, Abby Córdova, Dan Morey, Mark Peffley, Ellen Riggle, Steve Voss, Rick Waterman, and Mike Zilis. I want to also extend a big thank-you to my colleagues and professors at Florida State University, who provided instruction and support as I completed by PhD, including Christopher Reenock, Sean Ehrlich, Megan Shannon, Ryan Welch, and Brian Crisher. Also, Courtenay Conrad, Courtney Hillebrecht, Danny Hill, Chad Clay, Amanda Murdie, and Jackie DeMeritt, thank-you for your feedback on this book project and/or your continued support over the years. I am also incredibly grateful for the support of a fantastic group of scholars, including Cecily Hardaway, April Hughes, Kira Jumet, and Carla Guerron Montero, all of whom provided advice, guidance, accountability, and encouragement as I worked to complete this book.

Finally, I am grateful to my family and friends for their encouragement, support, and kindness to me over the years. I want to extend a big thank-you to my parents, Lyndon and Kathy Kacick, for their unwavering support in my academic pursuits. Also, Kaitlyn, Jake, Brantley, Chase, Jenny, Emily, Nancy, Keith, Amanda, Rob, and Jordan – thank you for helping me to stay focused on the important things in life. Finally, Justin, I am so lucky to have you as my biggest champion, friend, and partner. Not only did you kindly and patiently support me as I wrote this book, but you have helped me with any and all tech support, always offered a listening ear, and stuck by me through thick and thin – I am truly lucky to have you and Emerson (and our pups) in my life.

1

Introduction

In 1980, following a military coup in Bolivia, the Estrada brothers, Renato and Hugo, were detained near a control gate by a Bolivian military patrol while on their way to visit their sick grandfather. State officials proceeded to remove their belongings and beat and torture them. Following the beating, they were transferred by security forces to a military post, and then to a special security office (Scharrer, 2014a). After being sent to the security office, Renato disappeared. Reflecting on the incident, Hugo claims, "Since we entered the [security office], since then, I have never seen my brother again" (Amnesty International, 2014). To no avail, family members appealed to state authorities, requesting information, calling for an investigation, and filing several formal complaints throughout the 1980s. Finally, in 2003, Hugo requested that the Human Rights Commission in Bolivia investigate the disappearance, and in 2004, the Ombudsman of Bolivia filed a petition in the Inter-American Human Rights System on behalf of Renato (Scharrer, 2014a).

After 22 years of repeated state failures to adequately investigate and prosecute those responsible for the torture and disappearance of Renato, the case reached the Inter-American Court of Human Rights. In 2008, the Inter-American Court delivered a judgment, finding that Bolivia had violated several articles of the American Convention on Human Rights, including the right to life and the right to be free from torture.[1] Following the judgment, the state took several positive steps designed to remedy the rights abuse, including increasing resources for the Interinstitutional Council for the Clarification

---

[1] The articles violated included Article 4(1), Article 5(2), and Article 7, among several other articles. *Ticona Estrada v. Bolivia*, Merits, Reparations, and Costs, Judgment, Inter-Am. Ct. H.R. (ser. C) No. 191, 45(Nov. 27, 2008).

of Forced Disappearances (CIEDEF),[2] a necessity for the CIEDEF to carry out its mandate.[3]

Notably, following the Inter-American Court's judgment, physical integrity rights practices improved in Bolivia. The left panel of Figure 1.1 displays Bolivia's physical integrity rights practices before and after the 2008 adverse judgment. Physical integrity rights include freedom from torture, disappearance, political imprisonment, and extrajudicial killing. These data largely represent allegations of physical integrity abuse made in US State Department and Amnesty International human rights reports. Higher values indicate greater respect for rights, and lower values indicate worse respect for rights (Fariss, 2014). As shown in the left panel of Figure 1.1, respect for physical integrity rights was higher in the 4 years following the Inter-American Court judgment than in the 4 years prior, an indication that the adverse judgment deterred the future abuse of rights in Bolivia.

However, adverse regional human rights court judgments do not always deter future human rights abuses. In August 1974, Rosendo Radilla Pacheco, a musician and political and social activist from Guerrero, Mexico, was traveling with his 11-year-old son by bus from Atoyac de Álvarez to Chilpancingo, Guerrero. The bus underwent a search at a military checkpoint. All passengers were evacuated and only allowed to reboard after the search was completed. However, Rosendo was not allowed back on the bus and was arrested for his possession of *corridos*, traditional Mexican songs telling stories about oppression and the life of peasants (Khananashvili, 2014). Rosendo stated that his possession of the songs was not a crime, to which a soldier replied, "for the meantime, you're screwed" (Khananashvili, 2014, 1790). After his arrest, Rosendo was taken to the military barracks of Atoyac de Álvarez, where he was blindfolded and beaten. His family made repeated efforts to find him. Due to the repressive environment in Mexico, however, relatives and friends who worked for the state warned the family that they could face arrest by state officials if they attempted to pursue or formally file a criminal complaint.

It was not until 1992 that Rosendo's daughter filed the first criminal complaint, which was dismissed for lack of evidence. Subsequent complaints were filed every year from 1999 to 2001. After a series of failed investigations

---

[2] The Consejo Interinstitucional para el Esclarecimiento de Desapariciones Forzadas, or CIEDEF, is an institution designed to investigate and search for the remains of victims of enforced disappearances that occurred during the dictatorships of 1967 to 1982.

[3] See *Ticona Estrada v. Bolivia*, Monitoring Compliance with Judgment Inter-Am Ct. H.R., (February 23, 2011).

from 2005 to 2009, Rosendo was not located, nor was justice delivered for Rosendo or his family (Khananashvili, 2014). The case was submitted to the Inter-American Court of Human Rights, and in November 2009, the Court found the state to be in violation of several articles of the American Convention on Human Rights, including the articles guaranteeing the right to life and the right to be free from torture.[4]

Although the torture and disappearance in the case of *Radilla Pacheco v. Mexico* took place in the 1970s, like many cases before the Inter-American Court, the rights abuses addressed in the case were still occurring at the time of the 2009 judgment.[5] In fact, when asked about the relevance of the case to current human rights practices, the legal director of the Mexican Commission for the Defence and Promotion of Human Rights claims, "The Army has a history which has not been addressed ... and this omission is the source of the human rights violations being committed by the military today" (Peace Brigades International, 2010).

There is little evidence that the judgment influenced human rights practices in Mexico. The Mexican legislature paid lip service to the judgment by proposing a reform to the military justice system stipulating that the military should no longer have jurisdiction in cases related to forced disappearance, torture, and rape committed by soldiers against civilians. However, the Inter-American Court stated that the legislative reform did not go far enough. The Court demanded that the military justice system should only be granted jurisdiction over crimes committed by members of the military against members of the military.[6]

Consistent with the observations of the Inter-American Court, the evidence presented in Figure 1.1 shows that physical integrity rights in Mexico did not improve following the *Radilla Pachco v. Mexico* judgment. In fact, physical integrity rights practices declined in Mexico in the 4 years following the

---

[4] The Inter-American Court found Mexico had violated Article 5(1), 5(20), Article 3, and Article 4(10), among several others. *Radilla Pacheco v. Mexico*, Preliminary Objections, Merits, Reparations, and Costs, Judgment, Inter-Am. Ct. H.R. (ser. C) No. 209, (Nov. 23, 2009).

[5] One preliminary objection to the case lodged by the state of Mexico involved the Inter-American Court's jurisdiction: the state alleged that the Inter-American Court did not have jurisdiction in the case because the crime had taken place before Mexico accepted the jurisdiction of the Inter-American Court. The Inter-American Court found that disappearances were an ongoing human rights abuse in Mexico, and dismissed the state's objection. Furthermore, the Inter-American Court drew a distinction between instantaneous acts and continuous acts, or abuses that are ongoing, finding that forced disappearances represent a continuous act.

[6] See *Radilla Pacheco v. Mexico*, Monitoring Compliance with Judgment, Order of the Court, Inter-Am. Ct. H.R., (May 14, 2013).

4   Introduction

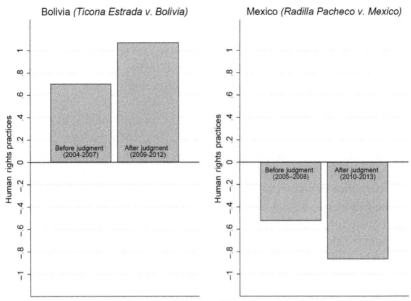

FIGURE 1.1. Average respect for physical integrity rights before and after adverse Inter-American Court judgments

Notes: Figure 1.1 displays the average level of physical integrity rights practices before and after the 2008 adverse Inter-American Court of Human Rights judgment in Bolivia in the left panel and before and after the 2009 adverse Inter-American Court of Human Rights judgment in Mexico in the right panel. Data on physical integrity rights are taken from Fariss (2014) and range from about −2 to +3 in the Americas.

adverse judgment. Moreover, in the year of the judgment (2009), disappearances were only occasionally taking place, but they increased in the years after the judgment (Cingranelli, Richards, and Clay, 2014).

The disparity in human rights practices following the adverse judgments in Bolivia and Mexico is puzzling and raises an important question: *Do adverse judgments rendered by regional human rights courts deter future abuses?* I argue that yes, adverse judgments rendered against a country can deter future human rights abuses, but only when the chief executive has the capacity and willingness to respond to the adverse judgment with human rights policy changes.

This book examines the conditions under which regional human rights courts improve human rights practices. Regional human rights courts render judgments in individual cases of human rights abuse, often because individuals and their families seek justice for a specific human rights violation. However, regional courts have a much broader mandate: Adverse judgments should discourage the commission of future human rights abuses by instilling fear of the consequences of continued abuse, that is, regional courts seek to deter further abuses. In fact, the European and Inter-American Courts of Human rights often require states to undertake measures of nonrepetition, including changes to laws, procedures, and administrative practices, designed to ensure that similar violations do not occur in the future (Hillebrecht, 2014).

A major contribution of this book is the focus on regional court *deterrence*. While many studies focus on compliance with regional human rights court orders (e.g., Hawkins and Jacoby, 2010; Hillebrecht, 2014), in this book, I examine regional court deterrence, or the effectiveness of regional courts. Studying deterrence provides better insight into the broad influence of regional human rights courts on future state human rights practices, as opposed to state compliance with a list of court orders. As I discuss in Chapter 2, there are two types of deterrence, general and specific. With general deterrence, states are deterred when they observe the consequences faced by other human rights–abusing states. Specific deterrence focuses on the rights-violating state; adverse judgments rendered against a rights-abusing state discourage that state from violating rights in the future. In other words, general deterrence captures the influence of the presence and activity of regional courts more generally on state human rights practices, while specific deterrence captures the influence of specific adverse judgments on the adverse judgment recipient's human rights practices. As I argue in more detail in Chapter 2, specific regional court deterrence is more likely to be effective than general deterrence because adverse judgments directly influence the recipient state's expectation of future adverse judgments and the costs thereof.

Despite the important deterrent mandate of regional human rights courts, like the European or Inter-American Courts of Human Rights, they face real and tangible enforcement challenges. States are sovereign, and as a result, there is no authority above the state to ensure enforcement of regional court judgments. The enforcement problem is even greater with respect to international or regional human rights law because international human rights agreements do not govern interactions among states, which often generate mutual cooperative benefits (e.g., trade benefits). Rather, international human rights law governs the state's relationship with its own citizens, and states do not receive the same type of cooperative benefits when they join an international (or regional) human rights agreement. That is, a trade agreement provides trade benefits for member states (e.g., tariff reduction, free trade). States recognize that to receive such trade benefits, cooperation in the trade regime is necessary, as states that fail to cooperate will lose access to such benefits. On the other hand, international human rights law is unique in that states agree to cooperate on policy that is largely domestic – the treatment of their own citizens. The decision by a state to withdraw or threaten to withdraw from the international human rights regime and engage in human rights abuses often has little influence on other member states. As a result, there are fewer mechanisms by which to enforce international human rights law than other types of international law.

As a result of these enforcement challenges, I argue that the chief executive plays a key role in the enforcement of adverse regional court judgments. As head of state, executive responsibility includes ensuring human rights policy changes following adverse regional human rights court judgments. In response to an adverse judgment, the executive adopts, administers, monitors, and enforces human rights policy, all of which are necessary for ensuring greater human rights protections.

That said, I argue that the executive may not make important human rights policy changes following an adverse judgment for at least two reasons. First, human rights policy change is *costly*, as it generates both material and political costs. For example, putting programs in place to monitor the behavior of state agents, like the police, may entail significant material costs (e.g., body cameras). Second, the executive may have *incentives* to maintain repressive policies. The executive often finds repressive policy to be a useful strategy for quelling the opposition, particularly when executive survival in office is threatened. Given the high costs of improving human rights practices and the incentives that executives have to repress, regional human rights courts face clear and tangible challenges to their ability to deter future human rights abuses. I argue that the executive is more likely to make human rights policy changes following an adverse judgment only when the executive has the *capacity* and *willingness* to make such changes.

Because policy change is costly, the executive must have the *capacity* to adopt, administer, monitor, and enforce human rights policy. So, *when does the executive have the capacity to respond to adverse judgments with human rights policy change?* I argue that the executive has greater capacity to protect some types of rights more than others. That is, the protection of civil and political rights is more feasible because it is more directly under the executive's control. Improving civil and political rights does not require the same amount of resource expenditure as improving other types of rights, like physical integrity rights. By analyzing data on adverse regional human rights court judgments involving different types of rights violations (i.e., civil and political rights violations and physical integrity rights violations), I demonstrate that the feasibility of human rights policy change directly influences the executive's capacity to respond to adverse regional court judgments. I further explain that the executive has a greater capacity to respond to adverse judgments with human rights policy change when the state has access to outside resources (e.g., international capital). When the executive has the confidence of creditors, fiscal flexibility to engage in human rights policy change grows. Examining data on state creditworthiness, which represents fiscal flexibility, I demonstrate that the ability to call on outside resources provides the executive with greater capacity to make human rights policy changes in response to adverse regional court judgments.

Moreover, because the executive has incentives to utilize repression, the executive must be *willing* to improve human rights, but *when will the executive be willing to respond to adverse judgments with human rights policy change?* I argue that executive willingness to undertake human rights policy change following adverse regional court judgments depends on pressure from the mass public, foreign economic elites, and domestic political elites. With respect to mass public pressure, the executive is more likely to make human rights policy changes following an adverse judgment when the executive is insecure in office and less likely to do so when the state faces threats to the political and social order. Leveraging evidence from data on election timing and executive vote share, I find that the mass public can generate pressure on the executive to respond to adverse judgments with human rights policy change. Furthermore, analyzing data on political stability and the absence of violence and terrorism shows that the mass public can also generate pressure on the executive to not undertake human rights policy change following an adverse judgment.

As for elite pressure, foreign elites push the executive to engage in human rights policy change following an adverse judgment when they condition access to economic resources on human rights practices. Using data on foreign direct investment, I show empirically that when the executive faces a potential loss of economic benefits, the executive is more likely to respond to adverse judgments with human rights policy change. Similar to foreign economic elites, domestic political elites such as domestic judges and legislators are also capable of generating pressure on the executive to prioritize human rights policy following an adverse judgment. Using data on national judicial power and the number of legislative veto players, I show evidence that under certain conditions, domestic political elites pressure the executive to change human rights policy in response to an adverse judgment. Taken together, focusing on executive capacity and willingness to respond to adverse regional court judgments provides important insights into the puzzle of when adverse judgments deter future human rights abuses.

The theoretical argument in this book stipulates that adverse regional human rights court judgments can deter future human rights abuses, but their deterrent influence depends on executive capacity and willingness to make human rights policy changes. While executive capacity and willingness are important for ensuring regional court deterrence, regional courts are unique institutions with a distinct influence on executive behavior. Although there are many types of international human rights law, regional human rights courts are particularly well suited to deter future human rights abuses. In the next section, I discuss several unique features of regional human rights courts and the important influence regional courts exhibit on state human rights practices.

1.1 WHY ARE REGIONAL HUMAN RIGHTS COURTS IMPORTANT FOR RIGHTS PROTECTION?

As part of the international human rights regime, regional human rights courts play a vital role in ensuring human rights protections. Whereas international human rights law generally plays an important role in setting international standards and encouraging domestic mobilization (Simmons, 2009), regional human rights courts have several unique features that make them particularly important for the protection of rights in the regions in which they render judgments. Regional human rights courts are the only supranational (operate above the level of the state) judicial bodies designed to hold states accountable for human rights abuses by rendering adverse judgments against states.[7] Because regional human rights courts have a truly unique responsibility and function, treating them as though they are roughly equivalent to other international human rights institutions means that scholars and practitioners miss the unique influence of these regional courts on state human rights practices. In this section, I discuss how regional courts fit into the larger international human rights regime as well as the key institutional design features that make regional courts uniquely suited to influence state human rights practices.

Despite the critical role that regional courts play in protecting human rights, like international human rights law more generally, they are unable to do so without domestic actors. International law suffers from an enforcement problem as there is no central authority to enforce legal commitments made by states. Enforcement of international *human rights* law is arguably even more problematic because whereas most international law governs relationships among states, international human rights law governs state-society relations. Enforcement mechanisms like reciprocity and retaliation help ensure enforcement of international law generally because states often receive positive

---

[7] The International Criminal Court represents an international court designed to hold *individuals* accountable.

benefits from their cooperation with other states. For example, membership in an international trade agreement or alliance provides economic or security benefits for both states involved. International human rights law, on the other hand, does not ensure such positive benefits. Rather, international human rights law is unique in that state cooperation involves agreeing to regulate behavior that is largely domestic, or the relationship between the state and society. Given significant enforcement challenges, the impact of international human rights law has been met with skepticism.

International human rights law presents a unique enforcement issue, and I argue that regional human rights courts are particularly well suited to address the enforcement challenge. Regional (or supranational) human rights courts represent international legal bodies charged with the promotion and protection of human rights. Regional human rights courts are *international* in nature, and when states accept their jurisdiction, regional courts have the authority and legal backing necessary to interpret international law (Alter, 2014). That is, regional courts are judicial bodies and have the authority to judge whether state behavior aligns with international law. Regional human rights courts are unique in this regard, as most international human rights treaties do not have corresponding courts with the power to interpret the law. Regional human rights courts are designed to ensure state accountability for human rights abuses. In this way, they are not designed to hold individuals criminally accountable, but rather, they hold states accountable by rendering adverse judgments against states and monitoring state human rights behavior postjudgment. By rendering adverse judgments, regional human rights courts are designed to deter future human rights abuses by the state.

Although there is some evidence that individuals are deterred as a result of domestic and foreign prosecutions (Sikkink, 2011) and as a result of the activity of the International Criminal Court (Jo and Simmons, 2016), the deterrent effect of regional human rights courts has not yet been explored. Regional human rights treaties, and the courts they establish, have been grouped alongside many United Nations treaties and treaty bodies as part of the state accountability model, whereby they represent institutions designed to hold the state, rather than individuals, accountable for human rights violations. Even though regional human rights courts share some similar features with international human rights treaties, regional human rights courts were designed to operate as distinct legal entities. As such, there is reason to expect that, unlike other international human rights treaties, regional human rights courts can deter future human rights abuses in the states where they render adverse judgments.

I argue that there are three key institutional design features that make regional human rights courts particularly effective in deterring future human rights abuses. Three key differences include (1) exclusive membership, (2) mechanism of influence (judgments rather than recommendations), and (3) institutional independence. First, membership in regional human rights treaties that establish regional human rights courts is more exclusive than membership in international human rights treaties. Exclusive membership means that membership is restricted to a subset of states that meet particular membership criteria. By their very nature, membership in regional human rights treaties (and their associated courts) is limited to a specific region. Like committees of experts that monitor compliance with international human rights treaties, regional court justices are relatively removed from the political and social context of countries where they make recommendations or render judgments (Cavallaro and Brewer, 2008). Arguably, however, regional courts are relatively less removed from the states with which they interact than are the committees of experts that comprise international human rights treaty bodies. Inter-American Court of Human Rights justices are nationals of states with membership in the Organization of American States (OAS), for example.[8] As a result, regional court justices have greater familiarity with the domestic legal and institutional structures of the states in which they render adverse judgments, including the public sentiment associated with particular cases and the domestic reception of adverse regional human rights court decisions by the public. Restricting membership to a regional subset of states ensures that regional court judges are more fully aware of interstate nuances and domestic political differences across states and are thus able to take these factors into consideration when evaluating state responses to regional courts.

Second, regional human rights courts have a unique mechanism of influence in that they render *judgments*, which distinguishes them from other international legal bodies like international human rights treaty bodies, which utilize *recommendations* to influence state human rights behavior. Unlike international human rights treaties, regional human rights courts (established by regional human rights treaties), render decisions against the state for specific human rights abuses. That is, regional human rights courts provide clear censure for human rights violations. Legal interpretation by a supranational judicial body, like a regional court, is arguably more difficult for the state to ignore than a series of recommendations from an international treaty body. For a regional court to render an adverse judgment, an individual petition must

---

[8] Though they are nationals of OAS member states, they are charged with international civil service.

1.1 Why Are Regional Human Rights Courts Important?

clear an admissibility stage, meet high standards of proof in a court of law, and be thoroughly examined by a panel of judges, lending adverse judgments substantial legitimacy. To be clear, regional human rights courts *do not* possess strong international enforcement mechanisms, but the clear legal censure provided by an adverse court ruling may be more difficult for political actors to overlook, particularly when compared to recommendations from international human rights treaty bodies. Even the names of the enforcement mechanisms used by treaty bodies and courts invoke distinct responses. *Recommendations* may be likened to suggestions that should be considered by the state, whereas a *judgment* is a final authoritative decision requiring reparations, or actions to remedy human rights abuses. Moreover, civil society actors (e.g., pro-rights advocates) and the public more generally gain more leverage when utilizing an adverse judgment for legal backing than they do when relying on state commitment to an international treaty, increasing their chances of successful mobilization following an adverse regional human rights court decision (Simmons, 2009).

Finally, regional human rights courts are relatively independent international institutions. As interpreters of the law, courts are generally considered to be apolitical in nature, looking to the law (and sometimes legal precedent) and the facts of the case and making an independent determination of whether a violation occurred. The public values the rule of law and checks and balances in government, and therefore values the court, as a means to prevent exploitation by the state (Weingast, 1997). Given that the public's preferences are not necessarily correlated perfectly with the government, the public uses courts as a cue for bad government behavior and as a tool to monitor and sanction that behavior (Carrubba, 2009). Public support is important for courts because it ensures that their decisions are upheld by political actors with enforcement power. Public support is more likely when the court is perceived to be a legitimate actor and when the court operates independent from other political actors.

Unlike national courts, regional human rights courts do not face the same threats to independence from other domestic political actors, such as the executive or legislature. However, regional courts may be susceptible to external political influence because regional human rights courts were, after all, created by states. One of the primary ways states may influence regional court independence involves the careers of judges (Voeten, 2012b, 17). Regional court judges are typically nominated by their home governments and elected by the regional governing body (e.g., Organization of American States). Regional court judges' concern for their careers opens the door to the potential for highly political appointment/election processes in which regional court judges represent the interests of their home country (Posner and Figueiredo, 2005). Furthermore, empirical evidence indicates that regional court justices may fear reappointment concerns for dissenting opinions (Voeten, 2009).

However, regional courts were designed to discourage undue state influence. For example, regional court justices are considered international civil servants and are not representatives of their home state (Pasqualucci, 2003, 10). In addition, European Court judges are nominated alongside two other candidates by their home states and are elected to 9-year nonrenewable terms (as of the adoption of Protocol 14 in 2010) by majority vote in the Parliamentary Assembly of the Council of Europe. The adoption of the fixed nonrenewable terms provides European Court judges substantial autonomy from the influence of their home states, as reelection concerns do not influence judicial decision making in the regional court. Inter-American Court judges are elected by the OAS General Assembly to 6-year terms, with the option of a one-term renewal. Although the Inter-American Court offers renewable terms, Inter-American Court (and European Court) judges are not elected directly by their home governments, which helps ensure that they remain accountable to constituents concerned with the advancement of human rights within the region, and not solely to constituents of their home state. Empirical evidence shows that European Court judges behave impartially in their decision making and are "politically motivated actors in the sense that they have policy preferences on how to best apply abstract human rights in concrete cases, not in the sense that they are using their judicial power to settle geopolitical scores" (Voeten, 2008, 417).

Relatively speaking, regional human rights courts are further insulated from the undue political influence that plagues other human rights institutions, such as the UN Human Rights Council, where states are members of the organization and state foreign ministers participate in meetings. As relatively independent bodies, regional human rights courts utilize the power of information to influence domestic actors. When a regional court renders an adverse judgment against a state, it imparts several key pieces of information to the domestic public and political actors. The adverse judgment communicates to the public and domestic political actors that human rights abuses are detectable. After all, regional human rights court judges evaluate the facts of the case and render an adverse judgment when sufficiently high evidentiary standards of proof have been met.[9] Adverse regional human rights court judgments also provide information on the facts of the case, including the

---

[9] For example, the European Court of Human Rights' evidentiary standards of proof require "beyond a reasonable doubt."

circumstances surrounding the case. This information allows the public and political actors to assess whether or not the abuse was due to a systematic policy failure and the general steps necessary to remedy the abuse. Systematic human rights policy failures often generate many victims, and as a result, adverse regional human rights court judgments also signal that future litigation is likely if human rights abuses continue. Institutional independence provides regional human rights courts with greater leverage to influence state human rights practices than other types of international human rights law.

International human rights institutions vary substantially in their institutional design. By studying regional human rights courts as theoretically and empirically equivalent to other international human rights legal bodies, scholars have missed the importance of key institutional design differences between these legal bodies in explaining variation in their influence on state human rights practices. Because of their more exclusive membership, mechanism of influence (adjudication, rather than recommendations), and institutional independence, regional human rights courts are arguably designed to be more effective in securing rights protections than international human rights treaties. As a result, domestic actors are inclined to take judgments coming from these courts seriously, and understanding when regional human rights courts deter is important for securing and maintaining rights protections globally.

Regional human rights courts, then, have the potential to influence domestic actors, particularly executive behavior. The argument advanced in this book highlights the important role of international political institutions as actors in international politics, as opposed to conceptualizing international institutions as forums designed solely to facilitate state interests or interactions (Gourevitch, 1978).[10]

1.2 COMPARING REGIONAL COURTS IN EUROPE AND THE AMERICAS

In this book, I leverage data on 1,275 adverse European Court of Human Rights judgments involving physical integrity rights violations from 1980 to 2012 and 121 adverse Inter-American Court of Human Rights judgments involving violations of physical integrity rights from 1989 to 2012, as well as human rights data to provide the first comprehensive analysis of the conditions under which decisions handed down by the two most active regional courts in the

---

[10] This has been termed the "second image reversed" as international factors influence domestic politics (Gourevitch, 1978).

world deter future human rights abuses. The activity of the regional human rights courts in Europe and the Americas is unique and unprecedented.[11] Whereas, most research on regional human rights courts focuses on the work or outcomes of one regional court at the expense of the other (e.g., Pasqualucci, 2003; Christou and Raymond, 2005; Cichowski, 2007; Cavallaro and Brewer, 2008; Keller and Stone-Sweet, 2008), I engage in a comparative approach (following Hawkins and Jacoby, 2010; Hillebrecht, 2014) for several reasons.

First, the European and Inter-American Courts possess unparalleled levels of authority and legitimacy in the international human rights regime, outpacing the activity of other regional or international human rights courts around the world.[12] To get a sense of the unprecedented level of activity of the European Court, Figure 1.2 shows the number of petitions alleging

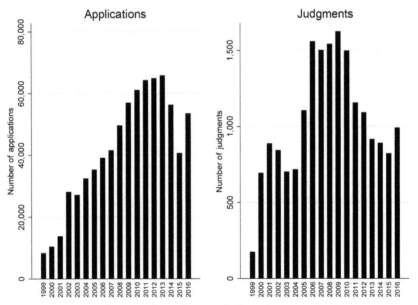

FIGURE 1.2. European Court of Human Rights applications and judgments
Notes: The left panel displays the number of petitions submitted to the European Court each year. The right panel displays the number of adverse judgments rendered by the European Court each year.

[11] The African Court on Human and People's Rights, established in 2004, delivered its first judgment in 2009, finding an application against Senegal inadmissible before the Court. African Court activity continues to increase; however, the AfCtHPR to date has only finalized and closed around 32 cases, making quantitative analysis of this Court's activity inherently difficult.
[12] The African Court on Human and People's Rights is discussed earlier. Similar regional human rights legal bodies do not exist in Asia or the Middle East.

human rights abuses received by the European Court over time in the left panel and the number of judgments rendered over time in the right panel (ECtHR, 2017). Strikingly, the European Court received between 40,000 to 60,000 applications per year over the past decade.[13] Further, the European Court rendered judgments (decisions on the merits) in around 1,000 to 1,500 cases a year over the past decade. Protocol 14, adopted in 2009, streamlined the processing of cases (particularly repetitive cases), by moving cases that deal with well-established case law of the Court more rapidly through a committee of judges in order to allow the Court to deal with the most important cases (Council of Europe, 2004). As a result, the right panel of Figure 1.2 shows a decline in the number of adverse judgments rendered in the past several years.

Beyond the sheer volume of cases, there is also variation in adverse judgments across states. Figure 1.3 shows the total number of adverse European Court judgments for each state from 1999 to 2016. Darker-colored states received more adverse judgments, and lighter-colored states received the fewest adverse judgments. The average number of judgments during the 1999 to 2016 time period was 288, while the median number was 92. The recipients of the largest number of adverse European Court judgments from 1999 to 2016 include Turkey (2,300), Russia (1,580), Italy (1,517), Romania (953), and Ukraine (886). The recipients of the fewest number of adverse European Court judgments from 1999 to 2016 are Monaco (2), Andorra (4), Liechtenstein (7), Iceland (10), and San Marino (10). Some states received few adverse judgments from the European Court because they did not become members of the Council of Europe (and the European Court) until much later in the time series covered by the data (e.g., Monaco), while other states likely received few adverse judgments because they are greater rights protectors (e.g., San Marino).

Like the European Court, the Inter-American Human Rights System has also become increasingly active over the past several decades. The left panel of Figure 1.4 displays the petitions alleging human rights abuses received by the Inter-American Commission, the body that processes human rights petitions, and the right panel shows the number of adverse judgments made by the Court over time. Figure 1.4 shows a steady increase in the number of applications in the Inter-American Human Rights System over time, with over 2,500 applications received in 2016. Judgments on the merits of the case have also grown, with 10 to 19 judgments rendered each year since 2004.

---

[13] The lower number of applications over the past few years may be attributed to the Court joining some applications that raise similar legal questions and considering them jointly (ECtHR, 2017).

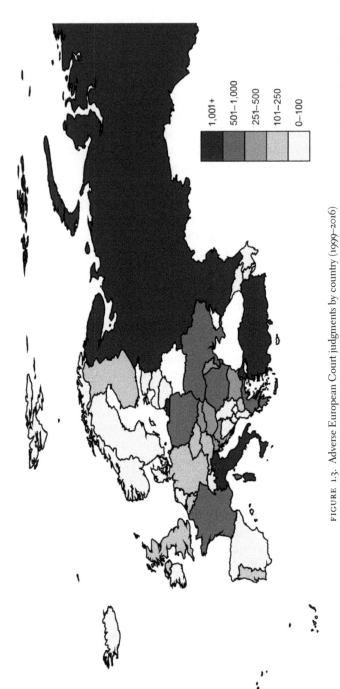

FIGURE 1.3. Adverse European Court judgments by country (1999–2016)

Notes: Figure 1.3 displays the total number of adverse judgments for each state from 1999 to 2016. Belarus and Kazakhstan are nonmembers. Darker-colored states received a greater number of adverse judgments, while lighter-colored states received fewer adverse judgments.

1.2 *Comparing Courts in Europe and the Americas* 17

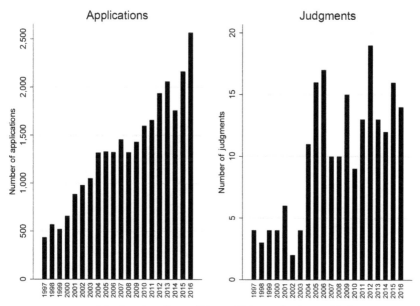

FIGURE 1.4. Inter-American Court of Human Rights applications and judgments
Notes: The left panel displays the number of petitions submitted in the Inter-American Human Rights System each year. The right panel displays the number of adverse judgments rendered by the Inter-American Court each year.

Like the European Court, the number of Inter-American Court judgments varies across states as well. Figure 1.5 shows the total number of adverse Inter-American Court judgments for each state from 1997 to 2016. Darker-colored states received more adverse judgments, and lighter-colored states received the fewest adverse judgments. The average number of judgments during the 1997 to 2016 time period was 9.7, while the median number was 6. The recipients of the largest number of adverse Inter-American Court judgments from 1997 to 2016 include Peru (39), Guatemala (25), Ecuador (20), Venezuela (18), and Colombia (17). The recipients of the fewest adverse Inter-American Court judgments from 1997 to 2016 are Barbados (2), Haiti (2), Uruguay (2), Costa Rica (3), and Nicaragua (3). The smaller number of judgments for each state in the Americas compared to Europe can be attributed to the presence and activity of another institution in the Inter-American human rights system, the Inter-American Commission on Human Rights. The Inter-American Commission examines petitions and makes recommendations to states prior to the submission of cases to the Inter-American Court. The process

FIGURE 1.5. Adverse Inter-American Court judgments by country (1997–2016)
Notes: Figure 1.5 displays the total number of adverse judgments for each state from 1997–2016. Darker-colored states received a greater number of adverse judgments, while lighter-colored states received fewer adverse judgments.

and procedures of the Inter-American Court are discussed in more detail in Chapter 3.

Second, making comparisons between the two regional human rights courts represents a worthwhile enterprise because doing so generates important policy prescriptions. The theoretical and empirical analyses in this book generate policy guidance by identifying the most important actors and institutions in the domestic political process for ensuring regional human rights court effectiveness. Furthermore, drawing comparisons across regions allows for learning and emulation across the two regional human rights legal bodies. That is, where differences in deterrence of adverse regional human rights court judgments exist across Europe and the Americas, learning and emulating the deterrence processes that works in the other region may be beneficial for securing greater respect for rights. For example, the evidence in this book suggests that the executive is more willing to respond to adverse judgments with human rights policy change in states with relatively higher levels of foreign direct investment inflows. This finding suggests that economic incentives are important for generating executive willingness, but this effect is particularly pronounced in states that are economically vulnerable, like many states in the Americas. Importantly, although many states in Europe are not economically vulnerable, economic incentives may play a role in European Court effectiveness in a subset of states in Europe. Moreover, comparing the differences in effectiveness across the European and Inter-American Courts has important implications for the design of international and regional institutions globally. For example, I show that several factors explain deterrence across both regions, like the role of the mass public in generating pressure on the executive to make human rights policy change, suggesting that the mass public may play an important role in deterrence of future human rights abuses by international human rights legal bodies more generally. Because the regional courts in Europe and the Americas operate in different contexts (e.g., level of development, history of abuses, strength of democratic institutions), the policy prescriptions generated from these regions have particular relevance for the proposed creation and establishment of new regional legal bodies in other regions around the world, including when and where they will be most effective.

Finally, despite some differences in the procedures and processes of the European and Inter-American Courts (on which I elaborate more in Chapter 3), the broad mandate of the European and Inter-American Courts is similar – to provide legal remedy for rights abuses and ensure that similar violations do not occur in the future. Importantly, both courts also face the same enforcement challenges. That is, in order to ensure that similar violations do not occur in the future, both regional courts must rely entirely on the state to implement their decisions. The similarities between the European and Inter-American Courts allows me to utilize a comparative research design, whereby the mandate and enforcement challenges faced by both courts is held constant. I am then able to explore the domestic political processes across states in both regions that are subject to each court's jurisdiction.

In both Europe and the Americas, domestic political challenges dampen the ability of the regional human rights court to ensure implementation of their decisions. Current scholarly work highlights domestic institutions that facilitate and constrain the achievement of respect for rights domestically (e.g., Davenport, 2007; Richards and Gelleny, 2007; Powell and Staton, 2009; Simmons, 2009; Conrad and Moore, 2010; Lupu, 2015). Drawing important insights from these works, I develop a theoretical framework to understand how the interests and interactions of various domestic political actors influences the likelihood of implementation of regional human rights court judgments and human rights policy changes in the postjudgment period. Theoretically, I expect the domestic political processes necessary to ensure policy change postjudgment to be similar across regions.

To summarize, making comparisons across the regional human rights courts in Europe and the Americas is appropriate because there are no regional legal bodies in existence today that match the authority and activity of the European Court in Europe and the Inter-American Court in the Americas. The sheer number of petitions received by each body illustrates the importance of regional human rights courts in both Europe and the Americas. Victims of human rights abuse are increasingly accessing these courts in pursuit of justice, and this pattern holds in both developed and developing countries. As a result, regional human rights courts have a unique opportunity to utilize their broad mandate to influence human rights practices and policies in different types of states. Also, drawing comparisons allows for policy prescription, as well as the opportunity for learning and emulation not only in Europe and the Americas, but in other regions of the world as well. Finally, the similar mandates and the similar enforcement challenges of both courts allows me to undertake a comparative approach, drawing inferences across both bodies about their ability to deter future human rights abuses.

1.3 ORGANIZATION OF THE BOOK

In Chapter 2, I lay out the full theoretical argument of the book. I begin by discussing the concept of regional court deterrence. In doing so, I discuss two different types of deterrence, general and specific, and argue that specific deterrence will be more effective in improving human rights abuses than general deterrence. I then elaborate on the role of the executive in the adoption, administration, monitoring, and enforcement of human rights policy, followed by a discussion of executive incentives to make human rights policy changes following an adverse regional human rights court judgment. Next, I discuss the costs faced by the executive for making human rights policy changes and the executive's incentives in maintaining a policy of repression. I proceed with a discussion of when the executive will have capacity to adopt, administer, monitor, and enforce human rights policy following an adverse judgment.

1.3 Organization of the Book 21

I focus on the feasibility of executive policy change and the executive's access to outside resources. Finally, I discuss when the executive will be willing to adopt, administer, monitor, and enforce human rights policy following an adverse regional court judgment. Specifically, I focus on pressure placed on the executive to make human rights policy changes by the mass public, foreign economic elites, and domestic political elites.

In Chapter 3, I draw an empirical distinction between general and specific deterrence and empirically assess general regional court deterrence. In order to examine deterrence by regional courts, it is important to understand how regional courts operate, and as result, I begin this chapter by describing the processes and procedures of the European and Inter-American Courts of Human Rights. Next, I describe the data I utilize in the analysis in Chapter 3 and subsequent chapters. I start with the outcome of interest, human rights practices (dependent variable), which captures regional human rights court effectiveness, or the extent to which the regional court deters future human rights abuses. In discussing effectiveness, I distinguish between two important concepts: compliance with regional court orders and regional court effectiveness. I argue that effectiveness is better captured by studying deterrence and present some descriptive analyses highlighting the difference between these two concepts.

I proceed in Chapter 3 by providing a descriptive summary of human rights practices (an indicator of effectiveness) and regional human rights court activity (judgments) in Europe and the Americas. Finally, I conduct an analysis of *general regional court deterrence*. To do so, I examine the influence of the *presence* of each regional court on respect for rights as well as the influence of the *activity* of each regional court on respect for rights. I conclude the chapter by presenting findings from the empirical analyses, finding little support for the general deterrent effect of the European Court in Europe and some support for the general deterrent effect of the Inter-American Court in the Americas. Given these inconsistent findings on general deterrence, I focus on specific deterrence in the remaining empirical analyses in this book.

Chapter 4 examines the role of state capacity in executive human rights policy change following an adverse regional human rights court judgment. Specifically, I test hypotheses capturing (1) the influence of the feasibility of human rights policy change on respect for rights following adverse regional court judgments and (2) the influence of fiscal flexibility on respect for rights following adverse judgments. With respect to the feasibility of policy change, I find that the executive is more likely to make policy changes that are feasible following an adverse regional human rights court judgment. More specifically, the executive is more likely to make civil and political rights policy changes than physical integrity rights policy changes in both Europe and the Americas. I also find that adverse judgments rendered in states with greater fiscal flexibility are associated with higher respect for rights than adverse judgments rendered in states with lower levels of fiscal flexibility.

Chapter 5 examines executive willingness to make human rights policy change following an adverse regional human rights court judgment as a result of mass public pressure. I empirically examine two hypotheses related to the role of the mass public in generating executive incentives to adopt comprehensive human rights policy change: (1) the role of executive job security as a result of the timing and competitiveness of the election and (2) the role of threats to the political and social order in generating executive incentives to adopt comprehensive human rights policy following an adverse regional human rights court judgment. I find that when the executive is insecure in office (prior to an election), an adverse judgment is significantly associated with human rights improvements. I also find that adverse regional human rights court judgments are associated with higher respect for rights when they occur prior to a *competitive* election. Turning to the second expectation, I find that executive adoption of comprehensive human rights policy is less likely when there are threats to the political and social order, including violence, terrorism, and crime. In considering these hypotheses together, when adverse judgments are rendered prior to an election year in politically stable states, respect for rights is likely to be higher than when an adverse judgment is rendered either prior to a nonelection year or when the state is politically unstable.

In Chapter 6, I examine the role of elites in generating executive incentives to make human rights policy change in response to adverse regional human rights court judgments. I look specifically at the influence of (1) foreign economic elites and (2) domestic political elites (national judges and legislators). First, with respect to foreign economic elites, I show that the threat of losing foreign investment or aid for failing to make human rights policy changes following an adverse judgment can sufficiently pressure the executive to adopt, administer, monitor, and enforce human rights policy. More specifically, I show that states with larger foreign direct investment inflows are more likely to have higher levels of respect for rights following an adverse regional human rights court judgment than states with lower levels of foreign direct investment.

With respect to domestic political elites, I argue and find evidence that national judicial power increases executive expectation of national judicial implementation of regional court orders. Consequently, I find that the executive is more likely to make human rights policy changes when the national judiciary is powerful. However, this finding is stronger and more consistent in the Americas than Europe, which I discuss in more detail in

Chapters 6 and 8. I also show in Chapter 6 that a relatively high number of legislative veto players with preferences different from the executive increases executive expectation of legislative implementation of regional court orders, though the results appear to be conditional on the number of judgments and type of abuse being examined, which suggests that the executive may take cues about the likelihood of legislative implementation from various legislative institutions (discussed more in Chapters 6 and 8).

In Chapter 7, I examine the joint influence of executive capacity and willingness and find that the deterrent effect of regional human rights courts is amplified in the presence of high capacity and high willingness. In other words, in states with high capacity executives, the presence of a highly willing executive amplifies the deterrent effect of the regional court. Similarly, in states with highly willing executives, the presence of high-capacity executives amplifies the deterrent effect of the regional court. However, the results indicate that capacity is more important in the amplification of regional court deterrence for highly willing executives in the Americas than in Europe, which may be due to more extensive capacity limitations in the Americas relative to Europe. I discuss this finding in more detail in Chapters 7 and 8.

Finally, Chapter 8 summarizes my theory and central findings. In this concluding chapter, I bring together the various empirical tests presented in Chapters 3–7 and draw important comparisons across the two regional legal bodies, highlighting the importance of particular actors for the effectiveness of the European and Inter-American Courts of Human Rights. In doing so, I discuss how differences in the domestic political institutional structure in Europe and the Americas or the institutional design differences in the European and Inter-American Courts explain differences in the strength of findings across the two regions. I then discuss several important policy implications that can be gleaned from the research in this book, particularly policy recommendations related to the design of effective international human rights law and regional courts more specifically. Finally, I discuss several important and promising paths for future research.

2

Explaining Regional Human Rights Court Deterrence

2.1 INTRODUCTION

To read the [European] Convention literally (Articles 41 and 46 ECHR, for example), one might conclude that the regime's legal system is primarily geared to delivering individual justice ... however ... today the Court behaves more as a general and prospective lawmaker than as a judge whose reach is primarily particular and retrospective. *(Keller and Stone-Sweet, 2008, 703)*

In May 2007, a bombing in the capital of Turkey (Ankara) killed nine people and injured 121 others. Turkish officials directed blame at the Kurdish rebels, specifically the Kurdistan Workers Party (PKK). Prime Minister Erdoğan suggested that the PKK was the key suspect in the bombing, stating, "We were worried that the terrorist organization could carry out such attacks in major cities" (Hacaoglu, 2007). In response to the looming domestic threats posed by Kurdish rebels, the Turkish government ramped up human rights abuses, specifically targeting (actual and suspected) members of the PKK. For instance, extrajudicial killings in Turkey occurred occasionally in the year of the bombing (2007), but increased in frequency in 2008 and 2009 (Cingranelli, Richards, and Clay, 2014). According to the Turkish government, in addition to the 657 terrorists killed, 49 civilians were killed and 252 injured in 2008. The US State Department noted in its 2008 report, "the number of civilian deaths and injuries significantly increased from 2007" (US State Department, 2009).

In response to the rampant human rights abuses committed by the Turkish government, the European Court of Human Rights has been particularly active in Turkey, rendering many adverse judgments related to systematic executions of Kurdish civilians, as well as the torture, forced displacement, arbitrary arrest, disappearance and deaths of Kurdish journalists, politicians, and activists. Despite these adverse judgments, human rights practices in Turkey remain dismal. In its 2017/2018 annual report on Turkey, Amnesty International noted that "dissent was ruthlessly suppressed, with journalists, political activists, and human rights defenders among those targeted ... and effective investigation of human rights violations by state officials was prevented by pervasive impunity" (Amnesty International, 2017). Because President Erdoğan has incentives to utilize repression to hold onto power, adverse judgments against Turkey have not generated executive incentives to make human rights policy changes.

On the other side of the world, executives have incentives to utilize repressive policies as well. In February 2018, Brazil's president, Michel Temer, issued a decree to put the military in charge of Rio de Janeiro's local police, a step not taken since Brazil's military dictatorship ended in the mid-1980s. Temer's decree was issued in response to rising crime rates in Brazil, particularly following an exceptionally violent Carnival (festival) in Rio de Janeiro, where crimes such as muggings, armed robberies, and violent confrontations ran rampant (Dilorenzo, 2018). In reference to rising crime, President Temer noted, "Organized crime nearly took over in the state of Rio de Janeiro. This is a metastasis that is spreading in our country and it threatens our people. That's why we decided on the [military] intervention ... Our administration will give a tough, firm answer" (Savarese, 2018).

Six months after the military was deployed in Rio de Janeiro, both the number of murders and people killed in police confrontations rose. Between February and July 2018, 738 people were killed in confrontations with the police in Brazil, up more than 35 percent from the previous year (Stargardter, 2018). Pedro Strozenberg of Rio's Public Defender's Office told the Associated Press in August, 2018, "In addition to the rights frequently violated, like entering homes (without a warrant), mistreatment and torture, there is an even more grave situation ... it's (allegations of) homicides, deaths, and bodies hidden in the forest" (Woody, 2018). Furthermore, soldiers who commit crimes (e.g., unlawful killings) during policing operations are not tried in civilian courts, giving the military justice system jurisdiction and substantial control over the consequences of human rights abuses (Savarese, 2018).

In the midst of rampant crimes rates, the Inter-American Court of Human Rights rendered several adverse judgments against Brazil, including the May 2017 *Favela Nova Brasília v. Brazil* adverse judgment, which dealt specifically with the lack of access to justice for the deaths of 26 youths and the torture and sexual assault of three girls during a police raid in 1995. In its ruling, the Inter-American Court recognized that the human rights violated in the adverse judgment against Brazil were part of an overall context of structural violence, specifically noting that "in Brazil, police violence represents a human rights challenge, especially in Rio de Janeiro" (CEJIL, 2017).[1] Despite the Inter-American Court's efforts in 2017, the state of Brazil (under Temer) has deliberately employed policies encouraging repression by state agents.

Repressive policies can be beneficial for executives, like Erdoğan in Turkey and Temer in Brazil, because repressive tactics can increase the chief executive's hold on power, thereby raising the likelihood of executive political survival. Utilizing repressive strategies against particular groups in society allows executives to signal to the public that the state is taking a tough stance on political threats (like in Turkey) or social threats (like in Brazil) in an effort to restore security and order in society. Should an executive make human rights policy changes in response to adverse judgments from a regional court like the European or Inter-American Court of Human Rights, the executive removes the ability to readily rely on repressive tactics in the future. Repressive incentives, coupled with a regional court's lack of enforcement power, give executives few incentives to respond to regional courts with human rights policy change, suggesting that regional courts are unlikely to deter future human rights abuses.

When will adverse regional human rights court judgments deter future human rights abuses? Adverse regional court judgments provide key information about state human rights abuses, and as such, adverse judgments represent a form of naming and shaming by a relatively independent international legal body. However, because international enforcement is weak at best, domestic actors play a key role in ensuring human rights policy change. As a result, the theory I present in this chapter explains variation in the deterrent effect of regional human rights courts as a function of domestic politics. Specifically, the executive acts as the authority on rights-related policy within the state. The executive, then, must find the benefits of making rights-related policy changes in response to adverse regional human rights court judgments to outweigh the costs of maintaining the status quo policy.

In this chapter, I develop a theory that specifies the conditions under which the executive has the capacity and willingness to adopt comprehensive human rights policy in response to adverse regional human rights court judgments. First, I argue that executive adoption of comprehensive human rights policy in response to an adverse regional human rights court judgment is more likely

---

[1] See *Favela Nova Brasília v. Brazil.* Preliminary Objections, Merits, Reparations and Costs, February 16, 2017.

when the executive has the *capacity* to make such policy changes, including the resources and political capital necessary to carry out policy change. Capacity generates greater opportunities to make human rights policy changes. I posit that capacity concerns arise when an adverse judgment involves physical integrity rights, as opposed to civil and political rights, because physical integrity rights abuses require greater capacity to remedy. I also theorize that the executive faces fewer capacity concerns when the state is fiscally flexible and has access to outside resources.

Second, while greater capacity to adopt comprehensive human rights policy is important for regional human rights court deterrence, the executive must also be *willing* to make such policy changes. For an adverse regional human rights court judgment to deter future human rights abuses, domestic actors must utilize these judgments to agitate for human rights policy change. When domestic actors place pressure on the executive to adopt comprehensive human rights policy, executive failure to respond with policy change threatens the executive's political survival. I argue that two sets of actors are important for threatening executive political survival, the mass public and elites. The mass public and foreign and domestic elites act as regional court allies, working to ensure that the executive responds to adverse regional human rights court judgments with the adoption of comprehensive human rights policy.

I posit that the mass public can generate executive incentives to adopt comprehensive human rights policy when the executive is insecure in office, particularly before a competitive election. I also argue that the mass public can pressure the executive not to adopt human rights policy. Public pressure in opposition to the adoption of human rights policy following an adverse regional court judgment is more likely when the state faces threats to the political and social order. Public support for human rights wanes in the face of such threats, which may explain the deterrence failures in Turkey and Brazil. In addition to the mass public, foreign economic elites may condition economic benefits on human rights practices and threaten the withdrawal of investment or aid when the state does not exhibit human rights improvements following an adverse judgment. Similarly, political elites create incentives for the executive to adopt comprehensive human rights policy. I posit that because they are independent and effective, powerful national judiciaries are more likely to implement adverse regional human rights court judgments than weak national judiciaries. I also hypothesize that legislatures with a relatively large number of veto players are more likely to implement adverse regional court judgments because a large legislative opposition is more likely to act as a check on executive behavior. When national judicial and legislative implementation are likely, the executive is more likely to make human rights policy changes in an effort to avoid blame for human rights policy failures.

In what follows, I begin by discussing the concept of deterrence. Drawing on the criminology literature, I apply the concept of deterrence to regional human rights courts. Next, I explain the role of the executive in responding to adverse regional human rights court judgments. I discuss the costs incurred by the executive for making comprehensive human rights policy change and executive preferences for repression. I then describe the influence of the regional court on executive incentives to repress, particularly the role that adverse regional human rights court judgments play in naming and shaming the state for human rights abuses. Finally, I develop several hypotheses related to executive capacity and willingness to adopt comprehensive human rights policy in response to adverse regional court judgments.

2.2 EXPLAINING REGIONAL HUMAN RIGHTS COURT DETERRENCE

In this book, I examine the conditions under which regional courts deter future human rights abuses. In order to examine when regional courts deter, it is necessary to define and conceptualize deterrence. Also, because deterrence has not yet been discussed in the context of regional human rights courts, it is necessary to extend and apply the concept of deterrence to them. Deterrence represents the act of discouraging crime by instilling fear of the consequences. I begin this section by discussing different types of deterrence (general and specific) and the process of deterrence, or the way regional courts generate prosecutorial and social consequences. Although these concepts and processes are developed in studies examining national legal systems, they are largely absent from studies of regional human rights courts. Following a broad discussion of deterrence, I discuss how the two types of deterrence and the mechanisms of deterrence apply to the activity of regional human rights courts.

2.2.1 *Two Types of Deterrence*

The study of criminal deterrence, or the act of discouraging crime by instilling fear of its consequences, has largely focused on deterrence in national justice systems, that is, the deterrent effect of legally imposed punishment on individual criminal behavior. Deterrence theory is based on an analysis of the costs and benefits of criminal behavior by would-be offenders. There are two types of deterrence: general and specific. General deterrence focuses on the prevention of crime by making examples of specific violators. With general deterrence, individuals are deterred when they observe the consequences faced by a specific law violator. Specific deterrence focuses on the individual who committed a crime. Punishment imposed on the law violator discourages that individual from committing criminal acts in the future. Stafford and Warr (1993) put it nicely, stating, "whereas general deterrence refers to the effects of legal punishment on the public (i.e. potential offenders), specific deterrence pertains to the effects of legal punishment on those who have suffered it (i.e. punished offenders)" (123).[2]

With respect to international or regional human rights courts, general deterrence takes place when the presence and activity of the court (globally or regionally) deters the commission of future human rights abuses by state actors. Specific deterrence, on the other hand, occurs when state actors are deterred from permitting or committing human rights abuse following the receipt of an adverse judgment. Studies of international courts and deterrence have largely focused on general deterrence by the International Criminal Court (ICC). For example, one study examines whether ratification of the Rome Statute of the ICC, as well as ICC actions more generally (preliminary investigations and prosecutions), are associated with a reduction in violence against civilians (Jo and Simmons, 2016). The ICC investigates and prosecutes only the most serious of crimes (e.g., genocide, crimes against humanity, war crimes), and although ICC activity has grown, assessing the specific deterrent effect of the court is not currently feasible due to the small number of observations (few convictions) and the gravity of the crimes involved. The ICC has opened investigations in 11 situations, it has publicly indicted 42 people, and three individuals are currently serving sentences.[3] Thus, for the few individuals convicted of genocide, crimes against humanity, and war crimes, most are unlikely to be placed in a position of power to commit such grave abuses in the future. In contrast to the ICC, regional human rights courts render hundreds of adverse judgments against states for human rights abuses short of genocide, crimes against humanity, and war crimes, giving regional human rights courts more opportunities to deter the commission of future human rights abuses in the states where they render judgments.

2.2.2 *The Deterrence Process*

Research in criminology examines whether courts and the punishments imposed in a court of law deter criminal behavior and generally focuses on

---

[2] See also Gibbs (1975, 32–39).
[3] Two others have finished their sentences, one has been acquitted, six have had charges dismissed, two have had charges withdrawn, one has their case declared inadmissible, and four died before trial. See www.icc-cpi.int/Pages/Main.aspx for more on the activity of the ICC.

two deterrent mechanisms: prosecutorial deterrence and social deterrence (Grasmick and Bryjak, 1980; Sikkink, 2011; Jo and Simmons, 2016). Prosecutorial deterrence is based on an individual expectation of future punishment for criminal behavior. In other words, the increased likelihood of punishment or the severity of punishment (including fines, incarceration, or even capital punishment) discourage the commission of future crimes. Criminologists have long debated the mechanism at work in ensuring prosecutorial deterrence, that is, whether the severity of punishment or the probability of punishment deters criminal behavior. However, a growing consensus has emerged that an increased probability of punishment, that is, the swiftness and certainty of punishment, is more important for deterrence than the severity of the punishment (von Hirsch et al., 1999; Nagin and Pogarsky, 2001; Leiman, 2009; Wright, 2010). Arguments highlighting the role of prosecutorial deterrence in the domestic criminology literature have been extended to international courts, specifically the International Criminal Court (ICC), an institution specifically designed to increase the probability of punishment through its authority to prosecute high-level officials for some of the most egregious crimes (e.g., genocide, crimes against humanity, war crimes) (Jo and Simmons, 2016). Empirical evidence indicates that actions undertaken by the ICC deter government officials from engaging in intentional civilian killing, resulting in a reduction in violence against civilians (Jo and Simmons, 2016).

Although studies generally find prosecutorial deterrence or the increased probability of punishment to be an important deterrent mechanism, there is also evidence that social deterrence may also discourage criminal behavior. Social deterrence occurs when legal actions, such as an adverse judgment, signal a violation of community norms and values. A violation of the law can create a social reaction, which may include stigmatization by society and shame for having committed the crime. Individuals may be ostracized or shunned by the community for criminal behavior, and this is often enough to discourage criminal behavior and deter potential offenders (Zimring and Hawkins, 1973). The law itself, and the interpretation of the law by courts, signals information about the norms and values of the community (Kahan, 1997). When an individual violates the law, he or she may face social consequences of an "informal, extralegal character, distinct from the likelihood of formal prosecution" (Jo and Simmons, 2016, 450). For example, individuals convicted of crimes may have more difficulty finding steady employment, are often not allowed to participate in the civic activities of the community, such as voting in elections, and may be required to register publicly as an offender. Turning to international courts, social deterrence appears to also play a role in dissuading the commission of future crimes. For instance, the International Criminal Court's actions are associated with fewer civilian killings by government forces when social pressures generated by the possible loss of foreign aid are present in the state (Jo and Simmons, 2016).

It is important to note the distinction between the concepts of social deterrence and socialization because although both concepts are related to the role of social factors in securing greater human rights protections, they are conceptually distinct. Social deterrence occurs when social consequences associated with breaking the law (i.e. committing a crime) prevent the commission of a crime in the future. Social consequences are generated through observed violation of the law, such as an adverse judgment. Socialization, on the other hand, is the *process* by which acceptable standards of behavior are established and human rights norms are identified, cascade, and become internalized by society. Socialization takes place over a long time frame through social learning about standards of appropriate conduct. Courts may be involved in the socialization process, particularly when they act as a catalyst by setting new legal standards, as was the case during the civil rights movement in the United States. In this book, my focus is not on socialization. Instead, I focus on deterrence, both prosecutorial and social, as a result of adverse regional human rights court judgments.

To extend deterrence arguments to regional human rights courts, in the following section, I first consider the two types of deterrence, general and specific. I argue that specific deterrence by a regional court is more likely to play a role in state human rights behavior than general deterrence. That is, regional human rights court judgments against states are more likely to deter future human rights abuses than the presence and general activity of the court within the region. I then discuss the role of prosecutorial and social deterrence in the context of regional human rights courts. I argue that both mechanisms play a role in deterring future human rights abuses through their effect on state agents and political actors.

2.2.3 *Regional Human Rights Court Deterrence: General and Specific*

General deterrence by the regional human rights court occurs due to the mere presence and activity of the regional court in the region. That is, the establishment of regional human rights courts should influence state human rights behavior. When a state is subject to the jurisdiction of the court and the state engages in human rights abuses, state actors know there is a nonzero probability of being the recipient of an adverse judgment, and political actors may adopt a policy of rights protection to avoid punishment by the court. In contrast to general deterrence, specific deterrence by a regional court occurs when an adverse regional court judgment targeting a specific state influences that state's human rights practices. That is, following receipt of an adverse judgment, the state is deterred by the actual experience of punishment, and, seeking to avoid the costs of future litigation, the state may adopt a policy of rights protection.

In the case of the regional human rights court, I argue that specific deterrence is more likely to deter future human rights abuses than general deterrence. Deterrence is more likely to work when the probability of punishment is relatively high. While the mere presence of the court increases the probability of punishment, the magnitude of the probability remains relatively low. State perceptions of the certainty of punishment are influenced by the presence of the court, but also by their experience with avoiding punishment (Stafford and Warr, 1993). For states that have not experienced punishment directly, their expectation of punishment remains low because only a relatively small number of human rights abuses result in an adverse judgment. The sheer number of petitions considered by the Inter-American Commission on Human Rights and the number of cases the Commission actually submits to the Inter-American Court of Human Rights illustrate the low probability of a petition being heard by the Court. In 2016, the Inter-American Commission received 2,567 petitions, published 5 reports on the merits of the case (including recommendations), and submitted 16 cases to the Court.[4] Whereas the European Court renders more adverse judgments than the Inter-American Court, thousands of petitions are found inadmissible by the European Court and consequently do not result in adverse judgments.[5]

Moreover, potential litigants face numerous hurdles in petitioning the regional court, including high material and legal costs, loss of working hours, as well as stigmatization and social consequences of bringing a case against the state. In addition to these costs, when victims of rights abuses are unsuccessful in petitioning the Court, they may face further ramifications by state officials implicated in the abuse. While the presence of the regional human rights court increases the probability of punishment from zero to nonzero, the magnitude of the increased probability is relatively low, as the likelihood of punishment is small.

---

[4] For more on the Commission, see www.oas.org/en/iachr/multimedia/statistics/statistics.html.
[5] See Figure 1.2 in Chapter 1.

However, regional human rights courts are more likely to influence future human rights practices through specific deterrence. When a state receives an adverse judgment, the probability of future punishment grows because the court (1) signals to the state that human rights abuses are detectable, (2) details the facts of the case in the published judgment, and (3) censures and subsequently monitors the state's violation of international law. First, adverse regional human rights courts signal to the state that human rights violations are detectable and adverse judgments are likely in the future if repressive behavior persists. Oftentimes, human rights abuses, particularly physical integrity rights abuses, are difficult to detect. The availability of evidence in cases involving physical integrity violations is often limited (Lupu, 2013a). For example, victims may not be available for testimony if they are being held by the government or have been killed. Also, the government has an interest in and the ability to hide human rights abuses. In fact, governments have used disappearances in the past as a repressive tactic precisely because disappearances provide greater plausible deniability by government officials. Disappearances in Argentina under the military junta in the late 1970s and early 1980s produced little evidence, as victims remained unaccounted for years later, making government responsibility difficult to determine. Regional human rights courts are legal entities, and as such, evidentiary requirements and standards of proof are higher when rendering an adverse judgment than they are for nongovernmental bodies or international treaty bodies when they generate allegations of abuse.

Legally demonstrating that an offense has occurred requires more extensive information and evidence than the naming and shaming done by nongovernmental organizations (NGOs). Although NGOs have developed reliable techniques to create awareness of human rights abuses more generally, "they are unlikely to be useful as evidence of specific violations of individual's rights" (Lupu, 2013a, 481). When a regional court renders an adverse judgment, it communicates that high standards of evidence were met, and because the court was able to make a legal determination in a particular case against the state, the likelihood of similar adverse judgments in the future remains high if human rights practices remain unchanged.

A second piece of information that adverse regional court judgments provide involves information on the facts of the case. When the regional court renders an adverse judgment, the judgment is published, along with a detailed description of the facts of the case and the events surrounding the human rights violation. Both the European and Inter-American Courts of Human Rights publish judgments in online databases, providing important information to civil society actors, social movements, and other potential litigants. In fact, both the European and Inter-American Courts often require recipient states to publish the judgment as part of the process toward achieving compliance. Information about the case published in the judgment may encourage mobilization efforts seeking to pressure the state (and specifically the executive) to adopt, administer, monitor, and enforce human rights policy.

Third, adverse regional court judgments provide information that the government violated international (and often domestic) law. As a form of naming and shaming, the court calls the state out for violating international law. However, beyond naming and shaming, the adverse judgment moves an alleged abuse into a place of concrete legal enforcement. An adverse judgment is a clear signal that the state has violated international law. In fact, the judgment itself indicates the specific articles and subarticles of the European or American Convention on Human Rights that were violated. An adverse judgment highlights the state's failure to defend international law and the failure of the domestic political process to adequately ensure rights protections guaranteed in international law.

This information increases the monitoring of state human rights practices by both international and domestic audiences. The regional court itself engages in extensive monitoring of implementation of the judgment. For example, the Committee of Ministers of the European Court requires states to submit reports detailing their efforts to implement a judgment and issues recommendations to states that fail to adequately implement the judgment. The Inter-American Court follows up with adverse judgment recipients by releasing compliance reports designed to explicitly note the state's efforts and failures to implement the judgment. The receipt of an adverse judgment ensures experience with punishment and subsequent monitoring, both of which are necessary for specific deterrence.

Empirical evidence also indicates that general deterrence is unlikely to secure human rights protections in the future. As I show in Chapter 3, the establishment and subsequent presence of regional human rights courts in Europe and the Americas have not produced improvements in respect for rights equally across all states in either region. Although data show that human rights practices have improved over time (Fariss, 2014), there is little evidence that the establishment of or membership in regional human rights courts served as a catalyst for this improvement. Notably, the end of WWII brought improvements in human rights to Europe at the same time as the establishment of the European Court. Also, improvements in human rights in the Americas coincided not only with the establishment of the Inter-American Court, but also with transitions to democracy taking place during the same period.

2.2.4 Regional Human Rights Court Deterrence: Prosecutorial and Social

Turning to the mechanisms underlying specific deterrence, I argue that both prosecutorial and social deterrence are important in ensuring future respect for rights. Notably, regional human rights courts are not designed to hold individuals accountable for criminal behavior in the same way that national courts, or even the International Criminal Court, hold individuals to account. I argue, however, that adverse regional human rights court judgments exhibit important prosecutorial and social deterrent effects on two important actors: state agents and political actors.

First, adverse regional human rights court judgments raise the likelihood of prosecution, which influences the behavior of state agents that can be implicated in human rights abuses (e.g., police, prison guards, members of the military). Given this, state agents are likely to be deterred when the regional court renders an adverse judgment against the state. States often must fulfill a specific set of orders designed to remedy the human rights abuse, and these orders may directly implicate individual state officials. For example, a regional court may require the state to prosecute a police chief or military official for the death or torture of an individual in custody. Recognizing that they may be tried (or retried) and prosecuted, individual state agents and members of the security forces may be deterred from engaging in human rights abuses in the future.

In addition to prosecutorial deterrence, adverse regional human rights court decisions may deter state agents through their ability to generate social consequences for the commission of crimes. When the state receives an adverse judgment, state agents responsible for the commission of rights violations examined by the regional court may face extralegal social consequences, including the loss of employment and stigmatization by their community. The adverse judgment, then, generates legal consequences for the abuse (i.e., trial, sentencing), as well as extralegal consequences, such as social ramifications resulting from the abuse. Moreover, the adverse judgment raises the probability that other state agents engaging in similar rights-related behavior will face consequences in the future. Adverse judgments are public, generating a high likelihood of international and public monitoring, and subsequently, increasing the likelihood of future litigation that directly implicates other state agents.

Second, and perhaps more important, adverse regional human rights court judgments deter through their influence on the behavior of political actors responsible for adopting and implementing comprehensive human rights policy. Political actors may be directly implicated in a human rights abuse and face direct punishment, particularly if abuses litigated by the regional court were a matter of state policy. In this case, the prosecutorial deterrence mechanism can be at work, as other political actors choose to distance themselves from a prior ruling coalition by adopting rights-respecting policy, and thereby ensuring future respect for rights.

However, social deterrence mechanisms are particularly consequential for political actors. Political actors may not be directly implicated when a regional human rights court renders an adverse judgment against the state. Instead, political actors can be indirectly implicated by an adverse judgment because the human rights abuse may have been committed on their watch. Similarly, even if a human rights violation was not committed while a particular political actor was in power, that political actor may want to signal to international and domestic audiences that similar human rights abuses will not be committed on his or her watch in the future. That is, regardless of whether political actors ordered state agents to engage in human rights abuses, governmental policy and oversight failed to prevent the human rights abuse from occurring.

Adverse regional human rights court judgments draw attention to failed government policies and oversight mechanisms, and political actors are more likely to be put under the microscope when it comes to rights protection following an adverse regional court judgment. The empirical record notes the important awareness-raising role of international human rights law. Citizens, the media, and opposition parties utilize adverse regional court judgments to pressure the government to change policy. International human rights law raises the rights consciousness of individuals and increases not only the value they place on rights, but also their probability of successful mobilization (Simmons, 2009). International human rights law creates a focal point and generates common goals around which individuals can mobilize (e.g., Carey, 2000; Dai, 2005). Nongovernmental organizations often refer to international obligations when mobilizing and draw on the influence of law to convince actors of the importance of an issue and ensure the state responds (Hafner-Burton and Tsutsui, 2005). Survey research even shows that citizens perceive the human rights conditions in their country more negatively when their country is shamed by the international community for human rights violations (Ausderan, 2014). Perhaps most notably, Hafner-Burton, LaVeck, and Victor (2016) show that activists believe NGOs would be less effective at reducing violations of core human rights in the absence of international law, and they see the most important component of international law as arising from accountability politics. Most research shows that international human rights law has clear effects on various domestic actors. Adverse regional human rights court judgments arguably provide an even stronger focal point for pro-rights advocates to use in mobilization efforts than other forms of international human rights law because adverse judgments represent a clear censure for human rights abuse, whereas international human rights treaties largely specify standards of behavior.

Human rights activists seek to use international law and regional human rights court litigation more specifically, to hold actors to account. As a result, continued human rights policy failures or additional regional court litigation can generate significant social, extralegal consequences such as international and domestic reputation costs. Moreover, political actors face a potential loss of political power for rights-related policy failures. Consequently, adverse regional human rights court judgments may encourage political actors to put mechanisms (i.e., policies/programs) in place to deter the abuse of human rights in the future. Once the state has been the recipient of an adverse judgment, if changes in human rights practices are not made, the likelihood of additional future litigation is high.[6] Given executive oversight of state officials often responsible for human rights abuses, the executive is uniquely suited to adopt policies designed to deter future human rights abuses and may have incentives to do so in an effort to appease international and domestic criticism, hold onto political power, and avoid future litigation.

Although regional human rights courts can exhibit important prosecutorial and social deterrent effects on state agents and political actors, regional human rights courts do not possess formal international enforcement authority. That is, following an adverse regional human rights court decision, there is little recourse internationally if an adverse judgment recipient does not follow through by making changes to human rights behavior. Regional human rights courts, then are unlikely to equally deter future human rights abuses across all states. Adverse regional human rights court judgments are more likely to work through prosecutorial and social deterrence mechanisms when domestic political actors have resources and incentives to make human rights policy change. In the next section, I turn to the role of the executive in responding to adverse regional court judgments. I argue that absent executive capacity and willingness to respond to adverse judgments with human rights policy change, the regional human rights court is unlikely to deter future human rights abuses.

---

[6] The sheer number of repeat or clone cases before the European Court is evidence of the high probability of future litigation when human rights practices do not improve following adverse judgments.

2.3 REGIONAL COURT DETERRENCE: THE ROLE OF THE EXECUTIVE

2.3.1 *Executive Implementation of Court Orders*

The executive is particularly important for ensuring the effectiveness of the regional court. The executive includes the leader and the various bureaucrats and state agents under his/her control. The chief executive plays an important role in regional court deterrence at two stages: implementation of regional court orders (compliance) and human rights policy changes (effectiveness). In this section, I focus on the role of the chief executive in implementing regional court orders tasked to the executive branch (compliance). In monitoring for compliance, the European Court does not give the state a specific checklist of orders with which to comply, but in an effort to ensure compliance, states often undertake some actions that are the responsibility of the executive branch. The Inter-American Court, on the other hand, provides the state with a checklist of steps to be taken to achieve compliance. Inter-American Court compliance orders generally do not name the actor charged with implementation. However, given the content of any individual compliance order, one can determine which state actor is charged with implementation (e.g., executive, judiciary) (Huneeus, 2012). Compliance orders directed at the executive may include tasks such as issuing a formal and public state apology, erecting a memorial to commemorate the victims, requiring large numbers of state officials to attend human rights training courses, or setting up a DNA database to help identify victims (Huneeus, 2012, 124).

The executive may also be charged with the payment of fair compensation (material or moral damages, legal costs and expenses). State compliance with orders requiring the payment of fair compensation is higher than compliance with other types of orders. For example, orders to amend or adopt new legislation (tasked to the legislature) have a compliance rate of 7 percent, and orders to investigate, identify, publicize, and punish perpetrators (generally tasked to the judiciary) have a compliance rate of 19 percent (Hawkins and Jacoby, 2010). Inter-American Court orders requiring payment of compensation (a task often carried out by the executive branch) have around a 40 to 43 percent compliance rate (Hawkins and Jacoby, 2010). Moreover, for Inter-American Court compliance orders tasked solely to the executive, states comply 44 percent of the time (Huneeus, 2012). With respect to the specific order of issuing an apology, states complied with the Inter-American Court 40 percent of the time. Even though compliance with regional court orders by the executive remains below 50 percent, compliance by the executive branch is still higher than compliance by other domestic actors (e.g., domestic judges and/or legislators). Higher rates of observed compliance by the executive branch may be a consequence of the relatively low costs of compliance orders tasked to the executive; Hawkins and Jacoby (2010) argue,

> it is probably easiest for the state to pay monetary damages or apologize and walk away ... although the monetary cost for such damages can be higher than some of the other actions required of states, monetary costs probably do not require as many political capital expenses, coordination efforts, or reputational expenses as some of the other types of reparations. (59)

Still, compliance rates, even by the executive branch, remain low. If international law can encourage mobilization and change citizen perceptions about respect for rights within a country, then one might expect higher compliance rates. However, there are several reasons that, despite the presence of adverse regional court judgments and subsequent compliance orders, compliance remains low. First, compliance orders tasked to the executive do not always entail "easy" tasks or tasks less difficult to implement than those given to other actors (Huneeus, 2012). The executive (and public ministry) is charged with the exhumation of disappeared victims or training state agents in human rights, both of which are costly for the executive branch, both in terms of material resources as well as the political capital necessary to secure such resources. As a result, one cannot assume that executive tasks are inherently easier to implement or that they manifest in lower levels of state human rights violations than orders tasked to other state actors. In fact, research shows that the difficulty of achieving compliance may in part be attributed to the number of political actors involved in the fulfillment of a compliance order. For instance, orders involving three actors – the executive, legislature, and public ministry – achieve a mere 2 percent compliance rate (Huneeus, 2012).

A second reason compliance remains low is because, following an adverse judgment, citizens, the media, and opposition groups are arguably more likely to be aware of human rights practices within the state (the deterrent effect of regional courts) than the level of compliance with specific orders of regional courts. Human rights practices represent an observable indicator of human rights policy changes. Despite executive fulfillment of compliance orders, such as issuing a formal apology or erecting a memorial, I contend that citizens, the media, and opposition groups are more likely to mobilize when human rights practices do not improve following an adverse judgment than they are when the executive fails to fulfill a compliance order.[7] While implementation of orders tasked to the executive branch encourage compliance, I argue that for regional courts to deter future human rights abuses, the executive must do more than implement the court's orders; the executive must make changes to human rights policy, which I discuss in more detail in the next section.

2.3.2 *The Executive and Human Rights Policy*

Executive implementation of regional court orders does not guarantee regional court deterrence or improvements in human rights practices. Although implementation of each compliance order is designed to remedy human rights abuses, compliance with some orders may not ensure that the necessary policy changes are undertaken to ensure regional court deterrence, or the effectiveness of the regional court. *Compliance* is conceptualized as conformity between state actions and a specific legal standard (Raustiala, 2000, 391). Focusing on the concept of *effectiveness* better captures the extent to which regional courts deter future human rights abuses. Effectiveness highlights the degree to which a legal rule or standard induces the desired change in behavior (Hawkins and Jacoby, 2010, 39). Examining the effectiveness of regional court decisions requires exploring the way court decisions translate into the domestic system, including the way regional court decisions inform the decisions of political actors, like the executive (Keller and Stone-Sweet, 2008, 24–26). Neyer and Wolf (2005) present the dichotomy between the two concepts well, noting,

> Compliance focuses neither on the effort to administer authoritatively public policy directives and the changes they undergo during this administrative process (implementation) nor on the efficacy of a given regulation to solve the political problem that preceded its formulation (effectiveness) ... Assessing compliance is restricted to the description of the discrepancy between the (legal) text of the regulation and the actions and behaviors of its addressees. Perfect compliance, imperfect implementation and zero effectiveness therefore are not necessarily mutually exclusive. (41–42)

Notably, scholars find that the modal category of compliance with regional court orders constitutes "partial" compliance (Hawkins and Jacoby, 2010).

---

[7] The extent to which citizens, the media, and opposition group are aware of regional court judgments varies across states. As a result, I take several factors into account in the subsequent empirical analyses to account for variation in public awareness of regional court judgments (e.g., freedom of speech, civil society strength).

In fact, Hillebrecht (2014) argues that states engage in "à la carte compliance, picking and choosing among the various measures," and empirical evidence indicates that states often comply only partially with individual court rulings and inconsistently across rulings (13). In fact, the European Court has a 49 percent compliance rate, and the Inter-American Court has a 34 percent compliance rate (Hillebrecht, 2014, 13). This indicates that states do not comply with individual orders with equal probability and rarely implement all orders from the regional court. In Chapter 3, I empirically examine the relationship between compliance and effectiveness, finding that the correlation between the two concepts is fairly low. The conceptual and empirical distinction between the two concepts suggests that compliance and effectiveness should be examined separately as outcomes of interest.

I contend that adverse regional court judgments are more likely to be effective (i.e., deter future human rights abuses) when the executive adopts and implements comprehensive human rights policy. The executive is primarily motivated by political survival and chooses a level of repressive effort designed to ensure survival in office. Greater levels of repression are valuable for the executive in the face of political instability or conflict (Davenport, Moore, and Armstrong, 2007). On the other hand, lower levels of repression may be more valuable for the executive in the face of international and/or domestic institutional constraints. The executive has substantial authority to regulate the level of repressive effort through (1) the adoption of coherent human rights policy, (2) the administration of such policy, (3) monitoring implementation of the policy, and (4) enforcing the policy. The first step involves executive adoption of a policy to protect rights. That is, the executive must decide to make rights protection a policy objective of the government and back the policy goal with sufficient resources to ensure rights protection.

After the adoption of policy, the second step is administration of the policy. Administration involves the dissemination of policy objectives, goals, and strategies to the various bureaucrats and state agents under the executive branch. Publishing and publicizing the policy are important for ensuring that state agents are informed of new policies and changes from prior policies. Administering and managing the dissemination of strategies designed to implement the policy ensures that state agents, particularly those charged with carrying out human rights policy, are not only aware of the existence of the policy, but also have guidance to carry out the new policy in the field. For example, to effectively administer human rights policy, the state may provide training in human rights to its police and military personnel. Such training programs often seek to help state agents identify and utilize appropriate interrogation techniques and educate law enforcement and security personnel on human rights standards.[8] Training of police and military personnel is important in securing rights protections, particularly by increasing their familiarity with international guidelines and international human rights standards, as well as the way in which human rights standards should be applied in the line of duty (Office of the United Nations High Commissioner for Human Rights, 2002).

Once policy is in place, the third step requires the executive to take proactive steps to monitor policy implementation.[9] Monitoring involves developing rules and institutions to ensure that the work of state agents does not involve human rights abuses. The executive likely does not monitor agents directly, but puts programs in place designed to ensure that policy is being carried out within the agency hierarchy (Alchian and Demsetz, 1972). For example, the executive may utilize on-site inspections of police and prison facilities by independent third parties or establish oversight mechanisms in military places of detention to discourage violations of the enacted policy.

In the final step, the executive engages in enforcement of the policy through the use of carrots or sticks. That is, when monitoring mechanisms find human rights abuses occurring, despite the existence of well-established human rights policy, there are legal repercussions for the abuse. Moreover, when monitoring mechanisms show effective domestic policy implementation and compliance by state officials, there may be rewards for state actors to encourage continued implementation of executive policy (e.g. promotion).

Despite low levels of state compliance, I argue that regional courts can still deter future human rights abuses, under certain conditions (described later). Although compliance with regional court orders and regional court deterrence may trend together (e.g., low compliance = low deterrence), there are reasons to expect that low levels of compliance may not necessarily produce low levels of deterrence as well. Many compliance orders tasked to the executive are important for providing victims with remedy for past human rights abuse and encouraging healing in society more broadly (i.e., paying reparations, erecting a memorial, or issuing an apology), and they are not necessarily designed to prevent future human rights abuses. Consider, for example, a regional court order to exhume the bodies of disappeared victims and return them to their families. Despite not executing this compliance order, the executive could still adopt, administer, monitor, and enforce human rights policy, and thereby

---

[8] Conrad and Moore (2010) call these types of actions *ex ante controls* on the behavior of state agents.
[9] Conrad and Moore (2010) call these types of actions *ex post controls* on the behavior of state agents.

deter future human rights abuses. The executive branch may fail to comply with this order due to the difficulty in locating disappeared victims or victim's families. The failure to comply with this order has little to do with the executive decision to adopt rights-respecting policy. That is, failure to fulfill the order to exhume victims' bodies does not prevent the executive from adopting, administering, monitoring, and enforcing rights policy.

Of course, some compliance orders are important for ensuring deterrence of future human rights abuses. Some regional court compliance orders entail various aspects of this four-step process (adoption, administration, monitoring, and enforcement of rights policy). However, for adverse regional court judgments to deter future human rights abuses, the executive must engage in all four steps: the adoption, administration, monitoring, and enforcement of human rights policy. For example, a compliance order charging the state with providing training to state agents is a part of the administration of human rights policy. However, absent the initial adoption of a coherent policy and subsequent monitoring and enforcement, fulfilling this order may have little influence on future respect for rights.

Importantly, because some compliance orders are designed to remedy past abuses rather than deter future abuses, the level of compliance does not directly influence executive decision making related to the adoption, administration, monitoring, and enforcement of future human rights policy. In other words, low levels of compliance do not necessarily directly inform the extent to which regional human rights courts deter future human rights abuses. Because compliance and deterrence do not necessarily overlap conceptually, understanding regional court deterrence is important in advancing our understanding of the broader effectiveness of regional human rights courts.

Given that executive human rights policy is important for ensuring future respect for rights (deterrence), this raises the question: *If executive adoption, administration, monitoring, and enforcement of human rights policy is important for securing future respect for rights, when will the executive make these policy changes?*

2.3.3 The Executive's Trade-Off

As noted earlier, I assume that the executive's primary interest is to stay in power, that is, to continue to hold the office of the executive. Executive choice of repressive effort is based on the extent to which the use of repression influences the executive's hold on power as well as the perceived costs and benefits of repression. Following an adverse regional court judgment, the executive faces a trade-off. On the one hand, adopting human rights policy change is costly and requires the executive to forgo the use of repressive policy in the future. On the other hand, the adoption of human rights policy appeases international and domestic audiences, thereby removing international and domestic backlash for failing to respect rights. In what follows, I weigh the costs and benefits of human rights policy change following an adverse regional human rights court judgment.

Costs of Human Rights Policy Change
First, continued repression may represent an attractive policy choice for the executive following an adverse regional court judgment because the implementation of human rights policy is costly, and repressive tactics can be a useful policy tool for the executive. The executive often chooses to maintain repressive policies because the adoption of policies designed to protect human rights is *costly* and requires the executive to divert important resources away from the provision of other important public goods necessary for political survival. As a result, the executive considers the material costs of adopting comprehensive human rights policy.

For example, the executive may incur substantial material costs in adopting comprehensive human rights policy and choosing a low level of repressive effort. Although *adopting* comprehensive human rights policy in and of itself may not entail high material costs, administering, monitoring, and enforcing human rights policy is very costly. Take, for example, the administration of human rights policy through executive implementation of human rights training programs for a state's police and military personnel. These programs are designed to train and educate state agents on human rights standards guaranteed in international and national law. Training programs are costly in that their full implementation typically requires the time and resources of many actors, including the support of nongovernmental organizations (NGOs), national human rights institutions (NHRIs), community-based organizations, and other human rights experts (Delaplace and Pollard, 2006).

Further, monitoring state agents is particularly costly for the executive. State agents under executive branch control often possess incentives that differ from the executive (i.e., wealth, survival), and this may drive repressive behavior (Mitchell, 2004). Principal-agent theory stipulates that state agents maintain a significant informational advantage over the principal (executive) because agents carry out policy in the field and are therefore well aware of the manner in which policy is implemented. The agents may choose to withhold certain pieces of information from the executive, particularly information regarding actions carried out in the field that do not coincide with the executive's delegated policy. The executive branch often faces significant information problems as a result. Increased monitoring and auditing of agent activities in the field help to alleviate some of these principal-agent problems, but these types of monitoring programs entail high costs. For preventive monitoring to be effective, it must involve regular in-depth visits to a range of facilities (e.g., remote locations, areas with vulnerable populations, or known places of interrogation), interviews with detainees, and discussions with staff (Bernath, 2010). Monitoring human rights violations may also involve improving the capacity of national human rights institutions (NHRIs) to collect, maintain, and disseminate data on human rights abuses within a particular country.[10] Material costs force the executive to divert important state resources away from the provision of other goods to ensure that state agents forgo the use of repression. By turning a blind eye to adverse regional court judgments, the executive does not have to divert substantial material resources toward stopping repression and can continue to expend resources on programs and policies the executive finds beneficial for maintaining power.

Beyond the costs of human rights policy change, the executive has a political interest in the continued use of repression. Methods of repression vary across states, with some states engaging in particular types of rights violations more than others. The executive values repressive tools as a means to maintain power or remain in office, so much so, that even the presence of particular democratic institutions have little effect on repressive policies when faced with violent internal dissent (Davenport, Moore, and Armstrong, 2007; Conrad and Moore, 2010). By adopting, administering, monitoring, and enforcing human rights policy, the executive is not able to readily rely on repressive policies and tactics that may have been utilized in the past to respond to domestic threats. That is, the executive must consider removing or ending the use of the particular tactics for which the state has been implicated by the regional court.

Forgoing the use of repressive tactics limits executive decision-making power. In order to maintain authority, the executive can choose to adopt other repressive tactics. However, the adoption of other repressive tactics may incur greater material costs. Research shows that international attention for one type of repressive tactic increases the leader's costs for continuing to use that type of repressive tactic (DeMeritt and Conrad, 2019), and as a result, the leader may have to reduce (or eliminate) the use of some types of repressive

---

[10] See www.apt.ch/en\/blog/good-internal-data-systems-are-important-in-prevention-of-torture/#.WYsZiIjyuM8 for more on the monitoring capacity of the NHRI in Timor Leste.

tactics (including those that are less costly) when shamed by the regional court. The material cost related to different types of rights violations make some tactics more cost effective than others (e.g., extrajudicial killing may be less costly than political imprisonment).[11] The choice of a repressive tactic or technique by the executive branch is likely (at least partially) determined by the cost-effectiveness of the tactic. When the executive adopts, administers, monitors, and enforces human rights policy in response to adverse regional court judgments, the executive limits the ability to utilize repression in the future, particularly when the executive's hold on power is threatened. Taken together, the executive faces costs for putting rights-respecting policies in place and often has an interest in the continued use of repression. In the face of an adverse regional human rights court judgment, the executive must balance these costs against the perceived benefits of human rights policy change.

Benefits of Human Rights Policy Change

Given the extant material costs associated with adopting comprehensive human rights policy, the executive's interest in repression as a policy tool, and the weak enforcement powers of the regional court, *how do adverse regional human rights court judgments influence executive decision making?* Moreover, how do adverse regional court judgments shift executive incentives toward making human rights policy change? In order to deter human rights abuse, an adverse judgment must make the benefits of human rights policy change outweigh the costs associated with changing human rights policy and forgoing the use of repression.

As discussed earlier in this chapter, adverse regional court judgments shine a light on human rights abuses by (1) making it widely known that human rights abuses are detectable, (2) producing reliable information on the events surrounding the abuse, and (3) publicly acknowledging that the state violated international law. As a result, an adverse judgment makes human rights issues salient and requires the executive to make decisions about future human rights policy. In making this policy decision following an adverse judgment, the executive considers the extent to which an adverse regional court judgment will influence executive tenure in office. Failure to respond to an adverse regional human rights court judgment can generate international and

---

[11] DeMeritt and Conrad (2019) refer to costs primarily in terms of material costs, rather than political costs. They argue that the *material* costs associated with repressive tactics vary. It may be expensive to imprison individuals, which requires extensive resources, such as food, water, and prison guards. On the other hand, extrajudicial killing may be less expensive, requiring fewer resources.

domestic backlash. Such backlash can threaten executive political survival. International backlash may result in pressure from international organizations, international nongovernmental organizations, and even other states to make human rights policy changes. Domestic backlash can come in the form of public or political elite pressure on the executive to institute human rights policy changes. Because the public generally expects the executive to uphold basic human rights, the failure to do so can result in a general loss of public support and have electoral ramifications. In an effort to avoid being implicated in human rights abuses, political elites may place pressure on the executive to make human rights policy changes in line with an adverse regional court judgment. The executive faces a clear trade-off in response to an adverse judgment: (1) continue to use repression to avoid the costs of policy change and to ensure continued access to repressive policies, while paying the cost of international and domestic backlash or (2) avoid international and domestic backlash by paying the costs of human rights policy changes and forgoing the use of future repression.

2.4 EXECUTIVE DECISION MAKING

In weighing the costs and benefits of human rights policy change following an adverse judgment, the executive can respond in several ways, including (1) ordering the continued abuse of rights, (2) turning a blind eye to rights abuses, or (3) taking actions to prevent human rights abuses (Conrad and Moore, 2010).[12]

The choice of executive policy depends on the extent to which the adverse judgment threatens executive tenure in office. In cases where executive tenure in office is not threatened by an adverse judgment, the executive may respond to the judgment with continued rights abuses or turn a blind eye to human rights abuses (points 1 and 2 listed earlier). Because regional human rights courts do not possess formal enforcement mechanisms, if the state is unwilling to make policy changes following an adverse regional court judgment, the regional court has little recourse to ensure behavioral changes. As a result, I contend that the regional court ruling *alone* does not generate sufficient threats to executive political survival. That is, international enforcement challenges give the executive incentives to ignore adverse regional court judgments.

---

[12] Even though Conrad and Moore (2010) focus on a specific human rights abuse (torture), their argument can apply to most rights abuses, particularly physical integrity abuses (the focus of the analyses in subsequent chapters), as well as civil and political rights abuses.

However, there are several conditions under which an adverse judgment can shift executive incentives toward human rights policy change. That is, under certain conditions, the executive finds responding to adverse regional court judgments by taking actions to prevent human rights abuses (point 3 listed earlier) to outweigh the costs of human rights policy change and forgoing the use of future repression. Generally, conditions that tip the scale toward executive rights protection following an adverse regional court judgment can be placed in two categories: (1) factors that influence the *capacity* of the executive to adopt, administer, monitor, and enforce human rights policy, and (2) factors that influence the *willingness* of the executive to adopt, administer, monitor, and enforce human rights policy. First, when the executive has greater capacity to engage in human rights policy change, the executive is less concerned about the substantial material costs of such policy changes. Higher-capacity executives are more likely to make human rights policy changes because the costs of policy changes do not require the executive to shift resources from the provision of other public goods to ensure human right protections. I argue that when policy changes required by the regional court are more feasible and when the state has access to outside resources, the executive will have a greater capacity to pay the costs associated with policy changes. When executive capacity is low, even a well-intentioned executive is less likely to respond to adverse regional court judgments. In addition, a low-capacity executive with an interest in continuing repressive policies may even appeal to capacity limitations as justification to key constituents for failing to make human rights policy changes.

Second, pressure from domestic actors, including the mass public and elites (foreign and domestic) influence the executive's interest in maintaining repressive policy. When the executive experiences pressure from the general public and elites to make human rights policy changes following an adverse regional court judgment, the executive's political survival may be threatened for failing to ensure human rights protections (e.g., Richards and Gelleny, 2007; Conrad and Ritter, 2013; Conrad, Hill, and Moore, 2017). As a result, pressure from the mass public and elites can shift executive incentives, and create an executive *willing* to adopt, administer, monitor, and enforce human rights policy. In the following sections, I discuss the influence of executive capacity and willingness to take actions to prevent human rights abuse following adverse regional court judgments.

2.4.1 Executive Capacity and Human Rights Policy

Because the adoption, administration, monitoring, and enforcement of human rights policy is costly, the executive must weigh the costs/benefits of ensuring effective human rights policy following an adverse regional court judgment. The adoption of comprehensive human rights policy entails significant costs. For example, putting in place monitoring programs is inherently costly, as is ensuring a system of rewards and punishments for state agents responsible for carrying out policy in the field. In principal-agent theory, the executive may instruct agents regarding human rights policy, and agents may fail to uphold the executive's instructions (termed agency loss) (e.g., Ross, 1973; Moe, 1984). State agents maintain an informational advantage over the executive because they carry out executive policy in the field. If agents do not have incentives to carry out executive policy, there is significant room for breakdown in the implementation of human rights policy. In many states, agents (e.g., police, civil servants) are poorly paid state employees and operate with little oversight; as a result, agents often have incentives to shirk (not carry out executive policy) (Englehart, 2009). This is further complicated by issues such as corruption in state agencies, making it difficult for the executive to maintain control over state agents (Englehart, 2009; Anagnostou and Mangui-Pippidi, 2014).

Although the executive might prefer to put in place comprehensive human rights policy following an adverse regional court judgment, as well as administer, monitor, and enforce such policy, capacity limitations often inhibit the executive's ability to ensure that state agents are effectively respecting rights. That is, the principal-agent problem among the executive and state agents is greater when the state faces capacity limitations. For example, poorly paid police may not share an executive's interest in human rights, particularly if there are financial gains for violating executive policy.

Because the adoption of comprehensive human rights policy is costly, an executive (well-intentioned or not) may not be capable of respecting human rights. As a result, shaming by a regional court is less likely to be effective when the state has limited capacity to make human rights policy changes. State capacity can be conceptualized as the ability of the state to project its power throughout its territory. With limited capacity, the executive is unable to administer, monitor, and enforce human rights policy throughout the country. For example, if an executive cannot monitor state agents in the field due to resource limitations, then there is little opportunity for an executive to put policy in place designed to improve human rights practices (Englehart, 2009). Similarly, states lacking capacity are likely to be bureaucratically inefficient, which makes them less likely to adhere to international human rights law (Cole, 2015). I argue that capacity concerns limit the executive's ability to make human rights policy changes following an adverse regional court judgment.

Capacity limitations inhibit executive human rights policy change following an adverse regional court judgment in two ways. First, given that most executives do not possess unlimited resources, the executive is more likely to make feasible human rights policy changes. Some types of rights are more feasible to remedy than others following an adverse judgment. I argue that capacity limitations are more likely to manifest in physical integrity rights policy changes than in civil and political rights policy changes because adopting, administering, monitoring, and enforcing physical integrity rights policy generates substantial principal-agent issues that must be addressed. Second, capacity limitations manifest when the executive has few resources to adopt comprehensive human rights policy. When the state has little access to additional outside resources (e.g., credit), the executive is less likely to adopt, administer, monitor, and enforce human rights policy following an adverse regional court judgment.

First, while the executive may have reputational incentives to make human rights policy changes in response to an adverse regional court judgment, some policy changes are inherently more feasible than others. Given the executive's prominence on the global stage and the reputation concerns discussed earlier, the executive may *want* to adopt, administer, monitor, and enforce human rights policy in response to an adverse regional court decision. However, executive *capacity* to make human rights policy changes varies by the type of rights abuse (Hafner-Burton, 2008). Moreover, in a similar vein, Voeten (2014) argues that some types of European Court judgments are implemented more slowly by countries because they are more difficult to implement. Consequently, I expect that executive capacity to make human rights policy reforms varies based on the type of rights abuse litigated in a regional court case and what is required of the state to adequately address the human rights abuse.

More specifically, reforms of political institutions, as well as reforms of bureaucratic and administrative procedures, may be easier for an executive to undertake and produce gains in respect for civil and political rights. Actions taken by the executive to guarantee civil and political rights include strengthening the electoral system to ensure free and fair elections, disseminating memoranda on new procedures regarding public access to government information and official documents, ensuring monitoring of surveillance activities and personal data collection by an independent oversight body, removing barriers to freedom of assembly, removing obstacles for electoral registration and the work of NGOs, and ensuring the permission of peaceful protests, among a number of other actions. Such actions may all be more feasible for an executive than reining in physical integrity abuses committed by state agents. The principal-agent problem is particularly problematic when it comes to limiting physical integrity abuses. To reform policy related to physical integrity abuses, the executive must ensure that state agents (e.g., law enforcement officials) are properly trained and educated on human rights standards and practices, as well as perform comprehensive post hoc monitoring of these agents, including places of detention where they work.

Take, for example, the 2006 Inter-American Court case of *Claude Reyes v. Chile*, which involved a denial of an applicant's request to state-held information without a legal basis or written decision explaining the reason for the refusal. The Inter-American Court concluded that Chile had violated Article 13 (freedom of expression), among a number of other articles of the American Convention on Human Rights. The Court then ordered Chile to:

> adopt the necessary measures to guarantee the protection of the right to access to State-held information, and these should include a guarantee of the effectiveness of an appropriate administrative procedure for processing and deciding requests for information, which establishes time limits for taking a decision and providing information, and which is administered by duly trained officials.[13]

In order to ensure that similar rights abuses do not occur in the future, the executive must undertake administrative reforms for processing and deciding on the merit of applications related to access to information. This type of administrative task is within the realm of executive branch control and entails management and administration of new procedures.

Contrast this case with the 2006 Inter-American Court case of *Miguel Castro-Castro Prison v. Peru*. In this case, around 135 female prison inmates, as well as about 450 male inmates, were subjected to violent attacks by prison guards and other state agents for 3 days at the Castro-Castro maximum security prison. Female inmates were subjected to solitary confinement, denial of medical care, humiliation, nudity, and physical and psychological abuse. The objective of state agents in the operation that led to these abuses was the transfer of women inmates to another prison. Many of the women attacked had been accused or sentenced for terrorism crimes or treason. The Inter-American Court found that Peru had violated Articles 4 (right to life) and 5 (right to humane treatment), among a number of other articles of the American Convention on Human Rights. The Court ordered the state to undertake reparations guaranteeing nonrepetition, designed to prevent future violations. Among a number of reparations orders, Peru was ordered to:

---

[13] See *Claude Reyes et al. v. Chile*, Merits, Reparations, and Costs. September 19, 2006. Series C No. 151. Para. 163.

design and implement, within a reasonable period of time, human rights education programs, addressed to agents of the Peruvian police force, on the international standards applicable to matters regarding treatment of inmates ...[14]

For the Inter-American Court to deter future human rights abuses following the case of *Miguel Castro-Castro Prison v. Peru*, the executive must adopt, administer, monitor, and enforce human rights policy. This involves adopting human rights education training programs for Peruvian police (as highlighted by the Inter-American Court), as well as monitoring the behavior of the Peruvian police force and enforcing the new policy (not stated directly by the Inter-American Court). Principal-agent problems can make enforcing human rights policy related to physical integrity abuses problematic, as agents' incentives may differ from those of the executive, and state agents maintain an informational advantage over the executive. Executive policy involves more than adopting and disseminating new administrative procedures; it involves ensuring that state agents understand international human rights standards and how to apply such standards on the job, as well as increasing the costs of violations enough to ensure that agents implement the policy on the ground.

The executive may want to make policy changes in response to an adverse regional court decision in an effort to avoid the extant reputation costs associated with being placed in the spotlight for the human rights abuse. However, executive capacity to adopt, administer, monitor, and enforce human rights policy is greater with respect to civil and political rights violations. Physical integrity rights abuses may be committed by actors who the executive has more difficulty reining in, particularly agents with interests and beliefs that do not align with executive policy. Regional courts, then, are more likely to be effective when judgments involve civil and political rights abuses, as opposed to physical integrity rights abuses. This suggests the following:

Hypothesis 1: *Adverse regional human rights court judgments involving civil and political rights abuses are associated with greater future respect for human rights than adverse judgments involving physical integrity abuses.*

Second, while no executive has *unlimited* resources to respond to an adverse judgment with the adoption, administration, monitoring, and enforcement of human rights policy, the executive's capacity to make such policy changes is

---

[14] See *Castro-Castro Prison v. Peru*, Merits, Reparations, and Costs. November 25, 2006. Series C No. 160. Opr. Para. 15.

greater when the state has *access to additional* resources available to ensure human rights protection. Adopting, administering, monitoring, and enforcing human rights policy is costly and may require the government to reallocate substantial resources away from other public goods to ensure rights protections. Because principal-agent theory stipulates that agents may have incentives to shirk, state agents may have incentives to violate rights. The executive can generate incentives for state agents to carry out human rights policy by adopting extensive monitoring programs and oversight mechanisms. Putting these types of programs in place may be prohibitively costly for some states, particularly states with few resources. When there are few resources available to ensure agents carry out rights-respecting policy, the executive may turn a blind eye to human rights abuses following an adverse regional court judgment and deny knowledge of such abuses. Few resources may also contribute to the executive ramping up rights abuses to silence oppressed groups and individuals. After all, when groups or individuals acquiesce, the executive can expect fewer appeals for better rights protections to the domestic or international legal system.

Access to resources ensures greater state capacity to make rights-related behavioral changes in response to adverse regional court judgments. As a result, it is important to consider the extent to which states can easily access additional resources. Research shows that states with flexible fiscal policies have greater access to resources and are less likely to resort to repressive policies (Clay and DiGiuseppe, 2017). States that hold favorable credit terms have a larger pool of resources from which to draw, including loans from international banks or bond issuances. Access to such resources provides greater fiscal flexibility than lenders of last resort, like the World Bank or International Monetary Fund, both of which place substantial conditions on lending. Sovereign credit allows governments to tap into new resources when there is a shock to the state's revenue or spending, like an adverse regional court judgment, without the strict loan requirements on loans from lenders of last resort. States that confront the demand for new revenue but cannot borrow must draw from other resources, reallocating funds and potentially leaving some government policies and programs unfunded (Clay and DiGiuseppe, 2017). Favorable credit terms offer the state the fiscal flexibility to respond to regional courts by instituting policies and programs designed to avoid agency loss. This argument suggests the following:

> **Hypothesis 2**: *Adverse regional human rights court judgments are associated with greater future respect for human rights when the state has greater capacity.*

2.4.2 *Executive Willingness and Human Rights Policy*

Although greater capacity provides the executive with the opportunity to adopt, administer, monitor, and enforce human rights policy, the executive must also be willing to make such policy changes. When an adverse regional court judgment threatens executive political survival, the executive is more willing to adopt comprehensive human rights policy. However, even though an adverse regional court judgment produces information that generates reputation costs, the judgment alone is unlikely to adequately threaten executive political survival, particularly because regional courts lack enforcement authority. For an adverse regional court judgment to deter future human rights abuses, domestic actors must utilize these judgments to agitate for human rights policy change. Two sets of domestic actors utilize adverse regional court judgments to pressure the executive to adopt comprehensive human rights policy and threaten executive political survival: (1) the mass public and (2) elites. The mass public and elites act as allies that work to ensure that the executive responds to adverse regional court judgments by adopting, administering, monitoring, and enforcing human rights policy. Under certain conditions, both the mass public and elites pressure the executive to respond to adverse regional court judgments with human rights policy change.

Mass Public Pressure and Executive Willingness

First, I argue that the mass public is more likely to influence executive incentives when the executive is insecure in office. The executive's primary motivation is to survive in office, and as a result, the executive must provide some combination of public and private goods to a domestic audience (Bueno de Mesquita et al., 2005). The domestic constituents of the executive demand respect for human rights, as they view human rights to be a critical component of democracy and attribute respect for rights to the national government (Hillebrecht, 2012, 969). The case of Mexico illustrates this claim, as research shows that Mexican citizens are more likely to support their democratically elected leaders when they believe that human rights are respected (Hillebrecht, Mitchell, and Wals, 2015). Human rights, then, represent an important public good provided by the executive in order to improve the likelihood of political survival.

An adverse regional court judgment signals to voters that the executive failed to respect rights. By making human rights policy changes (adopting, administering, monitoring, and enforcing human rights policy), the executive not only signals the importance of respect for rights, but also provides observable evidence of the changed policy as state human rights practices improve. For an adverse regional court decision to influence executive behavior, voters must condition their vote, to some extent, on respect for rights and adherence to international legal principles. Although voters may not make respect for rights a key electoral issue, voting solely according to this preference (Conrad, Hill, and Moore, 2017), international human rights law does play a role in voter behavior.

Empirical evidence finds that citizens do indeed respond to international human rights law and the work of human rights institutions. Research shows that when citizens are exposed to international law, they are less likely to support the use of torture (Wallace, 2013). Moreover, when precision and delegation in international law (i.e., potential for prosecution in an international court) are greater, public support for torture declines (Wallace, 2013). As a result, it is plausible that the activity of international human rights institutions (i.e., regional court judgments) influences public perceptions of respect for rights. That is, when a regional court renders an adverse judgment, public perception of respect for rights within the state declines. The extent to which the public pays attention to regional court litigation is debated, but Hillebrecht (2012) claims that "regular coverage of the Inter-American human rights tribunals in local newspapers and the engagement of domestic civil society groups with the Commission and Court suggest that audiences at home are paying attention to how their elected officials respond to the tribunal's rulings" (969). Taken together, these arguments suggest that voters are exposed to the work of bodies like regional human rights courts and their perceptions of respect for rights changes based on the activity of these international legal bodies.

The domestic environment plays a key role in the level of domestic threat experienced by the executive following an adverse regional court decision. Citizens can hold the executive accountable when they can credibly threaten removal from office. When the executive is directly elected into office by voters, the executive places greater importance on public goods provision, including respect for rights. On the one hand, direct election of the executive may encourage the executive to respond to the regional court by adopting, administering, monitoring, and enforcing human rights policy. Electoral institutions themselves create opportunities for the voting public to sanction leaders for human rights abuses or select leaders into office that are not likely to violate rights (Davenport, 2007). The electoral process may also be beneficial for the protection of rights. National presidential elections can encourage improvements in physical integrity rights (Richards and Gelleny,

2007)¹⁵ by providing an opportunity for open debate on political issues. Presidential elections often stimulate a stagnant political climate, allowing for greater dialogue among the public during elections and renewing interest in government human rights policies and practices (Richards and Gelleny, 2007).

On the other hand, elections may encourage repressive behavior. In countries where leaders are elected, there are often institutions in place that allow for and encourage contestation by the opposition, and the executive may have an interest in repressing the opposition. Also, presidential electoral systems may lead to exclusion of the opposition for fixed periods of time, creating a lack of executive accountability mechanisms and an increased probability of dissent by opposition groups (Richards and Gelleny, 2007). In the face of greater dissent, the office of president carries with it substantial independent power, which may encourage a governmental policy of repression in response to dissent (Richards and Gelleny, 2007). Moreover, recent research shows that the electorate does not inherently value rights protection for the population at large, but rather, individuals prefer that his/her *own rights* are not violated (Conrad, Hill, and Moore, 2017). As such, leaders may not be willing to change repressive policies in the presence of electoral contestation unless "a sufficient number of voters are willing to cast their ballot on that issue" (Conrad, Hill, and Moore, 2017, 5).¹⁶

Based on the conflicting findings of prior research, I argue that the role of executive elections on respect for rights is conditional on international human rights legal principles (like an adverse regional court judgment) and executive job security. With respect to the first condition, as noted earlier, research shows that following exposure to international law, the public is less likely to support the use of torture (Wallace, 2013). An adverse regional court decision represents a clear legal censure for rights abuse by an international body, which arguably influences voter perceptions and preferences for greater rights protection (Hillebrecht, 2012). Regarding the second condition, executive job security, I argue that the timing of elections plays a key role in whether the executive has incentives to appeal to large swaths of the population through greater rights protection. In the preelectoral period, the executive has incentives to appeal to the electorate at large, and if the state has been the recipient of an adverse regional court decision during this period, the executive has incentives to make policy changes before the election. However, in the postelectoral period, the

---

¹⁵ Even though Richards and Gelleny (2007) only focus on presidential elections, the arguments can plausibly be extended to elected officials in parliamentary systems as well.

¹⁶ Conrad, Hill, and Moore (2017) argue that voters are willing to tolerate repression of groups that are thought to be threatening (e.g., criminals, dissidents, marginalized individuals).

executive has few incentives to make policy changes in response to an adverse regional court judgment, as the executive is more secure in office.

As an example of the role of the election cycle in executive incentives, consider the 2006 Inter-American Court case of *Ximenes Lopes v. Brazil*. The victim, Damião Ximenes Lopes, was placed in the care of the Clinica de Repouso Guarapes in 1999 by his mother as a result of his psychiatric disorder. He died after being subjected to ill treatment and attacks from the clinic personnel 3 days after he was admitted. The Inter-American Court decided that Brazil was guilty of violating the physical integrity rights of the victim, as well as the right to access to justice and due process for the victim's family. The case generated a great deal of domestic interest, particularly from a state human rights commission, human rights organizations, psychiatric professionals, and the media (Cavallaro and Brewer, 2008, 790). The adverse Inter-American Court decision stimulated debate about public healthcare in Brazil and provided increased leverage for domestic groups to pressure the government to engage in policy change. Importantly, elections also took place in Brazil in 2006, and a runoff presidential election was held in October between incumbent Lula da Silva and challenger Geraldo Alckmin, in which the incumbent won a new 4-year term in office. According to repression data created by Fariss (2014), repression in the election year (2006) was lower than the average level of repression in the previous 5 years (2001–2005).[17] While this anecdote is simply illustrative, it does provide initial evidence of the importance of executive human rights policy change in response to an adverse regional court decision during an executive electoral cycle. The theoretical arguments and anecdotal evidence suggest the following:

Hypothesis 3: *Adverse regional human rights court judgments are associated with greater future respect for human rights in states where the executive is insecure in office.*

Second, the mass public can influence executive willingness to respond to adverse regional court judgments when the state faces threats to the political and social order. Threats to the political order include politically motivated violence, such as terrorism, while threats to the social order include violence more generally, such as violent crime. Unlike elections, however, in the face of threats to the political and social order, I argue that the executive has fewer incentives to adopt comprehensive human rights policy following an adverse regional court judgment. First, threats to the political and social order directly

---

[17] More specifically, the physical integrity rights score in 2006 was −0.996, while the average physical integrity rights score from 2001 to 2005 was −1.004 (Fariss, 2014).

threaten the executive's hold on power, and the executive is more likely to use repression, including physical integrity abuses, to quell the opposition (e.g., Davenport, 2007). Second, when the state faces political threats, the public may broadly support the abuse of rights under some circumstances. Torture, for example, largely targets particular subsets of the population, including marginalized groups, criminals, and dissidents (Rejali, 2007). When citizens demand protection from members of groups that they perceive to be threatening to the legal, social, or political order, elected officials have incentives to use repression to abuse weak and often disenfranchised groups (Conrad, Hill, and Moore, 2017, 2).

Public opinion research further supports this claim, showing that while just over 50 percent of Americans oppose the government's use of torture, Americans are considerably more supportive of government use of torture when it targets individuals who they perceive as threatening (e.g., detainees with an Arabic name and detainees suspected of terrorism) (Conrad et al., 2017). Because elected officials are accountable to voting constituents, they are highly sensitive to the public's perception of threatening groups in society. Criminals, dissidents, and marginalized individuals are the groups in society that are most likely to be tortured (Rejali, 2007) and because the public is more likely to find these groups threatening, the median voter will not prefer to protect the rights of individuals most at risk of torture. Elected officials, then, may prefer to utilize torture to signal to the voting public that they are taking a strong stance against threatening groups (Conrad, Hill, and Moore, 2017).[18]

For example, consider Trinidad and Tobago, a state that officially withdrew from the jurisdiction of the Inter-American Court over conflict involving Article 4 of the ACHR. In the 2002 case of *Hilare, Constantine and Benjamin v. Trinidad and Tobago*, the Inter-American Court found that the mandatory death penalty for those convicted of murder in Trinidad and Tobago violated the prohibition against the arbitrary deprivation of life in Article 4(1) and 4(2) of the American Convention. The Inter-American Court ordered Trinidad and Tobago to undertake several reforms designed to end the use of the death penalty, including reforming current legislation. The reform aimed to establish different categories or criminal classes for murder, in order to "ensure that the severity of the punishment is commensurate with the gravity of the act and the criminal culpability of the accused."[19] However, such legislation was not passed by the legislature or initiated by the executive.

---

[18] In fact, Conrad, Hill, and Moore (2017) find that electoral contestation is associated with a greater use of scarring torture (torture that leaves evidence of abuse on the body).

[19] See *Hilaire, Constantine, and Benjamin et al. v. Trinidad and Tobago*. Merits, Costs, and Reparations, June 21, 2002.

2.4 Executive Decision Making

Notably, the high murder rate in Trinidad and Tobago contributed to the formation of a public supportive of capital punishment as a way to remedy (and deter) the problem of murder on the island.[20] Trinidad and Tobago officially denounced the American Convention on Human Rights in 1999 and rejected the provisional measures ordered by the Inter-American Court in death penalty cases (Pasqualucci, 2003, 344). Given that the executive finds public support crucial to survive in office, executives pay close attention to public opinion regarding salient issues, including the extent to which the public perceives the presence of threats in society and whether court judgments conflict with public sentiment (Vanberg, 2005, 46).[21]

Following an adverse regional court judgment on a controversial human rights issue (like *Hilare, Constantine and Benjamin v. Trinidad and Tobago*), the executive is faced with two competing pressures, including (1) the adverse regional court judgment and (2) the public's perception of the domestic threat. The regional court sends a signal of government failure to respect rights, and the executive is directly responsible for the adoption of comprehensive human rights policy. The public's general concern for rights protection may make executive policy change likely. However, the executive is also concerned about the public's perception of national security and domestic threats. Importantly, in some states, the public may support the use of repression targeting subsets of the population. When there is a substantial threat to political and social order, the public is likely to support elected officials and leaders engaging in a policy of repression in the name of national security. The executive, then, is unlikely to make policy changes. However, when threats to political and social order are lower, the public is more likely to oppose human rights abuse, and the executive is more likely to undertake comprehensive human rights policy changes in response to an adverse regional court judgment. More specifically, I posit:

Hypothesis 4: *Adverse regional human rights court judgments are associated with greater future respect for human rights when there are few threats to political and social order.*

---

[20] In fact, one survey conducted by the Death Penalty Project indicated that 91 percent of Trinidad and Tobago's population support capital punishment (Hood and Seemungal, 2010).

[21] Where the public does not provide specific support for the (regional) court, implementing specific adverse regional court decisions becomes relatively more costly. If the public does not back the specific regional court decision, the public often continues to provide diffuse support for the regional court, or "general support for an institution qua institution, divorced from immediate reference to specific policy outputs" (Vanberg, 2005, 49). Although Vanberg (2005) refers specifically to domestic courts, specific and diffuse support can be extended to arguments regarding regional courts as well, as regional courts are likely to rely on the support of the public, particularly diffuse support, to ensure their legitimacy.

Notably, mass public pressure can exhibit conflicting effects on executive behavior. In the face of electoral incentives, I argue that the executive is more likely to make human rights policy changes following an adverse judgment. However, the presence of political and social threats are unlikely to generate public pressure on the executive to initiate human rights policy changes. In considering these two competing pressures on the executive together, I expect that the presence of an election is more likely to be effective in generating executive incentives to respect rights when threats to the political and social order are low. The presence of an adverse judgment prior to an election when threats to the political and social order are high is unlikely to generate executive willingness to make human rights policy changes. In fact, the executive may have incentives to ramp up human rights abuses prior to an election when political and social threats are high as a means to signal to the electorate that the executive is adequately dealing with such threats. I find support for this expectation in Chapter 5.

Elite Pressure and Executive Willingness

In addition to the mass public, elites act as allies to ensure that the executive responds to adverse regional court judgments by adopting, administering, monitoring, and enforcing human rights policy. Two types of elites can place pressure on the executive to make comprehensive human rights policy change following an adverse regional court judgment: (1) foreign economic elites and (2) domestic political elites.

First, foreign economic elites can threaten to withdraw important resources (e.g., investment, aid) from states that fail to protect rights. The withdrawal of important resources inhibits the ability of the executive to provide important public goods to constituents, which subsequently can threaten executive political survival. The threat of the loss of economic benefits for failing to respect rights creates strong incentives for the executive to make human rights policy changes to secure economic gains. Research shows that human rights practices are associated with foreign direct investment (FDI) (Richards, Gelleny, and Sacko, 2001; Blanton and Blanton, 2007; Garriga, 2016), preferential trade agreements (PTAs) (Hafner-Burton, 2005), and foreign aid (Lebovic and Voeten, 2009). More specifically, research shows that respect for human rights is higher in countries looking to attract FDI because respect for rights signals political stability and predictability, as well as reduces public criticism of firms investing in foreign countries (Blanton and Blanton, 2007). Good human rights practices may indirectly attract FDI by creating an environment less conducive to political violence and volatility (Sorens and Ruger, 2012), or by creating conditions for human capital development, an arguably valuable resource for a good investment climate (Blanton and Blanton, 2007).

Other research examines the influence of the international human rights *regime* on FDI. States and investors have reputation concerns when it comes to investment. States care about reputation because a good international reputation signals a stable investment climate, and states can enhance their reputation by being a party to international human rights treaties (Hafner-Burton, Tsutsui, and Meyer, 2008). Once the state has attracted FDI, it has an interest in maintaining the economic benefits of FDI, and as a result, respect for rights remains an important concern for states. Because investors can threaten to exit, the state must continue to signal to investors that their investment is secure and that the investment climate is stable and predictable.

Bad human rights practices may also directly influence FDI by harming companies' reputations (Blanton and Apodaca, 2007). Companies engage in reputation-building and restoration tactics in order to signal to audiences that they are undertaking socially responsible investments. In order to signal social responsibility, investors gather information from various sources on political stability and respect for rights (Garriga, 2016). Investors may then use a state's commitment to international human rights law to "shield themselves from eventual accusations and to deflect responsibility" (Garriga, 2016, 163). Research shows that participation in the international human rights regime has a positive effect on states' reputations, and ratification of international human rights treaties attracts FDI independent of the level of human rights violations (Garriga, 2016).

Although commitment to international human rights treaties provides an important signal for states seeking to attract investors and for investors seeking to demonstrate social responsibility, commitment to a regional court arguably allows states and investors to send a stronger signal to their respective audiences. Following the state decision to cede sovereignty to a regional court, the state remains vulnerable to litigation from the court. As a result, the court clearly censures the state for human rights abuses, often sending a signal of the presence of more systematic abuses within the country. In FDI host countries, adverse regional court judgments send a clear signal of the presence of state human rights violations. The failure to make behavioral changes following such litigation has the potential to harm the host state *and* investor's reputation, which may deter or detract FDI, and result in an economically disadvantageous outcome.

Foreign aid represents another economic benefit that may be at stake for failing to make human rights policy changes following an adverse regional court decision. Foreign aid can be an important resource for recipient countries, particularly when those in power rely on aid as a means to grant private and public goods to help them maintain power (Carnegie and Marinov, 2017). However, not all foreign aid is conditional on respect for rights, or even political liberalization. In fact, foreign aid allocations may be conditioned more strongly on strategic considerations, such as bureaucratic inertia (Carey, 2007) or political alliances (Alesina and Dollar, 2000). *Multilateral* aid, however, is often given through organizations dedicated to the promotion of democracy and human rights (e.g., World Bank or European Commission), and such organizations often condition foreign aid on respect for rights.

Multilateral aid institutions reduce aid in the presence of signals from the international community that a state is disregarding human rights norms. Research shows that condemnation of a state's human rights practices through the adoption of a United Nations Commission on Human Rights resolution produces a reduction in multilateral aid (but not bilateral aid) (Lebovic and Voeten, 2009). Adverse regional court judgments present another international shaming tool, and represent a clear legal censure for human rights abuse committed by a state. Failure to make human rights policy changes in response to adverse regional court decisions signals the absence of state intention to respect rights. This suggests the following:

> **Hypothesis 5**: *Adverse regional human rights court judgments are associated with greater future respect for human rights when economic benefits are conditional on human rights practices.*

In addition to foreign economic elites, domestic political elites can also pressure the executive to adopt, administer, monitor, and enforce human rights policy following adverse regional court judgments. National judges and legislators represent political elites important for regional court effectivness. Often, some of the measures required of the state by the regional court include actions typically carried out by the national judiciary, such as investigating violations, identifying individuals responsible, and imposing the appropriate punishment, as well as actions typically carried out by the domestic legislature, including adopting, amending, or repealing legislation (Burgorgue-Larsen and de Torres, 2011, 177–191).[22]

---

[22] Alter (2014, 20) calls actors such as domestic judges and legislators "compliance partners" because they can "embrace an [international court] ruling and thereby create compliance" (20).

In expectation of implementation efforts by the national judiciary and legislature, executive incentives to adopt, administer, monitor, and enforce regional court decisions increase. Following national judicial or legislative implementation, national judges or legislators can shift postjudgment responsibility to the executive. The executive then faces international and domestic shaming costs for failing to undertake human rights policy changes (adopt, administer, monitor, and enforce rights-respecting policy) despite national judicial or legislative implementation efforts in line with regional court orders. The chief executive would prefer to not have postjudgment responsibility shifted to the executive branch, and subsequently assume blame by international and domestic audiences for rights-related policy failures (Huneeus, 2012, 129). When faced with implementation efforts by the national judiciary and legislature, the executive faces a trade-off. Human rights policy changes are costly for the executive, but when the national judiciary and legislature have done their part by implementing regional court rulings and human rights practices have not improved, the executive bears the brunt of the responsibility. In order to avoid these costs, the executive is more likely to make policy changes in response to an adverse regional court decision when the probability of the national judiciary or legislature implementing regional court orders is high.

When will the executive expect national judicial implementation? Examining the politics of national justice systems or why and when judges are likely to implement regional court orders provides a better understanding of the likelihood of executive human rights policy change. National courts may find implementation of regional court orders to be costly. In fact, they often encounter procedural difficulties that make implementation of regional court orders difficult. For example, for a case to be admissible before a regional court, all domestic remedies must be exhausted, which means that adverse regional court decisions often contradict a prior national court ruling. The national judiciary, then, may face legitimacy costs, as well as obstacles associated with domestic criminal procedure, including statutes of limitations, double jeopardy, and amnesties (Kristicevic, 2007; Huneeus, 2012, 127). Most states do not specify through domestic legislation how regional court rulings will be implemented domestically, let alone how to handle national law that conflicts with orders from a regional legal body.[23]

---

[23] Peru and Colombia are exceptions; both states have passed legislation establishing specific steps that should be taken to implement regional court orders (Baluarte and DeVos, 2010, 85–88).

Even though national judicial implementation of regional court orders may entail substantial costs, there are many examples of the national judiciary abiding by regional court orders. In the case of *Bulacio v. Argentina*, the Inter-American Court ordered Argentina to prosecute a police chief, even though a trial absolving the police chief of criminal responsibility had already taken place. Argentina's Supreme Court implemented the Inter-American Court decision, despite the procedural obstacle posed by reopening a closed case domestically. In fact, there are numerous cases of domestic "judicial empathy" with judgments of the regional court (Burgorgue-Larsen and de Torres, 2011), but the story is more complex as a result of the substantial variation in national judiciaries across states. One important dimension along which national judiciaries vary cross-nationally is the strength of the national judiciary, or *judicial power*. Although judicial power in Argentina was relatively low throughout the 1990s,[24] substantial reforms to the judiciary began in 2003 when the Inter-American Court rendered the *Bulacio v. Argentina* decision, and judicial power grew substantially relative to other countries in the region.

I contend that national judicial power is important because it impacts the ability and willingness of the national judiciary to implement regional court orders. Judicial power has two components: independence and effectiveness. National judicial *independence* means that decision making in the national judiciary is free from external political influence, particularly other governmental actors (Kornhauser, 2002, 47). National judicial *effectiveness* captures whether national judicial decisions are implemented properly by the government. An effective national judiciary is influential, meaning that its decisions should be upheld by the government.[25] When the national judiciary is *independent*, national judges have a greater *ability* to implement regional court orders. The national court must be free from external political influence if it is to render decisions against state actors, particularly state agents (often under the umbrella of the executive branch) responsible for human rights violations (Simmons, 2009).

Consider the adverse Inter-American Court ruling in Peru related to the execution of prisoners at El Frontón prison in 2000. In its ruling, the Inter-American Court found that no statute of limitations applied to the crimes committed in El Frontón. In December, 2008, Peru's Constitutional Court upheld a lower court decision, which found that the statute of limitations had expired in this case. Following Peru's Constitutional Court decision, a

---

[24] According to the judicial power variable created by Linzer and Staton (2015), judicial power was below the median for the region in the 1990s.
[25] See Staton and Moore (2011) for further discussion of the concept of judicial power.

2.4 Executive Decision Making

lawyer for the Legal Defence Institute argued that the four magistrates who voted against the motion that statutory limitations do not apply to crimes against humanity "may have been susceptible to political pressure ... two of them – Javier Mesía and Fernando Calle – are known to be affiliated with the governing APRA party, while Ernesto Álvarez, whose view that no statute of limitations applied to the crime was already known, suddenly changed his vote" (Paez, 2008, 1). Because Peru's high court was not sufficiently independent from the state, the national court failed to implement the Inter-American Court order.

The second component of judicial power, judicial *effectiveness*, impacts the *willingness* of the national judiciary to implement regional court orders. National judiciaries encounter a potential implementation problem; they possess the formal power to rule against other institutions, but the substantive effect of these decisions generally depends on the way other political actors implement the decision (Vanberg, 2005, 19–20). For example, if the regional court holds a retrial for an individual based on a regional court order, the executive must ensure the enforcement of their national judiciaries' decision (Carrubba, 2005; Vanberg, 2005; Gauri and Brinks, 2008). Implementation requires cooperation among numerous domestic actors, including governmental actors whose actions courts have struck down (Vanberg, 2005, 6).

Research shows that citizens value implementation of national judicial decisions (e.g., Carrubba, 2005; Vanberg, 2005; Staton, 2006; Carrubba, 2009). The national judiciary provides an important check on the executive, and the public will support the rule of law, and therefore the court, in an effort to prevent exploitation by the state (Weingast, 1997, 260). Public support for the judiciary as an institution is called "diffuse support" or support for the court distinct from its policy output. Diffuse support is generated by the perception that courts represent institutions inherently different from other highly political institutions because they should act as impartial, apolitical actors, relying on the law to back their decisions (Vanberg, 2005, 52).

When the national court is *effective*, the public can use the court as a signal of bad government behavior. As a result, the public is more likely to hold elected officials (i.e., executive and legislators) accountable to implement national judicial decisions, which further enhances and maintains the public's support of the court. Public support for the national judiciary, then, increases the electoral cost to elected officials for failing to implement national judicial decisions, which consequently enhances the *effectiveness* of the national judiciary. In order to remain effective (i.e., ensure governmental actors implement national judicial decisions), the national judiciary has an interest in maintaining public support for the national court. Because citizen perceptions of human rights are susceptible to international human rights law (Wallace, 2013), national judges have an interest in upholding the check that the regional court places on the state in terms of respect for rights.

A powerful national judiciary, then, is more likely to implement regional court orders (i.e., investigate violations, identify individuals responsible, impose punishment). An *independent* national judiciary has a greater *ability* to implement regional court orders because it is relatively free to rule against the state. An *effective* national judiciary has a greater *willingness* to implement regional court orders because national judges recognize that citizen perceptions of human rights may change when an international human rights legal body condemns the state for rights abuse (Wallace, 2013) and by implementing regional court orders, the national judiciary increases the likelihood of continued public support for the national judiciary in the long term. Notably, the likelihood of executive policy change (adoption, administration, monitoring, and enforcement of rights-related policy) increases in expectation of national judicial implementation. As a result, when the national judiciary is relatively powerful, the executive is more likely to expect national judicial implementation of regional court orders, and the executive is more likely to make human rights policy changes as a result. This suggests the following:

> **Hypothesis 6**: *Adverse regional human rights court judgments are associated with greater future respect for human rights in states where the national judiciary is powerful (independent and effective).*

In addition to national judges, national legislators also represent important political allies for the regional court. The regional court often orders the state to carry out tasks that require legislative action, the most common being orders to amend, repeal, or adopt domestic laws to align with the regional court judgment. Orders requiring legislative action are common following regional court litigation, and implementation by the legislature is important, as national legislative changes are a vital step toward ensuring respect for rights in law. Although there may be gaps between the adoption (or amendment/repeal) of *law* and the realization of the law in *practice*, legislative changes represent an important condition for executive administration, monitoring, and enforcement of the law. I argue that in expectation of legislative implementation (i.e., adopting, amending, repealing national legislation), the executive is more likely to make human rights-related policy changes because once human rights legislative changes are in place and human rights practices do not improve, blame for human rights policy failures can easily be shifted to the executive. However, legislative implementation is not guaranteed because changing legislation is costly. Under what conditions are national legislators likely to implement adverse regional court judgments?

Traditionally, the presence of a large legislative opposition makes policy changes more difficult because the legislative opposition represents an additional veto point at which policy change can be blocked. The presence of a large legislative opposition with preferences that differ from those of the executive makes changes to the legal status quo more difficult (though not impossible) (Tsebelis, 2002). Policy stability, then, is the likely outcome in the face of a large legislative opposition, and legislative action may be stalled as the legislative opposition grows. Research shows that a large legislative opposition can also present challenges to constraining human rights violations, particularly torture. When torture represents the status quo policy, the legislative opposition can increase the challenge of policy adoption, including the adoption of programs designed to prevent or stop torture (Conrad and Moore, 2010).

The act of writing legislation or attending the legislative session and voting for its passage are not inherently costly. However, legislators do not always have an interest in legislative changes related to human rights, and legislators face significant procedural challenges to amending, repealing, or adopting legislation. Deliberation and contestation are built into legislative structure by design, which creates procedural problems in legislative implementation of regional court orders (Huneeus, 2012). In fact, compliance data show that compliance rates are lowest when Inter-American Court orders involve the amendment, repeal, or adoption of domestic laws or judgments (at only 7 percent), and this may be due to the feasibility of compliance. That is, compliance with orders such as the payment of monetary costs likely do not entail the same political capital expenses and coordination challenges as other types of reparation orders (Hawkins and Jacoby, 2010, 59).

Although a large legislative opposition (legislators with preferences opposing the executive) can have a negative effect on the likelihood of legislative changes, this negative effect is diminished in the presence of international human rights law. The presence of a large legislative opposition can make legislative implementation more difficult, but in the presence of international human rights law, the legislative opposition acts as an important constraint on the executive branch (Lupu, 2015).

In the presence of international human rights law, the legislative opposition can shift from preventing or blocking the passage of legislation to creating important legislation. The legislative opposition plays a key role in supporting adverse regional court judgments. Adverse judgments provide information to legislators about executive behavior. More specifically, opposition legislators have an interest in protecting groups they represent from human rights violations (Lupu, 2015). Not always able to fully monitor executive human rights policy and behavior, the legislative opposition can use adverse regional court judgments as an information shortcut because the judgment provides a detailed account of and clear censure for human rights abuse. When the regional court renders an adverse judgment, the legislative opposition uses this information to initiate policy change to ensure that the executive refrains from future rights abuses. The legislative opposition also has significant agenda-setting powers following an adverse regional court judgment, and the opposition is able to place (now salient) human rights issues on the legislative agenda by proposing legislative changes (Lupu, 2015). Relying on adverse regional court judgments as a legitimate record of rights abuse, the legislative opposition uses the adverse judgment to make human rights issues salient. The legislative opposition can point to the necessity of important legislative changes, such as the amendment, adoption, and repeal of existing legislation. Opposition legislators can also work to withhold funding and resources for the executive branch, where resources may be used for implementing repressive policies (Lupu, 2015).

Importantly, veto player theory highlights the institutional hurdle that a large legislative opposition creates for making human rights policy changes. Research shows that human rights policy changes are less likely in the face of a strong legislative opposition (Conrad and Moore, 2010). However, international human rights law (e.g., an adverse regional court judgment) generates politically usable information by members of the legislative opposition. Adverse regional court judgments communicate important information to the legislative opposition about executive behavior. The legislative opposition has incentives to demonstrate the distance between their policy objectives and executive policy, as well as take a strong stance against repression of the opposition's constituents (e.g., marginalized groups). Thus, the executive is more likely to expect legislative implementation of regional court orders when there is a significant legislative opposition with preferences that differ from the executive. As a result, I posit:

> **Hypothesis 7**: *Adverse regional human rights court judgments are associated with greater future respect for human rights in states with a large legislative opposition whose preferences differ from the executive.*

2.4.3 High Capacity, High Willingness, and Human Rights Policy

Each of the preceding theoretical expectations and hypotheses emphasizes the importance of executive capacity *or* executive willingness in regional human rights court deterrence. However, an additional implication of the theory is that adverse regional human rights court judgments are associated with greater respect for rights in the presence of high executive capacity *and* high executive willingness. I expect that an adverse regional court judgment is associated with greater respect for rights when the executive has high capacity, but this effect should be even greater when the executive is highly willing. For example, as executive access to outside resources grows (or the executive is fiscally flexible), I expect a greater likelihood of human rights policy change following an adverse regional court judgment. However, when the executive has access to outside resources and also faces a high likelihood of mass public pressure or elite pressure, the likelihood of executive adoption, administration, monitoring, and enforcement of human rights policy is amplified. In other words, the extent to which adverse regional human rights court judgments deter future human rights abuses in the presence of high-capacity executives is amplified when the executive is also highly willing. As a result, I posit:

Hypothesis 8a: *Adverse regional human rights court judgments are associated with greater future respect for human rights as executive capacity grows, but this effect is amplified as executive willingness grows.*

In addition, as indicated in Hypotheses 3–7, I also expect that adverse regional human rights court judgments will be associated with greater respect for rights when the executive is highly willing; however, the theory also suggests that the effect of executive willingness is greater as executive capacity grows. For example, when the executive expects to face mass public or elite pressure, I expect a greater likelihood of executive human rights policy change. The executive expects to face mass public pressure as a result of an upcoming election or few threats to the political and social order. The executive faces elite pressure when economic benefits are conditional on human rights practices, and the executive faces political elite pressure when the executive expects a high likelihood of national judicial or legislative implementation. However, when an executive is not only willing (due to mass public or elite pressure), but also has high capacity (e.g., access to outside resources), the likelihood of executive policy change grows. That is, adverse regional human rights court judgments are associated with greater respect for rights when the executive is highly willing, but this effect is amplified in the presence of high capacity (e.g., fiscal flexibility). Voeten (2014) suggests a similar expectation. Even though Voeten (2014) examines the influence of bureaucratic and legal infrastructure capacity on the time it takes a state to implement specific European Court judgments (as opposed to deterrence), he finds that high levels of bureaucratic and legal capacity will help willing executives (those facing political constraints) to implement judgments quickly. These findings suggest that capacity amplifies the effect of willingness in regional court deterrence as well. More formally, I expect:

> *Hypothesis 8b: Adverse regional human rights court judgments are associated with greater future respect for human rights as executive willingness grows, but this effect is amplified as executive capacity grows.*

Although I argue that adverse regional court judgments are likely to deter in the presence of high executive capacity and willingness, there are several reasons to examine the influence of executive capacity and executive willingness independently by testing Hypotheses 1–7. First, isolating the effects of executive capacity and willingness in regional court deterrence provides a more comprehensive test of the theory by allowing for examination of the relative importance of each indicator of executive capacity and willingness in regional court deterrence. Similarly, examining capacity and willingness independently allows for pragmatic interpretation of empirical results because assessing regional court deterrence becomes increasingly difficult in the presence of various interactions. Considering executive capacity and willingness jointly requires a multidimensional interaction that includes various measures of executive capacity and executive willingness in the presence of adverse judgments. Incorporating the complexity of this multidimensional process makes it difficult to assess and determine the importance of specific factors in regional court deterrence.

Second, despite examining the role of executive capacity and willingness in regional court deterrence independently in subsequent chapters, the empirical tests take into account both factors. The empirical tests examining the role of executive capacity on regional court deterrence take into account varying levels of executive willingness. That is, in examining whether characteristics of the adverse judgment (e.g., type of rights violated) are influential in regional court deterrence, I take into account (by controlling for) various indicators of executive willingness, such as electoral institutions, judicial power, and legislative opposition size, among others. Similarly, the theory and empirical tests examining the role of executive willingness on regional court deterrence take into account varying levels of executive capacity. More specifically, in examining whether pressure from the mass public or economic and political elites influence the likelihood of regional court deterrence, I take into account executive capacity by controlling for the type of rights violated (physical integrity) and an indicator of state capacity (GDP per capita).

By taking into account executive capacity and willingness in the empirical analyses, the empirical results show only moderate effects of the potential influence of either capacity or willingness, representing a conservative test of the theoretical expectations. In examining the influence of executive capacity on regional court deterrence, I pool together states with executives of high and low willingness.[26] Similarly, in examining the influence of executive willingness on regional court deterrence, I pool together states with executives of high and low capacity.[27] By pooling together high- and low-capacity executives in examining executive willingness and pooling together executives of high and low willingness in examining the role of executive capacity, I likely underestimate (rather than overestimate) the potential for executive capacity and willingness to influence regional human rights court deterrence.

2.5 CONCLUSION

In this chapter, I explained the conditions under which adverse regional human rights court judgments deter future human rights abuses. Figure 2.1 summarizes the theoretical framework and the empirical implications. The process begins with adverse regional human rights court judgments. Adverse regional court judgments bring human rights abuses to light by providing important information to the executive, political elites, and the general public. Adverse regional court judgments signal to the state that human rights violations are detectable, provide details surrounding the facts of the case, and communicate that there has been a violation of international (and likely domestic) law. Although the executive faces reputation costs for failing to adopt comprehensive human rights policy in response to an adverse regional court judgment, litigation alone is often not enough to offset the material and political costs associated with the adoption, administration, monitoring, and enforcement of human rights policy. The independent effect of the regional court is depicted at the top of Figure 2.1. I empirically examine the independent influence of the regional court on executive incentives to

---

[26] Results reported in Chapter 4 report the influence of executive capacity when indicators of executive willingness are held at their mean.
[27] Results reported in Chapters 5–6 report the influence of executive willingness when indicators of executive capacity are held at their mean.

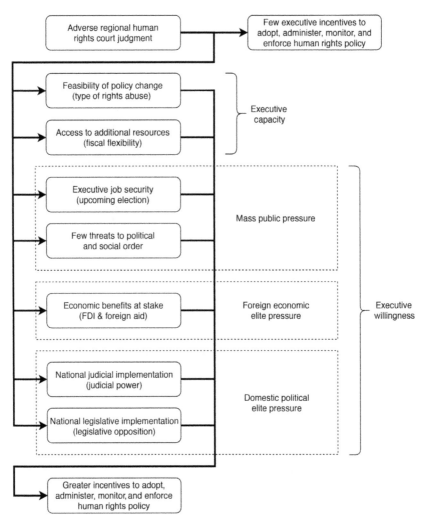

FIGURE 2.1. Theoretical framework and empirical implications

Notes: Figure 2.1 depicts the theoretical framework discussed in this chapter. The process begins with an adverse regional human rights court judgment, which is unlikely to independently generate executive adoption of comprehensive human rights policy due to extant costs of policy change and regional court enforcement challenges. However, each box displays the conditions under which the executive is more likely to adopt comprehensive human rights policy following an adverse regional human rights court judgment. Each condition is grouped into two broad categories: factors influencing executive capacity and factors influencing executive willingness to adopt, administer, monitor, and enforce human rights policy following an adverse regional human rights court judgment.

2.5 Conclusion

adopt, administer, monitor, and enforce human rights policy in Chapter 4 (when testing Hypothesis 1) and find little evidence that adverse regional court judgments independently influence executive human rights behavior.

Because the regional court has little independent influence on executive human rights policy, I argue that the executive is more likely to respond to adverse regional court judgments by adopting, administering, monitoring, and enforcing human rights policy when the executive has the capacity and willingness to do so. The executive does not have unlimited capacity and will need to divert resources away from the provision of other public goods in order to undertake human rights policy changes. Even well-intentioned executives with an interest in comprehensive human rights policy change may find it difficult to respond to an adverse regional court judgment. The costs of policy change coupled with capacity limitations produces a trade-off for the executive, and expending resources in the face of limited capacity may threaten executive political survival.

I argue that because most executives do not possess unlimited resources to change human rights policy, an executive is more likely to make such changes under particular circumstances. First, some types of rights are more feasible to remedy than others following an adverse judgment. The feasibility of human rights policy change following an adverse regional court judgment is greater with respect to civil and political rights than physical integrity rights. Civil and political rights policies are more directly in the executive's control. Therefore, undertaking reforms of bureaucratic and administrative procedures to guarantee respect for civil and political rights may be more feasible than reining in physical integrity rights abuses committed by state agents. Second, access to outside resources increases the executive's capacity to respond to adverse judgments with the adoption, administration, monitoring, and enforcement of human rights policy following an adverse regional court judgment. I argue that the executive is more likely to engage in human rights policy changes following an adverse judgment when the state is fiscally flexibility. Capacity considerations as a part of executive human rights policy decision making are depicted in two boxes at the top of Figure 2.1. I examine the role of capacity limitations more fully in Chapter 4.

Even though greater capacity provides the executive with the opportunity to adopt, administer, monitor, and enforce human rights policy, the executive must also be willing to make such policy changes. When an adverse regional court judgment threatens executive political survival, the executive is more willing to adopt comprehensive human rights policy. However, even though an adverse regional court judgment produces information that generates reputation costs, the judgment alone is unlikely to adequately threaten executive political survival, particularly because the regional court lacks enforcement authority. For an adverse regional court judgment to deter future human rights abuses, other actors must utilize these judgments to agitate for human rights policy change. Two sets of domestic actors can utilize adverse regional court judgments to pressure the executive to adopt comprehensive human rights policy: (1) the mass public and (2) elites. These two actors act as allies that work to ensure that the executive responds to adverse regional court judgments by adopting, administering, monitoring, and enforcing human rights policy. Under certain conditions, both the mass public and elites can tip the scale toward executive adoption of comprehensive human rights policy following an adverse regional court judgment.

The mass public influences executive willingness to respond to adverse regional court judgments when the executive is insecure in office due to an upcoming election and the state faces threats to the political and social order. However, unlike the election cycle, which can generate incentives for the executive to undertake human rights reforms following an adverse judgment, when the executive faces threats to the political and social order, the executive is less likely to have incentives to improve human rights policy. Threats to the political and social order directly threaten the executive's hold on power, and the public may even support the use of rights violations by the executive in an attempt to restore social and political stability. The center of Figure 2.1 depicts the role of mass public pressure in regional court deterrence. I empirically examine the role of mass public pressure in generating executive incentives to adopt, administer, monitor, and enforce human rights policy in Chapter 5.

In addition to the mass public, I also argue that foreign economic elites and domestic political elites influence executive incentives to adopt, administer, monitor, and enforce human rights policy following an adverse regional court judgment. First, foreign economic elites can threaten to withdraw important economic resources in the face of human rights policy failures. When the executive faces a potential loss of foreign direct investment or foreign aid for failing to adopt, administer, monitor, and enforce human rights policy following shaming by an adverse regional court judgment, the executive is more likely to make such policy changes. The center of Figure 2.1 displays the role of foreign economic elites. I empirically examine the role of foreign economic elites in executive willingness to adopt, administer, monitor, and enforce human rights policy in Chapter 6.

Second, political elites can pressure the executive to make human rights policy change in response to adverse regional court judgments. Regional courts often issue judgments that require actions typically carried out by domestic judges and legislators. Following national judicial or legislative implementation of regional court orders, national judges and legislators can shift postjudgment responsibility to the executive. When the executive fails to follow through with the adoption, administration, monitoring, and enforcement of human rights policy, despite the efforts of national judges and legislators, executive political survival is threatened as voters can attribute human rights policy failure to the executive. In expectation of implementation efforts by the national judiciary and legislature, the executive has incentives to adopt comprehensive human rights policy following an adverse regional court judgment. I argue that the executive expects implementation by the national judiciary when the national judiciary is powerful (independent and effective). National judicial independence grants the judiciary the ability to rule against the state. National judicial effectiveness makes judges more willing to rule against the state in an effort to behave as an effective check on the state and secure continued public support for the institution. In addition, I argue that the executive is more likely to expect national legislative implementation when there is a large legislative opposition with preferences that differ from those of the executive. Adverse regional court judgments provide the legislative opposition with important information about executive behavior and give national legislators leverage to act as a constraint on the executive. The bottom of Figure 2.1 displays the role of political elites in executive decision making. I empirically examine the role of political elites in executive willingness to adopt, administer, monitor, and enforce human rights policy in Chapter 6.

Finally, in Chapter 7, I empirically examine the influence of capable and willing executives on regional court deterrence. In doing so, I consider the influence of an indicator of executive capacity (fiscal flexibility) and several indicators of executive willingness (mass public pressure and elite pressure) on regional court deterrence. I expect that adverse regional human rights court judgments are more likely to deter future human rights abuses when the executive is both highly capable and highly willing, as opposed to when one of these indicators is low. In this chapter, I examine the combined role of the top and bottom of Figure 2.1 in regional human rights court deterrence.

In the next chapter, I begin my analysis by first describing the practices and procedures of the two regional courts of interest, the European and Inter-American Courts of Human Rights. I then describe and empirically present the primary variables of interest examined in subsequent chapters. Finally, I conduct the first of many empirical tests by looking at the general deterrent effect of the European and Inter-American Courts of Human Rights.

3

Examining Patterns of General Regional Court Deterrence

Poland joined the Council of Europe in 1991 and ratified the European Convention on Human Rights in 1993, thereby accepting the jurisdiction of the European Court of Human Rights. Following Poland's acceptance of the European Court's jurisdiction, respect for rights initially improved, before eventually declining. The left panel of Figure 3.1 displays Poland's respect for physical integrity rights in the years after Poland joined the Court (1993 to 1999). The vertical dashed line represents the year that Poland joined the European Court (1993). From 1993 to 1994, respect for rights continued to display a positive trend. However, from 1994 to 1996, respect for physical integrity rights appears to stagnate and in 1997, human rights practices begin to decline.

While the evidence suggests that the European Court's jurisdiction over Poland had little effect on Poland's human rights practices, evidence also suggests that rising European Court activity in the region played little role in prompting human rights policy changes in Poland. The European Court was particularly active from 2008 to 2012,[1] rendering 116 to 148 adverse judgments involving physical integrity rights of high-level importance each year. The right panel of Figure 3.1 displays Poland's respect for physical integrity rights during years of high levels of European Court activity in the region. The vertical dashed line represents the year (2010) in which the European Court was most active for the time period 1978 to 2012. The graph shows some slight improvements from year to year, but respect for rights stays fairly stagnant in Poland during this time period, despite heightened European Court activity.

Figure 3.1 shows little evidence in support of the general deterrent effect of the European Court of Human Rights in Poland. For general deterrence to

---

[1] In the 1978 to 2012 time period, the European Court was most active in the last 4 years, 2008 to 2012.

Examining Patterns of Court Deterrence 77

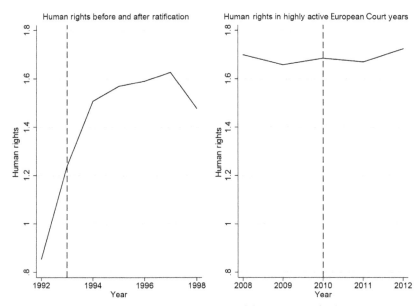

FIGURE 3.1. European Court general deterrence in Poland
Notes: Figure 3.1 displays Poland's level of respect for physical integrity rights. The left panel of Figure 3.1 displays Poland's respect for physical integrity rights before and after Poland joined the European Court. The solid line represents Poland's human rights score, while the vertical dashed line indicates the year Poland ratified the European Convention on Human Rights and submitted to the jurisdiction of the European Court of Human Rights. The right panel of Figure 3.1 displays Poland's respect for physical integrity rights in the years in which the European Court was most active during the 1978 to 2012 time period. The solid line represents Poland's physical integrity rights score and the vertical dashed line represents the year in which the European Court was most active during the 1978 to 2012 time period (2010).

occur, the presence and activity of the European Court in the region should be positively associated with human rights practices. With respect to European Court presence, Poland should be deterred from abusing human rights for fear of the consequences of future litigation following Poland's acceptance of the jurisdiction of the European Court. However, the patterns displayed in the left panel of Figure 3.1 do not support this argument. With respect to European Court activity, Poland should be sufficiently deterred from abusing human rights because of a greater threat of future litigation when regional court activity grows. However, the right panel of Figure 3.1 shows that even in the years in which the European Court was most active, Poland's physical integrity rights practices remained fairly stagnant.

Although the patterns displayed in Figure 3.1 do not support general European Court deterrence in Poland, I find anecdotal evidence of specific deterrence in Poland; that is, anecdotal evidence suggests that European

Court judgments *against Poland* are associated with improved human rights practices. In September 1993, Polish national Krzysztof Iwańczuk was serving a prison sentence for forgery of documents and use of counterfeit documents at Wroclaw prison in Poland. On September 19, Iwańczuk requested that the prison authorities allow him to vote in the parliamentary election at the voting facilities located at the prison. The prison guards took Iwańczuk to the guards' room and told him that in order to vote, he must get undressed and undergo a body search. After removing his clothes, the prison guards made humiliating remarks and then ordered him to strip naked. Iwańczuk refused, but continued to request permission to vote without a body search. In response, prison guards took him back to his cell without him being allowed to vote.

The case reached the European Court, and in the 2001 adverse judgment of *Iwańczuk v. Poland*, the European Court found that Iwańczuk had no criminal record and had been cooperative during his detention. The Court stated that while strip searches are sometimes necessary, they should be conducted appropriately, and in this case, the guard's behavior was intended to humiliate and amounted to degrading treatment. The European Court also found that the length of Iwańczuk's detention had been unreasonable. The Polish government took several steps to remedy the abuse, including the Ministry of Justice's adoption of an ordinance on safety in prisons in October 2003, which provided clear criteria on the circumstances in which a body search could be ordered in a prison setting. Notably, human rights practices in Poland improved 0.28 points in the 2 years following the adverse judgment (on a scale ranging around −3 to +5 in Europe) (Fariss, 2014). Also of note, prior to the judgment, torture took place occasionally, but torture was not practiced in the several years following the adverse judgment (Cingranelli, Richards, and Clay, 2014).

In Chapter 2, I argued that the mechanism of specific deterrence is more likely to prevent future human rights abuses than general deterrence. In this chapter, I examine patterns of general deterrence in both the European and Inter-American Courts of Human Rights. I find little systematic evidence of general deterrence in Europe and some limited support for general deterrence in the Americas. Although there is more work to be done on general deterrence in the Americas, these findings generally support examining specific deterrence in the subsequent chapters of this book.

In order to assess general deterrence, I begin by describing the data I utilize in the analysis in this chapter as well as subsequent chapters. I start with the outcome of interest, human rights practices (dependent variable), which captures regional human rights court effectiveness, or the extent to which regional human rights courts deter future human rights abuses. In the discussion of the outcome of effectiveness, I also argue that the concept of regional court effectiveness differs from compliance with regional courts. Using descriptive analyses, I find that these two concepts are not only conceptually different, but are also empirically distinct. This suggests that studies that focus only on compliance with regional human rights courts as an outcome of interest overlook an important way regional human rights courts influence state behavior – through deterrence of future human rights abuses. The distinction between compliance and effectiveness also suggests that it is important to theorize about these concepts separately, as the factors that explain compliance with the regional court may not explain regional court effectiveness, or the extent to which regional courts deter future human rights abuses.

Next, I present data capturing regional court behavior (explanatory variable). In this chapter, I use the year each state accepted the jurisdiction of each regional court as an indicator of general deterrence. I then examine the overall activity of regional courts by utilizing data on the number of adverse judgments rendered by each court in Europe and the Americas as additional indicators of general deterrence. I conclude the chapter by presenting findings from the empirical analyses, finding little support for the general deterrent effect of the European Court in Europe and limited support for the general deterrent effect of the Inter-American Court in the Americas. Given these findings on general deterrence, I focus on specific deterrence in the remaining empirical analyses in this book. However, before diving into the data and empirical analyses, it is important to understand how the regional courts in Europe and the Americas operate. In other words, in order to understand the extent to which regional human rights courts deter future human rights abuses, it is necessary to have a baseline understanding of their procedures, including similarities and differences across the European and Inter-American Courts of Human Rights. As a result, the next section focuses on the practices and procedures of both regional human rights courts.

3.1 PRACTICES AND PROCEDURES OF REGIONAL COURTS

3.1.1 *The European Court of Human Rights*

The European Convention on the Protection of Human Rights and Fundamental Freedoms (herein, European Convention), which protects a range of human rights, established the European Court of Human Rights. The European Court came into being in 1959 under the Council of Europe (COE), and 47 member states are parties to the convention.[2] Upon exhaustion of all domestic remedies, cases can be brought to the European Court by individuals, groups of individuals, law firms, or NGOs, among others specified in the convention, against states that have ratified the European Convention. The European Court hears cases involving violations of the European Convention by contracting parties. Once the European Court renders a judgment against a state, the state is charged with conceiving and executing steps to come into compliance with the Court.

While initially a separate body, the European Commission on Human Rights (also established by the European Convention) originally evaluated petitions and sent contentious cases to the European Court. However, the Commission quickly became overwhelmed by the volume of petitions, and the number of pending petitions was unsustainable. In 1998, the European Court underwent substantial reforms, including the adoption of Protocol 11, which eliminated the European Commission and worked to streamline the process for individual petitions to be evaluated, judged, and monitored.

With respect to European Court procedures, the process begins with petitioners exhausting all domestic remedies, which involves pursuing remedy through the domestic legal process, including the highest domestic court. The European Court then rules on the admissibility of the case, a major hurdle for any petition, as most petitions are dismissed at the admissibility stage largely as a result of the failure to exhaust all domestic remedies. Should the case clear the admissibility process, a chamber of seven judges rules on the merits of the case. Following an adverse judgment, the state has the opportunity to appeal through a Grand Chamber Judgment.

However, once the European Court hands down an adverse judgment, a Committee of Ministers (CM), also established by the European Convention and comprising states parties' Ministers of Foreign Affairs, monitors compliance with European Court rulings. The Committee asks states to report on measures taken to come into compliance and may also offer suggestions to states to encourage implementation of the judgment. The process of compliance with the European Court is "delegative," meaning that states must conceive of and execute steps they deem to be appropriate for achieving compliance (Hawkins and Jacoby, 2010). If the Committee of Ministers finds the state to have taken appropriate measures, the case is closed. However, if

---

[2] The European Union did not establish the European Court of Human Rights. All (27) members of the EU are members of the Council of Europe, but not all Council of Europe members are members of the EU. In 2010, member states acceded to Protocol 14, which provides for the European Union to accede and become party to the European Convention.

the CM deems that the state has taken less than a full account of the Court's judgment, it will make recommendations to the state to ensure compliance.[3]

As shown in Chapter 1, European Court activity has grown quite substantially over time. The large number of petitions received each year is largely due to repetitive cases or cases that address issues on which the Court has already adjudicated. These petitions largely originate from four Council of Europe states: Russia, Italy, Turkey, and Ukraine (ECtHR, 2017). Still, the number of cases examined by the European Court is unprecedented, and understanding the conditions under which adverse European Court judgments deter future human rights abuses is important not only for ensuring a lighter case load on the European Court, but also for ensuring better protections of human rights.

3.1.2 The Inter-American Court of Human Rights

The origins of the Inter-American Human Rights System trace back as early as 1948, with the adoption of the Declaration of the Rights and Duties of Man. The Organization of American States (OAS) established the Inter-American Commission on Human Rights (herein, Inter-American Commission) in 1959, followed by the drafting of the American Convention on Human Rights (herein, American Convention). The American Convention entered into force in 1978 and established the Inter-American Court of Human Rights to enforce and interpret the provisions of the Convention. The Inter-American Commission is charged with the promotion and protection of human rights and plays a large role in monitoring state human rights practices and examining individual petitions. The Inter-American Commission performs a variety of functions, including conducting country visits, researching and publishing reports on specific rights-related issues, and making recommendations to member states.

Regarding Inter-American Court procedures, all domestic remedies must be exhausted for a petition to be admissible in the Inter-American Human Rights System. However, in contrast to Europe, where applications are examined by judges of the European Court, the Inter-American Commission is responsible for processing and adjudicating individual petitions alleging human rights abuse. The Inter-American Commission decides on the admissibility of cases, largely by assessing whether domestic remedies have been exhausted. The Commission then gathers information, holds hearings, and negotiates friendly settlement agreements. Where friendly settlements

---

[3] The CM sometimes refers states to leading cases to assist in the steps necessary to ensure compliance.

cannot be reached, the Commission draws conclusions and publishes a report, including recommendations the state should undertake to facilitate compliance with the report's conclusions. If states do not comply within a specified period of time, the Commission may publish a second report or send the case to the Inter-American Court of Human Rights. Importantly, unlike the European Court, where individuals have direct access to the regional court, the Inter-American Commission makes the final determination regarding which cases reach the Court, and the Commission represents victims before the Court. Once a case reaches the Inter-American Court, the Court can rule on the admissibility, merits, and costs and reparations to be paid.

In contrast to the European Court, adverse judgments found by the Inter-American Court result in "compliance orders" or a list of specific steps the state must take to come into compliance with Court decisions (Hawkins and Jacoby, 2010). The Court monitors compliance with its judgments and relies on victims' representatives, the Inter-American Commission on Human Rights, and the state to submit reports on compliance. When full compliance is not observed, the Court issues compliance reports.

3.1.3 Comparing Practices and Procedures across Regional Courts

The European and Inter-American Courts of Human Rights differ substantially in their procedures for selecting cases, the mechanisms used for monitoring and securing state compliance with Court judgments, and the political and social context in which they operate. I return to the differences in practice and procedure of each regional legal body in the concluding chapter and suggest that some of the differences in practice and procedure may explain differences in deterrence of future human rights abuses. For example, because the Inter-American Court gives specific compliance orders that charge domestic actors like national judges and legislators with action, the public can more easily attribute blame for the lack of implementation to the appropriate domestic actors in the Americas. Because of this, national judges and legislators may have greater incentives to implement regional court orders in the Americas than national judges and legislators in Europe.

However, as discussed in Chapter 1, there are several important similarities between the regional courts, including their broad mandate (to protect human rights), mechanism of influence (binding legal judgments), and their independence (relative to other international human rights bodies). Another notable similarity between the European and Inter-American Courts involves the domestic political process necessary for cases to reach the court. Both the European and Inter-American Courts only deem cases admissible when all domestic remedies have been exhausted. The exhaustion of all domestic remedies opens up the opportunity for executive human rights policy changes prior to a case reaching the regional court. However, there are several reasons that executive policy change prior to an adverse regional human rights court judgment is unlikely.

First, domestic mobilization (by citizens, the media, and opposition groups) is unlikely following the failure of the national judicial system to remedy a human rights abuse because the lack of national legal backing provides little legal leverage to pro-rights advocates. If mobilization occurs during the national judicial process, then the executive could choose to adopt human rights policy changes prior to an adverse judgment being rendered by the European or Inter-American Court of Human Rights. Importantly, however, if a case reaches the regional court, the national judicial process likely failed the petitioner as the national judicial system did not effectively remedy a human rights abuse. As the case moves through the national judicial system, then, pro-rights advocates gain little legal leverage to utilize in their mobilization efforts. In other words, the national judicial system does not provide pro-rights movements with legal backing in their pursuit of human rights policy change. On the other hand, adverse judgments from an international legal body like a regional human rights court represent not only a clear censure for state-perpetrated human rights abuse, but also a signal that the state was wrong in the adjudication of the case. An adverse regional human rights court judgment provides clear leverage for pro-rights movements, representing a focal point on which pro-rights advocates can appeal in their mobilization efforts, which in turn encourages policy change among capable and willing executives.

Second, adverse judgments are rendered frequently in countries with capable and willing executives, providing empirical evidence that highly capable and willing executives do not necessarily preempt adverse regional court judgments by making human rights policy change prior to a judgment. If capable and willing executives engaged in human rights policy changes before the regional court rendered an adverse judgment, I would be less likely to find support for the hypotheses posited in Chapter 2 because capable and willing executives would rarely, if ever, be the recipients of adverse regional court judgments. I do not find that capable and willing executives are less likely to be adverse judgment recipients. Using executive capacity as an example, European states that receive adverse judgments have a higher level of fiscal flexibility than states that do not receive adverse judgments, an indication that capable executives are often the recipients of adverse judgments. Moreover, as noted in Chapter 2, judicial power represents an indicator of executive willingness, as strong judiciaries are more likely to implement regional court judgments, encouraging executive human rights policy change. Evidence shows that European states that receive adverse judgments have virtually the same average level of judicial power as European states that do not receive adverse judgments, an indication that willing executives are often the recipients of adverse judgments.

Finally, the executive faces a high degree of uncertainty regarding the likelihood of litigation, and because repression represents a useful policy tool, the executive is unlikely to adopt policies designed to prohibit the use of repression when the likelihood of an adverse judgment is nowhere near certain. Uncertainty about the likelihood of a case reaching the regional court is rooted in several factors. For one, evidence production costs and standards of proof necessary for the successful pursuit of complaints in a court of law are high, particularly with respect to physical integrity rights, as physical integrity abuses are not committed in public and often do not leave living victims (Lupu, 2013a). The high evidence production costs and standards of proof associated with physical integrity rights abuses make it difficult for victims to pursue cases in domestic courts, as well as regional courts, and can inhibit the ability of courts to rule against the state.

In addition to the dearth of evidence in many cases of physical integrity rights abuses creating executive uncertainty about the likelihood of being an adverse judgment recipient, the executive also faces information problems in assessing the probability of facing regional court litigation because individuals encounter obstacles in submitting applications to a regional human rights court, including legal costs and fear of further abuse. Moreover, most applications before regional courts do not become adverse judgments. Many cases are declared inadmissible and struck off the court's list of cases early in the process. As a result, the likelihood of litigation is relatively low, and executive information regarding the probability of litigation is incomplete. The executive cannot anticipate with certainty that rights abuse will result in an adverse regional (or even national) court judgment.

The Inter-American Human Rights System provides a good example of information problems and uncertainty of the likelihood of a case going before a regional court. States face some probability of a case being submitted to the Inter-American Court, particularly following the publication of an Inter-American Commission report. However, not all cases are submitted to the Court. The sheer number of petitions considered by the Inter-American Commission and the number of cases the Commission submits to the Court provide evidence of this small (albeit nonzero) probability. For example, in 2016, the Commission received 2,567 petitions, published 5 reports on the merits of the case (including recommendations), and submitted 16 cases to the Court. Considering the sheer volume of petitions submitted to the Inter-American Commission, the low probability of shaming by the Commission through a merits report, and the low likelihood that the Commission forwards the case to the Court, states do not expect a high probability that petitions and Commission reports will reach the Court. As a result, executives responsible for human rights abuse and repressive policies do not expect with high probability that they will be the recipients of adverse judgments and even capable and willing executives have few incentives to completely forgo the use of repression prior to the receipt of an adverse regional court judgment. To summarize, in terms of practice and procedure, the European and Inter-American Courts both operate as a complement to the national judicial system in that they render adverse judgments only when all domestic remedies have been exhausted. Importantly, despite the fact that human rights abuses examined by the regional court have been litigated at the national level, executive policy changes are unlikely prior to the regional court rendering an adverse judgment.

3.2 REGIONAL HUMAN RIGHTS COURT EFFECTIVENESS

Do regional human rights courts deter future human rights abuses? Because I am interested in the process by which adverse regional human rights court judgments deter future human rights abuses, the outcome of interest (dependent variable) used in the analyses is a measure of respect for human rights. I argue that regional human rights courts influence executive incentives to adopt, administer, monitor, and enforce human rights policy. When the executive engages in human rights policy change, human rights practices improve. Cross-national data on executive human rights policies do not exist and would be difficult to collect, as executive policies are often not available or formally documented. Respect for rights, though, provides a good indicator of executive policy change. When the executive adopts, administers, monitors, and enforces human rights policy, we should observe demonstrable human rights changes within the state.

Because regional human rights courts render adverse judgments related to many different types of rights abuse, I must choose the type of rights protection to be examined. I examine the influence of regional human rights courts on physical integrity rights practices for several reasons. First, analyzing respect for physical integrity rights provides a robust test of the hypotheses. Court cases involving respect for physical integrity rights face greater legal challenges than court cases involving other types of rights abuse. As noted earlier, the costs of producing legally admissible evidence and standards of proof are higher when it comes to physical integrity rights abuses (Lupu, 2013a). These costs are higher because evidence is often difficult to obtain in the case of physical integrity abuses as victims may be afraid to come forward or are no longer alive. Physical integrity cases also often involve criminal offenses, and the standard of proof in criminal claims is often higher than it is in civil claims due to the nature of criminal offenses (Lupu, 2013a). As a result, the state faces greater uncertainty about the facts and quality of cases involving physical integrity rights abuses, and this uncertainty can provide executives the necessary political cover to evade human rights policy changes following a regional court judgment. A second reason to examine physical integrity abuses in this study is because guaranteeing respect for physical integrity rights requires executive decision making and, importantly, changes in executive behavior, which is consistent with the policy changes necessary for regional court deterrence described in Chapter 2. For example, respect for the right to be free from torture is unlikely to occur absent proactive adoption and administration of training and monitoring programs for state agents (Conrad and Moore, 2010). A final reason to examine respect for physical integrity rights, as opposed to other types of rights abuses, is driven by practical considerations. Several excellent data collection projects have produced annual cross-national data on respect for physical integrity rights (e.g., Conrad, Haglund, and Moore, 2013; Cingranelli, Richards, and Clay, 2014; Gibney et al., 2016), and a recent study utilizes several of these datasets to generate estimates of the underlying latent concept of respect for physical integrity rights (Fariss, 2014), providing an excellent measure of physical integrity rights practices.

I utilize data on respect for physical integrity rights from Fariss (2014), which is based on a dynamic latent variable measurement model using 13 indicators of state human rights practices and accounting for changing standards of accountability, or the increased stringency with which organizations assess a government's human rights practices. The Fariss (2014) measure is based on the excellent data collection efforts of Cingranelli, Richards, and Clay (2014), Hathaway (2002), Conrad, Haglund, and Moore (2013), and Gibney et al. (2016), as well as several events-based datasets. Many of these datasets, particularly the standards-based datasets, use content analysis of US State Department Human Rights Reports and Amnesty International reports to collect human rights data.

The datasets used to produce the Fariss (2014) estimates (e.g., Cingranelli, Richards, and Clay, 2014; Gibney et al., 2016) code state human rights *practices*, not human rights policies or conditions (Cingranelli, Richards, and Clay, 2014). As a result, data used to create the latent estimates do not rely on court cases related to past abuses to assign human rights scores to countries. This distinction is important in order to avoid conceptual overlap between the independent variable (adverse court judgments) and the dependent variable (human rights practices).[4] In the empirical analyses (described later), I also lag the independent variable (1, 3, and 5 years), which means I assess the level of respect for rights in the years following an adverse judgment. The temporal separation means that human rights practices are not being evaluated in the year in which the judgment was rendered. The Fariss (2014) estimates range from about −2 to +5 in Europe and −2 to +3 in the Americas, with higher values on this variable representing greater levels of respect for rights and lower values representing lower levels of respect for rights.

Figure 3.2 displays the mean respect for physical integrity rights in Europe from 1980 to 2012 (left panel) and the Americas from 1987 to 2012 (right panel) for countries subject to the jurisdiction of the European and Inter-American Courts of Human Rights (using the Fariss [2014] physical integrity rights data). Noticeably, Figure 3.2 shows that on average, respect for physical integrity rights is higher in Europe than in the Americas. Over time, physical integrity rights range from around 1.6 to 2.1 in Europe on average, while over a similar time period, respect for physical integrity rights ranges from around −0.5 to +0.5 in the Americas on average. Also of note, respect for rights in the European sample shows a slight decline in the 1990s, which may be explained by the addition of new members to the Council of Europe (and therefore, the European Court). Many new member–states, including Croatia, the Slovak Republic, Serbia, and Azerbaijan, face more widespread rights-related concerns than the original members. On the other hand, respect for rights in the Americas steadily increased during the 1990s, which is likely due to the democratic transitions taking place within many countries in the Americas.

3.2.1 *Effectiveness versus Compliance*

In Chapter 2, I discussed several reasons why it is theoretically interesting to examine regional human rights court effectiveness (achieved through the process of deterrence), rather than compliance with the regional court, as the

---

[4] Notably, if there was conceptual overlap in the independent and dependent variables, my results would be biased toward the null. That is, if adverse judgments were used to code human rights data (which is not the case), states that received adverse judgments would receive lower human rights scores. I find that adverse judgments are not consistently negatively associated with human rights practices, particularly when the executive is capable and willing.

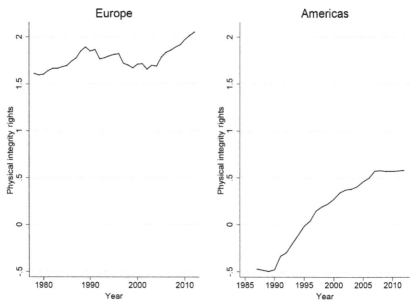

FIGURE 3.2. Mean physical integrity rights over time in Europe and the Americas
Notes: Figure 3.2 displays the mean physical integrity rights score from 1980 to 2012 in Europe and 1987 to 2012 in the Americas based on data from Fariss (2014). In comparing respect for physical integrity rights on the same scale, noticeably, respect for rights is higher in Europe than the Americas over the entire time period, indicating that there is more room for human rights improvement in the Americas than in Europe. As a result, effect sizes in the models predicting European Court deterrence of future rights abuses in Europe are likely to be smaller than effect sizes in the models predicting Inter-American Court deterrence of future rights abuses in the Americas.

primary outcome of interest. In addition to theoretical reasoning, empirical evidence also supports the need to examine regional human rights court effectiveness as the outcome of interest (dependent variable).

Table 3.1 displays the association between effectiveness and compliance using compliance data taken from the Compliance with Human Rights Tribunals (CHRT) Dataset (Hillebrecht, 2014), which measures compliance with the European and Inter-American Courts of Human Rights from 2008 to 2010. Compliance is reported in Table 3.1 as the percentage of total obligations with which states complied in individual cases related to physical integrity rights (PIR) abuses (row 1). The other rows in Table 3.1 report the percentage of obligations of each type of mandate with which states complied. Obligations related to financial reparations include payment of pecuniary and nonpecuniary damages, as well as costs and expenses. Examples of symbolic measures include public apologies, publishing the judgment, and commemorating

3.2 Regional Human Rights Court Effectiveness

TABLE 3.1. *Strength of association between compliance and effectiveness*

	European Court		Inter-American Court	
Percent complied	PIR (3-year change)	PIR (year coded change)	PIR (3-year change)	PIR (year coded change)
Total	0.0231	0.1495	−0.0202	0.0154
	(0.8350)	(0.2006)	(0.8660)	(0.9164)
	N = 84	N = 75	N = 53	N = 49
Financial reparations	0.0134	0.1399	0.0567	0.0367
	(0.9285)	(0.3830)	(0.6958)	(0.8088)
	N = 47	N = 41	N = 50	N = 46
Symbolic measures	0.0639	0.1260	−0.2364	**−0.3221**
	(0.6914)	(0.4573)	(0.1531)	**(0.0632)**
	N = 41	N = 37	N = 38	N = 34
Accountability	−0.0132	0.0035	−0.1689	−0.2373
	(0.9535)	(0.9879)	(0.2790)	(0.1403)
	N = 22	N = 21	N = 43	N = 40
Nonrepetition	−0.0011	0.1692	−0.0491	−0.0311
	(0.9940)	(0.2903)	(0.7897)	(0.8753)
	N = 46	N = 41	N = 32	N = 28
Individual measures	0.1063	0.1283	−0.0820	−0.1809
	(0.6129)	(0.5795)	(0.6199)	(0.2982)
	N = 25	N = 21	N = 39	N = 35

Notes: Table 3.1 shows the relationship between compliance and effectiveness. Rows display the percent of different types of compliance orders with which states complied, while columns display the change in respect for physical integrity rights (PIR) from the year of the judgment to 3 years postjudgment (columns 2 and 4) and the change in respect for physical integrity rights from the year of the judgment to the year compliance was coded (columns 3 and 5). Pearson's correlation coefficients, *p*-values (in parentheses), and sample size are displayed. Bolded values indicate statistical significance (but not strength of relationship).

victims, while examples of accountability include compliance with obligations to hold perpetrators accountable and (re)open domestic proceedings. Compliance with obligations of measures of nonrepetition include changing laws, procedures, and administrative practices. Finally, compliance with individual measures include recovering remains of victims and providing (mental) healthcare for the next of kin, among others.[5] Columns 2 and 4 of

---

[5] For more detailed descriptions of the types of compliance mandates, see Hillebrecht (2014, 50–51).

Table 3.1 display the correlation between compliance with various obligations and change in physical integrity rights from the year of the judgment to 3 years postjudgment according to the Fariss (2014) data on respect for physical integrity rights. Columns 3 and 5 of Table 3.1 display the correlation between compliance with various obligations and the change in the level of respect for physical integrity rights from the year of the judgment to the year in which compliance was coded.[6]

Table 3.1 displays several key pieces of information, including (1) the Pearson's correlation coefficient, which indicates the strength of the correlation; (2) a *p*-value, which indicates the statistical significance of the result ($p < 0.05$ represents the standard level of significance); and (3) the number of cases in each court used to calculate the correlation. The bold cells in Table 3.1 represent the cells in which there is a statistically significant association among the variables. However, to determine the strength of the relationship, I turn to the Pearson's correlation coefficient. The Pearson's correlation coefficient ranges -1 to $+1$, with higher values indicating a stronger correlation. Generally, according to Cohen (1988), a correlation coefficient greater than 0.5 represents a strong correlation, a correlation coefficient less than 0.5, but greater than 0.3 represents a moderate correlation, and a correlation coefficient less than 0.3 represents a small or weak correlation. In Table 3.1, there are no cells with strong correlations and only one cell with a moderate correlation. The moderate correlation is reported in Column 5. The change in respect for physical integrity rights from the year of the judgment to the year in which compliance was recorded is negatively and significantly correlated with symbolic measures (correlation coefficient of -0.3221). Perhaps states use compliance with symbolic measures as political cover for continued rights abuses.

If compliance and effectiveness were correlated strongly, compliance with measures of nonrepetition should be most highly associated with greater respect for rights, as measures of nonrepetition capture measures designed to prevent the occurrence of abuses in the future. However, compliance with most European and Inter-American Court obligations are weakly (and sometimes negatively) correlated with both changes in respect for rights 3 years postjudgment and changes in respect for rights from the time of the judgment to the year in which compliance was coded. The evidence presented in

---

[6] Results are robust to correlations among compliance and Cingranelli, Richards, and Clay (2014) data on respect for physical integrity rights. Results are also similar when examining the correlation between compliance and the change in respect for physical integrity rights from the year of the judgment to 1 and 5 years postjudgment.

Table 3.1 does not indicate that studying compliance is not a worthwhile endeavor, as many compliance orders involve remedies for a specific human rights abuse. Instead, future work should explore the processes of compliance and effectiveness jointly, as the relationship may not be as straightforward as assuming that greater compliance produces executive adoption, administration, monitoring, and enforcement of human rights policy following an adverse regional human rights court judgment.

While prior work examining compliance has been vital in advancing our understanding of the impact of regional human rights courts, the theory and empirical analyses in this book examine the deterrent effect of adverse regional human rights court judgments. Some scholars even claim that regardless of the rate of compliance with human rights court rulings, improvement in respect for human rights represents a good indication of an effective regional court, all else being equal (Posner and Yoo, 2005, 29). That is, to understand when the regional human rights court deters future human rights abuses, we must examine state human rights practices.

3.3 EXAMINING GENERAL DETERRENCE

Having determined that the outcome of interest is regional court effectiveness, or the level of respect for rights, I turn to measurement of the explanatory variable. As noted in Chapter 2, there are two types of deterrence: general and specific. I argued that general deterrence takes place when the presence of the regional court deters the commission of future human rights abuses by state actors. However, general deterrence can take another form; the regional court may also deter through its actions toward other states in the region. Moving beyond the mere presence of the court, this effect is based on a state's observation of the regional court's activity in other states in the region. In other words, as the regional court becomes more active, rendering a greater number of adverse judgments in the region, states are deterred from committing human rights abuses because they recognize that they face an increased probability of future litigation. Table 3.2 shows the mechanisms by which regional courts deter future human rights abuses in a state, here State A, as a function of general and specific deterrence.

I utilize two indicators to capture the general deterrent effect of the European and Inter-American Courts of Human Rights. First, I look to state commitment to the regional court. Once the state accepts the jurisdiction of the regional court, the state faces a threat of future judgments. Second, I look to the regional court's activity in the region using data on the presence of adverse European or Inter-American Court of Human Rights judgments.

TABLE 3.2. *Mechanisms through which State A is deterred by regional court*

Type	Mechanism
General	State A is deterred by the presence of the regional court.
	State A is deterred by the regional court's judgments against other states in the region.
Specific	State A is deterred by the regional court's judgments against State A.

Notes: Table 3.2 displays the two types of deterrence (general and specific), as well as two ways to observe general deterrence and one way to observe specific deterrence. General deterrence is examined more in this section. Specific deterrence is examined in Chapters 4–7.

In subsequent chapters, I assess specific deterrence using data capturing the presence of adverse judgments against each state.

Figure 3.3 displays the number of adverse physical integrity rights rulings from the European and Inter-American Courts of Human Rights over time in Europe and the Americas. Adverse judgments involving physical integrity abuses in Europe involve violations of Article 2 (right to life), Article 3 (prohibition of torture), Article 4 (freedom from slavery), and Article 5 (right to liberty and security) of the European Convention on Human Rights. Not all adverse European Court judgments are considered to be of equal importance. Judgments can be divided into four categories. Case reports represent judgments of the highest level of importance, and judgments are published or selected for publication in the Court's official *Reports of Judgments and Decisions*. Following case reports are cases of level 1, level 2, and level 3 importance. Level 1 judgments are those of high-level importance not included in case reports that make a significant contribution to development, clarification, or modification of the court's case-law. Judgments of level 2 importance are those that do not make a significant contribution to case-law but go beyond merely applying case-law and judgments of level 3 importance are judgments that simply apply existing case-law. I only include judgments from case reports (called key cases in the HUDOC database), judgments of level 1, and judgments of level 2 importance. I exclude judgments of level 3 importance because they only apply existing case law and do not communicate new information to the executive, political elites, or the general public. In fact, the European Court notes that level 3 judgments are of low importance and of little legal interest. As a result, the likelihood of level 3 judgments influencing the incentives of the executive is relatively low.

In addition, European Court judgments can involve substantive or procedural violations of the European Convention. A violation of the substantive

3.3 Examining General Deterrence

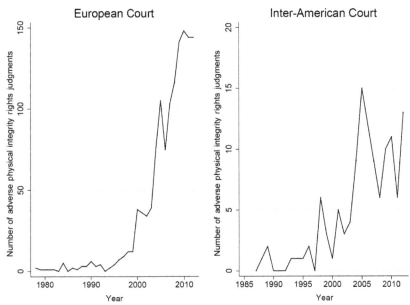

FIGURE 3.3. Number of adverse physical integrity rights judgments in Europe and the Americas over time

Notes: Figure 3.3 displays the annual number of adverse European Court (left panel) and Inter-American Court (right panel) judgments involving violations of physical integrity rights. For the European Court, adverse physical integrity rights judgments involve violations of Article 2 (right to life), Article 3 (prohibition of torture), Article 4 (freedom from slavery), and Article 5 (right to liberty and security) of the European Convention on Human Rights. For the Inter-American Court, adverse physical integrity rights judgments involve violations of Article 4 (right to life), Article 5 (right to humane treatment), and Article 7 (right to personal integrity) of the American Convention on Human Rights. In comparing the number of judgments by each Court, note that the y-axes in these figures are different. The number of adverse European Court judgments related to physical integrity rights ranges from 0 to 148 annually, while the number of adverse Inter-American Court judgments ranges from 0 to 15 annually.

aspect of Article 3 of the European Convention on Human Rights, for example, stipulates that the state engaged in torture or degrading treatment. A violation of the procedural aspect of Article 3 of the European Convention often indicates that the state failed to promptly, effectively, and publicly carry out an investigation or the investigation may not have been carried out by an independent agency alleged to have engaged in human rights abuse. I argue that violations of Article 3 of the ECHR should deter future human rights abuses regardless of whether the violation was substantive or procedural. European Court judgments alleging substantive violations call the state out directly for engaging in human rights abuses. European Court judgments alleging procedural violations indirectly call the state out for human rights abuse by noting the procedural problems the state faces in properly investigating an abuse, for example. Executive policy changes designed to curb future procedural violations are designed to effectively deter future abuses. For example, executive adoption, administration, monitoring, and enforcement of policies designed to ensure the proper investigation of cases of torture can influence the incentives of state agents in the future. Knowing that they will face proper investigations, state agents are likely to be deterred from engaging in torture and degrading practices in the future, which should lead to improvements in human rights. As a result, I include both substantive and procedural violations of Articles 2, 3, 4, and 5 of the European Convention.

To gather data on the European Court of Human Rights, I visited the HUDOC database of the European Court of Human Rights, performed searches of cases involving violations of the relevant articles of the European Convention for each state in the European Court sample (published in case reports, or classified as level 1 or level 2 importance), and recorded annual data.[7]

Adverse judgments involving physical integrity abuses in the Americas involve violations of Article 4 (right to life), Article 5 (right to humane treatment), and Article 7 (right to personal integrity) of the American Convention on Human Rights. Fortunately, data on Inter-American Court judgments involving physical integrity for the years 1989 to 2010 have been collected by Hawkins and Jacoby (2010). I expanded on these data by visiting the Inter-American Court website and recording case conclusions, including violations of the relevant articles for the years 2011 to 2012.

Of note in Figure 3.3 is the sheer volume of adverse judgments in Europe. The number of adverse judgments related to physical integrity abuses has grown substantially in recent years, particularly beginning in the 2000s. While the number of adverse judgments related to physical integrity abuses in the Americas is lower, there is a similar rise in the 2000s as well. The patterns in Figures 3.2 and 3.3 indicate that these two variables appear to be trending together, that is, we observe a rise in respect for rights at a similar time as the number of adverse judgments are rising.

Figures 3.4 and 3.5 display the regional distribution of adverse judgments involving violations of physical integrity in Europe and the Americas.[8]

---

[7] While Voeten (2007) has collected data on European Court case conclusions, the data are not formatted by country-year, and to my knowledge, do not extend beyond 2006. A recently released dataset by Cichowski and Chrun (2017) also has excellent data on European Court judgments, but these data were not publicly available at the time the analyses were performed.

[8] Maps presented in Chapter 1 display not only adverse judgments associated with physical integrity rights, but all types of rights violations.

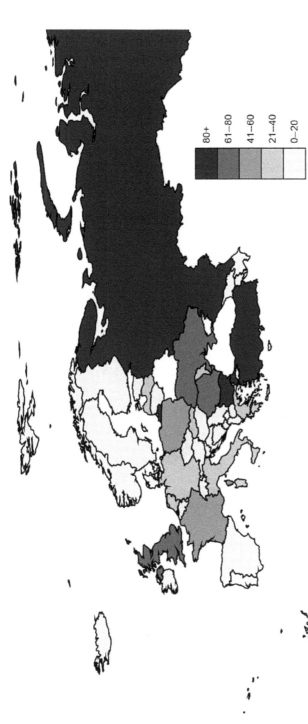

FIGURE 3.4. Number of adverse European Court physical integrity rights judgments (1980 to 2012)

Notes: Figure 3.4 displays the total number of adverse judgments involving physical integrity rights violations in Europe from 1980 to 2012. Adverse judgments related to physical integrity involve violations of Article 2 (right to life), Article 3 (prohibition of torture), Article 4 (freedom from slavery), and Article 5 (right to liberty and security) of the European Convention on Human Rights. Figure 3.4 only displays adverse judgments published in case reports or those of level 1 or level 2 importance. Darker states received a greater number of adverse judgments, while lighter states received fewer adverse judgments.

FIGURE 3.5. Number of adverse Inter-American Court physical integrity judgments (1989 to 2012)
Notes: Figure 3.5 displays the total number of adverse judgments involving physical integrity rights violations in the Americas from 1989 to 2012. Adverse judgments related to physical integrity involve violations of Article 4 (right to life), Article 5 (right to humane treatment), and Article 7 (right to personal integrity) of the American Convention on Human Rights. Darker states received a greater number of adverse judgements, while lighter states received fewer adverse judgments.

Figure 3.4 shows the total number of adverse European Court judgments involving physical integrity rights abuses for each state from 1980 to 2012. Figure 3.4 only displays adverse judgments published in case reports and those of level 1 and level 2 importance. Darker-colored states received more adverse judgments, and lighter-colored states received the fewest adverse judgments. The recipients of the largest number of adverse European Court judgments related to physical integrity rights abuse in Europe include Turkey,

3.4 *Evidence of General Regional Court Deterrence* 97

Russia, Bulgaria, Ukraine, and Romania. The recipients of the fewest number of adverse European Court judgments related to physical integrity rights abuse in Europe are Andorra, Montenegro, Monaco, Albania, and Norway. Some states received few adverse judgments from 1980 to 2012 because they did not become members of the Council of Europe (and come under the jurisdiction of the European Court) until much later in the time series covered by the data (e.g., Montenegro), while other states likely received few adverse judgments because they are better rights protectors (e.g., Norway).

Figure 3.5 shows the total number of adverse Inter-American Court judgments involving physical integrity abuses from 1989 to 2012. Like Figure 3.4, darker-colored states received more adverse judgments, while lighter states received fewer adverse judgments. While the total number of adverse physical integrity rights judgments in the Americas is fewer than in Europe, there is still variation within the region. The number of adverse judgments for each state ranges from 0 to 19 from 1989 to 2012. The states receiving the most adverse Inter-American Court judgments involving physical integrity abuses include Peru, Guatemala, Colombia, Venezuela, and Ecuador. States receiving the fewest number of adverse physical integrity rights judgments are Nicaragua, Chile, Costa Rica, Uruguay, and Barbados.

3.4 EVIDENCE OF GENERAL REGIONAL COURT DETERRENCE

3.4.1 *General Deterrence through Regional Court Presence*

To examine evidence of general deterrence, I first present descriptive statistics that show the level of respect for rights before and after states accepted the jurisdiction of each regional court. Figure 3.6 displays the mean and median level of respect for rights in Europe (left panel) and the Americas (right panel) before and after each regional court was established. The solid line in each panel depicts the mean level of respect for rights, and the dashed line depicts the median level of respect for rights. The vertical dotted line depicts the year in which each court was established, that is, the European Court was established in Europe in 1959, and the Inter-American Court was established in 1979 in the Americas.

In Europe, the mean level of respect for rights is significantly higher following the establishment of the European Court than prior to the European Court's establishment. Notably, however, respect for rights was growing in Europe prior to the establishment of the European Court (1955 to 1959), likely because of the end of WWII and the establishment of the United Nations and its subsidiary human rights bodies. Also of note, the median level of respect

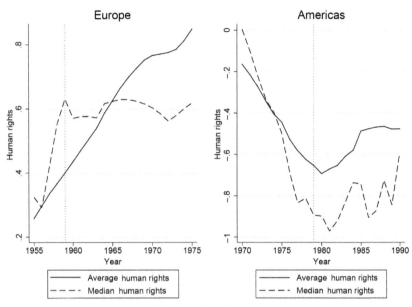

FIGURE 3.6. Level of respect for rights in Europe and Americas

Notes: Figure 3.6 displays the mean level of respect for rights (solid line) and median level of respect for rights (dashed line) in Europe (left panel) and the Americas (right panel) over time. The vertical dotted line represents the establishment of the European and Inter-American Courts of Human Rights.

for rights in Europe did not grow following the establishment of the European Court. In fact, the median level of respect for rights declines and then remains largely stagnant in the region. The difference in the patterns displayed in Europe (left panel) indicates that some countries showed large improvements in respect for rights, bringing the regional average of respect for rights higher. Turning to the Americas, the right panel of Figure 3.6 shows that respect for rights improved following the establishment of the Inter-American Court. However, the trend is not consistently positive over the years. For example, in 1985, there is a decline in the median level of respect for rights in the Americas, and the mean level of respect for rights becomes stagnant.

Because of the difference in the mean and median levels of respect for rights across the region, I present the variation in respect for rights within each region. Figure 3.7 displays the level of respect for rights (solid line) in 42 countries in the European sample.[9] The dashed vertical line represents

---

[9] Several countries are omitted due to missing human rights data in the year in which they accepted the jurisdiction of the court.

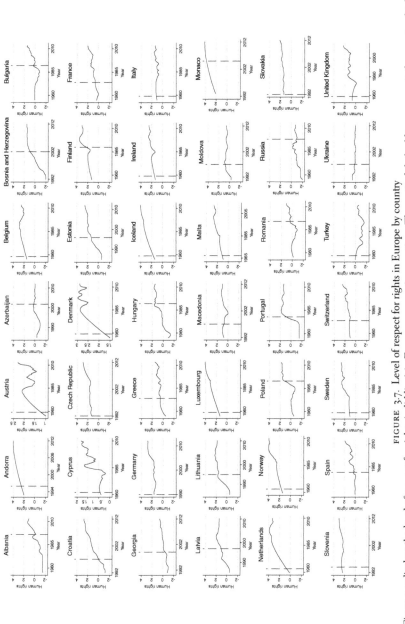

FIGURE 3.7. Level of respect for rights in Europe by country

Notes: Figure 3.7 displays the level of respect for rights (solid line) in European countries over time. The vertical dashed line represents the year in which each country ratified the European Convention on Human Rights and accepted the jurisdiction of the European Court. Several states are omitted because of missing human rights data in the year in which they ratified the European Convention, including Liechtenstein, Montenegro, San Marino, and Serbia.

the year in which each country ratified the European Convention on Human Rights and accepted the jurisdiction of the European Court. Although the European Court began operating in 1959, several states committed to the European Convention in the early 1950s (e.g., Belgium, Denmark, Iceland, Ireland, Italy). General deterrence is more likely to prevent future human rights abuses when the court is operational and there is a greater threat of future litigation. As a result, for states that ratified the European Convention prior to the European Court becoming operational in 1959, the dashed vertical line represents the year the court became operational (1959). While some states showed noticeable improvements in respect for rights following their commitment to the European Convention and Court (e.g., Croatia, Denmark, Iceland, Netherlands), others did not show much improvement in respect for rights (i.e., Azerbaijan, Czech Republic, Germany, Greece, Italy, Portugal, Russia, Turkey, United Kingdom). The variation in European state human rights practices following ratification of the European Convention suggests that the mere presence of the European Court in the region and the acceptance of the European Court's jurisdiction does not deter future human rights abuses, at least not evenly across states.

Turning to variation in the Americas, Figure 3.8 displays the level of respect for rights in each country under the jurisdiction of the Inter-American Court before and after accepting the jurisdiction of the Inter-American Court. The vertical dashed line represents the year in which a country accepted the jurisdiction of the Inter-American Court. Several countries ratified the American Convention on Human Rights and accepted the jurisdiction of the Inter-American Court prior to the Inter-American Court becoming operational in 1979. The vertical dashed line is placed at 1979 for countries that accepted the jurisdiction of the Inter-American Court on or before 1979 because general deterrence is more likely when the Inter-American Court is operational.

While several countries displayed an improvement in respect for rights following the establishment of the Court (i.e., Chile, Guatemala, Nicaragua, Uruguay), several countries also show little change in respect for rights, after the establishment of the Court (i.e., Brazil, Ecuador, Haiti, Panama, Peru, Venezuela). Notably, the Inter-American Court was established prior to the termination of several ongoing conflicts and prior to the establishment of democracy in several countries. The termination of conflict, peace settlements, and establishment of democracy may explain tangible human rights improvements at this time. Also of note, several countries that eventually show improvements in human rights over time did not show improvements for many years following the establishment of the Inter-American Court. For instance, despite being under the jurisdiction of the Inter-American Court for almost a

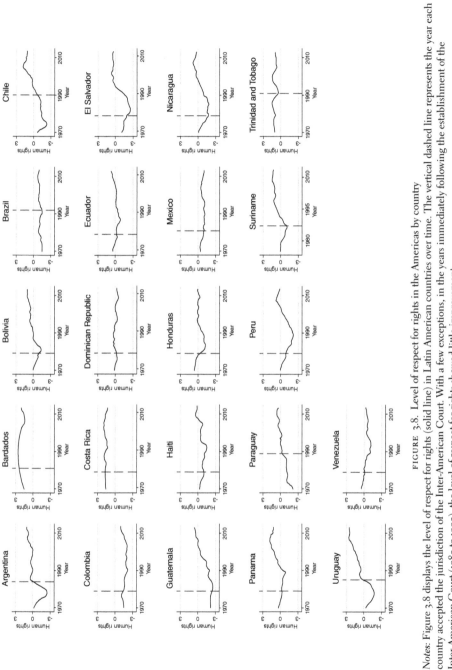

FIGURE 3.8. Level of respect for rights in the Americas by country

Notes: Figure 3.8 displays the level of respect for rights (solid line) in Latin American countries over time. The vertical dashed line represents the year each country accepted the jurisdiction of the Inter-American Court. With a few exceptions, in the years immediately following the establishment of the Inter-American Court (1980 to 1990), the level of respect for rights showed little improvement.

decade, El Salvador's and Peru's human rights practices remained low until around 1990.

Taken together, Figures 3.6–3.8 show little evidence that regional human rights courts deter future human rights abuses solely through their presence in the region. While there is some evidence of growth in respect for rights in Europe and the Americas following the establishment of the European and Inter-American Courts of Human Rights, there is less evidence of human rights improvements in the immediate term. That is, I find little improvement in respect for rights in the years immediately following membership in the regional organization and acceptance of the regional court's jurisdiction. Importantly, major political changes took place in both regions following the establishment of each Court. The end of WWII in Europe, the establishment of the United Nations, and subsequent adoption of the Universal Declaration of Human Rights meant that states were already increasing their commitment to international human rights in Europe when the European Court was established. In the Americas, several states emerged from violent conflicts throughout the 1980s and early 1990s, and many states transitioned to democratic forms of governance, providing greater room for growth in human rights. The variation in the findings across states in Figures 3.7 and 3.8 indicate that the influence of the mere presence of the regional court on state human rights practices may be conditional on several international and domestic factors (e.g. democracy), suggesting a path for future research on general regional human rights court deterrence.

3.4.2 General Deterrence through Regional Court Activity

Turning to the second indicator of general deterrence, I examine the influence of the activity of the European Court in Europe and the Inter-American Court in the Americas. That is, for general deterrence to occur, adverse regional court judgments against any state in the region should deter all other states from committing future human rights abuses. To examine general deterrence, I estimate a model that predicts the influence of the number of adverse regional court judgments rendered against all states in the region on respect for rights 1, 3, and 5 years postjudgment. The unit of analysis is the country-year, and the European sample includes all Council of Europe member states from 1980 to 2012. The sample excludes Montenegro, which became a member of the Council of Europe in 2007, but was not the recipient of an adverse European Court judgment related to physical integrity rights (the focus of the empirical analysis) until 2014. The Organization of American States (OAS) currently consists of 35 member-states, 23 of which are party to the American

Convention. Currently, 20 states recognize the contentious jurisdiction of the Inter-American Court.[10] I examine Inter-American Court judgments for those states under the jurisdiction of the Inter-American Court for the years 1989 to 2012.

To measure the outcome, respect for rights, I utilize the Fariss (2014) measure of respect for physical integrity rights (displayed in Figure 3.2), which is based on a latent variable measurement model and is continuous. The dependent variable captures the level of respect for rights at several points in time following an adverse judgment. I examine the level of respect for rights postjudgment, rather than a change in respect for rights (from the year of the judgment to several points in time postjudgment) for several reasons. First, the Fariss (2014) latent variable estimates are generated from a model in which physical integrity rights scores for a country in a particular year are dependent on the value of the same country in the previous year (304). The Fariss (2014) estimates are generated from a dynamic item-response model, which accounts for changing standards of accountability or more stringent standards on the part of monitoring agencies. That is, the dynamic model used to produce the human rights estimates accounts for the probability of observing and coding rights violations over time, as monitoring agencies that produce reports used to generate repression variables have greater access to information. As a result, the change in the Fariss (2014) human rights estimates is not an accurate depiction of the change in respect for rights from one year to the next because in generating estimates for year t, estimates for year t-1 are taken into account in the model. Another reason I utilize the level of respect for rights as the dependent variable is because interpreting the dependent variable is intuitive and straightforward. For most of the models estimated in this book, the results displayed show whether the presence of an adverse judgment is associated with higher levels of respect for rights across values of executive capacity and willingness.

Finally, rather than examining the level of respect for rights in the year of the judgment as the dependent variable, I lag the adverse judgment variable (independent variable) by 1, 3, and 5 years, which captures the level of respect for rights postjudgment. Through post estimation analyses, I then compare the level of respect for rights for adverse judgment recipients in the postjudgment period. This approach allows me to compare adverse judgment recipients' level of respect for rights, rather than comparing changes in respect for rights

---

[10] Trinidad and Tobago denounced the American Convention and the Inter-American Court, and Canada and the United States have not ratified the American Convention. Trinidad and Tobago, the United States, and Canada are omitted from the analysis.

within countries. However, if regional courts only rendered adverse judgments in states with high levels of respect for rights, the results would be biased. Biased results would show that adverse judgment recipients have higher levels of respect for rights, but this would be because they had relatively high levels of respect for rights prior to the adverse judgment being rendered.

Examining the level of respect for physical integrity rights for adverse judgment recipients and nonadverse judgment recipients shows that adverse judgment recipients do not have significantly higher or lower levels of respect for rights than nonadverse judgment recipients. The European Court renders more adverse judgments against states with lower respect for rights, rather than higher respect for rights. The average level of respect for rights in Europe is 1.79, and the average level of respect for rights for adverse European Court judgment recipients is 1.37 (Fariss, 2014). The average level of respect for rights in the Americas is 0.174, and the average level of respect for rights for adverse judgment recipients is 0.073 (Fariss, 2014). The evidence suggests that regional courts are not solely rendering adverse judgments against states with high levels of respect for rights. Rather, regional courts are more likely to render judgments against states with relatively lower levels of respect for rights.[11]

However, as a robustness check, I utilize the Cingranelli, Richards, and Clay (2014) physical integrity rights index to assess changes in the level of respect for rights. The Cingranelli, Richards, and Clay (CIRI) physical integrity rights index ranges from 0 to 8, with higher values indicating better respect for rights. Physical integrity rights include freedom from torture, disappearance, political imprisonment, and extrajudicial killing. A change in the CIRI physical integrity rights index represents a definitive increase or decrease in physical integrity rights practices (e.g., moving from frequent torture to occasional torture). In the empirical results that follow and for each hypothesis tested in subsequent chapters, I report the results for linear regression models utilizing an alternative dependent variable based on a change in respect for physical integrity rights. The 1-year change variable ranges from −4 to +3 in Europe and −4 to +6 in the Americas.

Given the nature of the dependent variable, I estimate linear regression models for both the European and Inter-American Court samples.[12] The

---

[11] This descriptive evidence suggests that using the level of respect for rights as the dependent variable will bias my results toward the null hypothesis.

[12] Models are robust to several different specifications, including a specification in which I use the Cingranelli, Richards, and Clay (2014) physical integrity rights index as a dependent variable as well as Bayesian hierarchical linear regression models. While selection is often a concern in studies examining the influence of international human rights law on state behavior, I do not utilize a selection model in these analyses and I discuss this challenge in more depth in Chapter 4.

3.4 Evidence of General Regional Court Deterrence

independent variable captures the number of adverse judgments in the region, excluding the number of adverse judgments directly received by the each state. Figure 3.3 displays the total number of adverse judgments in the region over time.[13] This variable captures the general deterrent effect of the regional court because it represents the court's activity in the region (total adverse judgments), while omitting the court's activity in each state (adverse judgments against each state).[14]

As discussed earlier in this chapter, the European and Inter-American Courts of Human Rights operate differently, particularly in their procedures and mechanisms for monitoring and securing state compliance. These differences provide justification for estimating individual models for each region. Within each region, the heterogeneity across states means that each country's baseline probability of making human rights policy changes in response to an adverse regional human rights court judgment is not the same, even after accounting for various control variables in the model. The growth in Council of Europe membership and European Court jurisdiction is a case in point, as many new members are regular rights violators (i.e., Serbia, Ukraine).

Rather than pooling all of the data together in the linear regression model, I account for unobserved heterogeneity across states by relaxing the assumption of a common intercept. More specifically, I utilize hierarchical modeling techniques by incorporating random intercepts in the model specification (Gelman and Hill, 2007, 259). By employing random intercepts, the model removes the restriction that the intercepts are constant across different observations, and treats the cross-sectional deviations from the common intercept as random, rather than estimable.[15] Also, because there are clusters of countries in the data, I cannot assume independence across observations. As a result, I utilize standard errors clustered on country. Additional model details, including descriptions of the control variables used in the analyses and full model results, are included in the Appendix to this chapter.

Figure 3.9 displays results for the primary variables of interest in the models. The figure displays coefficient estimates from the models (dots), which indicate the expected level of respect for rights, given the presence of an additional

---

[13] Adverse judgments in Europe only include key judgments and those of level 1 and level 2 importance.

[14] While the measure utilized in the model represents a count of the number of adverse judgments in the region, excluding the number of adverse judgments against each state, I control for the number of adverse judgments against each state in each model.

[15] Conducting a Breusch and Pagan Lagrangian Multiplier test shows that I can reject the null hypothesis that there is no significant difference across units, and the random effects model is appropriate.

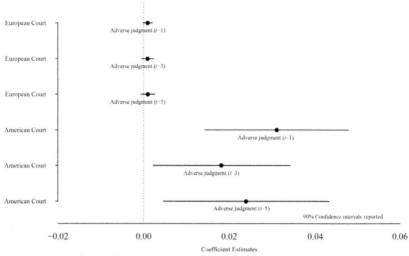

FIGURE 3.9. Predicted influence of adverse regional court activity on respect for rights
Notes: Figure 3.9 displays the influence of adverse regional court activity on respect for rights. Dots represent coefficient estimates, and lines represent 90 percent confidence intervals. The results displayed in Figure 3.9 indicate that the number of adverse judgments in Europe is not significantly associated with respect for rights; however, the number of adverse Inter-American Court judgments is positively and significantly associated with respect for rights in states in the Americas, providing some evidence in support of general deterrence in the Americas.

adverse regional human rights court judgment and controlling for various other factors. The line segments represent 90 percent confidence intervals, and they indicate that we can be 90 percent confident that the mean value of respect for rights is between the lines on the segment. A positive coefficient estimate with a 90 percent confidence interval that does not cross zero lends support to the hypothesis because it indicates that the number of adverse judgments by each regional court is positively associated with respect for rights 1, 3, and/or 5 years following the judgment(s).

There is little support for the role of general deterrence in Europe. The first three coefficient estimates in Figure 3.9 are substantively small, indicating that each additional adverse judgment by the European Court is associated with a fairly small increase in respect for rights 1, 3, and 5 years postjudgment. Moreover, the 90 percent confidence intervals all contain zero, indicating that we cannot be sufficiently confident that the relationship between adverse European Court judgments and respect for rights is positive.

In contrast, Figure 3.9 displays support for the role of general deterrence in the Americas. For example, each additional adverse judgment in the Americas is associated with 0.03 higher level of respect for rights 1 year after the adverse judgment and around 0.02 higher level of respect for rights 3 and 5 years following the adverse judgment on average. The average number of adverse judgments related to physical integrity rights in the Americas in a given year is around 4, suggesting that 1 year following the average number of adverse judgments in the region, respect for rights is around 0.12 higher in countries in the Americas than if there were no adverse judgments.

Taken together, I find limited support for the role of general deterrence. I assessed general deterrence in two ways. First, I examined the influence of the presence of the regional court on respect for rights. I find that the mere presence of the European and Inter-American Courts of Human Rights is not consistently associated with human rights improvements across states in Europe and the Americas. Second, I examined the activity of the regional court in each region by accounting for the number of adverse judgments rendered in the region. I find that the activity of the European Court is not positively and significantly associated with respect for rights in Europe. However, in the Americas, the activity of the Inter-American Court is positively and significantly associated with respect for rights. The influence of regional court activity on respect for rights more broadly in the Americas represents an important and understudied effect of regional human rights courts that deserves greater attention in future work.

3.5 CONCLUSION

In this chapter, I discussed and examined general regional human rights court deterrence. Before examining general deterrence empirically, I developed a research design to assess regional court deterrence. I discussed the outcome of interest examined in this chapter – as well as subsequent chapters – regional court effectiveness. In my discussion of regional human rights court effectiveness, I also distinguished conceptually and empirically between compliance and effectiveness. The descriptive statistics show that effectiveness and compliance are not only conceptually distinct (as argued in Chapter 2), but are also empirically distinct, that is, there is a low correlation between the two concepts.

The low correlation between compliance and effectiveness does not indicate that the study of compliance is unimportant. Compliance often provides remedy for specific human rights abuses and typically requires the payment of reparations and damages to individual victims of rights abuse. Compliance also represents an important way to capture the specific steps states take in responding to regional courts. The study of compliance provides leverage over questions related to strategic behavior by states, as domestic actors select some compliance orders over others or delegate compliance orders from the court's judgment to various domestic actors. Similarly, the study of compliance provides leverage over questions related to strategic behavior by regional courts and advances our understanding of the extent to which regional courts require different states to fulfill different types of orders. Effectiveness, on the other hand, allows scholars to assess the broader impact of regional courts and to study the decision-making and negotiation processes that political actors engage in regarding human rights policy change following an adverse judgment. In other words, effectiveness captures a key goal of regional courts: deterrence of future human rights abuses. The conceptual and empirical differences between the two concepts suggest that theorizing about the two concepts independently is necessary. Future research should consider the two concepts jointly, particularly the relative importance of some compliance orders over others for achieving effectiveness.

To empirically analyze general regional court deterrence, I first examined the influence of regional court presence on respect for rights and I found that the presence of the court in the region is not positively associated with better respect for rights. In fact, respect for rights in many states does not improve following ratification of regional treaties that establish courts and the acceptance of the regional court's jurisdiction. Next, I examined the influence of regional court activity by looking at the influence of the number of adverse judgments rendered by the regional court in the region on respect for rights and I found that the activity of the European Court is not significantly associated with greater respect for rights. However, the activity of the Inter-American Court is significantly associated with greater respect for rights. This is an important finding because it indicates that the Inter-American Court can have a powerful, albeit informal, influence on state human rights practices, by deterring human rights abuses across borders. While the general deterrent effect of regional courts is not the focus of this book, it represents an important avenue of future research, as the evidence suggests that Inter-American Court activity can influence state human rights practices, even when a judgment is not directed at a specific state.

The divergence in findings for general deterrence (based on regional court activity) in Europe and the Americas may be due to differences in the number of adverse judgments rendered in each region. The relatively small number of adverse judgments in the Americas may mean that states place more weight on each adverse judgment in the Americas than in Europe, where a relatively large number of judgments are rendered. In addition, with respect to the type of rights abuses and the institutional structure, the Americas represents a relatively homogenous region compared to Europe. States under the

3.5 Conclusion

jurisdiction of the Inter-American Court have relatively similar past experiences with repressive authoritarian regimes and subsequent democratic transitions. As a result, when states in the Americas observe adverse judgments rendered against other states in the region, they may expect a relatively high likelihood of facing litigation in the future if systemic problems that give way to rights abuses persist. States under the jurisdiction of the European Court, on the other hand, represent a relatively heterogenous group of states, ranging from strong rights-respecting democracies like Norway and Sweden to rights-violating states, like Turkey and Russia. As a result, adverse judgments against some European states may not be particularly pertinent to other states in Europe.

Notably, however, I argued in Chapter 2 that regional human rights courts are more likely to deter future human rights abuses through the mechanism of specific deterrence (i.e., adverse judgments rendered against State A deter future abuses in State A). Although I do not find support for general deterrence in Europe, I find some support for general deterrence as a result of Inter-American Court activity in the Americas. For general deterrence to take place, however, regional human rights courts must render judgments against individual states, and adverse judgments targeting individual states are necessary for specific deterrence to occur. Given the lack of support for general deterrence in the European Court context and the necessity of judgments against individual states for general deterrence to occur, I turn my attention to specific deterrence in the remaining chapters of this book. Notably, however, I account for regional court activity (the general deterrent effect of the regional court) in all subsequent models by including a variable representing the presence of adverse judgments rendered against all states within the region.

Importantly, I do not expect specific regional court deterrence to occur equally across states. In Chapter 2, I argued that the executive must have the capacity and willingness to respond to adverse judgments with the adoption, administration, monitoring, and enforcement of human rights policy. The next four chapters empirically examine the influence of specific regional court deterrence conditional on executive capacity (Chapter 4), executive willingness (Chapters 5 and 6), and in the presence of high executive capacity and willingness (Chapter 7).

4

Does the Executive have the Capacity to Respond to Adverse Judgments?

In Chapter 2, I argued that for adverse regional human rights court judgments to deter future human rights abuses, the executive must have the *capacity* to adopt, administer, monitor, and enforce human rights policy. Because human rights policy change is costly, the executive weighs the costs and benefits of adopting and implementing human rights policy following an adverse regional court judgment. I argued that capacity limitations can inhibit executive human rights policy change in two ways, as a result of feasibility and access to resources. First, the executive is more likely to undertake human rights policy changes that are more directly within executive control, or those that are more feasible. Second, the likelihood of executive human rights policy change is greater when the executive has access to outside resources available for ensuring human rights protections.

To begin empirically examining the role of state capacity in generating human rights policy change following an adverse regional human rights court judgment, I consider several judgments of the European and Inter-American Courts of Human Rights. To illustrate the importance of policy change feasibility in ensuring human rights policy changes, consider two European Court of Human Rights judgments against Turkey, *United Communist Party of Turkey and Others v. Turkey* and *Aydin v. Turkey*. The first case originated with the formation of the United Communist Party of Turkey in June 1990. By an order of the Constitutional Court in Turkey, the United Communist Party was dissolved in July 1991 on the grounds that by having the word *communist* in its name, it violated Turkish law and encouraged separatism in Turkey. Seven other political parties were dissolved around the same time, including the Socialist Party and the Freedom and Democracy Party.[1] The leaders of the dissolved parties were subsequently banned from leadership positions in other political parties in Turkey.

---

[1] All cases involving the dissolution of parties were considered jointly by the European Court.

In 1998, the European Court of Human Rights found Turkey in violation of several articles of the European Convention on Human Rights, including the right to freedom of assembly and association. In response to the adverse European Court judgment, Turkey lifted the bans on leaders and members of the dissolved parties, removed obstacles to reregistering the dissolved parties or registering similar parties, and even allowed the Communist Party to participate in the 2003 general election. These efforts, as well as several constitutional and legislative reforms allowed the European Court to close the case several years later.[2]

Contrast the *United Communist Party* case with the case of *Aydin v. Turkey*. In 1984, members of the Worker's Party of Kurdistan (PKK) tried to establish an independent Kurdish state within Turkey, which led to an armed struggle with Turkish security forces. During this time, security forces questioned a 17-year-old girl, Şükran Aydin, and her family. Şükran was taken with her father and sister-in-law to a detention center for three days, where she was beaten, stripped, and placed inside a tire and sprayed with high pressure water. She was then taken to an interrogation room and raped. After being returned to her village, Şükran and her family members went to the public prosecutor's office to report what happened. A medical examiner sent Şükran to two other doctors to conduct virginity tests to substantiate her claims. An investigation was opened, but there was no subsequent prosecution or conviction.

Following the failed domestic judicial procedure, the European Court of Human Rights rendered an adverse judgment against the state in 1997, finding the state to have violated several articles of the European Convention, including the right to be free from torture. Turkey responded by undertaking several measures to bring itself into compliance with the judgment. Notably, Turkey disseminated the European Court judgment, reduced the length of time a person could be held in police custody, introduced safeguards for those held in police custody, and implemented education programs for law enforcement.[3] However, upon examining the Turkish government's response, the Committee of Ministers of the European Court concluded that the state needed to "pursue with the greatest diligence their efforts to reorganize and improve the training of agents of the security forces in order to ensure respect for human rights in the performance of their duties" (Committee of Ministers, 1999). The Committee of Ministers made several other recommendations to

---

[2] See Appendix to Resolution CM/Res/DH(2007)100 for more on actions taken by Turkey to execute the judgment.
[3] See *Aydin v. Turkey*. Judgment, European Ct. H.R. September 25, 1997.

the state and published a second Interim Resolution in 2005 calling on the state to undertake several other reforms, without closing the case.

In these examples, the European Court of Human of Rights rendered adverse judgments related to two different human rights issues, the first (*United Communist Party of Turkey and Others v. Turkey*) involving a civil and political rights violation and the second (*Aydin v. Turkey*) involving a physical integrity rights violation. Following the *United Communist Party* adverse judgment, Turkey made policy changes related to freedom of assembly and association, which allowed the Committee of Ministers to eventually close the case. However, Turkey failed to make sufficient changes to guarantee freedom from torture following the *Aydin v. Turkey* case. These cases suggest that the policy changes required by the European Court may not be equally feasible across regional court cases. In this chapter, I empirically examine the feasibility of civil and political rights changes (e.g., allowing a political party to run in a general election) relative to the feasibility of physical integrity rights changes (e.g., ensuring state agents do not engage in future physical integrity abuses) following adverse regional human rights court judgments.

In addition to the role of policy change feasibility, access to outside resources also influences executive capacity to make human rights policy change following adverse regional court judgments. To illustrate the importance of access to outside resources, consider the 2011 adverse Inter-American Court of Human Rights judgment, *Lysias Fleury et al. v. Haiti*. In June 2002, two uniformed police officers arrived at the home of Mr. Lysias Fleury, a lawyer and human rights defender representing victims of domestic violence, sexual assault, child kidnapping, and illegal detention. The police officers accused Mr. Fleury of possession of a stolen water pump and despite denial of the accusations, the police engaged in a search of Mr. Fleury's home without a warrant (Frost, 2014). Mr. Fleury told the police officers that he worked as a lawyer and human rights defender, to which the police replied, "You work for human rights? You'll see." (Frost, 2014). Mr. Fleury was then struck several times and taken to a police station, where he was denied food and water and physically abused by the police. After being placed in a cell, Mr. Fleury suffered additional beating, including 64 blows to his body and 15 hits to the head, leaving him with several fractures, bruises, and 2 ruptured eardrums (Frost, 2014). Mr. Fleury was eventually released and hospitalized. After recovering for several months, Mr. Fleury did not return home, fearing for the safety of his family. In August 2002, the victim filed a formal complaint against the police officers responsible for his abuse. An investigation into the abuse was never opened and the individuals responsible were not prosecuted or punished.

In 2002, the victim filed a petition with the Inter-American Commission on Human Rights. In 2009, following a lack of response from the Haitian government, the Inter-American Commission submitted the case to the Inter-American Court. On November 23, 2011, the Inter-American Court rendered an adverse judgment against the state, finding the state to have violated Article 5 (prohibition of torture and cruel, inhuman, or degrading treatment), Article 7 (right to personal liberty), and Article 8 (right to a hearing within a reasonable time), among several other articles of the American Convention. The Inter-American Court placed a number of obligations on the state designed to remedy the human rights abuse, including ordering the state to conduct investigations and prosecute those responsible for the victim's abuse as well as publish the judgment (Frost, 2014). The Inter-American Court also placed obligations on the state designed to ensure human rights policy change, including charging the state with the implementation of mandatory courses as part of the general and continuing education of the Haitian National Police as well as the implementation of mandatory education for Haitian judicial officials (Frost, 2014). In November 2016, the Inter-American Court assessed Haiti's compliance with the adverse judgment, noting that the state had failed to provide any evidence of compliance with the Court's judgment by the extended deadline (April 30, 2016).[4]

As noted in Chapter 2, training and monitoring programs designed to ensure that similar abuses do not occur in the future are costly to implement and Haiti faces major capacity limitations, including limited access to outside resources. One way to capture a state's capacity is to look to the state's gross domestic product (GDP) per capita. The mean GDP per capita of states under the jurisdiction of the Inter-American Court from 1989 to 2012 was $4,172 U.S. dollars. The mean GDP per capita in Haiti for the same time period was $476 U.S. dollars. In the year of the adverse judgment, the average GDP per capita of states under the jurisdiction of the Inter-American Court was around $8,091 U.S. dollars, while the GDP per capita in Haiti was around $740. Another way to capture a state's access to outside resources is to look to a measure of a state's creditworthiness, as indicated by its Institutional Investor Country Credit Rating (IIR) (Clay and DiGiuseppe, 2017). The IIR measure ranges from 0 to 100, with 100 representing highly creditworthy states based on the anonymous opinions of experts in security and investment firms. The average IIR rating among states in the Americas from 1989 to 2012 was around 33, and Haiti's IIR for the same time period was around 12, a clear indication

---

[4] See *Lysias Fleury v. Haiti*, Monitoring Compliance with Judgment, Order of the Court, Inter-Am. Ct. H.R. Nov. 22, 2016.

that Haiti has few resources and little access to outside resources to make human rights policy changes. The Inter-American Court even noted Haiti's capacity limitations in its procedures, granting Haiti additional time to respond to the victim's petition due to the January 2010 earthquake, which "seriously affected the functioning of the State" (Frost, 2014, 1102). The evidence indicates that capacity limitations severely hampered the executive's ability to engage in human rights policy changes following the adverse Inter-American Court judgment in Haiti.

The preceding examples provide initial evidence in support of the importance of policy change feasibility and fiscal flexibility for regional human rights court deterrence. In the next section, I conduct a more systematic examination of the role of state capacity in executive human rights policy change following adverse regional court judgments (Hypotheses 1 and 2).

4.1 THE ROLE OF POLICY CHANGE FEASIBILITY

Adverse regional human rights court judgments may involve many types of human rights abuse, and the feasibility of policy change necessary for regional court deterrence varies by the type of rights abuse addressed in the judgment. (hypothesis 1). Take, for example, the 1996 case of *Manoussakis and Others v. Greece*.[5] In this case, several Jehovah's Witnesses were convicted for setting up and operating a place of worship without authorization from the Minister of Education and Religious Affairs. The European Court found that the applicant's conviction constituted interference with enjoyment of the right to freedom of religion. Following the judgment, the state undertook several measures designed to remedy the abuse, including granting permission for setting up and operating places of worship in all similar cases. The administrative practice became very stable following the European Court judgment and effectively prevented new violations.

Contrast the *Manoussakis and Others v. Greece* case with a case in Turkey, *Aksoy v. Turkey*. In this 1996 case, Zeki Aksoy was taken into police custody and detained for 14 days, where he was subjected to a form of torture known as "Palestinian hanging," whereby he was suspended from his arms. Aksoy alleged that he had been stripped naked, electrocuted in the genitals, kicked, slapped, and verbally abused.[6] The victim claimed to have lost use of his arms and hands following the torture. The European Court found that Turkey had

---

[5] See *Manoussakis and Others v. Greece*, Judgment, European Ct. H.R. September 20, 1996.
[6] See *Aksoy v. Turkey*, Judgment, European Ct. H.R. December 18, 1996.

violated the right to be free from inhuman or degrading treatment and the right to liberty. Following the failure to take adequate measures to remedy the abuse, the Committee of Ministers of the European Court ordered Turkey to undertake a number of measures, including orders to reorganize the basic management and training of police and ensure that the status of case law of the European Court was translated into daily practice for security forces.[7] Presumably, these efforts require extensive coordination on the part of the executive. That is, the executive must not only ensure that security forces are properly trained, but also that they carry out new regulations in practice, which requires extensive administrative and monitoring efforts. Compared to the policy change required in a case like *Manoussakis and Others v. Greece*, these types of reforms are relatively more costly for the executive to undertake. As these two case examples illustrate, it is relatively more feasible for the executive to undertake policy changes following an adverse regional human rights court judgment involving civil and political rights abuses, than an adverse judgment associated with physical integrity abuses.

4.1.1 Data and Methodology

Outcome Variables

I posit that adverse regional human rights court judgments involving civil and political rights abuses are more likely to be positively associated with respect for human rights than adverse judgments involving physical integrity abuses (Hypothesis 1). An important component of the research design is measuring the dependent variable, or the outcome of interest. Like the analyses in Chapter 3, I am interested in regional human rights court effectiveness. An effective regional human rights court deters future human rights abuses, and as a result, I need measures of human rights practices. To test Hypothesis 1, two dependent variables are needed, one measuring respect for physical integrity rights and a second measuring respect for civil and political rights.

With respect to physical integrity rights, I utilize the same measure of respect for physical integrity rights utilized in Chapter 3. Data on respect for physical integrity rights comes from Fariss (2014), which is based on a dynamic latent variable measurement model using 13 indicators of state human rights practices and accounting for changing standards of accountability, or the increased stringency with which organizations assess government human

---

[7] Committee of Ministers Interim Resolution ResDH(2005)43.

rights practices.[8] In order to make the physical integrity rights variable comparable to all of the civil and political rights dependent variables (discussed later), I rescale the respect for physical integrity rights variable so it ranges from 0 to 1 in both the European and Inter-American Court samples, with higher values on this variable representing greater respect for rights and lower values representing lower levels of respect for rights.

In addition to physical integrity rights data, I also need data capturing respect for civil and political rights. I utilize several different measures of civil and political rights abuses. The first variable, political civil liberties (*Political*), captures the extent to which political liberties are respected, with political liberties including freedom of association and expression. Data on political civil liberties comes from the Varieties of Democracy dataset (Coppedge et al., 2019), and represents an index created using Bayesian factor analysis including several indicators of political and civil liberties.[9] Second, I utilize a variable capturing freedom of association (*Association*) or the extent to which parties, including opposition parties, are allowed to form and participate in elections as well as the extent to which civil society organizations are able to form and operate freely. This variable is created using Bayesian factor analysis of several indicators of freedom of association (Coppedge et al., 2019). Third, I utilize a measure of freedom of discussion (*Discussion*), which captures the extent to which citizens are able to openly discuss political issues in private and public spaces. More specifically, this variable specifies the extent to which citizens are able to engage in private discussions, particularly on political issues, in private and public spaces, without fear of harassment by other members of the polity or the public authorities. All civil and political rights variables range from 0–1.

Explanatory Variables

I expect that adverse regional human rights court judgments involving civil and political rights abuses are positively associated with respect for human rights, and adverse judgments involving physical integrity abuses are not likely to be positively associated with respect for human rights. In order to

---

[8] The Fariss (2014) measure is based on the excellent data collection efforts of Cingranelli, Richards, and Clay (2014), Hathaway (2002), Conrad, Haglund, and Moore (2013), and Gibney et al. (2016), as well as several events-based datasets.

[9] The indicators included in the political civil liberties index include government censorship effort, harassment of journalists, media self-censorship, freedom of discussion for men and women, freedom of academic and cultural expression, barriers to parties, opposition parties, autonomy, civil society organization entry and exit, and civil society organization repression.

4.1 The Role of Policy Change Feasibility

examine this hypothesis, I need data that not only capture adverse regional human rights court judgments involving physical integrity abuses (like data used in Chapter 3), but also data that capture adverse regional human rights court judgments involving civil and political rights abuses. With respect to physical integrity rights, I utilize the same data examined in Chapter 3 on the presence of adverse European and Inter-American Court judgments related to physical integrity abuses. European Court judgments related to physical integrity involve violations of Article 2 (right to life), Article 3 (prohibition of torture), Article 4 (freedom from slavery), and Article 5 (right to liberty and security) of the European Convention on Human Rights. Like the analyses in Chapter 3, I utilize adverse judgments published in case reports or those of level 1 or level 2 importance. Adverse judgments involving physical integrity rights abuses in the Americas involve violations of Article 4 (right to life), Article 5 (right to humane treatment), and Article 7 (right to personal integrity) of the American Convention on Human Rights.

In order to gather data on adverse European Court judgments involving civil and political rights abuses, I use the same method used to gather data on physical integrity judgments. That is, I visited the HUDOC database and recorded adverse regional court judgments involving a violation of Article 9 (freedom of thought, conscience, and religion), Article 10 (freedom of expression), or Article 11 (freedom of assembly and association) of the European Convention on Human Rights. I gather case information for violations of Articles 9, 10, and 11 only for key cases or cases of level 1 or level 2 importance. Data on adverse Inter-American Court judgments involving civil and political rights for the years 1989 to 2010 come from Hawkins and Jacoby (2010). Like the data on Inter-American Court judgments involving physical integrity rights, I expanded on the civil and political rights data by visiting the Inter-American Court website, examining case conclusions, and recording the articles violated for the years 2011 to 2012. Violations of Article 12 (freedom of conscience and religion), Article 13 (freedom of thought and expression), Article 15 (right of assembly), and Article 16 (right of association) of the American Convention on Human Rights are included in the civil and political rights data. Figure 4.1 displays the number of adverse European Court judgments related to civil and political rights (solid line) and physical integrity rights (dashed line) from key cases or those of level 1 or level 2 importance from 1978 to 2012 in the left panel. The right panel of Figure 4.1 displays the number of adverse Inter-American Court judgments related to civil and political rights (solid line) and physical integrity rights (dashed line) from 1989 to 2012.

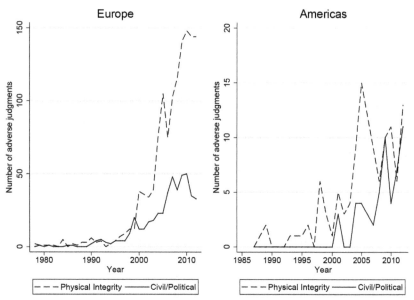

FIGURE 4.1. Number of adverse Civil/Political and Physical Integrity rights judgments in Europe and the Americas over time

Notes: Figure 4.1 displays the number of adverse judgments involving violations of civil and political rights (solid line) and physical integrity rights (dashed line) over time in Europe and the Americas. The left panel displays the number of adverse European Court judgments from key cases or those of level 1 or level 2 importance and the right panel displays the number of adverse Inter-American Court judgments. In comparing the number of judgments rendered by each Court, note that the y-axes in the panels are different. The number of adverse European Court judgments involving civil and political rights violations ranges from 0 to 50 annually, while the number of adverse Inter-American Court judgments involving civil and political rights violations ranges from 0 to 11 annually.

Empirical Models

I estimate several models to examine Hypothesis 1. The unit of analysis is the country-year, which allows me to capture the influence of adverse judgments in time t on respect for rights at several points in time in the future (e.g., $t+1$). I estimate several different models for the European and Inter-American Courts of Human Rights. Like the models examining general deterrence in Chapter 3, the European sample includes all Council of Europe member states from 1980 to 2012 (excluding Montenegro), and I examine Inter-American Court judgments for those states under the jurisdiction of the Inter-American Court for the years 1989 to 2012. Also like the models estimated in Chapter 3, I estimate linear regression models incorporating random intercepts and standard errors clustered on country. Additional model details, including a full description of the control variables used in the analyses

4.1 The Role of Policy Change Feasibility

and full model results for the figures presented in this chapter, are included in the Appendix to this chapter.

Because I have several measures of civil and political rights, I estimate three models to examine the civil and political rights expectation in Hypothesis 1. In the first model, I examine the influence of an adverse judgment involving a civil and political rights violation (lagged 1, 3, and 5 years) on respect for civil and political rights. This model represents an aggregate examination of the civil and political rights expectation in Hypothesis 1. For the European Court, I examine the influence of the number of adverse European Court judgments involving a violation of Article 9 (freedom of thought, conscience, and religion), Article 10 (freedom of expression), or Article 11 (freedom of assembly and association) of the European Convention on respect for civil and political rights (using the political civil liberties index as a measure of respect for civil and political rights). For the Inter-American Court model, I examine the influence of the number of adverse judgments involving violations of civil and political rights (Articles 12, 13, 15, and 16 of the American Convention on Human Rights) on respect for civil and political rights. More formally, the equation for the model is as follows:

$$Civil/Political\ Rights_{(t)} = b_0 + b_1\ Adverse\ Judgment_{(t-1)}$$
$$+ b_2\ Adverse\ Judgment_{(t-3)}$$
$$+ b_3\ Adverse\ Judgment_{(t-5)} + Controls_{(t-1)} + \varepsilon.$$

In the second and third models, I conduct disaggregated analyses of the civil and political rights expectation in Hypothesis 1. More specifically, in the second model, I examine the influence of the number of adverse regional court judgments related to freedom of association on respect for the right to freedom of association. For the European Court, this means that I examine the influence of adverse judgments involving violations of Article 11 (freedom of assembly and association) of the European Convention on the right to freedom of association. For the Inter-American Court, I examine the influence of violations of Article 16 (right to association) on respect for the right to freedom of association. In the third model, I examine the influence of the number of adverse judgments related to freedom of expression on the right to freedom of discussion. In the European Court sample, I examine the influence of an adverse judgment involving a violation of Article 10 (freedom of expression) on the right to freedom of discussion. In the Inter-American Court sample, I examine the influence of an adverse judgment involving a violation of Article 13 (freedom of expression) on the right to freedom of discussion. More formally, the equation for the European Court model involving freedom of association is specified here:

$$\text{Association}_{(t)} = b_0 + b_1 \text{ Article11 Violation}_{(t-1)} + b_2 \text{ Article11 Violation}_{(t-3)}$$
$$+ b_3 \text{ Article11 Violation}_{(t-5)} + \text{Controls}_{(t-1)} + \varepsilon.$$

Finally, in the fourth model, I examine the physical integrity rights expectation from Hypothesis 1. That is, I examine the influence of adverse judgments involving physical integrity rights abuse on respect for physical integrity rights. Like the civil and political rights models, I examine respect for physical integrity rights 1, 3, and 5 years following an adverse judgment. The equation for this model follows:

$$\text{Physical Integrity}_{(t)} = b_0 + b_1 \text{ Adverse Judgment}_{(t-1)} + b_2 \text{ Adverse Judgment}_{(t-3)}$$
$$+ b_3 \text{ Adverse Judgment}_{(t-5)} + \text{Controls}_{(t-1)} + \varepsilon.$$

A Brief Note on Selection

Research assessing the influence of international human rights law on state behavior has taken the selection problem associated with treaty commitment seriously (Hill, 2010; Lupu, 2013b). The selection problem is rooted in the idea that because states self-select into treaties, it is difficult to determine whether international treaties have a causal effect on the behavior of states. That is, changes in state behavior may not be caused by a treaty, but by the fact that states would have taken such actions anyway (Downs, Rocke, and Barsoom, 1996; Simmons, 1998).[10] Selection presents a problem for analyzing the influence of international human rights law on state behavior because states that commit to international human rights law may be different from states that do not. These differences may explain state decisions to select into an international treaty and their decision to repress citizens, which "makes it difficult to separate the effect of the treaty from the effect of the institutional features that led them to ratify" (Hill, 2010, 1168).

Selection would be a problem for these analyses if states that submit to the jurisdiction of the European and Inter-American Courts of Human Rights are different from states that have not in important ways. In the European context, all states that are members of the Council of Europe are subject to the jurisdiction of the European Court. The European Convention on Human Rights was adopted within the context of the Council of Europe, and all of the 47 member states are parties to the Convention and under the jurisdiction of the European Court. Nearly all European states have acceded to the Council of Europe, with the exceptions being Belarus and Kazakhstan, both of which

---

[10] Scholars have accounted for this problem by using Heckman selection models (Von Stein, 2005), matching (Hill, 2010), instrumental variables (Simmons, 2009), or spatial models (Lupu, 2013b).

have not addressed key human rights concerns. While the decision to join the Council of Europe places states under the jurisdiction of the European Court, member states receive access to an important decision-making body in Europe, assistance in democratic governance, and even a Development Bank. Also, every member of the European Union was first a member of the Council of Europe, meaning those with aspirations to accede to the EU find membership in the Council of Europe to be important. As a result, European states may find themselves under the jurisdiction of the European Court for reasons that have little to do with human rights concerns.

Turning to the Inter-American Court, there are 35 members of the Organization of American States (OAS), but currently only 20 members accept the jurisdiction of the Court. The members that have not accepted the jurisdiction of the Inter-American Court are quite diverse in terms of human rights practices, democratic consolidation, and size.[11] According to the Cingranelli, Richards, and Clay (2014) physical integrity rights index, for the OAS members that have accepted the jurisdiction of the Inter-American Court, the average level of respect for physical integrity rights is 4.3 (on a scale ranging from 0 to 8, with higher values indicating greater respect for rights). For those OAS member states that have not accepted the jurisdiction of the Inter-American Court, the average physical integrity rights score is 6.2 on the Cingranelli, Richards, and Clay (2014) physical integrity rights index.[12] Further, according to the Cingranelli, Richards, and Clay (2014) empowerment rights index, which includes several democratically oriented rights and ranges from 0 to 14, OAS member states that have not accepted the jurisdiction of the Inter-American Court score 11.32 on average, while those that have accepted the jurisdiction of the court score a 10.87.[13] These descriptive statistics provide some evidence that states under the jurisdiction of the Inter-American Court are not more democratic or better rights protectors than those not under the jurisdiction of the Inter-American Court.

Although more extensive research on selection into the European and Inter-American Courts is warranted, taken together, there is little evidence that those

---

[11] OAS member states that have not accepted the jurisdiction of the Inter-American Court include Antigua and Barbuda, Bahamas, Belize, Canada, Cuba, Dominica, Grenada, Guyana, Jamaica, Saint Kitts and Nevis, Saint Lucia, Saint Vincent and Grenadines, Trinidad and Tobago, and the United States. Venezuela denounced the American Convention in 2012, but because the adverse judgment data only extends to 2012, Venezuela is included in the analysis.
[12] Omitting the United States and Canada, the average physical integrity rights score for OAS members that have not accepted the jurisdiction of the Court is 6.0.
[13] The Cingranelli, Richards, and Clay (2014) empowerment rights index includes freedom of foreign and domestic movement, freedom of speech, freedom of assembly and association, workers' rights, electoral self-determination, and freedom of religion.

states that are a part of regional human rights courts are substantially different from states that are not part of the Court. In the Americas, where selection may be a larger concern, given the number of eligible states that have not accepted the jurisdiction of the Inter-American Court, states that have accepted the Court's jurisdiction have lower levels of respect for rights and are on par with nonmembers in terms of democratically oriented rights.

4.1.2 Evidence of Executive Capacity: Policy Change Feasibility

Figure 4.2 displays results for the primary variables of interest in the European Court models.[14] More specifically, Figure 4.2 displays coefficient estimates from the models (dots), which indicate the expected level of respect for rights in the presence of an adverse European Court judgment while controlling for various other factors. The line segments represent 90 percent confidence

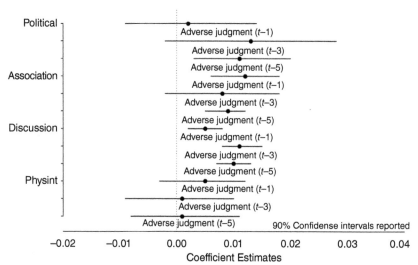

FIGURE 4.2. Predicted influence of adverse European Court judgments on respect for rights
Notes: Figure 4.2 displays the predicted influence of adverse European Court judgments involving civil and political rights on respect for civil and political rights and the influence of adverse European Court judgments involving physical integrity rights on respect for physical integrity rights. All dependent variables are rescaled to range from 0 to 1. The results show that adverse European Court judgments involving violations of freedom of association and freedom of discussion are positively and significantly related to respect for the corresponding rights. Adverse judgments involving physical integrity rights are not significantly associated with respect for physical integrity rights.

---

[14] Full model results are displayed in the Appendix.

4.1 The Role of Policy Change Feasibility

intervals, and they indicate that the probability of observing a value outside this interval is .10. A positive coefficient estimate with a 90 percent confidence interval that does not cross zero lends support to the hypothesis, as we can be relatively confident that adverse civil and political rights judgments are positively associated with civil and political rights.

The coefficient estimates from the aggregate models assessing the influence of European Court judgments involving all civil and political rights abuses and respect for civil and political rights are positive, but the confidence intervals for two of the adverse judgment variables contain zero ($t-1$ and $t-3$). The results for the aggregate civil and political rights models show limited support for Hypothesis 1. Adverse European Court judgments involving civil and political rights violations are significantly associated with respect for rights 5 years following an adverse judgment, but not 1 and 3 years following an adverse judgment.

Although the aggregate model results lend limited support to Hypothesis 1, the results for the disaggregated models (models 2 and 3) indicate that adverse European Court judgments involving violations of freedom of association (Article 11) are positively related to freedom of association 1 and 5 years following an adverse judgment in Europe. Similarly, adverse European Court judgments involving violations of freedom of expression (Article 10) are positively related to freedom of discussion 1, 3, and 5 years following the adverse judgment. The disaggregated model results lend support to Hypothesis 1, indicating that the executive is more likely to respond to adverse judgments with human rights policy change when the policy changes required are more feasible (e.g., involve civil and political rights violations). Although the results in Europe may appear substantively small, it is important to note that all the dependent variables range from 0 to 1, making even small changes relatively important. Despite the fact that there are larger confidence intervals around the estimates in the aggregate model, perhaps due to the various types of rights abuses included in the independent and dependent variables, the disaggregated models lend support to Hypothesis 1. As a robustness check, I estimated models with a variable capturing the change in civil and political rights from the year of the judgment to 1, 3, and 5 years after the judgment. The results (reported in the Appendix) show that an adverse judgment involving civil liberties and political rights is positively and significantly related to changes in civil and political rights 1, 3 and 5 years after the judgment.

Turning to physical integrity rights in Europe, the final model examines the influence of violations of the European Convention involving physical integrity rights abuses on respect for physical integrity rights. The results show that although the parameter estimates are positive, the 90 percent confidence intervals all cross the zero line, indicating that we cannot be sufficiently confident that adverse judgments involving physical integrity abuses are positively related to respect for physical integrity rights. Further analyses (not reported here) indicate that disaggregation of the measure of physical integrity rights does not produce statistically significant results either. For example, in a model estimating the influence of adverse judgments involving a violation of Article 3 of the European Convention (freedom for torture) on the right to be free from torture (Cingranelli, Richards, and Clay, 2014), results are not statistically significant at conventional levels of statistical significance ($p < 0.10$). An additional analysis (displayed in the Appendix) shows that an adverse judgment is not significantly related to the change in respect for physical integrity rights 1, 3, and 5 years following an adverse judgment.[15]

Turning to the Inter-American Court of Human Rights, Figure 4.3 displays results for the primary variables of interest in the Americas. Figure 4.3 displays coefficient estimates as dots and 90 percent confidence intervals as lines. Results reported in Figure 4.3 lend support to Hypothesis 1. The first three coefficient estimates show that adverse judgments related to civil and political rights (Articles 12, 13, 15, and 16) are positively and significantly related to respect for civil and political rights, with the exception of civil and political rights 5 years following an adverse judgment, where the 90 percent confidence interval just crosses the zero line. The models reporting disaggregated results also lend support for Hypothesis 1. Adverse judgments involving violations of freedom of association (Article 16) are positively and significantly related to freedom of association 1, 3, and 5 years following an adverse judgment. Similarly, adverse judgments involving freedom of expression (Article 13) are positively and significantly associated with freedom of expression. Additional analyses (reported in the Appendix) show that adverse judgments involving civil liberties and political rights are positively and significantly associated with changes in respect for civil liberties and political rights 3 and 5 years following an adverse judgment.[16]

The final results reported in Figure 4.3 show that adverse Inter-American Court judgments related to physical integrity rights are positively related to respect for physical integrity rights 1, 3, and 5 years following an adverse judgment. However, adverse judgments related to physical integrity rights are only positively *and significantly* associated with respect for physical integrity rights

---

[15] This analysis utilizes changes in the Cingranelli, Richards, and Clay (2014) physical integrity rights index as the dependent variable.
[16] The result for the role of an adverse judgment on the change in respect for rights 1 year postjudgment is positive, but does not achieve statistical significance.

4.1 The Role of Policy Change Feasibility

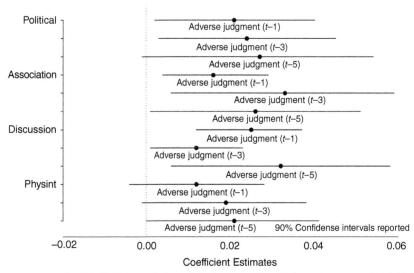

FIGURE 4.3. Predicted influence of adverse Inter-American Court judgments on respect for rights
Notes: Figure 4.3 displays the predicted influence of adverse Inter-American Court judgments involving civil and political rights on respect for civil and political rights and the influence of adverse Inter-American Court judgments involving physical integrity rights on respect for physical integrity rights. All dependent variables are rescaled to range from 0 to 1. The results show that adverse Inter-American Court judgments involving civil and political rights are positively and significantly related to respect for civil and political rights. Adverse judgments involving physical integrity rights are not significantly associated with respect for physical integrity rights 1 and 3 years following the adverse judgment.

5 years following an adverse Inter-American Court judgment, an indication that adverse judgments related to physical integrity rights take several years to produce physical integrity rights policy changes. This suggests that it may be less feasible for an executive to make physical integrity rights policy changes for a significant period of time after an adverse Inter-American Court judgment. As a robustness check, I estimated a model predicting the influence of an adverse judgment involving physical integrity rights on the change in respect for physical integrity rights 1, 3, and 5 years postjudgment (using changes in the Cingranelli, Richards, and Clay [2014] physical integrity rights index as the dependent variable). The results (displayed in the Appendix) are consistent, showing that adverse physical integrity rights judgments are insignificantly related to change in respect for rights 1 and 3 years postjudgment. Adverse physical integrity rights judgments are positively related to changes in respect for physical integrity rights 5 years postjudgment and just barely achieve conventional levels of statistical significance ($p < 0.10$ using a one-tailed significance test). The Inter-American Court results lend support to Hypothesis 1,

suggesting that the executive finds civil and political rights policy change following adverse regional court judgments to be more feasible than policy change involving physical integrity rights.

Taking together the anecdotal evidence, along with the aggregated and disaggregated analyses reported in Figures 4.2 and 4.3, the results provide evidence that following adverse regional human rights court judgments, the executive is more likely to make civil and political rights changes than physical integrity rights changes. While the type of rights violation for which the state has been implicated has direct implications for the feasibility of human rights policy change, the executive also faces capacity limitations as a result of the availability of outside resources, which I turn to in the next section.

4.2 THE ROLE OF FISCAL FLEXIBILITY

In addition to the role of policy change feasibility in executive capacity to make human rights policy change postjudgment, access to outside resources also plays a role in executive capacity to engage in human rights policy change. Consider Ukraine, a state under the jurisdiction of the European Court of Human Rights with very limited capacity. In 2012, the European Court rendered an adverse judgment against Ukraine in *Kaverzin v. Ukraine*. The applicant (Kaverzin) was given a life sentence in 2003 for aggravated murder. Kaverzin alleged to have been subjected to ill-treatment and torture at the hands of the police during and after his arrest. Medical specialists found evidence of abuse, including bruising to the chest, lower back, kidneys, face, and the back of the head. Further medical examination found bleeding in the eyeball and bruising and scratches to the chest, arms, and legs. The European Court rendered an adverse judgment against Ukraine in 2012 finding the state in violation of Article 3 (the right to be free from torture) of the European Convention. The European Court found that the situation in Ukraine was a result of systemic problems that would require the implementation of comprehensive and complex measures to resolve.[17]

In Ukraine's 2014 updated action plan, authorities noted that the state was working to establish a State Bureau of Investigations (SIB) in compliance with the new Criminal Procedure Code and pass laws that were in compliance with European standards.[18] However, by 2017, the State Bureau of Investigations was still not operational, and the Committee of Ministers noted that

---

[17] See *Kaverzin v. Ukraine*, Judgment (Merits and Just Satisfaction), European Ct. H.R. August 15, 2012.

[18] See Updated Action Plan on Measures to Comply with the Court's Judgment in the Case of *Kaverzin v. Ukraine*/Afensaiev Group of Cases. October 31, 2014.

Ukraine must take all necessary measures to ensure that the SIB become operational and able to conduct effective investigations.[19] Arguably, resource constraints in Ukraine limit the executive's ability to effectively undertake reforms required by the European Court. The European Committee for the Prevention of Torture and Inhuman or Degrading Treatment or Punishment (CPT) consistently notes the need for greater human and financial resources in its reports on Ukraine. States with little access to outside resources, such as foreign lending, face an even greater challenge in the provision of programs and policies designed to prevent torture and ill-treatment.

One measure of a state's access to outside resources is the state's creditworthiness, which can be assessed using the Institutional Investor Country Credit Rating (IIR) discussed earlier (Clay and DiGiuseppe, 2017). The IIR measure spans from 0 to 100, with 100 being a state that is highly creditworthy based on the anonymous opinions of experts in security and investment firms. The average IIR rating among states in the Council of Europe from 1980 to 2012 was 66.33, and Ukraine's average IIR for the same period was 29.30, further evidence that Ukraine lags far behind in terms of the amount of resources that can be dedicated to monitoring and oversight of state agents. In fact, Belousov et al. (2017) note that one of the key causes of impunity by law enforcement officers includes the lack of an efficient mechanism of investigation of torture and cruel treatment by law enforcement officers in Ukraine as well as the lack of professional training for law enforcement officials (82). The inability of the Ukrainian government to turn to outside resources to engage in human rights policy changes represents a clear capacity limitation and inhibits the ability of the executive to engage in the adoption, administration, monitoring, and enforcement of human rights policy.

4.2.1 Empirical Models

In Hypothesis 2, I posit a conditional relationship. That is, I expect that the influence of adverse regional human rights court judgments on respect for rights is conditional on executive capacity, or the state's level of fiscal flexibility. As a result, I create an interaction term including adverse regional human rights court judgments and fiscal flexibility. The adverse judgment variable is binary, in which a one represents one or more adverse regional court judgments and a zero represents the absence of adverse judgments. To measure fiscal flexibility, I follow Clay and DiGiuseppe (2017) and utilize

---

[19] See CM/Del/Dec(2017)1280/H46-35.

the Institutional Investor Country Credit Rating (IIR) described earlier. The IIR measure is lagged 1 year. The IIR measure is interacted with a variable measuring the presence of one or more adverse European or Inter-American Court judgments in a given year (1) or no adverse judgments in a given year (0).[20] To assess the effectiveness of the regional court, I estimate three models for both the European and Inter-American Courts of Human Rights. In the first model, I lag the adverse judgment variable 1 year; in the second model, I lag the adverse judgment variable 3 years; and in the third model, I lag the adverse judgment variable 5 years.[21] The following equation is an example of the model used to assess respect for rights 3 years postjudgment:

$$\begin{aligned}Respect\ for\ Rights_{(t)} = {} & b_0 + b_1\ Fiscal\ Flexibility_{(t-1)} * AdverseJudgment_{(t-3)} \\ & + b_2\ Fiscal\ Flexibility_{(t-1)} + b_3\ Adverse\ Judgment_{(t-3)} \\ & + b_4\ Adverse\ Judgment_{(t-2)} + b_5\ Adverse\ Judgment_{(t-1)} \\ & + Controls_{(t-1)} + \varepsilon.\end{aligned}$$

4.2.2 Evidence of Executive Capacity: Fiscal Flexibility

Figure 4.4 shows results for the primary variables of interest in the European Court models. The figure displays the influence of adverse European court judgments on respect for rights across the institutional investor country credit rating – an indicator of fiscal flexibility. The left panel of Figure 4.4 shows the predicted level of respect for rights 1 year following an adverse European Court judgment across values of fiscal flexibility. The center panel of Figure 4.4 shows the predicted level of respect for rights 3 years following an adverse European Court judgment across values of fiscal flexibility, and the right panel of Figure 4.4 shows the predicted level of respect for rights 5 years following an adverse European Court judgment across fiscal flexibility. To produce the predicted values, the adverse judgment variable is set to one, and all other variables are set to their mean or mode. Theoretically, I am interested in the conditional role of executive capacity on regional human

---

[20] Because the IIR measure is highly correlated with GDP per capita, I omit GDP per capita from the models.
[21] In order to identify the influence of an adverse judgment on respect for rights 5 years later, I also control for the presence of adverse judgments that occurred over the 5-year time period. I include variables capturing the presence of one or more adverse judgments 1, 2, 3, and 4 years before assessing respect for rights (i.e., adverse judgment (*t*-1), adverse judgment (*t*-2), adverse judgment (*t*-3), and adverse judgment (*t*-4)). For the model that assesses respect for rights 3 years postjudgment, I include the adverse judgment (*t*-1) and adverse judgment (*t*-2) variables in the model as control variables.

rights court deterrence. The theory stipulates that an adverse judgment is positively associated with respect for rights as fiscal flexibility grows. As a result, I present findings displaying the human rights practices of *adverse judgment recipients* across values of fiscal flexibility, rather than findings displaying the influence of fiscal flexibility in the absence of an adverse judgment (e.g., influence of fiscal flexibility on respect for rights for nonadverse judgment recipients).

Figure 4.4 shows that 1, 3, and 5 years following an adverse European Court judgment, the predicted level of respect for rights is lower at lower values of fiscal flexibility. In fact, 1 year following an adverse European Court judgment, the predicted value of respect for rights is 0.83 when the institutional investor country credit rating is 20 (low fiscal flexibility), but the predicted level of respect for rights grows to 2.26 when the institutional investor country credit rating is 90 (high fiscal flexibility). In other words, as fiscal flexibility grows from low to high, the predicted level of respect for rights grows by over 1.0 following an adverse European Court judgment. Importantly, the data show that several countries display a growth in fiscal flexibility over time. For example, Poland's fiscal flexibility increased 52.65 points from 1990 to 2008, evidence that state creditworthiness can improve over time. As the center and right panels illustrate as well, fiscal flexibility remains influential on the level of respect for rights 3 and 5 years following an adverse judgment, though the size of the confidence intervals indicate that 1 year postjudgment, we can be most confident that an adverse judgment is associated with higher levels of respect for rights as fiscal flexibility grows.

As a robustness check (displayed in the Appendix), I also estimated a model predicting the influence of adverse European Court judgments on the change in respect for rights 1 year postjudgment (using changes in the Cingranelli, Richards, and Clay [2014] physical integrity rights index as the dependent variable). The results (not reported here) show that fiscal flexibility is positively and significantly related with the change in respect for rights 1 year following an adverse judgment. In fact, 1 year following an adverse judgment, respect for rights is expected to increase by 0.35 (on a scale ranging from −4 to 3) as fiscal flexibility grows from low (20) to high (90).[22]

Turning to results for the Inter-American Court of Human Rights, Figure 4.5 displays the influence of at least one adverse Inter-American Court judgment on respect for rights across the IIR (an indicator of fiscal flexibility). The left panel of Figure 4.5 shows the predicted level of respect for rights 1 year

---

[22] Importantly, while the change may appear to be substantively small, there is less room for change in the level of respect for rights in Europe than in the Americas.

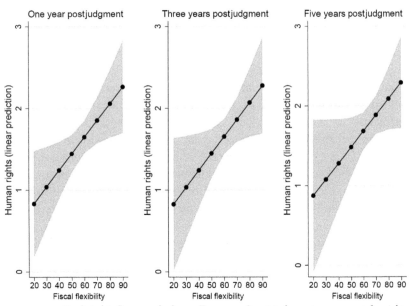

FIGURE 4.4. Predicted influence of adverse European Court judgments on respect for rights across fiscal flexibility

Notes: Figure 4.4 displays the predicted level of respect for rights 1 year (left panel), 3 years (center panel), and 5 years (right panel) following at least one adverse European Court judgment across the institutional investor country credit rating (an indicator of fiscal flexibility). Solid lines represent the predicted level of respect for rights in the presence of an adverse European Court judgment, and the shaded area represents 90 percent confidence intervals. The results show that adverse judgments are positively related to respect for rights as fiscal flexibility grows.

following an adverse Inter-American Court judgment across fiscal flexibility. The center panel displays the predicted level of respect for rights 3 years following an adverse Inter-American Court judgment, and the right panel displays the predicted level of respect for rights 5 years following an adverse Inter-American Court judgment across values of fiscal flexibility. To produce the predicted values, the adverse judgment variable is set to one and all other variables are set to their mean or mode. Figure 4.5 shows that the predicted level of respect for rights 1, 3, and 5 years following an adverse Inter-American Court judgment is higher when fiscal flexibility is high than when fiscal flexibility is low. In fact, the predicted level of respect for rights 1 year following an adverse Inter-American Court judgment when fiscal flexibility is low (10 on the IIR scale) is −0.36. When fiscal flexibility is high (70 on the IIR scale), the predicted level of respect for rights is 0.87 1 year following an adverse Inter-American Court judgment, which represents over a 1.0 change on the physical integrity rights measure (ranging around −3 to +3 in the Americas).

4.2 The Role of Fiscal Flexibility

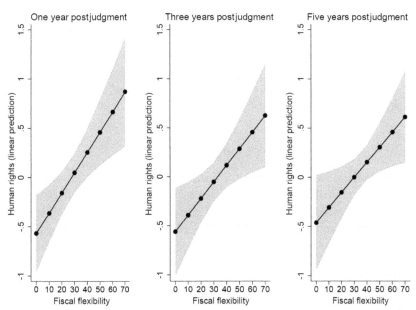

FIGURE 4.5. Predicted influence of adverse Inter-American Court judgments on respect for rights across fiscal flexibility

Notes: Figure 4.5 displays the predicted level of respect for rights 1 year (left panel), 3 years (center panel), and 5 years (right panel) following at least one adverse Inter-American Court judgment across the institutional investor country credit rating (an indicator of fiscal flexibility). Solid lines represent the predicted level of respect for rights in the presence of an Inter-American Court judgment, and the shaded area represents 90 percent confidence intervals. The results show that adverse judgments are positively related to respect for rights as fiscal flexibility grows.

As a robustness check, I also examine the influence of an adverse Inter-American Court judgment on the change in respect for physical integrity rights 1 year following the judgment (using changes in the Cingranelli, Richards, and Clay [2014] physical integrity rights index as the dependent variable). The results (displayed in the Appendix) show that an adverse Inter-American Court judgment is positively and significantly associated with changes in respect for rights 1 year following the judgment. In fact, physical integrity rights are expected to increase around 1.68 (on a scale ranging −4 to +6) in the year following an adverse Inter-American Court judgment when fiscal flexibility increases from low (10) to high (70).

The combination of the anecdotal evidence and results reported in Figures 4.4 and 4.5 lend support to Hypothesis 2 by showing that adverse regional court judgments are positively associated with rights as fiscal flexibility grows. In other words, the results support the notion that adverse judgments are more likely to generate executive human rights policy change when the executive has the capacity to adopt, administer, monitor, and enforce human rights policy. Importantly, executive capacity to ensure the implementation of human rights policy grows as the executive gains access to outside resources. Adverse judgment recipients with access to outside resources are more capable of making the necessary human rights policy changes to align with the regional court.

4.3 CONCLUSION

In this chapter, I argued that adverse regional human rights court judgments are more likely to deter future human rights abuses when the executive is *capable* of adopting, administering, monitoring, and enforcing human rights policy. I argued that executive capacity to make civil and political rights changes is greater than executive capacity to make physical integrity rights changes following an adverse regional court judgment. Civil and political rights improvements are more directly within the executive's control than are physical integrity rights improvements. I show that civil and political rights judgments are more strongly associated with human rights gains than physical integrity rights judgments in Europe and the Americas.

Beyond the feasibility of policy change, I also argued that the executive has greater capacity to adopt, administer, monitor, and enforce human rights policy when the state is fiscally flexible, that is, when the state has access to outside resources. I show that adverse judgments are positively related to respect for rights as the state's creditworthiness (institutional investor credit rating) increases. This effect is strongest 1 year postjudgment in Europe and the Americas, which indicates that the executive responds to adverse judgments with human rights policy change quickly when the executive has greater capacity. Access to outside resources allows the executive to engage in human rights policy changes in the immediate term following an adverse judgment. Access to outside resources becomes less important 3 and 5 years following an adverse judgment, meaning that if the executive has access to outside resources and the executive does not initiate human rights policy changes right away, the likelihood of policy change declines.

Taken together, the results show that executive capacity to make human rights policy changes plays an important role in regional human rights court deterrence. When the executive has the capacity to adopt, administer, monitor, and enforce human rights policy, the executive is more likely to respond to adverse judgments with human rights policy change. In addition to the role of executive capacity in regional court deterrence, I also argue that executive willingness plays a key role in regional court deterrence as well, and I turn to the role of executive willingness in the next two chapters.

5

Is the Executive Willing to Respond to Adverse Judgments? The Role of Mass Public Pressure

In Chapter 2, I argued that adverse regional human rights court judgments are more likely to deter future human rights abuses when the executive is *willing* to adopt, administer, monitor, and enforce human rights policy. I also argued that two sets of domestic actors utilize adverse regional human rights court judgments to pressure the executive to adopt comprehensive human rights policy: (1) the mass public and (2) economic and political elites. In this chapter, I focus on the role of mass public pressure on the executive to respond to adverse regional court judgments with human rights policy change.

To illustrate the role of the mass public in generating executive willingness to make comprehensive human rights policy changes following adverse regional court judgments, I begin by reviewing several cases before the European and Inter-American Courts of Human Rights. First, I look to the role of mass public pressure as a result of executive job security due to an upcoming election. The executive is more likely to be insecure in office prior to an election, and as a result, more *willing* to respond to pressure from the mass public to adopt and implement comprehensive human rights policy in response to adverse regional human rights court judgments. Consider the Inter-American Court case of *Gelman v. Uruguay*. The events leading up to the 2011 case of *Gelman v. Uruguay* began in 1976, when a pregnant university student, Mrs. María Claudia García Iruretagoyena Casinelli, and her husband, Mr. Marcelo Ariel Gelman Schubaroff, were detained in Buenos Aires, Argentina, by Uruguayan and Argentinean military commandos. The two were separated, and the husband was tortured in detention and eventually killed. María Claudia was transferred to a detention center where she gave birth to her child and was then forcefully disappeared. The daughter was given to an Uruguayan family. Obtaining justice through the national judicial system was unlikely, largely due to the approval of an amnesty law in 1986 that eliminated the investigation, trial, and sanction of police officers who had committed human rights violations before 1985 (Meisel and Tripodes, 2015).

The case eventually reached the Inter-American Court, and in 2011 the Court found that Uruguay had violated the American Convention on Human Rights, including articles related to the right to life, the right to humane treatment, and the right to personal liberty, among several other articles. The Inter-American Court ordered the state to identify, prosecute, and punish those responsible; determine the whereabouts of the victim; publish the judgment; create public access to state files on forced disappearances; and train judicial personnel in human rights, among several other orders.[1]

Notably, in June 2011, the president issued an order stating that the executive branch would no longer apply the amnesty law, and in August 2011, the president issued a decree creating an interministerial commission to monitor the state's compliance with the Inter-American Court's judgment.[2] What prompted the executive branch to undertake human rights reforms? I argue that executive job security played a role in the executive's willingness to make human rights policy changes. Presidential elections were held in 2009, and José Mujica, a member of the leftist Broad Front coalition, won the presidency. Many of the presidential orders following *Gelman v. Uruguay* took place during Mujica's term, and while Mujica was ineligible to run for election in 2014 due to constitutional term limits, his party (the Broad Front) campaigned strongly in favor of their candidate in 2014. In 2009, Mujica ran on a platform of scrapping the amnesty law. In the several years following the adverse Inter-American Court judgment and in the run-up to the 2014 presidential election, Mujica fulfilled many of the orders of the Inter-American Court in *Gelman v. Uruguay*, including prohibiting the application of the amnesty law, issuing a public apology, and erecting a plaque commemorating the victims. The state also made progress toward implementing human rights training programs for judicial personnel. In fact, Inter-American Court Judge Eduardo Ferrer Mac-Gregor Poisot appended a separate opinion in a compliance monitoring report touting the efforts of the state's executive and legislative branches to meet the Inter-American Court obligations.

Of importance, the executive's actions were largely consistent with Broad Front constituent preferences. While there was a public divide over the amnesty law, with 53 percent voting in favor of the amnesty law and 47 percent opposed to the law in the 2009 referenda, Broad Front constituents largely

---

[1] *Gelman v. Uruguay*, Merits and Reparations, Judgment, Inter-Am. Ct. H.R. Feb. 24, 2011.
[2] *Gelman v. Uruguay*, Monitoring Compliance with Judgment, Order of the Court, Inter-Am. Ct. H.R. Mar. 20, 2013.

favored repealing the law (Soltman, 2013).³ Although the Supreme Court ruled that the legislation repealing the amnesty law was unconstitutional in 2013, Mujica's efforts to repeal the amnesty law were not unnoticed by constituents, particularly those of the Broad Front coalition. The Broad Front won the 2014 election in a second-round vote with 56.63 percent of the votes.

Despite contention over the amnesty law among the general public, the Broad Front's base of supporters were largely opposed to the amnesty law. As a result, the executive undertook actions to repeal the law, an order of the Inter-American Court. Importantly, repeal of the amnesty law allowed for the investigation, trial, and prosecution of many state officials responsible for human rights abuses, and arguably deterred the commission of human rights abuses by state officials in the future. In fact, there is evidence that human rights practices in Uruguay improved following the adverse judgment (Fariss, 2014). The Inter-American Court case in Uruguay suggests that the executive was willing to make policy changes following an adverse Inter-American Court judgment based on pressure from the public at large, particularly in an election period. While Mujica was ineligible to run for a second term, the president's party, the Broad Front, had incentives to maintain support from their constituents and appeal to their winning coalition – particularly in the run-up to executive elections.

While an upcoming election creates incentives for executive adoption, administration, monitoring, and enforcement of human rights policy in response to adverse regional human rights court judgments, the presence of threats to the political and social order can generate executive incentives to utilize human rights abuses in response to threats. Consider, for example, the response of European countries to the Global War on Terror, particularly as it pertains to immigration and detention policies. Although human rights researchers often assume that the mass public is generally supportive of human rights, citizens of European countries also recognize that like national courts, the European Court operates as a counter-majoritarian institution, protecting the rights of minorities, including immigrants and suspected terrorists. The Global War on Terror, coupled with the rise of populist and nationalist movements in many European countries, has contributed to public failure to support some European Court judgments, particularly judgments that protect the rights of minorities perceived as threatening by large segments of the mass public.

---

³ In fact, when the legislature voted on repealing the law in 2011, the vote was split, with all members of the Broad Front voting for the annulment of the amnesty law.

Consider, for example, the case of *Mubilanzila Mayeka and Kaniki Mitunga v. Belgium*. In 2002, Tabitha, a five year old Congolese national was traveling with her Dutch uncle from the Democratic Republic of the Congo to Brussels, Belgium. Upon arrival at the international terminal in Brussels, she was detained because she did not have the necessary documents to enter Belgium. Tabitha's uncle returned to the Netherlands, and her mother, who had been granted refugee status, remained in Canada. A lawyer was appointed to assist Tabitha. Tabitha was detained for 2 months in an immigration center for adults before being deported back to the Democratic Republic of the Congo. The mother and child filed an application with the European Court of Human Rights and in 2006, the European Court issued a judgment against Belgium finding that the child's detainment, detention (without her parents in a center for adults), and subsequent deportation violated the prohibition of inhuman treatment and the right to liberty and security, among several other articles.[4] Because large segments of the population perceive minorities, like immigrants, asylum seekers, and refugees, as a threat to the political and social order, many European countries have adopted strict immigration policies and laws. Consequently, the likelihood of executive human rights policy change in response to adverse European Court judgments is low.

In addition to the public controversy around European Court cases involving immigration, the political climate also sparked controversy around European Court judgments involving deportation of suspected terrorists, creating problems for European Court deterrence. The European Court has rendered adverse judgments against states for deportation of individuals at risk of ill-treatment. Italian courts, for example, ordered the deportation of Tunisian national Ben Khemais to Tunisia in 2006, where he was sentenced by a military court to 10 years' imprisonment for membership in a terrorist organization. Khemais lodged an application with the European Court, and following the 2009 case of *Ben Khemais v. Italy*, Khemais was extradited to Tunisia despite the European Court order to stay the applicant's deportation pending a decision. Similarly, in the 2012 case of *Labsi v. Slovakia*, an Algerian man (Mustafa Labsi) residing in Slovakia had his request for asylum denied several times by the Migration Office, as the applicant was found to represent a security risk to the Slovak Republic.[5] The case eventually reached the Supreme Court in Slovakia, which upheld earlier decisions, and Labsi's asylum application was again denied. Labsi was deported to Algeria despite facing risk of ill-treatment (and a death sentence). Following the deportation,

---

[4] See *Mubilanzila Mayeka and Kanki Mitunga v. Belgium*, Judgment, European Ct. H.R. January 12, 2007.

[5] See *Labsi v. Slovakia*, Judgment, European Ct. H.R. September 24, 2012.

Interior Minister Robert Kalinak claimed, "It's a victory of common sense and a guarantee of safety for our citizens" (Terenzani, 2010). The European Court found the state in violation of several articles of the European Convention, including Article 3 (freedom from torture and ill-treatment) on account of the applicant's expulsion to Algeria. Disregard for the European Court's rulings are common when states face social and political threats, notably the threat of terrorism. Such threats in society reduce public support for rights protection, including rights upheld by regional human rights courts. Therefore, as threats to the political and social order persist postjudgment, the executive has few incentives to adopt comprehensive human rights policy.

These examples provide anecdotal evidence of the role of mass public support in generating executive willingness to adopt, administer, monitor, and enforce human rights policy following an adverse regional human rights court judgment. Executive willingness to respond to pressure from the mass public to protect rights following an adverse regional court judgment is greater when executive job security is threatened, particularly during an election cycle. However, executive willingness to adopt comprehensive human rights policy is lower when states face threats to the political and social order because segments of the executive's winning coalition may support withholding rights from groups viewed as threatening. In this chapter, I find that adverse regional human rights court judgments before elections, particularly competitive elections, are more likely to deter future human rights abuses. I also find that adverse regional court judgments are less likely to deter future human rights abuses when there are threats to the political and social order in society. In what follows, I provide several illustrative examples that support the theoretical argument, conduct empirical tests, and draw conclusions about the role of executive willingness to adopt, administer, monitor, and enforce human rights policy following an adverse regional court judgment as a result of mass public pressure.

5.1 DATA AND METHODOLOGY

In this chapter, I analyze the relationship between the executive, the mass public, and regional human rights courts. To do so, I begin by discussing several anecdotes that support the theoretical argument. I then display results from quantitative analyses in support of the general argument. I utilize the dependent variable described in Chapter 3, a measure of respect for physical integrity rights from Fariss (2014). Higher values represent greater respect for rights, while lower values indicate worse respect for rights. I assess the level of respect for rights at several points in time following an adverse regional human rights court judgment. Like the previous empirical chapters, I also examine the robustness of the results by discussing results from models estimated using an additional dependent variable, the change in respect for physical integrity rights from the year of the judgment to several years after the judgment (using changes in the Cingranelli, Richards, and Clay [2014] physical integrity rights index).

The primary independent variable used in the analyses in this chapter captures the presence of adverse European or Inter-American Court of Human Rights judgments (described in more detail in Chapter 3). I utilize a binary variable in which the presence of at least one adverse European or Inter-American Court judgment in a country-year takes on a value of one and zero otherwise. As described in Chapter 3, I only examine European Court judgments published in case reports or judgments of level 1 or 2 importance. I exclude judgments of level 3 importance because they only apply existing case law and do not communicate new information to political actors.

I estimate several models to test Hypotheses 3 and 4 in this chapter. The samples and model specifications are also similar to those examined in Chapter 4 (linear regression models with random intercepts and standard errors clustered on country). A list of control variables and full model results are included in the Appendix to this chapter.

5.2 REGIONAL COURT DETERRENCE IS CONDITIONAL ON MASS PUBLIC SUPPORT

5.2.1 *The Role of Executive Job Security*

To begin examining the role of mass public support in generating executive willingness to adopt comprehensive human rights policy following an adverse regional human rights court judgment (Hypothesis 3), I look to the role of executive job security as a result of an upcoming election. I expect that adverse regional human rights court judgments will be associated with better respect for rights in states where the executive or the executive's party is insecure in office due to an upcoming election. Consider the 2008 case of *Heliodoro Portugal v. Panama*. Heliodoro Portugal, a proponent of a movement opposed to the military regime (the Revolutionary Unity Movement), was detained and taken to one of the country's secret interrogation and torture centers in 1970. Following a transfer to the Tocumén Barracks, Portugal disappeared and was never heard from again. In 1990, after democracy was restored, the case was investigated, and remains of a victim were found at the Tocumén Barracks, showing signs of brutal mistreatment. DNA testing revealed that the human remains belonged to Portugal (Marinova, 2015). In 2008, the Inter-American Court of Human Rights found that Panama had violated several articles of the American Convention on Human Rights and ordered the state to investigate, prosecute, and punish the responsible parties; publish the judgment; provide medical care; and reform legislation to define forced disappearance and torture as crimes consistent with international law. When compliance was assessed in 2010, the Inter-American Court found that the state had complied with several of the Court's orders, including issuing a public apology in February 2009.[6]

Notably, Panama held a general election in May 2009. Although the Panamanian constitution prohibits consecutive second terms of the presidency, the popular current president, Martin Torrijos of the Democratic Revolutionary Party, supported Minister of Housing Balbina Herrera's run on the Democratic Revolutionary Party's ticket in 2009. While Torrijos's political survival did not depend on making human rights policy changes following the adverse Inter-American Court judgment, the party hoped to hold onto power in the next election. Responding to the Inter-American Court with human rights policy change was one way to appeal to voters and increase the Democratic Revolutionary Party's chances of success. Evidence shows that following the 2008 adverse judgment, Panama's physical integrity rights score improved. In fact, according to human rights data (ranging from about −2 to +3 in the Americas), Panama's physical integrity rights score following the 2008 adverse judgment was 1.65 (in 2009), higher than the average over the previous decade (1.57) (Fariss, 2014).

As another example, consider the 1992 case of *Zambrano Vélez et al. v. Ecuador*. In 1992, Ecuador's Navy, Air Force, and Army carried out an operation under a state of emergency during a period of high terrorist group activity. During the operation in the city of Guayaquil, the armed forces entered the houses of Wilmer Zambrano Vélez and two other victims. The three victims were shot and killed by state agents (Samyan, 2017). In 2007, the Inter-American Court found the state in violation of several articles of the American Convention on Human Rights, including the article prohibiting the arbitrary deprivation of life and the article specifying the procedural requirements to suspend rights, among others.[7] The Inter-American Court ordered the state to investigate, identify, prosecute, and punish those responsible; acknowledge responsibility; publish the judgment; adopt adequate legislation; and implement programs of education in human rights, along with several other orders.

[6] *Heliodoro Portugal v. Panama*, Monitoring Compliance with Judgment, Inter-Am. Ct. H.R. April 20, 2010.
[7] *Zambrano Vélez et al. v. Ecuador*, Merits, Reparations, and Costs, Judgment. Inter-Am. Ct. H.R. July 4, 2007.

In 2009, the Court assessed compliance with the judgment, finding that the state had partially complied with several orders, including the requirement to acknowledge responsibility, which was done by the state's Minister of Justice and Human Rights on television. Legislative reforms were also undertaken to modify the National Security Law regarding states of emergency. The state also held pilot programs on international standards for judicial protection with the aim of providing adequate training of law enforcement and judicial officers.[8]

Also taking place in Ecuador following the adverse Inter-American Court judgment was the 2009 general election. The incumbent candidate, Rafael Correa of the PAIS Alliance (a democratic socialist political party), was reelected, the first reelection of a president since 1975. Importantly, following the adverse Inter-American Court decision in 2007, respect for physical integrity rights in Ecuador improved, from 0.186 in 2007 to 0.324 in 2008 and 0.441 in 2009 (on a scale ranging from −2 to +3 in the Americas).

The examples in Panama and Ecuador provide initial evidence that executive insecurity in office due to an upcoming election can generate executive incentives to make human rights policy changes following adverse regional human rights court decisions. In other words, the anecdotal evidence suggests that the presence of adverse regional human rights court judgments prior to an election can generate executive job insecurity, prompting the executive to adopt comprehensive human rights policy, and thereby deterring future human rights abuses. In the following section, I turn to a more systematic analysis of Hypothesis 3.

5.2.2 Evidence of Executive Willingness: Executive Job Security

To test Hypothesis 3, I utilize two measures of executive electoral incentives. First, I argue that election timing matters in explaining regional human rights court deterrence. When the executive is insecure in office, as is often the case before an election, the executive is more likely to make human rights policy changes in an attempt to appeal to the electorate at large following shaming as a result of an adverse regional human rights court judgment. To test the influence of executive electoral incentives, I utilize a binary variable capturing whether a presidential election took place during the year (Coppedge et al., 2019). The adverse regional human rights court judgment is lagged 1, 2, and 3 years to examine the influence of the adverse judgment at three points in time prior to an election.

---

[8] *Zambrano Vélez et al. v. Ecuador*, Monitoring Compliance with Judgment, Inter-Am. Ct. H.R. May 22, 2009.

5.2 Regional Court Deterrence Is Conditional

In Chapter 4, I estimated models utilizing 1-, 3-, and 5-year lags of the adverse judgment variable. To examine the influence of election timing on respect for rights, I do not utilize a 5-year lag because I do not expect the presence of an adverse judgment 5 years prior to an election to be influential in respect for rights. First, term limits often mean that executives are unlikely to hold office for 5 years without facing a reelection bid. Second, when executive electoral rules provide for terms longer than 5 years, the presence of an adverse judgment 5 years prior to an election is unlikely to influence executive incentives because the executive is relatively secure in office 5 years prior to an election.

I estimate several models in each region. In the first set of models, I examine the influence of the presence of an adverse regional human rights court judgment 1 year before an election on respect for rights in an election year. Then, to compare the influence of an adverse judgment that takes place before an election year with the influence of an adverse judgment that occurs prior to a nonelection year, I estimate models examining the influence of adverse regional human rights court judgments on respect for rights in the following year, but only for cases in which no election was held. The split sample models can be written more formally as follows:

$$Respect\ for\ Rights_{(t)} = b_0 + b_1\ Adverse\ Judgment_{(t-1)} + Controls_{(t-1)}$$
$$+ \varepsilon \quad (if\ Election_{(t)} = Yes)$$

$$Respect\ for\ Rights_{(t)} = b_0 + b_1\ Adverse\ Judgment_{(t-1)} + Controls_{(t-1)}$$
$$+ \varepsilon \quad (if\ Election_{(t)} = No)$$

I estimate a second set of models to capture the influence of an adverse judgment that occurs 2 years prior to an election/nonelection year on respect for rights. Because the executive may not have sufficient time to respond to an adverse judgment with the adoption of comprehensive human rights policy when the judgment is rendered in the year prior to an election, I examine the influence of adverse regional human rights court judgments *2 years before an election* on respect for rights in an election year. I then estimate models examining the influence of adverse regional human rights court judgments on respect for rights *2 years before a nonelection year*.[9] The two models can be written as follows:

---

[9] In order to identify the influence of an adverse judgment 2 years prior to an election on respect for rights, I also control for the presence of other adverse judgments that occurred 1 year prior to the election.

$$\text{Respect for Rights}_{(t)} = b_0 + b_1 \text{ Adverse Judgment}_{(t-2)} + b_2 \text{ Adverse Judgment}_{(t-1)}$$
$$+ \text{Controls}_{(t-1)} + \varepsilon \quad (\text{if Election}_{(t)} = \text{Yes})$$
$$\text{Respect for Rights}_{(t)} = b_0 + b_1 \text{ Adverse Judgment}_{(t-2)} + b_2 \text{ Adverse Judgment}_{(t-1)}$$
$$+ \text{Controls}_{(t-1)} + \varepsilon \quad (\text{if Election}_{(t)} = \text{No})$$

Finally, I estimate a third set of models to capture the influence of an adverse judgment that occurs 3 years prior to an election/nonelection year on respect for rights. I estimate models examining the influence of adverse regional human rights court judgments on respect for rights 3 years before an election and 3 years before a nonelection year.[10] The two models can be written as follows:

$$\text{Respect for Rights}_{(t)} = b_0 + b_1 \text{ Adverse Judgment}_{(t-3)} + b_2 \text{ Adverse Judgment}_{(t-2)}$$
$$+ b_3 \text{ Adverse Judgment}_{(t-1)} + \text{Controls}_{(t-1)}$$
$$+ \varepsilon \quad (\text{if Election}_{(t)} = \text{Yes})$$
$$\text{Respect for Rights}_{(t)} = b_0 + b_1 \text{ Adverse Judgment}_{(t-3)} + b_2 \text{ Adverse Judgment}_{(t-2)}$$
$$+ b_3 \text{ Adverse Judgment}_{(t-1)} + \text{Controls}_{(t-1)}$$
$$+ \varepsilon \quad (\text{if Election}_{(t)} = \text{No})$$

There were 93 presidential elections held in Europe and 111 presidential elections held in the Americas during the time period covered by the analyses.[11] A description of control variables and full model results are presented in the Appendix. Although in what follows I present substantive results from split sample models, models estimated with interaction terms produce similar results. I present model results utilizing an interaction term of an adverse judgment and election year, rather than split sample models, in the Appendix.

Figure 5.1 displays results for the European Court models; the figure reports coefficient estimates (as dots) and 90 percent confidence intervals (as lines). Figure 5.1 shows little support for the role of the election in generating executive (here, presidential) incentives to adopt comprehensive human rights policy in line with adverse European Court judgments. The coefficient estimates and confidence intervals show that adverse European Court judgments are not significantly associated with respect for rights 1, 2, or 3 years before an election or nonelection year. As a robustness check, I estimated models predicting the influence of an adverse judgment on the

---

[10] In order to identify the influence of an adverse judgment 3 years prior to an election on respect for rights, I also control for the presence of other adverse judgments that occurred 1 and 2 years prior to the election.

[11] There are fewer observations reported in the models due to missing data.

5.2 Regional Court Deterrence Is Conditional

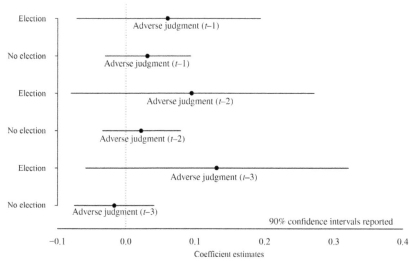

FIGURE 5.1. Predicted influence of adverse European Court judgments on respect for rights before election

Notes: Figure 5.1 displays coefficient estimates (as dots) and 90 percent confidence intervals (as lines) for the influence of adverse European Court judgments on respect for rights 1, 2, and 3 years before an election and nonelection year. The results show that adverse European Court judgments in the 3 years prior to an election are not significantly associated with respect for rights.

change in respect for physical integrity rights 1, 2, and 3 years postjudgment (using changes in the Cingranelli, Richards, and Clay [2014] physical integrity rights index as the dependent variable). The results (not reported here) are largely consistent with those reported in Figure 5.1. Adverse European Court judgments are insignificantly related to *change* in respect for rights 1, 2, and 3 years postjudgment in both election and nonelection years. The only exception to this finding is when an adverse judgment is rendered 1 year before a nonelection year, in which case an adverse European Court judgment is negatively and significantly related to the change in respect for rights from the year of the judgment to the following nonelection year.

Coefficient estimates for the Inter-American Court are displayed in Figure 5.2. The results for the Inter-American Court show that the presence of an adverse Inter-American Court judgment 2 years before an election is positively and significantly associated with respect for rights. Also of note, adverse Inter-American Court judgments 1 year before an election year and 3 years before an election year are not significantly associated with respect for rights. An adverse judgment 1 or 2 years before a nonelection year is not significantly associated with greater respect for rights either. However, the

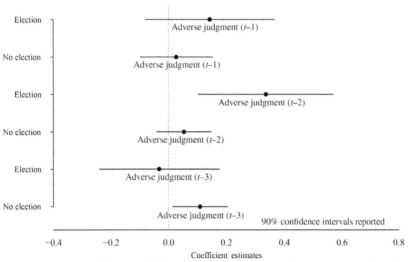

FIGURE 5.2. Predicted influence of adverse Inter-American Court judgments on respect for rights before election

Notes: Figure 5.2 displays coefficient estimates (as dots) and 90 percent confidence intervals (as lines) for the influence of adverse Inter-American Court judgments on respect for rights 1, 2, and 3 years before an election and nonelection year. While adverse Inter-American Court judgments are not significantly associated with respect for rights 1 year or 3 years prior to an election, adverse Inter-American Court judgments are positively and significantly associated with respect for rights 2 years prior to an election year.

presence of an adverse judgment 3 years before a nonelection year is positively associated with respect for rights, though the effect is substantively quite small. Perhaps this result is driven by the lingering effects of the prior election. For example, if an election is held every five years, then 3 years prior to a nonelection year may also be closely following an election year, and human rights policies adopted before the last election may still be in place.

Like the European Court, I also estimated models predicting the influence of adverse Inter-American Court judgments 1, 2, and 3 years prior to an election on the change in respect for physical integrity rights from the year of the judgment to the year of the election. The results are largely consistent with the results reported in Figure 5.2. Specifically, adverse Inter-American Court judgments 1 year prior to an election year are insignificantly associated with the change in respect for rights from the year of the judgment to the election year. Additionally, adverse Inter-American Court judgments 3 years prior to an election are insignificantly related to the change in respect for rights from the year of the judgment to the year of the election. However, also consistent with the results reported in Figure 5.2, adverse Inter-American Court judgments

5.2 Regional Court Deterrence Is Conditional

2 years prior to an election are positively and significantly associated with the change in respect for rights from the year of the adverse judgment to the year of an election. The results (reported in Table C.7 of the Appendix) show that an adverse Inter-American Court judgment 2 years before an election is associated with a 0.436 increase in respect for rights from the year of the adverse judgment to the year of the election. Two years prior to a nonelection year, adverse Inter-American Court judgments are not significantly associated with a change in respect for rights.

Given that the only positive and significant finding in support of Hypothesis 3 reported in Figures 5.1 and 5.2 is the presence of an adverse Inter-American Court judgment 2 years prior to an election, I investigate this finding further. However, rather than running a split sample model, I utilize an interaction term including adverse regional human rights court judgments and the presence of an executive (presidential) election. In order to capture the influence of the adverse judgment 2 years prior to an election, the adverse judgment variable is lagged 2 years. The equation for can be written formally as follows:

$$\text{Respect for Rights}_{(t)} = b_0 + b_1 \text{ Executive Election}_{(t)} * \text{Adverse Judgment}_{(t-2)} \\ + b_2 \text{ Executive Election}_{(t)} + b_3 \text{ Adverse Judgment}_{(t-2)} \\ + b_4 \text{ Adverse Judgment}_{(t-1)} + \text{Controls}_{(t-1)} + \varepsilon.$$

The left panel of Figure 5.3 displays the predicted level of respect for rights during an election and nonelection year. The dots represent the predicted level of respect for rights and the lines represent 90 percent confidence intervals. All other variables in the model are set to their mean (for continuous variables) or mode (for binary or ordinal variables). When an adverse Inter-American Court judgment is rendered prior to an election year, the predicted level of respect for rights is about 0.30 higher (on a scale ranging from −2 to +3) than when the Inter-American Court renders a judgment prior to a nonelection year. While there is a slight overlap in the 90 percent confidence intervals in the left panel of Figure 5.3, estimating contrasts of margins shows that the contrast between election and nonelection in the presence of an adverse judgment is 0.30 (0.138 to 0.463, 95 percent confidence interval).

The right panel of Figure 5.3 displays the influence of an adverse Inter-American Court judgment rendered 2 years prior to an election/nonelection year on the change in respect for rights from the year of the judgment to the year of the election/nonelection (using changes in the Cingranelli, Richards, and Clay [2014] physical integrity rights index as the dependent variable). The dots represent the predicted change in respect for rights, and the lines

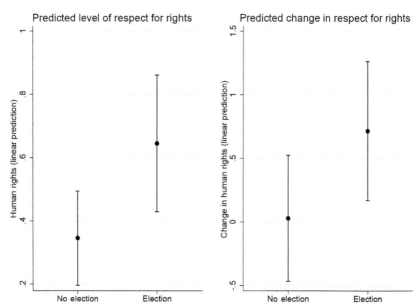

FIGURE 5.3. Predicted influence of adverse Inter-American Court judgments on respect for rights two years prior to election / non-election year

Notes: The left panel of Figure 5.3 displays the influence of an adverse Inter-American Court judgment 2 years prior to an election year and a nonelection year on the level of respect for rights and the right panel displays the influence of an adverse Inter-American Court judgment 2 years prior to an election or nonelection year on the change in respect for rights. The dots represent the predicted level of or change in respect for rights, and the lines represent 90 percent confidence intervals. All other variables are set to the mean or mode.

represent 90 percent confidence intervals. All other variables in the model are set to their mean (for continuous variables) or mode (for binary or ordinal variables). The results show that when an adverse judgment is rendered 2 years prior to a nonelection year, the predicted change in physical integrity rights is around 0.03. However, when an adverse judgment is rendered 2 years prior to an election year, the predicted change in physical integrity rights is around 0.72 (on a scale ranging from −4 to +6). Like the results in the left panel, the results presented in the right panel of Figure 5.3 display some overlap in the 90 percent confidence intervals. However, the contrast of predictive margins shows that the contrast between election and nonelection in the presence of an adverse judgment is 0.69 (0.116 to 1.26, 95 percent confidence interval). Full model results are presented in the Appendix (Table C.7).

The findings displayed in Figures 5.2 and 5.3 lend support to Hypothesis 3, but the reliable findings are largely limited to the influence of adverse Inter-American Court judgments on respect for rights 2 years prior to an election

5.2 Regional Court Deterrence Is Conditional

year. Notably, there are important differences between elections that are not captured by simply examining the presence or absence of an election. Some elections are highly competitive, where a candidate wins by only a small margin, whereas others are not competitive, in which one candidate wins by a landslide. Executive job security is more likely to be threatened in the face of a competitive election. Presumably, presidential candidates that win by a large margin do not expect the election to be competitive, and because the election is noncompetitive, there are fewer incentives to adopt comprehensive human rights policy following an adverse regional human rights court judgment. The executive does not expect to lose office and is less concerned with responding to mass public pressure to make human rights policy changes following an adverse regional court judgment as a result. Conversely, when the executive expects to lose office by a large margin, there are few incentives to undertake costly human rights policy changes prior to an election because the executive would expend substantial effort to make policy changes with little payoff.

However, presidential candidates that win by a relatively smaller margin recognize that the election is competitive, and the candidate seeking to stay in office has incentives to adopt comprehensive human rights policy in response to adverse regional human rights court judgments to appeal to the public's interest in human rights. Even for executives that have reached their term limit, the executive still has incentives to ensure that the newly elected executive comes from the executive's current party. As a result, even outgoing executives have party-driven incentives to respond to adverse regional human rights court judgments in expectation of a competitive election.

Looking beyond the mere presence of an election to capture executive job security, I estimate models that take into account variation in the competitiveness of the election; more specifically, I examine the percentage of the vote received by the winning candidate (Coppedge et al., 2019). The low values on this variable indicate that the candidate won by a smaller margin, and the high values on this variable indicate that the candidate won by a larger margin. To test the role of electoral competitiveness in generating executive incentives to adopt, administer, monitor, and enforce human rights policy, I create an interaction term between the vote share of the presidential election winner and the presence of at least one adverse judgment 1, 2, and 3 years before an election. I estimate three different models for the European and Inter-American Courts of Human Rights. In the first model, I examine the influence of an adverse judgment (lagged 1 year) and electoral competitiveness on respect for rights in the election year. In the second model, I examine the influence of an adverse judgment (lagged 2 years) and electoral competitiveness on respect for rights in the election year. Finally, in the third model, I examine the influence of an adverse judgment (lagged 3 years) and electoral competitiveness on respect for rights in the election year. The following equation is an example of the model used to assess respect for rights 3 years postjudgment:

$$\text{Respect for Rights}_{(t)} = b_0 + b_1 \text{ Vote Share}_{(t)} * \text{Adverse Judgment}_{(t-3)}$$
$$+ b_2 \text{ Vote Share}_{(t)} + b_3 \text{ Adverse Judgment}_{(t-3)}$$
$$+ b_4 \text{ Adverse Judgment}_{(t-2)} + b_5 \text{ Adverse Judgment}_{(t-1)}$$
$$+ \text{Controls}_{(t-1)} + \varepsilon.$$

Figures 5.4 and 5.5 display the influence of adverse regional court judgments on respect for rights across the vote share of the largest vote-getter in an executive election. The left panel of Figures 5.4 and 5.5 shows the influence

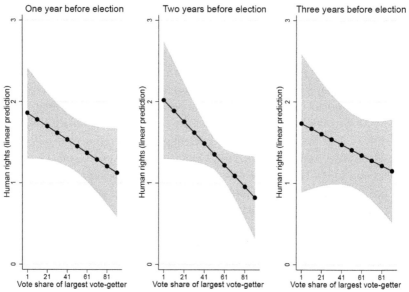

FIGURE 5.4. Predicted influence of adverse European Court judgments on respect for rights across electoral competitiveness

Notes: Figure 5.4 displays the influence of an adverse European Court judgment 1 year prior to an executive election (left panel), 2 years prior to an executive election (center panel), and 3 years prior to an executive election (right panel) across the vote share of the largest vote-getter on respect for rights in the election year. Lines represent the predicted level of respect for rights in the presence of an adverse European Court judgment, and the shaded area represents 90 percent confidence intervals. The center panel shows that when vote share of the largest vote-getter in an executive election is low (i.e., the election is more competitive), an adverse judgment 2 years before an election is associated with higher respect for rights than when the vote share of the largest vote-getter is high (i.e. the election is less competitive).

5.2 Regional Court Deterrence Is Conditional

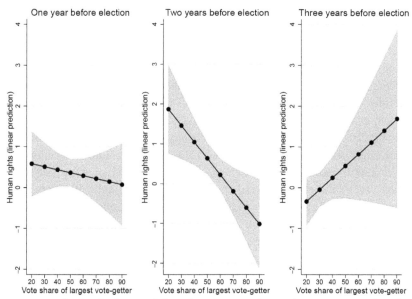

FIGURE 5.5. Predicted influence of adverse Inter-American Court judgments on respect for rights across electoral competitiveness

Notes: Figure 5.5 displays the influence of an adverse Inter-American Court judgment 1 year prior to an executive election (left panel), 2 years prior to an executive election (center panel), and 3 years prior to an executive election (right panel) across the vote share of the largest vote-getter on respect for rights in the election year. Lines represent the predicted level of respect for rights in the presence of an adverse Inter-American Court judgment, and the shaded area represents 90 percent confidence intervals. The center panel shows that when vote share of the largest vote-getter in an executive election is low (i.e., the election is more competitive), an adverse judgment 2 years before an election is associated with higher respect for rights than when the vote share of the largest vote-getter is high (i.e. the election is less competitive).

of an adverse judgment in the year before an election on respect for rights in the election year across values of executive vote share, the center panel 2 years before an election, and the right panel 3 years before an election.

Figure 5.4 displays results for the European Court sample and shows that the predicted level of respect for rights is lower as the vote share of the largest vote-getter increases. In fact, in the presence of an adverse judgment 1 year before an election, the predicted value of respect for rights is 1.70 when the vote share of the largest vote-getter is 21 percent, and the predicted value of respect for rights is 1.12 when the vote share of the largest vote-getter is 91 percent.

The effect is even more striking 2 years prior to an election. The center panel of Figure 5.4 shows that in the presence of an adverse European Court judgment 2 years prior to an election, the predicted level of respect for rights is 1.75 when the vote share of the largest vote-getter is 21 percent (more competitive election), and the predicted level of respect for rights is 0.822 when the vote share of the largest vote-getter is 91 percent (less competitive election), a difference of 0.93 on the human rights measure (ranging from around −2 to +4 in Europe).[12] The right panel of Figure 5.4 shows wider 90 percent confidence intervals, an indication that we can be less confident about the role of electoral competitiveness when an adverse judgment occurs 3 years prior to an election.

In order to examine the robustness of the results, I also analyze the influence of adverse European Court judgments 1, 2, and 3 years before an election on the *change* in respect for physical integrity rights from the year of the judgment to the year of the election using changes in the Cingranelli, Richards, and Clay (2014) physical integrity rights index as the dependent variable. The substantive results (displayed in Table C.11 of the Appendix) display a negative trend in that adverse European Court judgments are negatively associated with the vote share of the largest vote-getter, though the size of the confidence intervals mean we should interpret these results with some caution. That is, as the election becomes less competitive (vote share of the largest vote-getter grows), adverse European Court judgments 1, 2, and 3 years prior to an election are negatively associated with the change in respect for rights from the year of the judgment to the year of the election. For example, when an adverse European Court judgment occurs 2 years prior to an election, the predicted change in respect for rights from the year of the judgment to the year of the election is 0.180 (on a scale ranging from −4 to +3) when the election is highly competitive (vote share of the largest vote-getter is 21 percent). However, the presence of an adverse European Court judgment 2 years prior to an election is associated with a −0.052 change from the year of the adverse judgment to the year of the election when the election is not competitive (vote share of the largest vote-getter is 91 percent). This finding suggests that when an executive anticipates a highly competitive election, the executive has incentives to address constituent preferences for greater rights protection in response to adverse judgments that occurred 2 years before the election.

Turning to results for the Inter-American Court, a similar pattern emerges. Consistent with the Inter-American Court findings discussed earlier on election timing, adverse Inter-American Court judgments are more likely to be effective 2 years prior to a competitive election. The left panel of Figure 5.5 shows that although the influence of an adverse judgment 1 year prior to an election across vote share is negatively associated with respect for rights, there is little substantive difference in respect for rights across values of

---

[12] The predicted value of respect for rights at each value of executive vote share is statistically different from zero ($p < .000$).

vote share. However, the center panel shows that an adverse Inter-American Court judgment 2 years prior to an election is associated with better respect for rights, particularly when the election is highly competitive. For example, in the presence of an adverse judgment 2 years before an election, the predicted value of respect for rights is 1.87 when the vote share of the largest vote-getter is 20 percent, and the predicted value of respect for rights is −0.605 when the vote share of the largest vote-getter is 80 percent (a difference of 2.48 on the human rights measure). Like the results for the European Court, the right panel of Figure 5.5 shows that the presence of an adverse judgment 3 years prior to an election is not significantly associated with respect for rights.

Examining the robustness of the findings using changes in the Cingranelli, Richards, and Clay (2014) physical integrity rights index as the dependent variable shows little support for the role of electoral competitiveness in Inter-American Court effectiveness. The results, reported in Table C.11 of the Appendix, show that adverse judgments 1, 2, and 3 years prior to an election are not significantly associated with changes in respect for rights from the year of the judgment to the year of the election. Considering the findings for the Inter-American Court reported in Figures 5.3 and 5.5, as well as from models predicting the level of respect for rights and changes in respect for rights following adverse Inter-American Court judgments, one might conclude that the *presence and timing of elections* in the Americas is more important for Inter-American Court effectiveness than the *competitiveness of elections*. That is, executives in the Americas appear to find it electorally beneficial to respond to adverse Inter-American Court judgments prior to an election regardless of executive expectations about electoral competitiveness.

Taken together, these results indicate that elections generate executive incentives to adopt comprehensive human rights policy following adverse regional court judgments. The presence of an adverse Inter-American Court judgment 2 years before an election is associated with greater respect for rights. Further, the competitiveness of an election is important for generating executive incentives to adopt, administer, monitor, and enforce human rights policy following adverse European and Inter-American Court judgments. The findings show that as the election becomes more competitive (vote-share of the largest vote-getter is relatively low), an adverse judgment is associated with higher respect for rights than when the election was not competitive (vote-share of the largest vote-getter is relatively high). More specifically, the results indicate that when an adverse judgment is rendered 2 years prior to a competitive election, the predicted level of respect for rights is significantly higher in the election year than is the predicted level of respect for rights when an adverse judgment is rendered 2 years prior to noncompetitive executive elections. In other words, the regional court is more likely to deter future human rights abuse when an adverse judgment is rendered 2 years prior to a competitive election in both Europe and the Americas.

5.2.3 The Role of Threats to the Political and Social Order

In Chapter 2, I argued that executive willingness to adopt, administer, monitor, and enforce human rights policy is conditional on the presence of threats to the political and social order (Hypothesis 4). Two countries in the Americas provide excellent illustrations of this process. Trinidad and Tobago and Barbados are both countries that have been involved in Inter-American Court cases involving the mandatory application of the death penalty in the national judicial system. The mandatory application of the death penalty stipulates that anyone convicted of murder is sentenced to death, and national judges have little discretion to consider the circumstances of the case. In Chapter 2, I discussed the case of *Hilaire, Constantine, and Benjamin et al. v. Trinidad and Tobago*. In this case, Indravani Ramjattan was subjected to domestic abuse by her common law husband, Alexander Jordan. Ramjattan formed a relationship with another man, Denny Baptiste, and became pregnant with his child. Jordan (the common-law husband) abused Ramjattan, causing her to flee the house and move into Baptiste's home. Upon discovering that Ramjattan was living with Baptiste and a second man (Hilaire), Jordan broke into Baptiste's home and took Ramjattan back to live with him, where she suffered further domestic abuse. Ramjattan called on Hilaire and Baptiste to rescue her, and Hilaire and Baptiste went to Jordan's house and beat him to death. Hilaire and Baptiste were convicted and sentenced to death under the mandatory death penalty for murder law. Ramjattan was convicted and sentenced to death for murder as well, a conviction that was overturned due to international pressure (Bendinelli, 2015). Several other individuals, all sentenced to death under the mandatory death penalty, submitted petitions through the Inter-American Human Rights System, joining the petition of *Hilaire, Constantine, and Benjamin et al. v. Trinidad and Tobago*.

In 2002, the Inter-American Court found that the Trinidad and Tobago had violated several articles of the American Convention on Human Rights, including the right to life. Trinidad and Tobago was ordered to undertake several major reforms. The state failed to comply with any of the Inter-American Court orders.[13] Notably, respect for physical integrity rights declined

---

[13] Although Trinidad and Tobago denounced the Inter-American Court in 1999, the court still claimed jurisdiction for cases involving rights abuses while Trinidad and Tobago was under the jurisdiction of the court.

steadily in Trinidad and Tobago following the adverse judgment, an indication that the executive did not engage in human rights policy changes. According to the measure of physical integrity rights used in this chapter (Fariss, 2014), in the 4 years before the Inter-American Court ruling, Trinidad and Tobago scored a 1.51 on respect for physical integrity rights (a scale ranging around −2 to +3 in the Americas), while in the 4 years after the adverse judgment, Trinidad and Tobago scored a 0.921.

Contrast the case in Trinidad and Tobago with the case of *Boyce et al. v. Barbados.* In 1999, four men (Lennox Ricardo Boyce, Jeffrey Joseph, Rodney Murray, and Romaine Bend) went to a public basketball court and got into a fight with Marquelle Hippolyte. The men then chased Hippolyte down and beat him with pieces of wood. All four men were arrested and sent to prison. A few days later, Hippolyte died as a result of a blood clot from the beating, and the four men were charged with murder. Two of the men, Murray and Bend, entered guilty pleas for manslaughter and were sentenced to 12 years in prison. Boyce and Joseph pled not guilty and denied participating in the beating of Hippolyte. In 2001, both Boyce and Joseph stood trial, where they were found guilty of murder and sentenced to death by hanging, as the mandatory punishment for murder (Coveney, 2014).[14] The victims were originally held at Glendairy prison until it was destroyed by a fire in 2005. The conditions in prison were dire, and the victims were forced to use slop buckets for urination and defecation; ventilation was also poor, and inmates were held in their cells for at least 23 hours a day for over 4 years (Coveney, 2014). Following the fire in 2005, the inmates were held in cages at Harrison's Point Temporary Prison (Coveney, 2014).

The victim's petitions to the Inter-American Court alleged several violations, including violations of the right to life and the right to humane treatment. In 2007, the Inter-American Court found that Barbados had violated several articles of the American Convention on Human Rights, including the prohibition of arbitrary deprivation of life and death penalty limitations (Article 4) and the prohibition against torture (Article 5). The Inter-American Court ordered Barbados to commute the death sentence of one of the victims, make prison reforms ensuring that prison conditions align with the American Convention on Human Rights, and adopt legislative measures to comply with the American Convention.[15]

---

[14] The case of *Boyce et al. v. Barbados* also involves the imposition of the mandatory death sentence for murder for several other individuals.
[15] See *Boyce et al. v. Barbados*, Preliminary Objections, Merits, Reparations, and Costs, Judgment, Inter-Am. Ct. H.R. Nov. 20, 2007.

In 2011, the Inter-American Court assessed Barbados's compliance with the regional court decision, finding that the state had commuted the death sentence of one of the victims and had taken steps to adopt and implement measures to improve prison conditions.[16] In 2014, Barbados committed to removing the mandatory death penalty and proposed an amendment to the Offences against the Person Act, by creating a discretionary death penalty, under which persons could be sentenced to death *or* imprisonment for life. Of note, respect for physical integrity rights changed in Barbados following the the 2007 case. According to the Fariss (2014) data, respect for rights has steadily improved in Barbados following the adverse judgment. In 2007, Barbados scored a 1.46 (on a scale ranging from around −2 to +3 in the Americas), while in the 4 years after the judgment, the average level of respect for physical integrity rights in Barbados increased to 1.60.

While Trinidad and Tobago has completely rejected Inter-American Court recommendations, Barbados has made strides toward implementation. The human rights improvements in Barbados provide evidence of the presence of executive human rights policy change following the regional court judgment, while the lack of improvement in human rights practices in Trinidad and Tobago suggests that the executive did not engage in human rights policy change following the adverse judgment. One key difference between these two countries is political stability. According to the World Bank's political stability and absence of violence/terrorism measure (ranging from around −2.3 to +1.25 in the Americas), the average level of political stability in Barbados from 2001 to 2012 was 1.07, and the average level of political stability in Trinidad and Tobago was −0.089 for the same time period. Also telling is the homicide rate in each country. The median homicide rate per 100,000 in Trinidad and Tobago from 2001 to 2012 was around 27.45, while the median homicide rate in Barbados for the same time period was 9.2. The median homicide rate in the region was 14.1 per 100,000, meaning Barbados's homicide rate was below the median, and Trinidad and Tobago's homicide rate was above the median for the region.

The public in Trinidad and Tobago is largely supportive of the death penalty as well. In fact, a 2010 survey shows that 91 percent of Trinidadians are in favor of the death penalty (Hood and Seemungal, 2010).[17] Support for the death penalty is lower in Barbados, and according to a 2010 survey in Barbados, 79 percent of respondents support the death penalty, with 50 percent supporting the death penalty only in some circumstances. Support for the

---

[16] See *Boyce et al. v. Barbados*, Monitoring Compliance with Judgment, Order of the Court, Inter-Am Ct. H.R., Nov. 21, 2011.

[17] This number declines when considering the mandatory death penalty.

death penalty in Barbados was much higher in 1999 (around 82 percent) and declined in 2004 to around 65 percent. Wickham (2010) notes that "this surplus support [in 1999] is perhaps not genuine but represents people who are otherwise uncertain about this punishment, but migrate to the supportive category in reaction to a crime wave which they believe that the death penalty could address" (1). The slight increase in support (79 percent) in 2010 (from 65 percent in 2004) may be attributed to high-profile crimes that resulted in the deaths of six women and the outrage that followed (Thompson, 2010).

These anecdotes provide evidence for the importance of political and social stability in executive willingness to adopt, administer, monitor, and enforce human rights policy following adverse Inter-American Court judgments. Lower levels of political and social stability, as evidenced by higher homicide rates in Trinidad and Tobago, generate public support for a government willing to take a strong hand, notably through application of the death penalty. In Barbados, political and social stability are relatively higher and the homicide rate is relatively lower, leading to a public relatively less supportive of the death penalty. The political survival of the executive is highly contingent on public support. When the public does not support human rights policy changes ordered by the Inter-American Court, the executive is unlikely to make such changes, as illustrated in the case in Trinidad and Tobago.

These anecdotes provide initial evidence in support of Hypothesis 4, which states that executive willingness to adopt comprehensive human rights policy is lower when the state faces threats to the political and social order. The public is generally supportive of an executive taking a strong stance against political and social threats. Subsequently, the public is more likely to support the abuse of human rights of particular segments of the population perceived as representing political and social threats. In the next section, I turn to quantitative analyses to provide a more systematic examination of Hypothesis 4 in Europe and the Americas.

5.2.4 *Evidence of Executive Willingness: Threats to the Political and Social Order*

When a state faces threats to the political and social order, the public often supports the executive taking a heavy-handed approach to protecting citizens, and this may include the abuse of human rights. As a result, the public will not likely support the adoption of comprehensive human rights policy following adverse regional human rights court judgments, particularly when rights policy protects groups in society perceived as threatening by the majority (e.g., criminals, dissidents).

Hypothesis 4 is conditional, and as a result, I create an interaction term including adverse regional human rights court judgments and threats to the political and social order. To measure threats to the political and social order, I rely on the World Bank's political stability and absence of violence/terrorism measure (World Bank, 2014). This variable captures perceptions of the likelihood of political instability and/or politically motivated violence, including terrorism, with higher values representing greater levels of political stability and lower values representing lower levels of political stability. The political stability measure is lagged 1 year and is interacted with a variable measuring the presence of one or more adverse European or Inter-American Court judgments in a given year (1) or no adverse judgments in a given year (0). To assess the effectiveness of the regional court, I estimate three models for both the European and Inter-American Courts of Human Rights. In the first model, I lag the adverse judgment variable 1 year; in the second model, I lag the adverse judgment variable 3 years; and in the third model, I lag the adverse judgment variable 5 years.[18] The following equation is an example of the model used to assess respect for rights 3 years postjudgment:

$$\begin{aligned} Respect\ for\ Rights_{(t)} = &\ b_0 + b_1\ Political\ Stability_{(t-1)} * Adverse\ Judgment_{(t-3)} \\ &+ b_2\ Political\ Stability_{(t-1)} + b_3\ Adverse\ Judgment_{(t-3)} \\ &+ b_4\ Adverse\ Judgment_{(t-2)} + b_5\ Adverse\ Judgment_{(t-1)} \\ &+ Controls_{(t-1)} + \varepsilon. \end{aligned}$$

Beginning with Europe, Figure 5.6 summarizes the results of the influence of political stability on respect for rights following an adverse European Court judgment. Figure 5.6 shows the predicted level of respect for rights across values of political stability 1 year following an adverse European Court judgment (left panel), 3 years following an adverse judgment (center panel), and 5 years following an adverse judgment (right panel). The left panel of Figure 5.6 shows that in the year following an adverse judgment, the predicted value of respect for rights is −0.51 when political stability is at its lowest and 2.57 when political stability is at its highest. The middle panel of Figure 5.6 indicates that when political stability remains at its lowest 3 years following an

---

[18] In order to identify the influence of an adverse judgment on respect for rights 5 years later, I also control for the presence of other adverse judgments that occurred over the 5-year time period. I include variables capturing the presence of one or more adverse judgments 1, 2, 3, and 4 years before assessing rights (i.e., adverse judgment $(t-1)$, adverse judgment $(t-2)$, adverse judgment $(t-3)$, and adverse judgment $(t-4)$). For the model that assesses respect for rights 3 years postjudgment, I include the adverse judgment $(t-1)$ and adverse judgment $(t-2)$ variables in the model as control variables.

5.2 Regional Court Deterrence Is Conditional

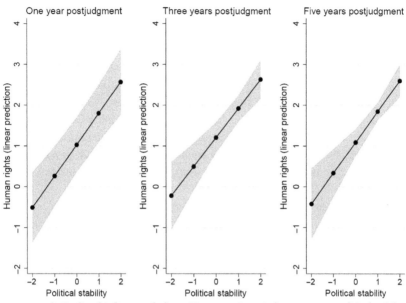

FIGURE 5.6. Predicted influence of adverse European Court judgments across political stability
Notes: Figure 5.6 displays the level of respect for rights 1 year (left panel), 3 years (center panel), and 5 years (right panel) following an adverse European Court judgment across values of political stability. Lines depict the predicted level of respect for rights in the presence of one or more adverse European Court judgments, and the shaded area represents 90 percent confidence intervals. Figure 5.6 shows that political stability is positively associated with respect for rights 1, 3, and 5 years post–European Court judgment.

adverse European Court judgment, the predicted level of respect for rights is −0.220. However, when political stability is at its highest 3 years following an adverse European Court judgment, the predicted level of respect for rights is around 2.63. Finally, the right panel of Figure 5.6 shows that when political stability remains low 5 years following an adverse European Court judgment, the predicted level of respect for rights is −0.25, and when political stability is high 5 years following an adverse European Court judgment, respect for rights is around 2.77.

The results reported in Figure 5.6 are consistent with Hypothesis 4, showing that when political stability remains low up to 5 years following an adverse judgment, the predicted level of respect for rights is relatively low as well. However, as political stability improves following an adverse European Court judgment, respect for rights is significantly higher. In fact, moving from the lowest to the highest level of political stability is associated with a 2.98 average increase in respect for rights 1, 3, and 5 years postjudgment. Also of note, respect for rights looks similar at low levels of political stability 1 year, 3 years, and 5 years after an adverse European Court judgment. When a country faces political *instability*, including violence and terrorism, the adverse judgment is associated with persistently low levels of respect for rights, despite the presence of an adverse European Court judgment. Similarly, at high levels of political stability, respect for rights is significantly higher 1, 3, and 5 years postjudgment and this effect is fairly consistent, with the predicted level of respect for rights ranging from 2.57 to 2.63 in the 5 years following an adverse judgment. This evidence suggests that when the country remains politically stable for up to 5 years after an adverse European Court judgment, the executive is more likely to adopt and implement persistent human rights policy changes.

As a robustness check, I also examine the influence of adverse European Court judgments on the *change* in respect for rights from the year of the judgment to 1, 3, and 5 years following the judgment using changes in the Cingranelli, Richards, and Clay (2014) physical integrity rights index as a dependent variable. The results (reported in Table C.15 of the Appendix) show that at low levels of political stability, adverse European Court judgments are associated with negative changes in respect for rights. As political stability grows, the predicted change in respect for rights also grows. For example, 1 year following an adverse judgment, the predicted change in respect for physical integrity rights from the year of the judgment to the year after the judgment is −2.10 at low levels of political stability and 0.885 at high levels of political stability (on a scale ranging from −4 to +3). These results provide additional evidence that executive willingness to make human rights policy changes is greater when political stability is relatively high.

Turning to the Inter-American Court, Figure 5.7 displays the level of respect for rights 1 year following an adverse Inter-American Court judgment in the left panel, 3 years following an adverse judgment in the center panel, and 5 years following an adverse judgment in the right panel. The left panel shows that in the year following an adverse Inter-American Court judgment, the predicted level of respect for rights is −0.058 when political stability is relatively low. When political stability is relatively high, the predicted level of respect for rights is around 0.759, a difference of 0.817. The center and right panels show that this effect becomes even more striking 3 and 5 years postjudgment. That is, when political stability remains low 3 years postjudgment, respect for rights drops to −0.743, and the expected value is similar 5 years postjudgment. However, when political stability is relatively high 3 and 5 years postjudgment, respect for rights is significantly higher than at low levels of political stability (1.37 3 years postjudgment and 1.41 5 years postjudgment).

5.2 Regional Court Deterrence Is Conditional

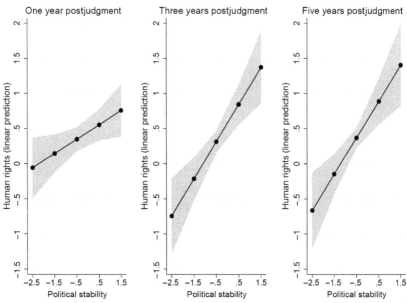

FIGURE 5.7. Predicted influence of adverse Inter-American Court judgments across political stability

Notes: Figure 5.7 displays the level of respect for rights 1 year (left panel), 3 years (center panel), and 5 years (right panel) following an adverse Inter-American Court judgment across values of political stability. Lines represent the predicted level of respect for rights in the presence of one or more adverse Inter-American Court judgments and the shaded area represents 90 percent confidence intervals. The results show that political stability is positively associated with respect for rights 1, 3, and 5 years post–Inter-American Court judgment. Notably, the results displayed in Figure 5.7 show important long-term effects of adverse Inter-American Court judgments in politically stable states, as the level of respect for rights is higher at high levels of political stability 3 and 5 years post–Inter-American Court judgment relative to 1 year post–Inter-American Court judgment.

Figure 5.7 provides support for Hypothesis 4 in that the predicted levels of respect for rights 1, 3, and 5 years post–Inter-American Court judgment is lower at low levels of political stability and significantly higher at high levels of political stability. Interestingly, when political stability is high, adverse judgments are associated with greater respect for rights 3 and 5 years after the judgment than 1 year postjudgment. In addition, Figure 5.7 shows that when political stability is low, the predicted level of respect for rights is lower 3 and 5 years postjudgment than 1 year postjudgment. Perhaps when political instability persists 3 and 5 years after an adverse judgment, the judgment becomes less politically salient over time, and public pressure to abide by an adverse judgment wanes in light of persistent political instability. That is, any initial human rights policy efforts by the executive in light of an adverse judgment may be abandoned in the face of persistent political and social threats in the 3 and 5 years following an adverse judgment.

In an effort to examine the robustness of the results, I also estimate a model predicting the change in respect for physical integrity rights using changes in the Cingranelli, Richards, and Clay (2014) physical integrity rights index as the dependent variable. The results, which are reported in Table C.15 of the Appendix, lend support to the hypothesis. An adverse judgment is associated with greater changes in respect for physical integrity rights 1, 3, and 5 years postjudgment as political stability grows. For example, an adverse Inter-American Court judgment is associated with a -1.32 change in respect for physical integrity rights (on a scale ranging from -4 to $+6$) from the year of the judgment to 5 years postjudgment when political stability is low. However, when political stability is high, an adverse Inter-American Court judgment is associated with a 2.31 change in respect for physical integrity rights from the year of the judgment to 5 years postjudgment.

Figures 5.6 and 5.7 lend support to Hypothesis 4 by showing that adverse European and Inter-American Court judgments are associated with lower levels of respect for rights when threats to the political and social order are present in society. The results lend support to the importance of political stability in executive willingness to adopt, administer, monitor, and enforce human rights policy following adverse regional human rights court judgments. To summarize, when political stability is low, executive adoption of comprehensive human rights policy following an adverse regional human rights court decisions is unlikely. As a result, when states are facing threats to the political and social order, adverse regional human rights court judgments are less likely to deter future human rights abuses than when a state faces few political and social threats.

5.2.5 *Examining the Conflicting Effects of Mass Public Support*

Because the empirical tests of Hypotheses 3 and 4 find conflicting effects for the role of the mass public, I conduct additional analyses to examine the role of adverse regional court judgments prior to an election at varying levels of political stability. I expect that regional court deterrence is highly likely when adverse judgments occur prior to an election (or competitive election) in countries with high levels of political stability. I also expect that adverse judgments are least likely to deter future human rights abuses when they occur prior to a nonelection (or noncompetitive election) year in countries with low levels of political stability.

TABLE 5.1. *Predicted human rights scores in the presence of adverse European Court judgment at different combinations of electoral competitiveness and political stability*

	Competitive election	Noncompetitive election
Political stability (high)	2.42	1.72
	(1.87, 2.97)	(1.37, 2.08)
Political stability (low)	0.261	−0.438
	(−0.597, 1.12)	(−1.09, 0.219)

Notes: Table 5.1 shows the predicted human rights score in the presence of an adverse European Court judgment, highly competitive and noncompetitive elections, and high and low levels of political stability. An election is considered competitive when the judgment took place before a competitive election year (largest vote-getter received 10 percent of the vote). An election is considered noncompetitive when the judgment took place prior to a noncompetitive election year (largest vote-getter received 90 percent of the vote). Political stability (high) indicates that political stability is high (set at 90th percentile) and Political stability (low) indicates that political stability is low (set at 10th percentile). Ninety percent confidence intervals are displayed in parentheses.

For the European Court, I estimate an additional model examining the influence of adverse European Court judgments prior to competitive elections at high and low levels of political stability.[19] Table 5.1 displays the predicted level of respect for rights in the presence of an adverse judgment when elections are competitive or noncompetitive and political stability is high or low.[20]

The results presented in Table 5.1 show the importance of competitive elections and political stability in the effectiveness of adverse European Court judgments. Table 5.1 shows that the predicted value of respect for rights in the presence of an adverse judgment prior to a competitive election in states with high levels of political stability is 2.42. The predicted level of respect for rights declines when one of these factors is missing. In the presence of an adverse judgment, high political stability, and a *noncompetitive election*, respect for rights declines to 1.72. The decline in respect for rights is even starker when political stability decreases. In the presence of an adverse judgment, a

---

[19] In the model, I include the electoral competitiveness and political stability variables and set them to high and low levels in postestimation analyses. Full model results are displayed in Appendix C.
[20] In the postestimation analysis, I set political stability to the 10th percentile (−0.54) to capture low political stability. For high political stability, I set political stability to the 90th percentile (1.40). Highly competitive elections are those where the largest vote-getter received 10 percent of the vote, and noncompetitive elections are those where the largest vote-getter received 90 percent of the vote. All other variables are set to their mean or mode.

competitive election, and *low political stability*, the predicted level of respect for rights is 0.261. The results also show that either the presence of an election or an improvement in political stability is associated with improvements in the effectiveness of adverse European Court judgments. When both are absent (upcoming competitive election and political stability), respect for rights is lower (−0.438) than when one or both are present. While there is some overlap in the 90 percent confidence intervals, the predicted level of respect for rights in the presence of an adverse judgment at most values of competitive elections is statistically significant ($p < 0.10$) for both high and low levels of political stability. There is no overlap in the confidence intervals when utilizing a slightly less stringent confidence interval level (80 percent).

Turning to the Inter-American Court, I estimate an additional model examining the influence of adverse Inter-American Court judgments prior to an election at high and low levels of political stability. Unlike the European Court, the findings presented earlier in this chapter show that the *presence* of an election is positively associated with respect for rights 2 years following an adverse Inter-American Court judgment. Therefore, rather than look at competitive elections, I present results from models taking into account whether an adverse Inter-American Court judgment took place prior to an election. Table 5.2 displays the predicted value of respect for rights in the presence of an adverse Inter-American Court judgment prior to an election or nonelection year, at high and low levels of political stability.[21]

The results presented in Table 5.2 show that the predicted level of respect for rights in the presence of an adverse judgment prior to an election year at high levels of political stability is 2.08. In the presence of an adverse judgment prior to a *nonelection year* at high levels of political stability, the predicted level of respect for rights declines to 0.602. Political stability is highly important for Inter-American Court deterrence, as even in the presence of an adverse judgment prior to an election, the predicted value of respect for rights when *political stability is low* is −0.965, which is around three points lower under similar circumstances at high political stability.

Political stability before an election is particularly important for Inter-American Court deterrence of future rights abuses as well. The results in Table 5.2 show that when political stability is low before an election, the predicted level of respect for rights is −0.965, but when political stability is low before a nonelection year, the predicted level of respect is higher (0.402). When political stability is low and the state has received an adverse Inter-

---

[21] All other variables are set to their mean or mode.

TABLE 5.2. *Predicted human rights scores in the presence of adverse Inter-American Court judgment, the presence/absence of election, and high/low political stability*

	Election	No election
Political stability (high)	2.08	0.602
	(1.51, 2.64)	(0.376, 0.828)
Political stability (low)	−0.965	0.402
	(−1.57, −0.364)	(0.038, .765)

Notes: Table 5.2 shows the predicted human rights score in the presence of an adverse Inter-American Court judgment, presence/absence of an election, and high and low levels of political stability. Election indicates that the judgment took place before an election year. No election indicates that an adverse judgment took place before a nonelection year. Political stability (high) indicates that political stability is high (1.0), and Political stability (low) indicates that political stability is low (−2.0). Ninety percent confidence intervals are displayed in parentheses.

American Court judgment prior to an election, the executive faces a trade-off between continuing or even ramping up abuses to manage political and social threats or adopting human rights policy to align with the Inter-American Court judgment. The results indicate that in an effort to appeal to the broad electorate prior to an election, the executive is more likely to double down on rights abuses in response to political and social threats than to adopt rights-respecting policy in response to an adverse Inter-American Court judgment. Importantly, when political stability is low prior to an election, the executive has incentives to ramp up rights abuses in an effort to signal to the public that the government is taking a strong stand against political and social threats, and this is particularly important in the run-up to the election. Furthermore, Inter-American Court judgments can deter rights abuses, particularly before an election, but judgments during this time period are likely to be ignored when the country faces high levels of political instability. This finding suggests that the Inter-American Court may be more effective in rendering adverse judgments in countries with low levels of political and social stability in years following the election, when the executive is more secure in office.

Taken together, the results show that the combination of an adverse judgment prior to an election in politically stable countries is associated with the highest likelihood of regional court deterrence as a result of mass public pressure. With respect to Europe, the predicted level of respect for rights in the presence of an adverse judgment prior to a noncompetitive election year in politically stable countries is lower than when the judgment occurs before a competitive election. However, respect for rights declines even further in the presence of an adverse judgment prior to a noncompetitive election when the country is politically unstable. With respect to the Inter-American Court, the predicted level of respect for rights in the presence of an adverse judgment prior to an election year is significantly higher at high levels of political stability than low levels of political stability. However, the presence of an adverse judgment prior to an election year at low levels of political stability is associated with lower levels of respect for rights than when the adverse judgment occurs prior to a nonelection year. This indicates that when the Inter-American Court renders adverse judgments prior to elections, the influence on respect for rights is highly conditional on the level of political and social stability in the country.

5.3 CONCLUSION

In this chapter, I argued that adverse regional human rights court judgments are more likely to deter human rights abuses when the executive is *willing* to adopt, administer, monitor, and enforce human rights policy. I argued that the mass public represents an important actor for generating pressure on the executive to adopt comprehensive human rights policy following adverse regional human rights court judgments. I find that the executive is more likely to adopt comprehensive human rights policy following an adverse judgment when executive job security is low. The presence of an adverse Inter-American Court judgment 2 years prior to an election year is associated with greater respect for rights than the presence of an adverse Inter-American Court judgment 2 years prior to a nonelection year. I also show that the presence of an adverse European Court judgment 2 years before an election is associated with greater respect for rights when the executive expects to face a competitive election as opposed to a noncompetitive election.

Second, while the mass public may generate pressure on the executive to adopt comprehensive human rights policy in response to an adverse regional court judgment prior to an election (when executive job security is threatened), the mass public may also place pressure in the opposite direction. When a state faces threats to social and political stability, the executive is unlikely to respond to adverse regional court judgments with comprehensive human rights policy change because the executive prefers to reserve repressive policies and tactics to address social and political threats. Furthermore, the public may prefer that the executive utilize repressive policies in response to such threats in society. I find that respect for rights is relatively low several years following adverse regional court judgments when political stability is low, but as political stability grows, adverse regional court judgments are associated with higher respect for rights.

Finally, with respect to mass public support generally, I show that adverse judgments prior to an election in politically stable countries are associated with higher respect for rights than if an adverse judgment occurs prior to a noncompetitive election year or the state is politically unstable. While both election timing/competitiveness and political stability are important for regional human rights court deterrence, political instability is particularly detrimental for respect for human rights following an adverse judgment. That is, the combination of an upcoming (competitive) election and political instability following an adverse judgment is associated with lower levels of respect for rights than the combination of no upcoming (competitive) election and political stability.

In this chapter, I argued that the mass public can place pressure on the executive to adopt, administer, monitor, and enforce human rights policy following an adverse judgment, and I find that mass public pressure to make human rights policy change is likely prior to an election, but unlikely when the state faces political and social instability. Beyond the mass public, the executive is also responsive to political pressure from elites, including economic and political elites. In the next chapter, I turn to the role of economic and political elites in generating pressure on the executive to adopt, administer, monitor, and enforce human rights policy following adverse regional court judgments.

6

Is the Executive Willing to Respond to Adverse Judgments? The Role of Elite Pressure

In the previous chapter, I examined the role of mass public pressure on the executive to adopt, administer, monitor, and enforce human rights policy following adverse regional human rights court judgments. However, in Chapter 2, I also noted that economic and political elites are important in generating executive willingness to make human rights policy changes. When economic and political elites have an interest in executive human rights policy change postjudgment, executive willingness to adopt, administer, monitor, and enforce human rights policy grows. To illustrate the importance of economic and political elites, I begin by looking to several cases before the European and Inter-American Courts of Human Rights.

Beginning with the role of economic elites, I argue that when the executive faces a loss of economic benefits for failing to make human rights policy changes in line with adverse regional court judgments, executive willingness to make such policy changes is greater. Economically vulnerable states are most susceptible to economic elite pressure. Economic vulnerability manifests when states rely on foreign investment or aid as a significant portion of their revenue for public goods provision. When states face a high likelihood of withdrawal of economic benefits for the failure to respect rights, the executive has incentives to make human rights policy changes.

Consider the Inter-American Court case of *Rochac Hernández and Others v. El Salvador*. A series of forced disappearances took place in the 1980s in El Salvador in the context of an armed conflict. In the events leading up to the Inter-American Court case, state and armed forces kidnapped five children during counterinsurgency operations. The families filed many formal complaints, including a petition before the Constitutional Chamber of the Supreme Court of El Salvador, but the state did not carry out effective investigations. These disappearances did not represent isolated incidents. In

April 2014, an estimated 926 registered cases of missing children were reported (International Justice Resource Center, 2014). In 2014, the Inter-American Court issued an adverse judgment against El Salvador, finding that the state had violated several articles of the American Convention, including the right to humane treatment, the right to personal liberty, and the right to a fair trial, among others. The Inter-American Court ordered the state to undertake several reforms, including opening investigations, searching for disappeared children, adopting adequate measures to guarantee justice, publishing the judgment, and training police and other state officials, among several other orders. Although El Salvador has yet to fulfill all of these orders, the state carried out serious search efforts to determine the whereabouts of the children, publicly accepted international responsibility, and paid reparations, costs, and expenses. In 2016, the Supreme Court overturned the Amnesty Law, opening the door to prosecute state officials involved in disappearances, and in September 2017, El Salvador's president established a National Commission to Search for Disappeared Persons through an executive order. The Inter-American Court's ruling in 2014 provided a legal basis for the subsequent policy changes by the judiciary and executive in El Salvador.

Contrast the case in El Salvador with the 2006 case of *Montero Aranguren et al. v. Venezuela*. Following an attempted coup in Venezuela in November 1992, 37 detainees at the Detention Center of Catia were extrajudicially executed, which led to a prison riot. The prison guards intervened, using excessive force and shooting indiscriminately at the detained. All told, 63 prisoners died, 52 were injured, and 28 disappeared (Yeung, 2016). The case reached the Inter-American Court of Human Rights, and in 2006, the Court found the state in violation of several articles of the American Convention on Human Rights, including the right to life and the right to physical, mental, and moral integrity, along with several other articles.

The Inter-American Court subsequently ordered the state to investigate the facts of the case, deliver the bodies of several victims to their next of kin, and adopt legal and administrative standards to prevent further rights abuses, among other measures. Several years following the judgment, the Inter-American Court found that the state had partially fulfilled several orders but had yet to fully fulfill most orders. For example, the state initiated legislative reforms, but none were approved, and the state took initial steps to improve prison conditions, but reforms did not move beyond the planning stage. Venezuela also failed to fulfill several other measures altogether. The state did not conduct an investigation into the massacre or initiate proceedings against the perpetrators, nor did the state locate and deliver the bodies of the victims or attempt to publicly acknowledge responsibility.[1] In 2011, the Inter-American Court noted that Venezuela had not reported any progress to the Court since 2009.[2]

In considering the different responses of El Salvador and Venezuela to the Inter-American Court, one key difference between the two states involves the level of dependence on economic elites. El Salvador faces substantial economic challenges and has one of the slowest-growing economies in Central America. The net total official development assistance and development aid received by El Salvador in 2014 (when the case was before the Inter-American Court) was $98,070,000, and this number rose to $129,200,000 in 2016 (World Bank, 2017). In Venezuela, net official development assistance and official aid received was $57,690,000 in 2006 (the year of the adverse judgment), but this number declined to $43,130,000 by 2014 (World Bank, 2017). Due to its struggling economy, the government of El Salvador is relatively more concerned with maintaining foreign investment and aid inflows. I argue that to signal a stable political environment and a dedication to upholding human rights, El Salvador is more likely to respond to international human rights legal commitments, including adverse judgments from the Inter-American Court.

On the other hand, Venezuela is less economically vulnerable as a result of a strong oil economy. Crude oil makes up 95 percent of Venezuela's exports and 50 percent of the country's GDP, and for many years, Venezuela's oil economy flourished, decreasing Venezuela's dependence on foreign (bilateral and multilateral) aid. However, in recent years, oil revenues have declined. The theory on which I elaborate in Chapter 2 predicts that greater economic vulnerability in Venezuela, including a growing reliance on multilateral and foreign aid, is associated with a greater likelihood of human rights policy change following adverse Inter-American Court judgments. However, Venezuela denounced the American Convention on Human Rights in 2012, making an assessment of Venezuela's response to the Inter-American Court due to its current economic conditions unobservable.

In addition to economic elites, I also argue that political elites influence executive willingness to adopt, administer, monitor, and enforce human rights policy following an adverse regional human rights court judgment. To illustrate the importance of political elites, consider the role of the national judiciary in several regional court cases. In December 1991, antiriot police

---

[1] See *Montero Aranguren et al. v. Venezuela*, Monitoring Compliance with Judgment. Order of the Court, Inter-Am, Ct. H.R. Nov. 17, 2009.

[2] *Montero Aranguren et al. v. Venezuela*, Monitoring Compliance with Judgment. Order of the Court, Inter-Am. Ct. H.R. Aug. 30, 2011.

used smoke bombs and tear gas grenades against demonstrators during violent clashes in Pamplona, Spain. Iribarren Pinillos was seriously injured when struck by a smoke bomb fired at very short range by police. Pinillos's face was burned and paralyzed on the left side. Criminal proceedings ended when Spanish courts ruled that it was not possible to identify the person who had fired the smoke bomb. Pinillos was certified disabled in May 1997. Domestic investigations were opened, but the investigating judge closed the case twice claiming that Pinillos had been participating in violent disturbances and that the identity of the police officer who threw the smoke bomb was unknown.

The case reached the highest court in Spain, which ruled that the actions of the security forces were legitimate and the injuries suffered by Pinillos were due to chance (Amnesty International, 2009). Pinillos filed a petition with the European Court of Human Rights, claiming interference with his physical and mental integrity as a result of the disproportionate nature of police reaction. In 2009, the European Court found that Spain violated Article 3 (among several articles), claiming that Spanish Courts fell short in their investigation of the events that led to injuries sustained by Pinillos.[3] Following the European Court judgment, the Spanish Constitutional Court adopted the European Court case law through several national court judgments involving complaints of ill-treatment by police officers. In its judgments, the Spanish Constitutional Court noted the seriousness of the prohibition of torture and ill-treatment and emphasized that effective judicial protection must be guaranteed through effective investigation. The Spanish Constitutional Court also established several rules for carrying out investigations of such matters in its case law.

However, national judicial implementation of adverse regional human rights court judgments is not guaranteed. In the case of *Saadi v. Italy*, the European Court found Italy in violation of its obligations under Article 3 of the European Convention, prohibiting the return or extradition of individuals to states where they face a risk of torture or inhuman or degrading treatment. In this particular case, Nassim Saadi, a Tunisian national in Italy on a residence permit, was arrested on suspicion of involvement with international terrorism in 2002. Saadi was convicted *in absentia* of membership in a terrorist organization and incitement to terrorism and subsequently sentenced to 20 years imprisonment. In 2006, a Deportation Order was issued by the Minister for the Interior stating that Saadi was threatening national security as a result of his active role in a terrorist organization in Italy. Saadi applied for political asylum, claiming to be at risk of torture and political and religious reprisals if

[3] See *Iribarren Pinillos v. Spain*, Chamber Judgment. European Ct. H.R. Jan. 8, 2009.

returned to Tunisia. His application for asylum was deemed inadmissible on the ground that he represented a danger to national security.

Saadi then lodged an application against Italy with the European Court, claiming that his deportation would represent a violation of the European Convention, including exposing him to a risk of ill-treatment and torture under Article 3. Italy sought assurances from the government of Tunisia that Saadi would not be subjected to torture or inhuman treatment. The Tunisian government provided diplomatic assurances (with references made to Tunisian domestic laws and accession to international treaties), but the European Court did not find them to qualify as adequate assurance. In 2008, the Grand Chamber of the European Court found Italy in violation of Article 3 of the European Convention.[4] In addition, following the Saadi case, the Second Chamber of the European Court unanimously found Italy in violation of Article 3 of the European Convention in *Ben Khemais v. Italy*, another case involving deportation of a Tunisian citizen. Unlike the case of Saadi, Ben Khemais was deported to Tunisia before the European Court could issue its judgment, an indication that the European Court judgment had little effect in the Italian Constitutional Court.[5]

In addition to national judiciaries, national legislatures are often charged with implementation of regional court judgments as well. Take, for example, the 2010 case of *Gomes Lund et al. ("Guerrilha do Araguaia") v. Brazil*, where the Inter-American Court found that Brazil was responsible for enforced disappearances of communist guerillas in the 1970s. From 1972 to 1975, 60 guerilla members were disappeared and 22, including Julia Gomes Lund, were killed (Williams, 2016). The Inter-American Court found that enforced disappearances are continuous or permanent in nature, meaning that the act begins at abduction and continues until the victim or information about the victims is released, allowing the court to consider the facts of the case regardless of the date (Williams, 2016).[6] The Inter-American Court judgment included an order to adopt new legislation codifying the crime of enforced disappearances. By 2014, Brazil had not yet adopted legislation criminalizing enforced disappearances. Similarly, following the 2009 case of *Radilla Pacheco v. Mexico*, the Inter-American Court found Mexico's enforced disappearance legislation to be inadequate. The Mexican legislature's implementation of the judgment was slow, but in 2017, Mexico's lower house of Congress approved

---

[4] See *Saadi v. Italy*. Grand Chamber Judgment. European Ct. H.R. Feb. 28, 2008.
[5] See *Ben Khemais v. Italy*. Chamber Judgment. European Ct. H.R. Feb. 24, 2009.
[6] See *Gomes Lund et al. ("Guerrilha do Araguaia") v. Brazil*, Preliminary Objections, Merits, Reparations, and Costs, Judgment, Inter-Am. Ct. H.R. Nov. 24, 2010.

a forced disappearance law. Like implementation by the national judiciary, implementation by the national legislature varies considerably across states.

Although regional human rights courts often do not specify national courts or national legislatures by name as the institutions charged with carrying out the orders of regional human rights courts, the content of regional court orders typically invokes a response from the national judiciary or legislature. Judicial remedy is a requirement in many regional human rights courts judgments. In fact, reparations orders requiring national judicial action are growing in frequency over time (Huneeus, 2012).[7] Regional court orders to the national justice system most often include the call for a renewed or new criminal investigation, but also include orders involving due process safeguards, requests to nullify an existing sentence, and requests to reinstate judges (Huneeus, 2012, 503). Orders may also specify how existing law should or should not be applied in national courts.

In addition to orders involving the national judiciary, regional courts often order the state to reform their legal systems to meet international standards on human rights and ensure those standards are fulfilled domestically in practice. Regional court orders invoking a response from national legislatures include calls for the amendment, repeal, or adoption of national legislation. Legislative reforms are a common requirement of regional human rights courts. For example, in a series of cases before the Inter-American Court, the Court ordered several states to repeal existing amnesty laws.[8]

Importantly, however, neither judicial nor legislative implementation are guaranteed. As the cases of *Iribarren Pinillos v. Spain* and *Saadi v. Italy* show, the likelihood of national judicial implementation varies across states. Similarly, as the cases of *Gomes Lund et al. ("Guerrilha do Araguaia") v. Brazil* and *Radilla Pacheco v. Mexico* show, legislative implementation varies considerably across states as well. Understanding national judicial and legislative implementation is important because as I argued in Chapter 2, the executive behaves in expectation of implementation by national judges and legislators. That is, when the executive expects national judicial and legislative implementation, executive willingness to adopt, administer, monitor, and enforce human rights policy grows.

I argued in Chapter 2 that the executive is more likely to expect national judicial implementation when the national judiciary is relatively powerful

---

[7] Huneeus (2012) shows that before 1990, the Inter-American Court did not issue any orders to national judiciaries; however, by 2005, the Inter-American Court was issuing orders to national judiciaries in about 66 percent of its cases.

[8] See, for example, *Barrios Altos v. Peru* Merits, Judgment, Inter-Am. Ct. H.R. Mar. 14, 2001.

because the national judiciary has a greater ability and willingness to implement adverse regional human rights court judgments. I also argued in Chapter 2 that legislative implementation of adverse regional human rights court judgments is more likely in the presence of a large legislative opposition with preferences that differ from the executive because the adverse judgment provides the legislative opposition with leverage to engage in legislative changes. In this chapter, I find that regional human rights court deterrence is more likely when the national judiciary is powerful. I also find that adverse regional human rights court judgments are more likely to deter future human rights abuses in the presence of a large legislative opposition with different preferences from the executive. In what follows, I provide several illustrative examples of the theoretical argument, conduct empirical tests, and draw conclusions about the role of executive willingness to adopt, administer, monitor, and enforce human rights policy following adverse regional human rights court judgments.

6.1 DATA AND METHODOLOGY

The analyses in this chapter examine the relationship between the executive, elites (economic and political), and regional human rights courts. To do so, I begin by discussing several anecdotes that support the theoretical argument. I then display results from quantitative analyses of the role of economic and political elites in regional court deterrence. Similar to Chapters 4 and 5, the dependent variable is a measure of respect for physical integrity rights (Fariss, 2014). Higher values represent greater respect for rights, while lower values indicate worse respect for rights. I assess the level of respect for rights at several points in time following an adverse regional human rights court judgment. The primary independent variable used in the analyses in this chapter is also the same as the independent variable used in Chapters 4 and 5, the presence of an adverse European or Inter-American Court of Human Rights judgment. I utilize a binary variable in which the presence of at least one adverse European or Inter-American Court judgment in a country-year takes on a value of one and zero otherwise. Like Chapters 4 and 5, I only examine the presence of adverse European Court judgments published in case reports and those of level 1 or level 2 importance, as those judgments convey new information to domestic political actors about rights abuses.

I estimate several models to examine Hypotheses 5, 6, and 7. Like the models in Chapters 4 and 5, the unit of analysis is the country-year, and I estimate three different models for both the European and Inter-American samples to examine each hypothesis. In the first model, I examine the influence of an adverse regional human rights court judgment (at time t-1) on respect for rights 1 year after the judgment (at time t). In the second model, I examine the influence of an adverse judgment (at time t-3) on respect for rights 3 years after the judgment (at time t) and in the final model, I examine the influence of an adverse regional court judgment (at time t-5) on respect for rights 5 years after the judgment (at time t). The samples and model specifications are also similar to those examined in Chapters 4 and 5 (linear regression models with random intercepts and standard errors clustered on country). A description of control variables and full model results are included in the Appendix to this chapter.

6.2 REGIONAL COURT DETERRENCE IS CONDITIONAL ON ECONOMIC ELITE SUPPORT

6.2.1 *The Role of Economic Elite Support*

In Chapter 2, I argued that executive willingness to make human rights policy change following an adverse regional human rights court judgment is conditional on pressure from economic elites. To illustrate the importance of economic elites, consider the state of Bolivia. In 2002, the Inter-American Court rendered an adverse judgment against Bolivia in the case of *Trujillo Oroza v. Bolivia*. In 1971, José Carlos Trujillo Oroza, a 21-year-old philosophy student, was arrested without a court order and transferred to a prison compound. After visiting her son, the victim's mother noticed that he had been subjected to physical torture. Specifically, she observed that he had lost several fingernails and had been beaten by someone using an object with a sharp edge (Scharrer, 2014b). In February 1972, the victim's mother was informed that her son was transferred to a police station for questioning, but Trujillo Oroza was disappeared by the government and the victim's mother never saw her son again.

In 2002, the Inter-American Court found that the state violated several articles of the American Convention on Human Rights, including the right to life (Article 4) and the prohibition of torture and cruel, inhuman, and degrading punishment (Article 5), among other articles. The court issued several reparations orders, including ordering the state to determine the victim's whereabouts, publish the court's judgment, train law enforcement personnel, and undertake legislative reforms (e.g., criminalizing forced disappearances), among other orders (Scharrer, 2014b).[9] In 2004, the Inter-American Court established that the state fully complied with several measures, including

---

[9] See *Trujillo Oroza v. Bolivia*, Reparations, and Costs, Judgment, Inter-Am. Ct. H.R. Feb. 27, 2002.

training law enforcement personnel, and in 2007 the state passed legislation criminalizing forced disappearances.[10] In considering the deterrent effect of the Inter-American Court, I look to Bolivia's respect for physical integrity rights following the Inter-American Court judgment. According to Fariss (2014), Bolivia's physical integrity rights score (on a scale ranging around −2 to +3) was 0.5728 in the year of the judgment (2002). Five years following the judgment, Bolivia's respect for physical integrity rights was higher (0.847).

Importantly, Bolivia was heavily dependent on foreign aid in the early 2000s. Between 1971 and 1981, Bolivia incurred more than three billion dollars in foreign debt. In the mid-1980s, Bolivia was facing a severe debt crisis and began to look for assistance from multilateral agencies like the International Monetary Fund (IMF) and the World Bank. Attached to loans from international organizations like the IMF are a series of conditions, including austerity measures such as requirements to privatize public services and reduce social spending. Between 2000 and 2005, Bolivia was heavily dependent on foreign aid and loans. In the early 2000s, Bolivia owed large debts to several multilateral aid agencies, as well as several countries, like the United States. At the end of 2005, Bolivia owed 5.3 billion dollars to foreign creditors, 7.5 percent of which was owed to other governments and the rest owed to multilateral development banks.

Maintaining good working relationships with multilateral aid agencies was in the interest of the Bolivian government, as many aid organizations began to forgive the foreign debt in which Bolivia was entrenched. For example, two billion US dollars was forgiven under the Heavily Indebted Poor Countries (HIPC) program, and the IMF forgave another 300 million US dollars of debt in 2005, while the World Bank began discussions to forgive another 1.8 billion US dollars in 2006 (US State Department, 2006). Based on the OECD data on aid from multilateral agencies, Bolivia received 206.54 million US dollars in 2002 and 384.59 million US dollars in 2003. Bolivia received well above the average aid received by other countries in the region. The average amount of aid received in 2002 in the Americas was around 34 million US dollars, and the average in 2003 was around 54 million US dollars. The economic incentives at stake in Bolivia in the early 2000s, notably the need to maintain a reputation of good governance and respect for rights in order to continue to receive development dollars, likely generated incentives for the Bolivian government to comply with many orders from the Inter-American Court, as well as to make changes to human rights policies.

---

[10] See *Trujillo Oroza v. Bolivia*, Monitoring Compliance with Judgment, Order of the Court, Inter-Am. Ct. H.R. Nov. 17, 2004.

However, more recently, Bolivia's economic incentives are changing, and dependence on the IMF and World Bank are declining as the Bolivian government pursues its own economic policy based on increasing government royalties from the country's hydrocarbon reserves. In July 2017, Bolivia's president Evo Morales claimed in a tweet that "These organizations [the IMF and World Bank] dictated the economic fate of Bolivia and the world. Today we can say that we have total independence from them" (Telesur, 2017). Moving forward, Bolivia may have weaker incentives to respond to adverse Inter-American Court judgments by making human rights policy changes based on economic incentives or dependence on multilateral aid agencies.

6.2.2 Evidence of Executive Willingness: Economic Elites

In Chapter 2, I argued that regional human rights courts are more likely to deter future human rights abuses when the executive is economically vulnerable. When foreign direct investment inflows comprise a large share of gross domestic product or the state is highly dependent on development assistance and aid, the executive is more economically vulnerable. States that receive relatively large inflows of FDI or development assistance are more likely to have an interest in signaling a politically stable climate to international investors and multilateral aid agencies. To test this hypothesis (Hypothesis 5), I am interested in examining a conditional relationship, meaning that I expect adverse regional human rights court judgments are associated with stronger human rights practices, but this relationship depends on economic vulnerability. Therefore, to estimate the models, I create an interaction term of the presence of one or more adverse European or Inter-American Court judgment (lagged 1, 3, and 5 years) and foreign direct investment. I focus on foreign direct investment in the analyses, rather than foreign aid, as examining FDI inflows allows me to compare the findings across Europe and the Americas. Countries in both Europe and the Americas exhibit substantial variation in foreign direct investment inflows, while development aid and assistance in the European context exhibits less variation (many European countries receive little or no development assistance). As noted earlier, to measure adverse regional human rights court judgments, I utilize a binary variable capturing whether an adverse judgment took place in a given year (1) or not (0). To measure FDI, I utilize a 3-year moving average of foreign direct investment inflows as a percentage of GDP, taken from the World Bank's World Development Indicators (World Bank, 2017). In the European Court model, I take the logged value of FDI because FDI is highly right-skewed in Europe. FDI in the Inter-American sample is less skewed, so I rely on the 3-year moving average of FDI in the

Americas.[11] I also include a number of control variables to take into account alternative explanations of human rights abuses, as well as several variables that may signal a stable investment climate to foreign investors (e.g., internal conflict, the presence of democratic institutions). As noted earlier, a full description of control variables is provided in the Appendix. I estimate three different models for the European and Inter-American Courts of Human Rights. In the first model, I examine the influence of an adverse judgment (lagged 1 year) on respect for rights 1 year after the judgment. In the second model, I examine the influence of an adverse judgment (lagged 3 years) on respect for rights 3 years after the judgment. Finally, in the third model, I examine the influence of an adverse judgment (lagged 5 years) on respect for rights 5 years after the judgment.[12] The following equation is an example of the model used to assess respect for rights 3 years postjudgment:

$$Respect\ for\ Rights_{(t)} = b_0 + b_1\ FDI_{(moving\ average\ in\ t)} * Adverse\ Judgment_{(t-3)}$$
$$+ b_2\ FDI_{(moving\ average\ in\ t)} + b_3\ Adverse\ Judgment_{(t-3)}$$
$$+ b_4\ Adverse\ Judgment_{(t-2)} + b_5\ Adverse\ Judgment_{(t-1)}$$
$$+ Controls_{(t-1)} + \varepsilon.$$

Beginning with the European Court results, Figure 6.1 displays results from the three European Court models. More specifically, Figure 6.1 displays the predicted level of respect for rights 1 year (left panel), 3 years (center panel), and 5 years (right panel) following an adverse European Court judgment. The line represents the predicted level of respect for rights, and the shaded area represents 90 percent confidence intervals. All other variables in the model are set to their mean (for continuous variables) or mode (for binary or count variables). The left panel of Figure 6.1 shows a clear upward trend, indicating that 1 year following an adverse judgment, the level of respect for rights grows as FDI inflows increase. Notably, the confidence interval bands are fairly wide at high and low levels of FDI in the left panel.

However, the results presented in the center and right panels of Figure 6.1 lend support to the hypothesis. The trend displayed in the center and right panels of Figure 6.1 is positive, indicating that as FDI inflows (as a percentage

---

[11] The moving average captures trends in FDI over time, rather than a single estimate for each year. This smooths out noise in the data from outlying years and by taking into account the level of investment in the surrounding years, better captures a country's general level of economic vulnerability in a given year.

[12] In the model utilizing the 3-year lag, I control for adverse judgments lagged 1 and 2 years. In the model utilizing the 5-year lag, I include control variables for adverse judgments lagged 1, 2, 3, and 4 years.

6.2 Deterrence Is Conditional on Economic Elite 177

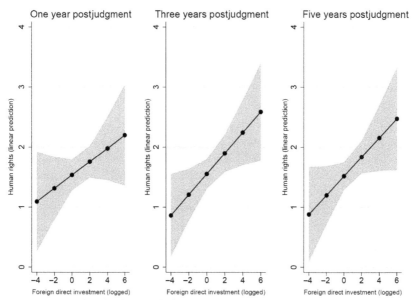

FIGURE 6.1. Predicted influence of adverse European Court judgments on respect for rights across FDI

Notes: The left panel of Figure 6.1 displays the predicted level of respect for rights 1 year postjudgment, the center panel 3 years postjudgment, and the right panel 5 years postjudgment across FDI net inflows as a percentage of GDP (logged). Lines represent the predicted level of respect for rights and the shaded area represents 90 percent confidence intervals. The results show that when FDI makes up a larger percentage of GDP, the predicted level of respect for rights is significantly higher 3 and 5 years following an adverse European Court judgment.

of GDP) increase, the predicted level of respect for rights is higher in the 3 and 5 years following an adverse European Court judgment than when FDI inflows are low. Beginning with the center panel, 3 years following an adverse European Court judgment, the predicted level of respect for rights is 0.86 when FDI inflows are low, and the predicted level of respect for rights is 2.59 when FDI inflows are relatively high. Five years following an adverse judgment, the predicted level of respect for rights is similar to the level of respect for rights 3 years following an adverse judgment at low and high values of FDI. These results indicate that high levels of FDI inflows are associated with greater respect for rights, but only several years after a judgment. Perhaps economic elite pressure is delayed in the aftermath of an adverse European Court judgment. Economic elites may not be able to credibly threaten withdrawal of FDI if human rights practices do not change 1 year following an adverse judgment. However, when the executive fails to make human rights policy change in the 3 and 5 years following an adverse

European Court judgment, economic elites can prepare for and credibly threaten exit. That is, economic elites can credibly threaten the withdrawal of investments with the intention to move them somewhere with a stronger rights-respecting reputation and potentially greater political stability. In expectation of delayed withdrawal, the executive may continue to utilize repression until the threat of withdrawal becomes higher.

As a robustness check, I examine the influence of adverse European Court judgments on the change in respect for rights from the year of the judgment to 1, 3, and 5 years following the judgment using changes in the Cingranelli, Richards, and Clay (2014) physical integrity rights index as a dependent variable. The results (reported in Table D.5 of the Appendix) show that at low levels of foreign direct investment, adverse European Court judgments are associated with negative changes in respect for rights. However, as FDI grows, the predicted change in respect for rights increases. For example, 3 years following an adverse European Court judgment, the predicted change in respect for rights from the year of the judgment to 3 years later is −0.524 (on a scale ranging from −4 to +3) when FDI makes up a low percentage of GDP. However, the predicted change in respect for physical integrity rights from the year of the judgment to 3 years after the judgment is 0.658, when FDI makes up a large percentage of GDP. Although the relationship is strongest 3 years following an adverse judgment, the trend in the change in respect for rights as FDI grows is positive 1 and 5 years following an adverse judgment as well.

Turning to the Inter-American Court, Figure 6.2 displays the predicted level of respect for rights across values of FDI inflows 1 year (left panel), 3 years (center panel), and 5 years (right panel) following an adverse Inter-American Court judgment. Like Figure 6.1, Figure 6.2 displays the predicted level of respect for rights as solid lines, and the shaded area represents 90 percent confidence intervals. The results show a positive trend, indicating that as FDI inflows increase, the predicted level of respect for rights also increases following an adverse Inter-American Court judgment.

The wider confidence interval bands in the right panel indicate that we cannot be confident that higher levels of FDI inflows are associated with greater respect for rights 5 years postjudgment. Perhaps because states in the Americas are more economically vulnerable in general, executives are more likely to respond to adverse judgments with human rights policy change in the immediate term (1 and 3 years postjudgment) to ensure a continued stable investment climate. The executive may find it necessary to appease investors in the short term by adopting and implementing human rights policy changes in response to the regional court, but may resort back to repression

6.2 Deterrence Is Conditional on Economic Elite 179

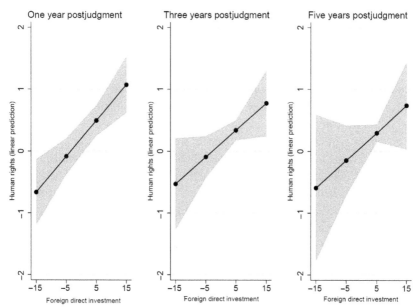

FIGURE 6.2. Predicted influence of adverse Inter-American Court judgments on respect for rights across FDI

Notes: The left panel of Figure 6.2 displays the predicted level of respect for rights 1 year postjudgment, the center panel 3 years postjudgment, and the right panel 5 years postjudgment across FDI net inflows as a percentage of GDP. Lines represent the predicted level of respect for rights and the shaded area represents 90 percent confidence intervals. The results show that when FDI makes up a larger percentage of GDP, the predicted level of respect for rights is significantly higher 1 and 3 years following an adverse Inter-American Court judgment.

in the longer term. Nevertheless, 1 year following an adverse Inter-American Court judgment, the predicted level of respect for rights is 1.07 at high values of FDI net inflows, but the predicted level of respect for rights is −0.66 at low values of FDI net inflows, a difference of 1.73.[13]

In order to examine the robustness of the results, I estimate additional models that predict the influence of adverse Inter-American Court judgments on the change in respect for rights from the year of the judgment to 1, 3, and 5 years postjudgment. To do so, I utilize changes in the Cingranelli, Richards, and Clay (2014) physical integrity rights index as the dependent variable. Substantive results are reported in Table D.5 of the Appendix. The results are similar to those reported in Figure 6.2, showing that when FDI makes

---

[13] Results from models estimated using official development assistance from multilateral aid agencies as an indicator of economic vulnerability yield similar results for the Inter-American Court sample.

up a relatively small percentage of GDP, the predicted change in respect for physical integrity rights is lower than when FDI makes up a relatively large percentage of GDP. Like the model results presented in Figure 6.2, the results are strongest for a 1-year change (change in respect for rights from the year of the judgment to 1 year later). More specifically, when FDI makes up a relatively small percentage of GDP, the predicted change in respect for rights from the year of the judgment to 1 year postjudgment is −1.93 (on a scale ranging from −4 to +6). However, when FDI makes up a relatively large percentage of GDP, the predicted change in respect for rights from the year of the judgment to the year following the judgment is 1.59. The results indicate that when FDI inflows are relatively low in the Americas, an adverse judgment is associated with a negative changes in respect for rights the year after the judgment, but when FDI inflows are relatively high in the Americas, an adverse judgment is associated with positive changes in respect for rights the year after the judgment. The trend for the change in respect for rights 3 and 5 years postjudgment is positive, but the results are statistically insignificant.

Notably, pressure from economic elites in the Americas appears to more immediately generate executive willingness to adopt, administer, monitor, and enforce human rights policy than in Europe. That is, high values of FDI inflows are more strongly associated with greater respect for rights 1 and 3 years postjudgment in the Americas, but FDI inflows are more strongly associated with greater respect for rights 3 and 5 years postjudgment in Europe. Perhaps because states in the Americas are more economically vulnerable than states in Europe on average, executives in the Americas may find it more important to send a strong signal to foreign investors about the stability of the investment climate in the wake of shaming by an international court. An adverse Inter-American Court judgment sends a strong signal about potential systematic human rights failures, and an executive likley has an interest in hastily adopting comprehensive human rights policy to signal to investors the continued stability of an investment. Importantly, whereas executives in the Americas are more likely to find the need to promptly send a signal of stability to economic elites following adverse Inter-American Court judgments, executives in Europe are less vulnerable to economic pressure in the immediate term. As a result, European states are more likely to wait until the threat of withdrawal becomes more credible several years after adverse judgments in Europe, and human rights policy is unlikely to change until 3 to 5 years postjudgment.

The anecdotal evidence from Bolivia combined with the statistical analyses for Europe and the Americas together provide evidence for the importance of economic factors in generating executive incentives to make human rights policy change following adverse regional court judgments. In other words, evidence indicates that adverse European and Inter-American Court judgments are positively associated with respect for rights in the Americas when foreign direct investment inflows are relatively high. While evidence shows that economic elites can place pressure on the executive to adopt, administer, monitor, and enforce human rights policy following an adverse regional court judgment, political elites are also important in generating executive willingness to adopt comprehensive human rights policy. In the next section, I turn to the role of political elites, specifically national judges and legislators.

6.3 REGIONAL COURT DETERRENCE IS CONDITIONAL ON POLITICAL ELITE SUPPORT

6.3.1 *The Role of National Judicial Support*

In Chapter 2, I argued that executive willingness to adopt, administer, monitor, and enforce human rights policy following an adverse regional human rights court judgment is conditional on support from political elites, including national judges and legislators. In this section, I look at the role of the national judiciary in generating executive willingness to adopt and implement comprehensive human rights policy following an adverse regional human rights court judgment. To demonstrate the importance of the national judiciary, consider two states in the Americas and their divergent responses to adverse judgments from the Inter-American Court of Human Rights: Venezuela and Argentina. In December 1999, major rainfall caused severe flooding and landslides in the State of Vargas in Venezuela. The state of Venezuela dispatched security forces to maintain order. Instead, security forces engaged in arbitrary arrests, inhuman treatment, and forced disappearances. Among the victims was Oscar José Blanco Romero, who was detained and beaten by security forces after they forcibly entered his home. The same day, another victim, José Francisco Rivas Fernández, was beaten and detained while at a shelter for victims of the flooding. Two days after these events, officers from another branch of the state security forces entered the home of a third victim, Roberto Javier Hernández Paz, without a search warrant, and detained, arrested, and shot the victim (Benson, 2015). The whereabouts of all three victims remain unknown.

Following extensive appeals through the domestic criminal judicial process, relatives of the victims were unable to locate the victims, and investigations were closed for lack of information. The case was submitted to the Inter-American Court of Human Rights in June 2004. In November 2005, the Inter-American Court issued an adverse judgment against the state of

Venezuela, finding Venezuela to have violated several articles of the American Convention on Human Rights, including articles related to the right to life; the prohibition of torture and cruel, inhuman, or degrading treatment; and the right to personal liberty and security, among several other articles. The Inter-American Court ordered the state to investigate, prosecute, and punish those responsible; locate the victims and exhume, identify, and return their remains; publish the judgment; and reform legislation, among numerous other orders.[14] In 2009, the Inter-American Court found that the state had failed to comply with many of the obligations required by the judgment.[15] In fact, the Inter-American Court found that 3 years following the judgment, there was almost total noncompliance with the obligations ordered by the Inter-American Court, including the obligation to investigate, prosecute, and punish those responsible for violations, an order requiring action by the domestic judiciary.

Looking to evidence of regional court deterrence, respect for physical integrity rights in Venezuela in the postjudgment period remained dismal. The average level of respect for physical integrity rights in Venezuela in the 4 years prior to the Inter-American Court judgment was −0.532 (on a scale ranging from around −2 to +3 in the Americas) and in the 4 years following the adverse Inter-American Court judgment, respect for rights was −0.593 (Fariss, 2014). Moreover, in the year of the judgment, Venezuela practiced torture frequently, and in the 4 years following the adverse judgment, Venezuela continued to practice torture frequently (Cingranelli, Richards, and Clay, 2014).

As I argue in Chapter 2, judicial power represents a key factor in explaining regional court deterrence. Venezuela is notoriously recognized for the national judiciary's lack of independence. In 2003, following the threat of a coup, President Hugo Chavez began taking steps to control the country's judicial branch – this included expanding the Supreme Court from 20 to 32 members and adopting legislation making the ability for the executive to pack the court much easier. Judges have little security over their tenure, and judges have also been dismissed for their decisions on politically controversial cases in Venezuela (Human Rights Watch, 2004). According to a measure of judicial power created by Linzer and Staton (2015), Venezuela's average judicial power score (on a measure ranging from 0 to 1) was 0.355 in the 4 years after the adverse Inter-American Court judgment, while the average level of judicial

---

[14] See *Blanco Romero et al. v. Venezuela*, Merits, Reparations and Costs, Inter-Am. Ct. H.R. Nov. 28, 2005.

[15] See *Blanco Romero et al. v. Venezuela*, Monitoring Compliance with Judgment, Order of the President of the Court, Inter-Am. Ct. H.R May 18, 2009.

power in the region in the same 4 years was 0.564. Given Venezuela's weak judiciary, I argue that the national judiciary is unlikely to implement regional court orders, which is evidenced in the failure to investigate, prosecute, and punish those responsible in the *Blanco Romero et al. v. Venezuela* case. As a result of the lack of implementation of the national judicial order, the executive is unlikely to make policy changes including the adoption, administration, monitoring, and enforcement of human rights policy postjudgment.

Contrast the Inter-American Court case in Venezuela with an Inter-American Court case in Argentina. In 1999, Argentine Federal Police arrested and detained around 73 individuals after tickets sold out for a rock concert taking place near a stadium in Buenos Aires. Among those arrested was 17-year-old Walter Bulacio, who was subsequently taken to a police juvenile detention facility and severely beaten (Chang, 2016). Early the next morning, Walter Bulacio was transferred to a hospital, where he was diagnosed with a concussion. Walter Bulacio informed the physician that he was beaten in police custody. Several days later, Walter Bulacio died of injuries sustained while beaten in police custody. The autopsy indicated that Walter Bulacio sustained blows to his face, legs, and soles of his feet from a hard instrument (Chang, 2016). Criminal charges were filed against the police captain in Argentine courts, but after a number of delays, no definitive judgment was ever rendered. The case of *Bulacio v. Argentina* reached the Inter-American Court in 2003, and the Court found that the state had violated Article 4 (right to life), Article 5 (right to humane treatment), and Article 7 (right to personal liberty) of the American Convention, among a number of other articles.[16] The Inter-American Court ordered the state, among a number of other reparations orders, to investigate and punish those responsible. The state complied with the obligation and reopened the investigation into the victim's detention and death. The Supreme Court overturned an appeal judgment whereby the criminal action brought against a defendant for the aggravated illegal imprisonment of Walter Bulacio was dismissed under the statute of limitations.

The actions of Argentina's Supreme Court may be explained by the interests of domestic judges to maintain public support for the Court. Even after the democratic transition in Argentina in the 1980s, the executive maintained substantial control over the judiciary. For example, Carlos Menem was elected president in 1989 and subsequently expanded the Supreme Court from five to nine members and chose the four new justices. The Senate then approved

---

[16] See *Bulacio v. Argentina*, Merits, Reparations, and Costs, Judgment, Inter-Am. Ct. H.R. Sept. 18, 2003.

the nominated justices during a secret parliamentary session in which the opposition was not invited. In the 2000s, the judicial branch underwent major reforms, and the Argentine Supreme Court became largely independent from the executive branch. Reforms were made to the Judicial Council, which oversees the promotion and impeachment of justices, and several of Menem's justices were removed or resigned. The national judiciary also underwent substantial reforms to the nomination procedure and a reduction in the number of justices. Turning to respect for physical integrity rights in Argentina, in the 4 years before the *Bulacio v. Argentina* case, Argentina's average physical integrity rights score was 0.146 (on a scale ranging from around −2 to +3), while in the 4 years following the adverse judgment, the average physical integrity rights score was higher, at 0.753 (Fariss, 2014). Although the anecdotal evidence from Venezuela and Argentina lends initial support for the role of the national judiciary in generating executive incentives to make human rights policy changes (Hypothesis 6), in the next section, I conduct systematic empirical tests of Hypothesis 6.

6.3.2 *Evidence of Executive Willingness: National Judiciaries*

The national judiciary hypothesis (Hypothesis 6) is conditional; that is, I expect adverse regional human rights court judgments to be positively related to respect for rights when the national judiciary is relatively powerful. To test Hypothesis 6, I create an interaction term including adverse regional human rights court judgments and judicial power. I rely on a measure of judicial power created by Linzer and Staton (2015). A judge is considered powerful if "her decisions reflect her evaluation of the legal regard (autonomous decision-making)" and her decisions "are respected by government officials who disagree with them (effective decision-making)" (12). Linzer and Staton (2015) create a latent variable measurement model using eight indicators of judicial independence. I interact the judicial power measure with a variable measuring the presence of one or more adverse regional human rights court judgments (1) or no adverse judgments in a given year (0). As noted earlier, I also include a number of control variables in the models. A full list of control variables is provided in the Appendix. I estimate three different models for the European and Inter-American Courts of Human Rights. In the first model, I examine the influence of an adverse judgment (lagged 1 year) on respect for rights 1 year after the judgment. In the second model, I examine the influence of an adverse judgment (lagged 3 years) on respect for rights 3 years after the judgment. Finally, in the third model, I examine the influence of an adverse judgment (lagged 5 years) on respect for rights 5 years after

6.3 Deterrence Is Conditional on Political Elite

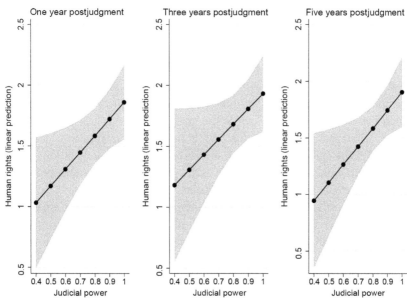

FIGURE 6.3. Predicted influence of adverse European Court judgments across judicial power
Notes: The left panel of Figure 6.3 displays the predicted level of respect for rights 1 year postjudgment, the center panel 3 years postjudgment, and the right panel 5 years postjudgment across judicial power. Lines represent the predicted level of respect for rights and the shaded area represents 90 percent confidence intervals. Figure 6.3 indicates that 1, 3, and 5 years post–European Court judgment, the level of respect for rights increases as judicial power grows. Table 6.1 displays disaggregated model results, using respect for the right to be free from torture as the dependent variable.

the judgment.[17] The following equation is an example of the model used to assess respect for rights 3 years postjudgment:

$$\begin{aligned}\text{Respect for Rights}_{(t)} = {} & b_0 + b_1 \text{ Judicial Power}_{(t-1)} * \text{Adverse Judgment}_{(t-3)} \\ & + b_2 \text{ Judicial Power}_{(t-1)} + b_3 \text{ Adverse Judgment}_{(t-3)} \\ & + b_4 \text{ Adverse Judgment}_{(t-2)} + b_5 \text{ Adverse Judgment}_{(t-1)} \\ & + \text{Controls}_{(t-1)} + \varepsilon.\end{aligned}$$

Beginning with findings from the European Court, Figure 6.3 displays the predicted level of respect for rights 1 year (left panel), 3 years (center panel), and 5 years (right panel) postjudgment across values of judicial power. The solid line represents the predicted level of respect for rights, and the shaded area displays 90 percent confidence intervals. All other variables in the model

---

[17] In the model utilizing the 3-year lag, I control for adverse judgments lagged 1 and 2 years. In the model utilizing the 5-year lag, I control for adverse judgments lagged 1, 2, 3, and 4 years.

are set to their mean (for continuous variables) or mode (for binary or count variables). Figure 6.3 displays a positive trend, that is, for adverse European Court judgment recipients, the predicted level of respect for rights is higher as judicial power grows and the predicted level of respect for rights is lower as judicial power declines. More specifically, 5 years following an adverse European Court judgment, the predicted value of respect for rights is 1.92 when judicial power is high, while the predicted value of respect for rights is 0.95 when judicial power is low. While the trend displayed in Figure 6.3 is positive, the confidence intervals are fairly wide, particularly at low levels of judicial power, which is likely due to the presence of few countries in the European sample with low levels of judicial power.

I also estimate a model predicting the influence of adverse European Court judgments on the change in respect for physical integrity rights using changes in the Cingranelli, Richards, and Clay (2014) physical integrity rights index as the dependent variable. Substantive results are reported in Table D.9 in the Appendix and lend support to the hypothesis. An adverse judgment is associated with greater changes in respect for physical integrity rights 1, 3, and 5 years postjudgment as judicial power grows, though the results are strongest 1 year following an adverse judgment, an indication that the strength of the judiciary sends a credible signal to the executive of the likelihood of judicial implementation in the immediate aftermath of an adverse judgment. That is, human rights policy changes are likely to take place fairly quickly in the presence of a strong domestic judiciary. More specifically, the results show that an adverse judgment is associated with a -0.569 change (on a scale ranging from -4 to $+6$) in respect for physical integrity rights from the year of the judgment to the year following the judgment when judicial power is low. On the other hand, an adverse European Court judgment is associated with a 0.394 change in respect for physical integrity rights from the year of the judgment to the year following the judgment when judicial power is high. The trend is positive 3 and 5 years postjudgment, indicating that the predicted change in respect for physical integrity rights grows as judicial power grows. However, the confidence intervals are fairly wide 3 and 5 years postjudgment, indicating that these findings should be treated with some caution.

The preceding analyses aggregate the influence of all adverse European Court judgments associated with the physical integrity rights articles of the European Convention and respect for physical integrity rights broadly. Because of the relatively large confidence intervals, particularly at low values of judicial power, I conduct a more direct test of the hypothesis for the European sample. I examine the influence of adverse judgments related to a specific article of the European Convention on respect for one type of

6.3 Deterrence Is Conditional on Political Elite 187

physical integrity abuse. In this disaggregated model, I examine the influence of adverse European Court judgments related to torture on the right to be free from torture. This analysis provides a more direct test of the hypothesis by directly linking adverse judgments involving violations of Article 3 of the European Convention (freedom from torture) to state torture practices. In addition, the disaggregated analysis has the added benefit of more directly capturing executive decision making. Torture violations may occur as a result of principal-agent problems, whereby state agents have an informational advantage over the executive regarding their use of torture as well as incentives to shirk. For the executive to manage this principal-agent problem, the executive must take proactive measures, and if the executive has adopted a policy of respect for rights, administered the policy, and put in place the appropriate monitoring and enforcement programs, then torture violations should be relatively lower.

In the disaggregated model, I utilize a dependent variable that captures respect for the right to be free from torture and ill-treatment. Data for these analyses come from the Cingranelli, Richards, and Clay (2014) dataset. The torture variable is coded on a three-point scale, where a zero indicates that torture is practiced frequently, a one indicates that torture is practiced occasionally, and a two indicates that torture is not practiced/unreported.[18] The independent variable of interest is an interaction between an adverse judgment finding a violation of Article 3 of the European Convention and judicial power (lagged 1 year). I also estimated models examining respect for the right to be free from torture 3 and 5 years postjudgment and the results are similar to those reported here.

Given the nature of the dependent variable, I estimate ordered logistic regression models. The full model results are included in the Appendix to this chapter (Table D.6).[19] I show the marginal predicted probability of being in each category of the torture variable in the year following the receipt of at least one adverse European Court judgment that found a violation of Article 3 of the European Convention, across values of judicial power in Table 6.1. The values in Table 6.1 represent the predicted probability of frequent torture, occasional torture, and no torture. The values in parentheses represent 90 percent confidence intervals. To generate the values, all other variables are set to their mean or mode.

---

[18] There are 415 country-years with a value of two, 366 country-years with a value of one, and 190 country-years with a value of zero in the sample.

[19] Model results remain similar when I estimate random effects ordered logistic regression models.

TABLE 6.1. *Predicted probability of torture following adverse European Court judgments (Article 3 – Freedom from torture) across judicial power*

Judicial power	Frequent torture	Occasional torture	No torture
Low	0.179 (0.004, 0.354)	0.742 (0.638, 0.846)	0.079 (0.000, 0.160)
Medium	0.034 (0.008, 0.060)	0.618 (0.494, 0.742)	0.348 (0.203, 0.493)
High	0.006 (0.001, 0.010)	0.227 (0.122, 0.332)	0.767 (0.659, 0.876)

Notes: Table 6.1 shows the predicted probability of frequent torture, occasional torture, and no torture across judicial power and 90 percent confidence intervals (in parentheses). Low judicial power represents a 0.4, medium judicial power represents a 0.7, and high judicial power represents a 1.0 on the judicial power measure. Table 6.1 shows that adverse European Court judgments related to torture (Article 3 of the European Convention) are associated with lower levels of torture when judicial power is higher.

The results in the second column of Table 6.1 show that there is little difference in the probability of practicing frequent torture across high and low values of judicial power. The third column of Table 6.1 shows the predicted probability of occasionally practicing torture in the year following an adverse European Court judgment (finding a violation of Article 3 of the European Convention) for low, medium, and high values of judicial power. At low levels of judicial power, the probability of practicing torture occasionally in the year following an adverse European Court judgment (violation of Article 3) is around 0.74. However, at high levels of judicial power, the predicted probability of practicing torture occasionally in the year following an adverse European Court judgment (violation of Article 3) is lower (around 0.23).

Finally, the last column of Table 6.1 shows the predicted probability of not practicing torture in the year following an adverse European Court judgment (violation of Article 3) for low, medium, and high values of judicial power. At low levels of judicial power, the probability of not practicing torture in the year following an adverse European Court judgment related to Article 3 is around 0.08. However, at high levels of judicial power (1.0), the probability of not practicing torture in the year following the finding of a violation of Article 3 by the European Court is around 0.77. The results displayed in Table 6.1 show that in the year following the finding of a European Court violation of Article 3 (prohibition of torture), the probability of not practicing torture is high, but only in states with strong national judiciaries.

6.3 Deterrence Is Conditional on Political Elite

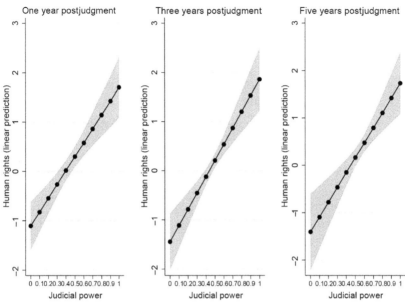

FIGURE 6.4. Predicted influence of adverse Inter-American Court judgments across judicial power

Notes: The left panel of Figure 6.4 displays the predicted level of respect for rights 1 year postjudgment, the center panel 3 years postjudgment, and the right panel 5 years postjudgment across judicial power. Lines represent the predicted level of respect for rights and the shaded area represents 90 percent confidence intervals. Figure 6.4 lends support to Hypothesis 6, as adverse Inter-American Court judgments are associated with greater respect for rights at relatively high levels of judicial power and the deterrent effect is consistent 1, 3, and 5 years postjudgment.

Turning to results for the Inter-American Court, the solid line in Figure 6.4 displays the predicted level of respect for rights 1 year (left panel), 3 years (center panel), and 5 years (right panel) following adverse Inter-American Court judgments across judicial power. The shaded area represents 90 percent confidence intervals. All other variables are set to their mean (for continuous variables) or mode (for binary or count variables). Figure 6.4 lends support to Hypothesis 6. The left panel shows that 1 year following an adverse Inter-American Court judgment, the predicted level of respect for rights is −1.10 when judicial power is at its lowest. However, when judicial power is at its highest, the predicted level of respect for rights is 1.70 (a difference of around 2.8 points). The results are consistent for 3 and 5 years postjudgment, an indication that adverse judgments are positively associated with respect for rights when judicial power is high for at least 5 years after a judgment has been rendered. In support of Hypothesis 6, the predicted level of respect for rights is higher at high levels of judicial power than low levels of judicial power, and the difference is substantively important.

To examine the robustness of the results, I estimate an additional model examining the influence of adverse Inter-American Court judgments on the change in respect for physical integrity rights. To measure change in respect for physical integrity rights, I utilize changes in the Cingranelli, Richards, and Clay (2014) physical integrity rights index from the year of the judgment to 1, 3, and 5 years postjudgment as the dependent variable. The substantive results, which are reported in Table D.9 of the Appendix, provide additional support for the hypothesis. An adverse Inter-American Court judgment is associated with greater changes in respect for physical integrity rights 1, 3, and 5 years postjudgment as judicial power grows. More specifically, an adverse Inter-American Court judgment is associated with a −1.94 change in respect for physical integrity rights (on a scale ranging from −4 to +6) from the year of the judgment to 3 years postjudgment when judicial power is low. However, when judicial power is high, an adverse Inter-American Court judgment is associated with a 2.63 change in respect for physical integrity rights from the year of the judgment to 3 years postjudgment. Results from models estimated with a change dependent variable are also robust when the adverse judgment variable is lagged 1 and 5 years, that is, adverse Inter-American Court judgments are associated with significantly higher changes in respect for physical integrity rights from the year of the judgment to 1 and 5 years postjudgment when judicial power is relatively high.

The combination of substantive case narratives in Venezuela and Argentina, the aggregate empirical analyses for the Inter-American Court sample, and the disaggregated analyses for the European Court sample lend strong support for the argument that national judicial power is associated with a higher likelihood of national judicial implementation and a greater likelihood of executive adoption, administration, monitoring, and enforcement of human rights policy. In the aggregate analysis, the results are stronger in the Americas than in Europe. However, finding evidence in Europe is more difficult because judicial power and respect for rights are both relatively high in Europe, which easily mutes some of the effects. By more directly testing the hypothesis using violations of Article 3 (prohibition of torture) and respect for the right to be free from torture, I find greater evidence of the role of judicial power in ensuring adverse European Court deterrence of future human rights abuses. Finding evidence that the national judiciary can influence executive willingness to adopt comprehensive human rights policy, in the next section, I turn to the role of an additional set of political elites for regional court deterrence, national legislators.

6.3.3 *The Role of National Legislative Support*

I argued in Chapter 2 that adverse regional human rights court judgments are associated with greater respect for rights in the presence of a large legislative opposition with preferences that differ from the executive (Hypothesis 7). To illustrate the importance of legislative veto players in regional human rights court deterrence, consider the state of Mexico. In Chapter 1, I discussed the case *Radilla Pacheco v. Mexico*. To briefly recap, Rosendo Radilla Pacheco and his 11-year-old son were traveling by bus to Chilpancingo, Guerrero, when the bus was stopped at a military checkpoint. Passengers were forced to exit the bus, and soldiers went through their belongings. At a second military checkpoint, soldiers once again inspected passenger's belongings and Radilla Pacheco was arrested for his possession of corridos (traditional folk songs). Radilla Pacheco was taken to a military barracks, where he was subsequently abused and beaten. Following his detention, family members were unable to locate Radilla Pacheco (Khananashvili, 2014).

The case reached the Inter-American Court in 2008 after a series of filed complaints and failed investigations. In 2009, the Inter-American Court rendered an adverse judgment against the state of Mexico in *Radilla Pacheco v. Mexico*, finding the state in violation of several articles of the American Convention on Human Rights, including the right to personal liberty and security, the prohibition of torture, and the prohibition of arbitrary deprivation of life, along with several other articles. Among the many orders required of Mexico was the reform of the constitution and legislation. One important legal reform required of the state was the adoption of an adequate definition of the crime of enforced disappearance of persons.[20] The Inter-American Court found Mexico's federal definition of the crime to be inadequate because it failed to recognize the many potential perpetrators of forced disappearance or the forms of participation state agents can have in the crime.

By 2015, the legislature had fallen short in implementing the Inter-American Court judgment. In February, 2015, the United Nations Committee on Enforced Disappearances (UNCED) found that some Mexican states had not yet codified the crime of disappearance or did so with varying sentences

---

[20] *Radilla Pacheco v. Mexico*, Preliminary Objections, Merits, Reparations, and Costs, Judgment, Inter-Am. Ct. H.R. Nov. 23, 2009.

(Saenz, 2010).[21] In October 2017, Mexico's lower house of Congress, the Chamber of Deputies, approved a Forced Disappearance law. Lawmakers approved the law unanimously, with 361 voting in favor. Although still awaiting Senate approval, the legislative implementation in Mexico is a significant step moving forward. What explains the decision of the Mexican legislature to implement the Inter-American Court judgment and adopt legislation?

Exploring Mexico's domestic legislative process sheds light onto the timing of Mexico's legislative change. The size of the legislative opposition with preferences different than the executive increased in 2015. A new president was elected in Mexico in 2012, Enrique Peña Nieto, of the Institutional Revolutionary Party (PRI). The PRI took control of both chambers of the legislature, winning 57 seats in the Senate and 212 seats in the Chamber of Deputies. The PRI also allied with a smaller party, the Ecologist Green Party of Mexico (PVEM), giving the PRI near-majority in the Chamber. In the 2015 midterm elections, the PRI lost seats in the Chamber of Deputies, winning 203 seats. As a result, the president's party (PRI) lost some control in the lower house.

Turning to the data, I look to a well-known indicator of political constraints from the Political Constraints Index (POLCON) Dataset (Henisz, 2002). This measure captures difficulties executives face in making policy changes, including the presence of legislative opposition groups. The measure comes from a spatial model, ranging from 0 to 1. Since 2012, political constraints have increased in Mexico from 0.400 for the 2010 to 2012 time period to 0.583 by 2015. The increase in political constraints may explain the priority placed on implementation of the adverse judgment and the eventual passage of legislation in 2017. Also of note, political constraints may not tell the entire story of Mexico's legislative implementation. Several other factors discussed in the chapters of this book may also be at play. For example, a general election was held in 2018 which, based on Hypothesis 3 (examined in Chapter 5), likely generated executive and legislative incentives to pass legislation in 2017. Also, based on Hypothesis 4 (examined in Chapter 5), political and social instability likely played a role in delayed legislative implementation. Mexican drug cartels and the Mexican military rely extensively on violence, including forced disappearances, to maintain control. Such heightened political and social instability may explain the substantial delay in implementation. Despite these alternative explanations, the data provide some evidence

---

[21] More specifically, 12 Mexican states had failed to incorporate the crime of enforced disappearance into their criminal code, and 16 had laws that failed to meet international standards (Saenz, 2010).

that a large legislative opposition played a role in the legislative implementation and, subsequently, the executive decision to adopt comprehensive human rights policy.

Given the relatively smaller legislative opposition faced by the executive in 2012, executive expectation of legislative implementation remained low, resulting in few executive incentives to make human rights policy change. Evidence shows that in the time since the Inter-American Court ruling, enforced disappearances in Mexico remained high, and there is some evidence that enforced disappearances increased over time (Saenz, 2010). In 2014, there were approximately 5,098 reported disappearances (GOV.UK, 2015), breaking the record for the number of annual disappearances set in the previous year by 584 (Bargent, 2014). Repression more generally in Mexico also continued to rise following the 2009 adverse Inter-American Court judgment. According to the Fariss (2014) measure of respect for physical integrity rights (ranging from −2 to +3), Mexico scored a −0.758 in 2009 (the year of the *Radilla Pacheco v. Mexico* judgment). By 2012, Mexico's physical integrity rights score declined to −0.939.

The delayed legislative implementation in the case of *Radilla Pacheco v. Mexico* can be explained by changes in the size of the legislative opposition with preferences different from the executive. This anecdote lends support to the role of the legislative opposition in ensuring regional human rights court deterrence. Given this initial anecdotal evidence, in the next section, I systematically examine the role of the size of the legislative opposition in the likelihood of legislative implementation, and therefore executive adoption, administration, monitoring, and enforcement of human rights policy.

6.3.4 Evidence of Executive Willingness: National Legislatures

To formally reiterate the legislative opposition argument, I argue that as the size of the legislative opposition with preferences different than the executive grows, adverse regional court judgments are associated with greater respect for rights. Adverse regional court judgments generate information about executive behavior. As a result, groups and the media engage in increased monitoring of executive repression (Lupu, 2015). The legislative opposition can use the information produced by an adverse regional court judgment to build momentum around the passage of legislation to monitor the executive. The hypothesis is conditional, and as a result, I create an interaction term capturing the presence of an adverse regional human rights court judgment and a measure of opposition in the legislature. Following Lupu (2015), I utilize the *PolCon iii* measure of political constraints developed by Henisz

(2002). The measure captures the feasibility of policy change as a result of interactions between political actors, including the party composition of the executive and legislative branches. The measure is based on a spatial model that includes the presence of effective legislative veto players, the extent to which those veto players are controlled by parties different than the executive's party (alignment across branches of government), and the extent to which the majority controlling each veto player is cohesive. The Henisz (2002) measure is appropriate because it captures the effectiveness of the legislative opposition in overturning policy, specifically the legislative opposition with preferences different from the executive.[22]

The legislative opposition variable is interacted with a variable measuring the presence of one or more adverse regional human rights court judgments (1) or no adverse judgments in a given year (0). The control variables utilized in the models are described in more detail in Appendix D. I estimate three different models for the European and Inter-American Courts of Human Rights. In the first model, I examine the influence of an adverse judgment (lagged 1 year) on respect for rights 1 year after the judgment. In the second model, I examine the influence of an adverse judgment (lagged 3 years) on respect for rights 3 years after the judgment. Finally, in the third model, I examine the influence of an adverse judgment (lagged 5 years) on respect for rights 5 years after the judgment.[23] The following equation is an example of the model used to assess respect for rights 3 years postjudgment:

$$\begin{aligned}Respect\ for\ Rights_{(t)} = {} & b_0 + b_1\ Leg\ Opposition_{(t-1)} * Adverse\ Judgment_{(t-3)} \\ & + b_2\ Leg\ Opposition_{(t-1)} + b_3\ Adverse\ Judgment_{(t-3)} \\ & + b_4\ Adverse\ Judgment_{(t-2)} + b_5\ Adverse\ Judgment_{(t-1)} \\ & + Controls_{(t-1)} + \varepsilon.\end{aligned}$$

Figure 6.5 displays the predicted level of respect for rights 1 year (left panel), 3 years (center panel), and 5 years (right panel) postjudgment across values of the political constraints variable (the legislative opposition). The solid line represents the predicted level of respect for rights 1, 3, and 5 years following at least one adverse European Court judgment and the shaded area displays 90 percent confidence intervals. All other variables in the model are set to their mean (for continuous variables) or mode (for binary or count

---

[22] The results reported here are robust to the use of a measure capturing the extent to which opposition parties are able to exercise oversight over the governing party in the legislature, taken from Coppedge et al. (2019).

[23] In the model utilizing the 3-year lag, I control for adverse judgments lagged 1 and 2 years. In the model utilizing the 5-year lag, I control for adverse judgments lagged 1, 2, 3, and 4 years.

6.3 Deterrence Is Conditional on Political Elite

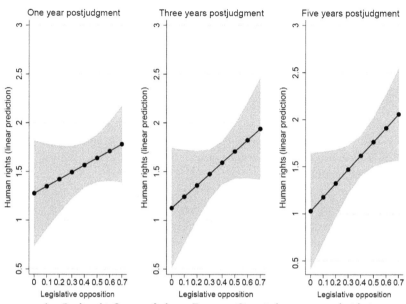

FIGURE 6.5. Predicted influence of adverse European Court judgments across legislative opposition

Notes: The left panel of Figure 6.5 displays the predicted level of respect for rights 1 year postjudgment, the center panel 3 years postjudgment, and the right panel 5 years postjudgment across the legislative opposition. Lines represent the predicted level of respect for rights and the shaded area represents 90 percent confidence intervals. Figure 6.5 shows that European Court judgments are associated with higher levels of respect for rights as the size of the legislative opposition with preferences different from the executive grows.

variables). The trend in Figure 6.5 is positive, indicating that for adverse European Court judgment recipients, the predicted level of respect for rights is higher as the effective legislative opposition grows and the predicted level of respect for rights is lower as the size of the effective legislative opposition declines. Full model results are reported in the Appendix in Tables D.10, D.11, and D.12. Importantly, the constituent term for legislative opposition shows that the size of the legislative opposition is negatively associated with respect for rights (absent an adverse European Court judgment). However, as the results in Figure 6.5 show, the relationship between the legislative opposition and respect for rights trends positive, but only in the presence of an adverse European Court judgment.

The effect is stronger 3 and 5 years following an adverse European Court judgment than 1 year following the judgment. Making legislative changes in line with adverse regional court judgments is inherently difficult given the nature of the legislature as a deliberative body. The executive likely expects delayed implementation by the legislature (in the presence of a large legislative opposition), and (all else equal) the executive may delay the adoption of comprehensive human rights policy as a result. Notably, 5 years following an adverse judgment, the predicted value of respect for rights is 2.05 when there is a relatively large legislative opposition with preferences that differ from the executive. However, the predicted value of respect for rights is 1.02 when the size of the legislative opposition with preferences that differ from the executive is relatively low, which is around one point lower than the level of respect for rights in the presence of a relatively large legislative opposition.

I also examine the robustness of the results by estimating a model that examines the influence of adverse European Court judgments on the change in respect for physical integrity rights using the Cingranelli, Richards, and Clay (2014) physical integrity rights index as the dependent variable. Substantive results are reported in Table D.13. The results are largely similar to those reported in Figure 6.5, showing that the predicted change in respect for physical integrity rights following an adverse judgment is greater as the size of the legislative opposition grows. For example, an adverse European Court judgment is associated with a −0.170 change in respect for physical integrity rights (on a scale ranging from −4 to +3) from the year of the judgment to 1 year postjudgment when the legislative opposition is small. However, when the legislative opposition is large, the predicted change in respect for physical integrity rights from the year of the judgment to 1 year postjudgment is 0.289. Of note, however, the predicted changes reported in the Appendix have 90 percent confidence intervals that include zero, which means that the influence of adverse European Court judgments and the legislative opposition on the change in respect for physical integrity rights should be interpreted with some caution.

Although Figure 6.5 displays a positive trend, the confidence intervals are relatively wide 1, 3, and 5 years postjudgment. As a result, I estimate a disaggregated model in an effort to more directly examine the role of the legislative opposition. The preceding analyses aggregate all adverse European Court judgments associated with the physical integrity rights articles of the European Convention and respect for physical integrity rights broadly. As an additional test of Hypothesis 7, I conduct a disaggregated analysis; I examine the influence of adverse European Court judgments related to torture on the right to be free from torture. Similar to the disaggregated model used to test the national judiciary hypothesis (Hypothesis 6), I utilize a dependent variable that captures respect for the right to be free from torture and ill-treatment. Data for

TABLE 6.2. *Predicted probability of torture following adverse European Court judgments (Article 3 – Freedom from torture) across size of the legislative opposition*

Legislative opposition	Frequent torture	Occasional torture	No torture
Small	0.079	0.741	0.180
	(0.000, 0.178)	(0.633, 0.850)	(0.000, 0.377)
Medium	0.026	0.565	0.409
	(0.006, 0.047)	(0.423, 0.707)	(0.250, 0.567)
Large	0.009	0.306	0.685
	(0.000, 0.017)	(0.153, 0.459)	(0.525, 0.845)

Notes: Table 6.2 shows the predicted probability of frequent torture, occasional torture, and no torture across the size of the legislative opposition and 90 percent confidence intervals (in parentheses). A small legislative opposition represents a 0.1, a medium legislative opposition represents a 0.4, and a large legislative opposition represents a 0.7 on the legislative opposition variable. Table 6.2 shows that adverse European Court judgments related to torture (Article 3 of the European Convention) are associated with lower levels of torture when the legislative opposition is larger.

these analyses come from the Cingranelli, Richards, and Clay (2014) dataset. The independent variable of interest is an interaction between an adverse judgment finding a violation of Article 3 of the European Convention and the legislative opposition variable (lagged 1 year). I also estimated models assessing respect for the right to be free from torture 3 and 5 years postjudgment, and the results look similar to those reported here.

I estimate an ordered logistic regression model. The full model results are included in the Appendix to this chapter (Table D.10).[24] I report the marginal predicted probability of being in each category of the torture variable for a country in the year following the receipt of at least one adverse European Court judgment finding a violation of Article 3 of the European Convention, for varying sizes of the legislative opposition (small, medium, and large) in Table 6.2.

Table 6.2 conveys several pieces of information. First, the table shows that there is little difference in the probability of practicing frequent torture across a large and small legislative opposition, which may be due to few states in Europe frequently practicing torture. Table 6.2 (column 3) also shows the predicted probability of occasionally practicing torture in the year following an adverse European Court judgment (finding a violation of Article 3 of the European Convention) across the size of the legislative opposition. When

---

[24] Model results remain similar when I estimate random effects ordered logistic regression models.

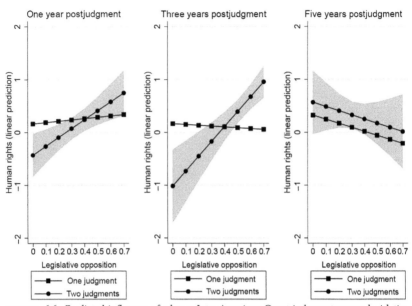

FIGURE 6.6. Predicted influence of adverse Inter-American Court judgments across legislative opposition

Notes: The left panel of Figure 6.6. displays the predicted level of respect for rights 1 year postjudgment, the center panel 3 years postjudgment, and the right panel 5 years postjudgment across the legislative opposition. Lines represent the predicted level of respect for rights following a single adverse judgment (squares) and following two adverse judgments (circles), while the shaded area represents 90 percent confidence intervals. Figure 6.6 shows that the presence of two adverse Inter-American Court judgments is associated with higher levels of respect for rights as the size of the legislative opposition with preferences different from the executive grows.

the legislative opposition is small, the predicted probability of practicing torture occasionally in the year following an adverse Article 3 European Court judgment is 0.74 and when the size of the legislative opposition is large, the probability of practicing occasional torture is 0.31 following an adverse European Court judgment. Finally, the last column of Table 6.2 shows the predicted probability of not practicing torture in the year following the finding of an adverse European Court judgment (violation of Article 3) across the size of the legislative opposition. When the legislative opposition is small, the probability of not practicing torture in the year following an adverse European Court judgment (Article 3 violation) is around 0.18. However, when the legislative opposition is large, the probability of not practicing torture in the year following an adverse European Court judgment (Article 3 violation) is 0.69, which is around 0.51 higher than when the legislative opposition is small.

Turning to the Inter-American Court, the results are summarized in Figure 6.6, which shows the level of respect for rights 1 year postjudgment (left panel), 3 years postjudgment (center panel), and 5 years postjudgment (right panel) across the legislative opposition. The results are not as straightforward for the Inter-American Court. Unlike the European Court, *the number of adverse Inter-American Court judgments* matters more for ensuring respect for rights than the mere presence of an adverse judgment and a large legislative opposition. As a result, I present results displaying the influence of one and two adverse judgments on respect for rights across the size of the legislative opposition. One adverse judgment is not associated with higher values of respect for rights when the legislative opposition is large. Rather, the presence of two adverse Inter-American Court judgments is associated with significantly higher values of respect for rights 1 and 3 years postjudgment when the size of the legislative opposition with preferences different from the executive is large. More specifically, 3 years following a single adverse Inter-American Court judgment, the level of respect for rights is 0.056 when the size of the legislative opposition is large, and this value is not much different than the predicted level of respect for rights when the size of the legislative opposition is small (0.165). However, 3 years following *two adverse judgments*, the predicted level of respect for rights is 0.954 when there is a large legislative opposition, as opposed to −1.01 when the legislative opposition is small. Perhaps the presence of two adverse judgments provides more information on human rights policy failures to the legislative opposition, giving the opposition additional leverage in advocating for legislative implementation of adverse judgments.

Also of note in Figure 6.6, the results show that the size of the legislative opposition makes little difference 5 years postjudgment. If the legislative opposition has not used the adverse judgment as a means to initiate legislative changes for 5 years after a judgment, the judgment may no longer be salient enough to generate support for legislative implementation. Subsequently, the executive may no longer expect a strong likelihood of legislative implementation, which means the executive has fewer incentives to adopt, administer, monitor, and enforce human rights policy. Furthermore, the executive may also look to other legislative institutions for signals about the likelihood of legislative implementation, including the number of opposition parties, the cohesiveness of the legislative opposition, the presence of an upcoming legislative election, and the presence of subnational government, all of which are subject to change 5 years following an adverse judgment.

In order to examine the robustness of the results, I estimate an additional model examining the influence of adverse Inter-American Court judgments on the change in respect for physical integrity rights using changes in the Cingranelli, Richards, and Clay (2014) physical integrity rights index as the dependent variable. Substantive results from this model are reported in the Appendix (Table D.13). The results are similar to those reported in Figure 6.6. That is, the trend is positive, indicating that the predicted change in respect for physical integrity rights grows following an adverse Inter-American Court judgment as the size of the legislative opposition increases. Also, the findings are stronger in the presence of two adverse judgments as opposed to a single adverse judgment. For example, the predicted change in respect for physical integrity rights is −3.00 (on a scale ranging from −4 to +6) 3 years following two adverse Inter-American Court judgments when the legislative opposition is small. However, the predicted change in respect for rights grows to 3.68 3 years following two adverse judgments when the legislative opposition is large.

Because the results show that the influence of a single adverse Inter-American Court judgment on respect for rights is weak, I conduct an additional analysis for the Inter-American Court to more directly test the hypothesis. The preceding analyses aggregate all adverse Inter-American Court judgments finding violations of the physical integrity articles of the American Convention and respect for physical integrity rights broadly (i.e., extrajudicial killing, torture, disappearance, and political imprisonment). I conduct an additional analysis by examining the influence of adverse judgments related to political imprisonment on the right to be free from arbitrary arrest and political imprisonment. This provides a more direct test of the hypothesis by linking adverse judgments related to Article 7 of the American Convention, which specifies the right to personal liberty and the prohibition on arbitrary arrest and imprisonment, to state political imprisonment practices. Whereas I look at the influence of adverse European Court judgments related to torture in the European sample, I examine freedom from political imprisonment in the Americas because there is more variation in the level of political imprisonment in the Americas than there is variation in torture. More specifically, there are few country-years in the Americas with no torture, making it hard to accurately predict the influence of the legislative opposition and adverse regional court judgments on freedom from torture.[25]

In the disaggregated Inter-American Court model, I utilize a dependent variable that captures respect for the right to be free from political imprisonment. Data for this analysis come from the Cingranelli, Richards, and Clay (2014) dataset. The political imprisonment variable is coded on a three-point scale, where a zero indicates many political imprisonments occurred, a one indicates

---

[25] There are only 24 country-years in which states did not torture in the Americas, and half of those years are in Costa Rica and Uruguay.

TABLE 6.3. *Predicted probability of political imprisonment following adverse Inter-American Court judgments (Article 7 – Freedom from political imprisonment) across size of the legislative opposition*

Legislative opposition	Many political imprisonments	Some political imprisonments	No political imprisonments
Small	0.047 (0.001, 0.094)	0.415 (0.197, 0.633)	0.538 (0.278, 0.797)
Medium	0.020 (0.007, 0.033)	0.242 (0.140, 0.345)	0.738 (0.626, 0.849)
Large	0.008 (0.000, 0.019)	0.120 (0.001, 0.238)	0.872 (0.744, 0.999)

Notes: Table 6.3 shows the predicted probability of many political imprisonments, some political imprisonments, and no political imprisonments across the size of the legislative opposition and 90 percent confidence intervals (in parentheses). A small legislative opposition represents a value of 0.1, a medium legislative opposition represents a value of 0.4, and a large legislative opposition represents a value of 0.7 on the legislative opposition variable. Table 6.3 shows that adverse Inter-American Court judgments related to political imprisonment (Article 7 of the American Convention) are associated with fewer political imprisonments when the legislative opposition is larger. Notably, there is slight overlap in the 90 percent confidence intervals at high and low values of the legislative opposition variable.

some political imprisonments occurred, and a two indicates that there were no political imprisonments.[26] The independent variable of interest is an interaction between the presence of at least one adverse judgment involving a violation of Article 7 of the American Convention (prohibition on arbitrary arrest) and the legislative opposition (lagged 1 year). A model examining the influence of adverse judgments related to political imprisonment on the right to be free from political imprisonment 3 years postjudgment looks similar to the results presented here.

Given the nature of the dependent variable, I estimate an ordered logistic regression model. The full model results are included in the Appendix to this chapter.[27] The marginal predicted probability of being in each category of the political imprisonment variable in the year following the receipt of at least one adverse Inter-American Court judgment finding a violation of Article 7 of the American Convention for various sizes of the legislative opposition

---

[26] There are 78 country-years with a value of zero, 148 country-years with a value of one, and 269 country-years with a value of two.
[27] Model results remain similar when I estimate random effects ordered logistic regression models.

is displayed in Table 6.3. The values in Table 6.3 indicate the predicted probability of many political imprisonments, some political imprisonments, and no political imprisonments, and the values in parentheses represent 90 percent confidence intervals. To estimate the predicted probabilities in Table 6.3, all other variables are set to their mean or mode (for binary or ordinal variables).

Table 6.3 conveys several important pieces of information. First, the table shows that the probability of many political imprisonments is close to zero for various sizes of the legislative opposition (second column). Second, column 3 of Table 6.3 shows that the probability of some political imprisonment in the year following an Inter-American Court finding of a violation of Article 7 is around 0.42 when the size of the legislative opposition is small; however, the predicted probability of some political imprisonments in the year following an Inter-American Court violation of Article 7 is lower when size of the legislative opposition is large (around 0.12).

Finally, the last column of Table 6.3 displays the predicted probability of no political imprisonments in the year following the finding of an adverse Inter-American Court judgment (violation of Article 7) across the size of the legislative opposition. The results show that the probability of no political imprisonments in the year following an adverse Inter-American Court judgment related to Article 7 is around 0.54 when the legislative opposition is small. However, when the legislative opposition with preferences that differ from the executive is large, the probability of no political imprisonments in the year following the finding of a violation of Article 7 by the Inter-American Court is higher (0.87). Notably, although the trend reported in Table 6.3 is positive, indicating that as the size of the legislative opposition grows, the probability of no political imprisonments grows, there is a slight overlap in the 90 percent confidence intervals at low and high values of the legislative opposition, which means we should interpret the disaggregated results with some caution.

For the European and Inter-American Courts, the executive may consider several legislative institutions in combination when making an assessment of the likelihood of legislative implementation of adverse regional court judgments. That is, although the size of the legislative opposition sends an important signal about the likelihood of legislative implementation, the size of the legislative opposition should be considered alongside other legislative institutions. That is, the size of the legislative opposition may represent an important signal of legislative willingness to make legislative changes. But, the cohesiveness of the legislative opposition also sends a signal to the executive of the ability of the legislature to make legislative changes, and perhaps the cohesiveness of the legislative opposition sends a stronger signal to the executive than the mere size of the legislative opposition.

The combination of the anecdotal evidence of an Inter-American Court judgment in Mexico and the aggregated and disaggregated empirical analyses for each sample provide support for Hypothesis 7, showing that the legislative opposition is associated with a higher likelihood of national legislative implementation and a greater likelihood of executive adoption, administration, monitoring, and enforcement of human rights policy. The results suggest that adverse judgments provide important information to the legislative opposition and as the size of the legislative opposition with preferences different from the executive grows, an adverse judgment is positively related to respect for rights. Notably, the aggregate results for the European Court are not strong. However, the disaggregated results for the European Court are strong and significant. Also of note, the aggregate results for the Inter-American Court are only positively and significantly related to respect for rights in the presence of two adverse judgments (1 and 3 years postjudgment), an indication that in the Americas, the legislative opposition is unable to leverage a single adverse judgment to agitate for legislative changes that align with the regional court. The disaggregated model results display a positive trend, indicating that adverse judgments involving political imprisonment are associated with better respect for the right to be free from political imprisonment as the size of the legislative opposition grows, but just fail to reach conventional levels of statistical significance.

6.4 CONCLUSION

In this chapter, I argued that adverse regional human rights court judgments are more likely to deter future human rights abuses when the executive is *willing* to adopt, administer, monitor, and enforce human rights policy as a result of elite pressure. I argued that there are two sets of elites important for generating executive willingness: economic elites and political elites. With respect to economic elites, I show that states that have relatively large foreign direct investment inflows have higher levels of respect for rights following adverse regional court judgments than states with lower levels of foreign direct investment inflows. The evidence suggests that the executive has a greater willingness to adopt, administer, monitor, and enforce human rights policy following an adverse regional court judgment when the state is vulnerable to a loss of economic benefits, like FDI. The findings indicate that executives in the Americas, perhaps due to a greater level of economic vulnerability than in Europe, are more likely to respond to adverse judgments with human rights policy change 1 to 3 years following the judgment. In Europe, FDI is more strongly associated with better human rights practices 5 years after an adverse judgment (than 1 or 3 years after an adverse judgment), an indication that European states may be less economically vulnerable to a loss of foreign investment for human rights policy failures, and as a result, European states with high FDI inflows are less likely to respond to adverse judgments for several years.

Turning to the role of political elites, I argue that the executive is more likely to adopt comprehensive human rights policy in expectation of national judicial or legislative implementation of regional court judgments. I find evidence that national judicial implementation is more likely when the national judiciary is relatively powerful. The interaction between regional and national courts is particularly important as national courts are the place where individuals go to pursue a remedy for human rights abuse. National courts are the first stop on the road to justice when human rights have been violated. The importance of national judicial implementation cannot be understated; Keller and Stone-Sweet (2008) highlight this interaction in the European context nicely:

> The European Court of Human Rights then becomes the guardian of the application of the European Convention on Human Rights by the Constitutional and Supreme Courts ... the system also needs to count on the possibility of reopening domestic proceedings when a violation of the Convention has been acknowledged by the European Court of Human Rights ... Ultimately, only if these elements work together will the full effectiveness of the European Convention on Human Rights in national legal orders be realized. (446)

I provide evidence that national judicial power raises executive expectation of national judicial implementation, and as a result, the executive is more likely to adopt, administer, monitor, and enforce human rights policy. The empirical evidence presented in this chapter indicates that the national judiciary is important in both Europe and the Americas, suggesting that if regional human rights courts are to deter future human rights abuses, national judicial implementation is a vital piece of the puzzle.

In addition to national judges, I argue that national legislators represent another set of political elites important for generating executive incentives to adopt, administer, monitor, and enforce human rights policy. I find evidence that national legislative implementation is more likely as the size of the legislative opposition grows. Although the legislative opposition generally has an independently negative effect on rights protection (e.g., Conrad and Moore

(2010)), adverse regional human rights court judgments play an important informational role, providing information to legislators about executive human rights policy failures. The legislative opposition, then, utilizes adverse judgments to build support for the creation of new rights-respecting legislation. I find limited support for the role of the legislative opposition in European Court deterrence. More specifically, 3 and 5 years following an adverse European Court judgment, the size of the legislative opposition is positively associated with higher levels of respect for rights in Europe, though the results indicate that this finding should be interpreted with some caution. When I look at adverse judgments associated with freedom from torture and the right to be free from torture in Europe, I find that following an adverse European Court judgment, the legislative opposition is significantly associated with a lower probability of no torture incidences. This result may indicate that the legislative opposition relies on a clear signal of human rights policy failure (e.g., an adverse judgment finding a violation of the right to be free from torture) when pressing for legislative changes associated with torture.

In the Americas, the relationship is not as straightforward. The legislative opposition is important for regional court deterrence in the Americas, but only when the Inter-American Court has rendered at least two adverse judgments against a state in a given year. This finding suggests that the presence of at least two adverse judgments provides the legislative opposition with greater leverage in its deliberations regarding implementation of Inter-American Court judgments. That is, the legislative opposition can place greater pressure on the executive to adopt comprehensive human rights policy following two adverse Inter-American Court judgments rather than one. Further, I find evidence that adverse judgments associated with freedom from arbitrary arrest and detention are associated with a higher probability of fewer political imprisonments in the Americas in the presence of a large legislative opposition, though these results should be interpreted with some caution as the results just fail to achieve statistical significance.

The results for the role of the legislative opposition highlight an important problem for the likelihood of legislative implementation. By design, legislatures are deliberative bodies, and action is relatively more difficult. The institutional design problem is highlighted nicely by Huneeus (2012). She argues,

> Executives are top-down institutions designed to carry out action. Legislatures are designed for democratic deliberation and contestation. To pass a law, a majority vote must be negotiated and a series of procedural hurdles passed.

> One only has to see the differences in structure to predict that legislatures will be slower and less likely to implement [regional] Court orders. (517)

The executive may expect a relatively low likelihood of legislative implementation simply due to the legislative process. As a result, a strong legislative opposition is important in ensuring a greater likelihood of legislative implementation and subsequently greater executive willingness to adopt, administer, monitor, and enforce human rights policy. Not only is legislative implementation of regional court orders inherently difficult due to the design of legislatures, but the executive also likely looks to various signals of the likelihood of legislative implementation, including, but not limited to, the cohesiveness and ideology of the legislative opposition. If the legislative opposition is made of several parties with preferences that differ from those of the executive, but those parties do not agree on the appropriate legislation to address an adverse court judgment, the executive may expect a low likelihood of legislative implementation. Or, the opposition party platform and ideology may play a role in the likelihood of legislative implementation. For example, far-right parties may have preferences that differ from those of the executive, but may have little interest in the rights protection of minorities, arguing instead for the need to protect the safety and interests of the majority.

Considering the political elite results alongside one another, the results indicate that the national judiciary is a promising path for ensuring regional human rights court deterrence. Although legislative implementation can also influence executive willingness to engage in policy change, thereby deterring future human rights abuses, the baseline probability of legislative implementation is relatively low. The legislature sends many signals of the likelihood of legislative implementation, making it difficult for the executive to determine the likelihood of legislative implementation. The size of the legislative opposition, therefore, likely sends a noisy signal to the executive and exhibits only a marginal effect on executive incentives and decision making.

7

Amplified Regional Court Deterrence: High Executive Capacity and High Executive Willingness

In the previous chapters, I show that adverse regional human rights court judgments are likely to deter future human rights abuses when the executive is highly capable *or* highly willing. I argue, however, that the deterrent effect of regional human rights courts will be amplified in the presence of high executive capacity *and* high executive willingness. To illustrate that regional human rights court deterrence is amplified in the presence of both high capacity and high willingness, consider several cases before the European and Inter-American Courts of Human Rights.

First, Germany represents a Council of Europe member state with relatively high executive capacity and willingness to make human rights policy changes in response to adverse European Court judgments. Take, for example, a rights abuse that occurred in 1993 when police officers attempted to arrest a suspected drug dealer, Abu Bakah Jalloh. During the attempted arrest, Jalloh swallowed a tiny bag he had in his mouth. The police found no drugs on Jalloh and ordered that he be given an emetic, a medicine to induce vomiting, in order to force him to regurgitate the bag. Jalloh refused to take the medication, and four police officers held him down while the doctor inserted a tube through his nose and administered the medication by force. As a result, Jalloh regurgitated a small bag of cocaine and was subsequently placed in detention and charged with drug trafficking. Jalloh's lawyer alleged that the evidence against Jalloh was obtained illegally, that the police and doctor responsible for administering the emetic were guilty of causing bodily harm, and that the administration of the medication was disproportionate under the Code of Criminal Procedure. The case eventually reached the European Court of Human Rights. In 2006, the European Court rendered an adverse judgment in the case of *Jalloh v. Germany*, finding Germany in violation of the right to be free from inhuman and degrading treatment, among several other articles.

Germany represents a state with considerable capacity relative to other states in the Council of Europe. While the mean per capita GDP among Council of Europe member states in 2006 amounted to 29,538 US dollars (median of 19,773 US dollars), per capita GDP in Germany in 2006 amounted to 36,447 US dollars. Germany also represents a very creditworthy state, with substantial access to outside resources. In fact, although the mean institutional investor credit rating (ranging from 0 to 100) in the Council of Europe in the several years prior to 2006 was 65.78 (median of 68.25), the institutional investor credit rating in Germany was 92.27 (median of 92.60). In addition to high capacity, Germany also represents a country with heightened executive willingness to make human rights policy changes. Germany is a politically stable country, an indication that the mass public is likely to support the protection of rights. According to the World Bank's political stability and absence of violence measure, Germany is above the mean for the region, averaging 0.85 in the several years leading up to the adverse judgment, while the mean political stability and absence of violence measure in Council of Europe member states was 0.57 (World Bank, 2014).[1]

Following the adverse judgment in Germany, high capacity and high willingness translated into the deterrence of future human rights abuses. Following the *Jalloh v. Germany* judgment, Germany not only paid reparations to the victim, but also responded by banning the practice of administering emetics to obtain evidence in several of the German states and city-states where it had been used (e.g., Berlin, Bremen, Hamburg, Hessen, and North Rhine-Westphalia). Adopting, administering, monitoring, and enforcing such a policy is costly both in terms of material costs and the expense of political capital. When the executive is capable and willing, changes to human rights practices are more likely. Notably, human rights practices in Germany improved following the adverse judgment. According to the Fariss (2014) latent respect for physical integrity rights measure, Germany averaged 1.75 (on a scale ranging from about −2 to +4) in the 4 years leading up to the adverse judgment (2002–2005). In the 4 years following the adverse judgment (2007–2010), Germany averaged 2.67 on respect for physical integrity rights.

Contrast the case of Germany with an example of a state with either diminished capacity or willingness. Venezuela represents a state where an executive has relatively high capacity, but little willingness to make human rights policy changes following an adverse regional court judgment. From 2001 to 2005, supporters of President Hugo Chavez in Venezuela engaged in a series of attacks on and harassment of journalists of Globovisión. President

---

[1] See *Jalloh v. Germany*, Grand Chamber Judgment. European Ct. H.R. Jul. 11, 2006.

Chavez was temporarily displaced from power in 2002, and in response, Chavez organized local support groups called Bolivarian Circles to support his political agenda. Chavez support groups resorted to violence against anti-Chavez demonstrators. During a presidential broadcast in 2004, President Chavez labeled Globovisión an enemy of the state (Tello, 2016).

Numerous reports of attacks on journalists and failed state investigations occurred during this time period. For example, on January 9, 2002, about 30 men surrounded Globovisión camera assistant Alfredo José Peña Isaya, journalist Beatriz Adrián García, and Jorge Paz Paz in their car. The group of men assaulted the camera team and beat José Peña Isaya. Globovisión filed a formal complaint with the National Directorate of Common Crimes, but the Prosecutor's Office requested the proceedings be closed in 2006 (Tello, 2016). As another example of a failed investigation into attacks on journalists, Mayela León Rodríguez and cameraman Jorge Paz Paz were covering a broadcast of President Chavez's weekly radio and television program in January 2002 when a group of assailants wearing Chavez-endorsed insignia attacked the news team. Globovisión filed a formal complaint with the National Directorate of Common Crimes as well as the Ombudsman Office and Prosecutor's Office, but there are no records of any further investigations (Tello, 2016). In another incident in May 2004, Globovisión journalists and camera team were beaten with a pipe while covering a recall election in Caracas despite security guard and Metropolitan police presence. Although Globovisión filed a formal complaint, proceedings were closed in 2007 (Tello, 2016).

In 2009, the Inter-American Court rendered an adverse judgment against Venezuela, *Perozo et al. v. Venezuela*, finding Venezuela in violation of several articles of the American Convention, including the right to physical, mental, and moral integrity (Article 5) and the right to seek, receive, and impart information and ideas (Article 13). The Inter-American Court noted that although the actions of government supporters did not implicate the state directly, a state may be held responsible for those actions when private individuals act as state agents, and the state may be responsible for statements from high-ranking public officials.[2]

At the time of the adverse judgment, Venezuela represented a state of relatively high capacity, meaning that the executive was capable of responding to the adverse judgment with human rights policy change. For many years, Venezuela was one of the world's largest exporters of oil. The Venezuelan Central Bank reported that the government received around 325 billion US

---

[2] See *Perozo et al. v. Venezuela*, Preliminary Objections, Merits, Reparations, and Costs, Inter-Am. Ct. H.R. Jan. 28, 2009.

dollars through oil production from 1998 to 2008. Moreover, although income inequality in Venezuela is high, Venezuela's GDP per capita at the time of the adverse judgment was relatively higher than the rest of the region. In 2009, average per capita GDP in the Americas was around 6,500 US dollars, while per capita GDP in Venezuela amounted to 11,534 US dollars. In terms of creditworthiness, Venezuela's institutional investor credit rating (IIR) was fairly close to the average for the region prior to the adverse judgment (a few points below the average IIR for the region). Generally, Venezuela had the capacity to respond to an adverse judgment with human rights policy change.

However, executive willingness to respond to adverse Inter-American Court judgments in Venezuela was low at the time of the 2009 judgment. As discussed earlier, facing several coup attempts, demonstrations, and strikes, the Chavez regime resorted to repression in the period prior to the adverse judgment. According to the World Bank's political stability and absence of violence indicator, at the time of the adverse judgment (2009), Venezuela scored -1.28, while the average political stability and absence of violence in the Americas in 2009 was -0.29 (World Bank, 2014). Given the low level of political stability in Venezuela, the executive had few incentives to engage in human rights policy changes, and as the anecdotal evidence suggests, the Chavez regime resorted to repression as a means to hold on to power.

Following the 2009 adverse judgment, the Inter-American Court placed several obligations on the state, including conducting effective investigations and criminal proceedings, as well as implementing measures to prevent restrictions on information dissemination. In 2015, the Court noted in its compliance report that despite being sent five requests to submit a compliance report, the state had failed to provide any information on measures taken to comply with the judgment.[3] According to the Fariss (2014) human rights data, respect for physical integrity rights improved slightly in Venezuela following the adverse judgment, from -0.499 in 2009 to -0.418 3 years later (2012), though notably, political stability improved slightly from 2009 to 2012 in Venezuela as well, giving the executive an increased, albeit small, willingness to respond to the adverse judgment by making human rights improvements. The case of Venezuela provides anecdotal evidence that when high capacity to make human rights policy change is not met with high levels of willingness, the likelihood of regional court deterrence declines. In other words, while adverse Inter-American Court judgments can deter future human rights abuses in the

---

[3] See *Perozo et al. v. Venezuela*, Monitoring Compliance with Judgment, Order of the Court, Inter-Am Ct. H.R. Nov. 20, 2015.

presence of high capacity, the deterrent effect of the regional court is greater when the executive also has high willingness.

Compare the cases of Germany and Venezuela with a third state. Slovakia represents a state where the executive has relatively low capacity and relatively high willingness to respond to adverse European Court judgments with human rights policy change. In February 2002, a waitress of non-Roma origin refused to serve a drink to a person of Roma origin in a village bar. Romani people face substantial discrimination and represent a traditionally marginalized group in many European countries. Following the refusal to serve a drink, an argument erupted, and later in the evening a group of men went to a Roma settlement and physically assaulted three Roma from the bar. Police arrived at the settlement about a half hour later and in the coming weeks, the police opened an investigation into the incident. The investigation was extended to look for a possible racial motive behind the attacks. In April, the investigator suspended the investigation, claiming that no evidence had been established to bring charges against a specific person. Despite renewed investigations and appeals, the domestic judicial criminal process failed to hold perpetrators to account, and an application was lodged with the European Court of Human Rights in 2003. In 2012, the European Court found in the case of *Koky and Others v. Slovakia* that the authorities had violated the procedural aspect of Article 3 of the European Convention for not carrying out an effective investigation into the incident.[4]

Slovakia represents a state of relatively low capacity. The average per capita GDP in Slovakia in the 4 years prior to the 2012 adverse European Court judgment was 17,383 US dollars (median of 17,207 US dollars), while the average per capita GDP in the region during the same years was 34,489 US dollars (median of 23,063 US dollars). Slovakia also lags behind other countries in the region when it comes to creditworthiness, with less access to outside resources than other European countries. The average institutional investor credit rating (ranging from 0 to 100) in Council of Europe member states in the several years prior to the 2012 adverse judgment was 66.4 (median of 70.03), while the average rating in Slovakia for the same time period was 59.74 (median of 61.2). Despite relatively diminished capacity, Slovakia represents a state with relatively high willingness to respond to adverse European Court judgments. In the 4 years prior to the 2012 adverse judgment, Slovakia scored a 1.02 on the World Bank's political stability and absence of violence measure, while the average in the region for the same time period was 0.54 (World Bank, 2014). As I argued in Chapter 2, the executive is more likely to face pressure from

---

[4] See *Koky and Others v. Slovakia*, Judgment. European Ct. H.R. Jun. 12, 2012.

the mass public to adopt human rights policy changes post–European Court judgment in politically stable states. Also of note, the median FDI net inflows as a percentage of GDP in Slovakia was on par with the other Council of Europe member states in the decade prior to the adverse judgment. Slovakia's median FDI net inflows from 2002 to 2012 made up around 4.6 percent of GDP, while other Council of Europe member states' median FDI net inflows made up around 5.5 percent of GDP, an indication that the executive may have experienced pressure from economic elites to adopt human rights policy change following adverse European Court judgments.

Because of heightened executive willingness to engage in human rights policy change in Slovakia, several important human rights policy changes were adopted there following the *Koky and Others v. Slovakia* adverse judgment. Slovakia undertook several important changes, including the adoption of a new Code of Criminal Procedure guaranteeing efficient course of criminal investigation among other legislative protections, additional training of prosecutors and judges, and the establishment of specialized police units dealing with racially motivated criminal offences.[5] According to the Fariss (2014) latent respect for physical integrity rights measure, respect for physical integrity rights improved by a small margin in Slovakia following the adverse judgment, from an average of 1.63 (on a scale ranging from about −2 to +4) in the 4 years prior to the adverse judgment (2009 to 2012) to 1.70 in the 4 years following the adverse judgment (2013 to 2016).

Despite these marginal improvements in rights protections, there is some evidence that executive capacity hindered the executive's ability to adopt the necessary policy changes to effectively prohibit inadequate investigations in the future. In 2015, the United Nations' Committee Against Torture expressed concern over the low number of complaints, prosecutions, and convictions in cases involving violence against Roma in Slovakia and continued to make recommendations regarding the need for the state to carry out prompt, impartial, and thorough investigations in such cases. The Committee Against Torture also expressed concern over the absence of comprehensive statistical data on complaints, investigations, prosecutions, and convictions in cases of ill-treatment and torture, a task requiring substantial resources on the part of the state (United Nations Committee Against Torture, 2015). The case of Slovakia suggests that high executive willingness can produce executive human rights policy change following adverse European Court judgments, but in the absence of high capacity, regional human rights court deterrence

---

[5] See DH-DD(2016)1324 Communication from the Slovak Republic concerning the case of Koky and Others against the Slovak Republic.

may remain limited, that is, the European Court may fail to achieve its full potential to deter future human rights abuses.

Finally, consider Guatemala, a state where the executive has relatively low capacity and low willingness to respond to adverse regional human rights court judgments. On March 12, 1992, Bámaca Velásquez, a commander of one of the guerilla groups that comprised the Guatemalan National Revolutionary Unit, was captured and tortured in an armed encounter with the Guatemalan Army. Bámaca Velásquez was last seen tied to a metal bed and after a long domestic judicial battle, the body of Bámaca Velásquez was never found (Hassan, 2014). The case eventually reached the Inter-American Court and in 2000, the Inter-American Court rendered an adverse judgment in *Bámaca Velásquez v. Guatemala*, finding that the state had violated several rights in the American Convention, including the right to personal liberty (Article 7), the right to humane treatment (Article 5), and the right to life (Article 4).[6]

Guatemala represents a state of relatively low capacity and willingness. With respect to capacity, at the time of the Inter-American Court judgment (2000), the average per capita GDP in the Americas was 3,657 US dollars, while the per capita GDP in Guatemala was 1,650 US dollars. According to the United Nations' human development index, which includes three indicators of development (life expectancy at birth, education, and gross national income), Guatemala ranked 124 out of 173 countries in 2000, and the level of development has not improved significantly, as Guatemala ranked 127 out of 189 states in 2017. Moreover, Guatemala represents a country of relatively low creditworthiness, an indicator of access to outside resources. While the average institutional investor credit rating (ranging from 0 to 100) in the Americas in the year of the judgment was 37.65, Guatemala's rating was 34.05.

Turning to willingness, Guatemala has a long history of political instability, including a 36-year civil war (1960 to 1996), during which the Guatemalan military held power and over 200,000 people were killed or disappeared. A legacy of violence and harassment persisted in the years following the conflict, and according to the US State Department, the number of threats against judicial personnel, journalists, and human rights workers increased significantly in 2000, generating a heightened sense of public insecurity (US State Department, 2001). According to the World Bank (2014), the average level of political stability in the region was −0.01 in the year of the judgment, while the level of political stability in Guatemala in the same year was −0.77. Heightened levels of political stability generate few executive incentives to

---

[6] See *Bámaca Velásquez v. Guatemala*, Judgment, Inter-Am. Ct. H.R. Nov. 25, 2000.

respond to an international legal body, like the Inter-American Court with human rights policy change. Also of note, judicial power remained relatively low in Guatemala. As I argued in Chapter 2, states with strong national judiciaries are more likely to implement adverse regional court judgments, leading to a greater likelihood of executive human rights policy change. The US State Department noted that the judicial system in Guatemala was ineffective, with national judges subject to intimidation and corruption (US State Department, 2001). According to Linzer and Staton's (2015) judicial power measure, the average level of judicial power in 2000 in the region was 0.560 (on a scale from 0 to 1), while the level of judicial power in Guatemala was 0.416. The relatively low likelihood of judicial implementation of an adverse judgment provides few incentives for the executive to make human rights policy changes.

Following the judgment, the Inter-American Court ordered Guatemala to undertake a number of orders, including orders to conduct a thorough and effective investigation into the disappearance of the victim, locate the victim's remains and return them to the next of kin, publish the judgment, and adopt human rights norms and humanitarian law into domestic law, among several other orders. In monitoring compliance, the Court found that by 2007 the state had only partially complied with obligations to adopt legislative measures and enforce international standards at the domestic level. The Court also noted that the state had not yet located and exhumed the remains of the victim.[7] According to Fariss (2014), respect for physical integrity rights improved slightly following the adverse judgment, from -0.359 in 2000 to -0.248 in 2001. However, respect for physical integrity rights in Guatemala remained below the average level of respect for physical integrity rights in the Americas. That is, in the years following the 2000 adverse judgment (2001 to 2005), the average level of respect for physical integrity rights in the Americas was 0.393, while the average level of respect for physical integrity rights in Guatemala for the same time period was -0.043. Finally, according to Cingranelli, Richards, and Clay (2014), the level of disappearances in Guatemala remained the same (occasional) for several years following the adverse judgment.

The preceding examples provide an indication that capacity and willingness play an important complementary role in regional human rights court deterrence. When both are present, the likelihood of executive adoption, administration, monitoring, and enforcement of human rights policy becomes increasingly likely. When an executive has high capacity, high levels of willingness amplify the deterrent effect of regional human rights courts.

---

[7] See *Bámaca Velásquez v. Guatemala*, Monitoring Compliance with judgment, Inter-Am. Ct. H.R. Jul. 10, 2007.

Similarly, when an executive has high willingness, high capacity amplifies the deterrent effect of regional human rights courts.

7.1 EVIDENCE OF HIGH EXECUTIVE CAPACITY AND WILLINGNESS

I expect that the effect of high executive capacity will be amplified in the presence of high executive willingness (Hypothesis 8a), and I expect that the effect of high executive willingness will be amplified in the presence of high executive capacity (Hypothesis 8b). To test Hypotheses 8a and 8b, I create an interaction term including three variables: the presence of an adverse regional human rights court judgment, an indicator of executive capacity, and an indicator of executive willingness. For the adverse regional court judgment, I utilize a binary variable in which the presence of at least one adverse European or Inter-American Court judgment in a country-year takes on a value of one or zero otherwise. The adverse judgment variable is lagged 1 year.[8]

To capture executive capacity, I utilize the indicator of fiscal flexibility used in Chapter 4 for both the European and Inter-American Courts. Following Clay and DiGiuseppe (2017), I utilize the Institutional Investor Credit Rating (IIR), which spans 0 to 100, with 100 being a state that is highly creditworthy based on the anonymous opinions of experts in security and investment firms. The IIR variable is lagged 1 year. Although I examine two indicators of executive capacity in Chapter 4, feasibility of policy change and fiscal flexibility, I rely exclusively on fiscal flexibility (IIR) as an indicator of executive capacity in this analysis. There are empirical advantages to utilizing fiscal flexibility (IIR), rather than the feasibility of policy change operationalized as the type of human rights violation on which the court renders a judgment (e.g., civil and political or physical integrity), as an indicator of executive capacity. By utilizing the IIR, I can directly compare high and low levels of executive capacity (high and low levels of IIR) in the same model. Using the type of rights violation on which the court ruled (policy change feasibility) requires comparing capacity across two separate models with different dependent variables, where a model using respect for civil and political rights as a dependent variable represents high capacity, and a model using respect for physical integrity rights as a dependent variable represents low capacity.

To capture executive willingness, I rely on two indicators utilized in Chapters 5 and 6, one capturing executive willingness as a function of mass public pressure and another capturing executive willingness as a function of

---

[8] Although I do not present results using 3- and 5-year lags here, they look similar to results from models with 1-year lags.

elite pressure. For mass public pressure, I utilize the World Bank's political stability and absence of violence/terrorism measure (used in Chapter 5) (World Bank, 2014). Although I examine two indicators of mass public pressure in Chapter 5, I utilize the political stability measure in this analysis, rather than the measure of election timing (capturing executive job security) because the findings for political stability as an indicator of mass public support were consistent across the European and Inter-American Courts. I expect that when a state experiences fewer threats to the political and social order (high political stability), the executive is more willing to respond to adverse regional court judgments with human rights policy change. The political stability measure is lagged 1 year. The following equation represents a model used to assess the influence of adverse European and Inter-American Court judgments conditional on executive capacity (IIR) and willingness as a function of mass public pressure (political stability).

$$\begin{aligned} \textit{Respect for Rights}_{(t)} = & \, b_0 + b_1 \, \textit{Adverse Judgment}_{(t-1)} * \textit{Fiscal Flexibility}_{(t-1)} \\ & * \textit{Political Stability}_{(t-1)} \\ & + b_2 \, \textit{Adverse Judgment}_{(t-1)} * \textit{Fiscal Flexibility}_{(t-1)} \\ & + b_3 \, \textit{Adverse Judgment}_{(t-1)} * \textit{Political Stability}_{(t-1)} \\ & + b_4 \, \textit{Fiscal Flexibility}_{(t-1)} * \textit{Political Stability}_{(t-1)} \\ & + b_5 \, \textit{Adverse Judgment}_{(t-1)} + b_6 \, \textit{Fiscal Flexibility}_{(t-1)} \\ & + b_7 \, \textit{Political Stability}_{(t-1)} + \textit{Controls}_{(t-1)} + \varepsilon. \end{aligned}$$

As I argued in Chapter 2, executive willingness is the result of mass public pressure and elite pressure. As a result, I examine a second indicator of executive willingness as a function of elite pressure. Because the findings for elite pressure are less consistent across the European and Inter-American Court models, I utilize different indicators of elite willingness for the European and Inter-American Court models. The European Court results presented earlier in this chapter show that *economic elite* pressure is positively associated with executive human rights policy change following an adverse European Court judgment. To capture economic elite pressure in Europe, I utilize the same measure used to test Hypothesis 5, the logged 3-year moving average of foreign direct investment inflows as a percentage of GDP (World Bank, 2017). The adverse judgment variable, IIR variable (capacity), and FDI variable (willingness) are interacted. The adverse judgment variable is lagged 3 years because the results reported in Chapter 6 show that FDI as an indicator of executive willingness is most effective in generating executive incentives to make human rights policy changes 3 years following an adverse European Court judgment. The following equation represents the model used to assess

7.1 Evidence of High Executive Capacity

the influence of adverse European Court judgments conditional on executive capacity (IIR) and willingness as a function of economic elite pressure (FDI inflows as a percentage of GDP).

$$\begin{aligned}
\text{Respect for Rights}_{(t)} = {} & b_0 + b_1 \, \text{Adverse Judgment}_{(t-3)} * \text{Fiscal Flexibility}_{(t-1)} \\
& * \text{FDI}_{\text{(moving average in } t)} \\
& + b_2 \, \text{Adverse Judgment}_{(t-3)} * \text{Fiscal Flexibility}_{(t-1)} \\
& + b_3 \, \text{Adverse Judgment}_{(t-3)} * \text{FDI}_{\text{(moving average in } t)} \\
& + b_4 \, \text{Fiscal Flexibility}_{(t-1)} * \text{FDI}_{\text{(moving average in } t)} \\
& + b_5 \, \text{Adverse Judgment}_{(t-3)} + b_6 \, \text{Fiscal Flexibility}_{(t-1)} \\
& + b_7 \, \text{FDI}_{\text{(moving average in } t)} + \text{Controls}_{(t-1)} + \varepsilon.
\end{aligned}$$

For the Inter-American Court model, I utilize an indicator of executive willingness based on political elite pressure, specifically pressure from the national judiciary. The Inter-American Court results presented in Chapter 6 show that political elite pressure (from national judges) is positively associated with human rights policy change following adverse Inter-American Court judgments. I utilize the measure of judicial power used to test Hypothesis 6, created by Linzer and Staton (2015), whereby judicial power means judges engage in independent and autonomous decision making. The adverse judgment variable, IIR variable, and judicial power variable are interacted. The adverse judgment variable is lagged one year because the results reported in Chapter 6 show that judicial power as an indicator of executive willingness is effective in generating executive incentives to make human rights policy changes 1, 3, and 5 years following an adverse Inter-American Court judgment. Results from models where the adverse judgment variable is lagged 3 and 5 years look similar to those reported below. The following equation displays the model used to examine the influence of adverse Inter-American Court judgments conditional on executive capacity (IIR) and willingness as a function of political elite pressure (judicial power).

$$\begin{aligned}
\text{Respect for Rights}_{(t)} = {} & b_0 + b_1 \, \text{Adverse Judgment}_{(t-1)} * \text{Fiscal Flexibility}_{(t-1)} \\
& * \text{Judicial Power}_{(t-1)} \\
& + b_2 \, \text{Adverse Judgment}_{(t-1)} * \text{Fiscal Flexibility}_{(t-1)} \\
& + b_3 \, \text{Adverse Judgment}_{(t-1)} * \text{Judicial Power}_{(t-1)} \\
& + b_4 \, \text{Fiscal Flexibility}_{(t-1)} * \text{Judicial Power}_{(t-1)} \\
& + b_5 \, \text{Adverse Judgment}_{(t-1)} + b_6 \, \text{Fiscal Flexibility}_{(t-1)} \\
& + b_7 \, \text{Judicial Power}_{(t-1)} + \text{Controls}_{(t-1)} + \varepsilon.
\end{aligned}$$

Like the models estimated in the preceding chapters, I utilize linear regression models with random intercepts and standard errors clustered on country. A full list of control variables and full model results are displayed in Appendix E.

7.1.1 Regional Court Deterrence: The Effect of Executive Capacity in the Presence of High/Low Willingness (Hypothesis 8a)

Hypothesis 8a stipulates that adverse regional court judgments are associated with greater respect for rights as executive capacity grows, but this effect is amplified as executive willingness grows. Figure 7.1 displays the predicted level of respect for rights following adverse regional court judgments across executive capacity at high and low levels of executive willingness. To generate the figure, all other variables in the model are set to their mean or mode.

The first row of Figure 7.1 displays the influence of adverse European Court judgments across capacity using two indicators of executive willingness, mass public pressure (upper-left panel) and economic elite pressure (upper-right panel). Beginning with the results for Hypothesis 8a using mass public pressure as an indicator of executive willingness (upper-left panel of Figure 7.1), I generate the predicted level of respect for rights for adverse judgment recipients across values of fiscal flexibility (capacity) when political stability (willingness) is low (-2) and when political stability is high (2). Two conclusions about European Court deterrence can be drawn from the results presented in the upper-left panel of Figure 7.1. First, the results show that when executive capacity is low (20), the predicted level of respect for rights is -0.338 when executive willingness is low. However, at low levels of capacity, the predicted level of respect for rights increases to 1.63 when executive willingness is high. These results indicate that a willing European executive (facing few threats to the political and social order) is substantially more likely to make human rights policy change, even when executive capacity is low. Second, the upper-left panel of Figure 7.1 shows that when executive capacity is high (IIR of 90), the predicted level of respect for rights is -0.961 when executive willingness is low (political stability value of -2), but the predicted level of respect for rights increases to 3.14 when executive willingness is high (political stability of 2). The results in the upper-left panel of Figure 7.1 show that human rights policy change following an adverse European Court judgment is most likely to occur when executive capacity and willingness are high. However, executive willingness to make human rights policy change following adverse European Court judgments is particularly important for European Court deterrence, as willing executives with low capacity are more

7.1 *Evidence of High Executive Capacity*

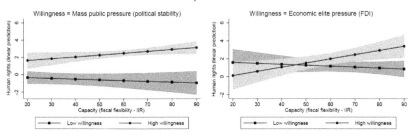

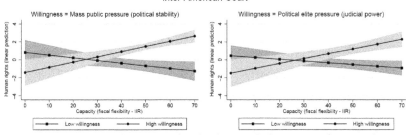

FIGURE 7.1. Testing Hypothesis 8a: Predicted influence of adverse regional court judgments across executive capacity for high and low levels of executive willingness

Notes: The upper-left panel of Figure 7.1 shows the predicted level of respect for rights 1 year post–European Court judgment across values of executive capacity (fiscal flexibility) when executive willingness (political stability) is low (value of −2) and when executive willingness is high (value of 2) for adverse European Court judgment recipients. The upper-right panel of Figure 7.1 shows the predicted level of respect for rights 3 years post–European Court judgment across values of executive capacity (fiscal flexibility) when executive willingness (logged foreign direct investment) is low (value of −4) and when executive willingness is high (value of 6) for adverse European Court judgment recipients. The lower-left panel of Figure 7.1 shows the predicted level of respect for rights 1 year post–Inter-American Court judgment across values of executive capacity (fiscal flexibility) when executive willingness (political stability) is low (value of −2.5) and when executive willingness is high (value of 1.5) for adverse Inter-American Court judgment recipients. The lower-right panel of Figure 7.1 shows the predicted level of respect for rights 1 year post–Inter-American Court judgment across values of executive capacity (fiscal flexibility) when executive willingness (judicial power) is low (value of 0.1) and when executive willingness is high (value of 0.9) for adverse Inter-American Court judgment recipients.

likely to adopt human rights policy changes than unwilling executives of low capacity.

As a second test of Hypothesis 8a for the European Court, the upper-right panel of Figure 7.1 displays the influence of adverse European Court judgments across executive capacity (fiscal flexibility) at high and low levels of executive willingness, in which willingness is conceptualized as economic elite pressure (measured as logged foreign direct investment 3 years postjudgment). To generate the predicted values in the upper-right panel of

Figure 7.1, I estimate the predicted level of respect for rights for adverse judgment recipients across values of fiscal flexibility (capacity) when logged foreign direct investment (willingness) is low (−4) and when logged FDI is high (6). All other values in the model are set to their mean or mode.

The upper-right panel shows that at high levels of executive capacity (value of 90 on the IIR measure), the predicted level of respect for rights is 3.40 when executive willingness is high (value of 6 for logged FDI), while the predicted level of respect for rights is only 0.871 when executive willingness is low (value of −4 for logged FDI) and the difference is statistically significant. However, when executive capacity is low (value of 20 on the IIR measure), there is no statistically significant difference in the level of respect for rights at high and low values of executive willingness. The results indicate that for states that are highly incapable of making human rights policy change, policy change is unlikely regardless of the level of executive willingness (as a function of economic elite pressure).

While the top row of Figure 7.1 presents the results from a hypothesis test of Hypothesis 8a for the European Court, the bottom row presents results from a hypothesis test of Hypothesis 8a for the Inter-American Court. The bottom row of Figure 7.1 displays the predicted level of respect for rights for adverse Inter-American Court judgment recipients across values of executive capacity at high and low levels of executive willingness due to mass public pressure (bottom left panel) and due to political elite pressure (bottom right panel). To generate the values in the lower-left panel of Figure 7.1, I examine the predicted level of respect for rights for adverse Inter-American Court judgment recipients across values of executive capacity (fiscal flexibility) when executive willingness (political stability) is low (−2.5) and when executive willingness (political stability) is high (1.5). All other variables in the model are set to their mean or mode. The results show that at high levels of executive capacity, the predicted level of respect for rights is 2.65 when executive willingness is high (value of 1.5 on political stability), but declines to −1.25 when executive willingness is low (value of −2.5 on political stability). At low levels of executive capacity, there is no statistically significant difference in the predicted level of respect for rights at high and low values of executive willingness. This means that following adverse Inter-American Court judgments, highly incapable executives have a low likelihood of human rights policy changes regardless of the level of executive willingness (as a function of mass public pressure). Even a willing executive is unlikely to make human rights policy change following an adverse Inter-American Court judgment if the executive does not have the capacity to do so.

7.1 Evidence of High Executive Capacity

As a second test of Hypothesis 8a in the Inter-American Court context, the bottom right panel of Figure 7.1 shows the influence of adverse Inter-American Court judgments across capacity for high and low values of executive willingness, measured as political elite pressure (judicial power). The predicted values in the lower-right panel of Figure 7.1 are generated by estimating the predicted level of respect for rights for adverse judgment recipients across fiscal flexibility (capacity) when judicial power is low (0.1) and when judicial power is high (0.9). The results show that 1 year following an adverse Inter-American Court judgment, the predicted level of respect for rights is 2.30 when executive capacity is high (70 on the IIR measure) and when executive willingness is high (value of 0.9 on judicial power measure). Following adverse Inter-American Court judgments, the predicted level of respect for rights declines to −0.923 when executive capacity is high (70 on IIR measure) and executive willingness is low (value of 0.1 on judicial power measure). This means that despite the presence of a high-capacity executive, adverse Inter-American Court judgments are less likely to deter future human rights abuses when the executive is unwilling than when the executive is willing. The results also show that when executive capacity is low (0 to 10 on the IIR measure), there is no statistically significant difference in the predicted level of respect for rights regardless of the level of executive willingness. For incapable executives, even a high degree of willingness is unlikely to generate human rights policy changes following an adverse Inter-American Court judgment.

7.1.2 Regional Court Deterrence: The Effect of Executive Willingness in the Presence of High/Low Capacity (Hypothesis 8b)

In Hypothesis 8b, I posit that adverse regional court judgments are associated with greater respect for rights as executive willingness grows, but this effect is amplified in the presence of high executive capacity. Figure 7.2 shows the predicted level of respect for rights following adverse regional court judgments across executive willingness at high and low levels of executive capacity. Like Figure 7.1, the predictions are generated by setting all other variables to their mean or mode. The first row of Figure 7.2 shows the extent to which the European Court deters future human rights abuses. In the upper-left panel, I show the predicted level of respect for rights across executive willingness as a function of mass public pressure (political stability) when executive capacity is low (IIR value of 20) and when executive capacity is high (IIR value of 90) following adverse European Court judgments. The results reported in the upper-left panel indicate that the predicted level of respect for rights following

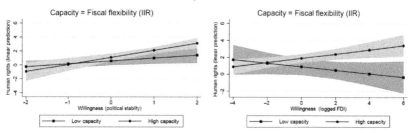
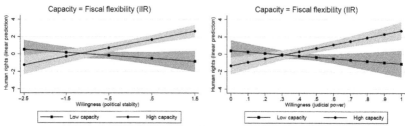

FIGURE 7.2. Testing Hypothesis 8b: Predicted influence of adverse regional court judgments across executive willingness for high and low levels of executive capacity

Notes: The upper-left panel of Figure 7.2 shows the predicted level of respect for rights 1 year post–European Court judgment across values of executive willingness (political stability) when executive capacity is low (value of 20) and when executive capacity is high (value of 90) for adverse European Court judgment recipients. The upper-right panel of Figure 7.2 displays the predicted level of respect for rights 3 years post–European Court judgment across values of executive willingness (logged foreign direct investment) when executive capacity (fiscal flexibility) is low (value of 20) and when executive capacity is high (value of 90) for adverse European Court judgment recipients. The lower-left panel of Figure 7.2 shows the predicted level of respect for rights 1 year post–Inter-American Court judgment across values of executive willingness (political stability) when executive capacity is low (value of 10) and when executive capacity is high (value of 70) for adverse Inter-American Court judgment recipients. The bottom right panel of Figure 7.2 displays the predicted level of respect for rights 1 year post–Inter-American Court judgment across values of executive willingness (judicial power) when executive capacity (fiscal flexibility) is low (value of 10) and when executive capacity is high (value of 70) for adverse Inter-American Court judgment recipients.

adverse European Court judgments is highest at high values of executive capacity and willingness. However, at high levels of executive willingness, the predicted estimates for high and low capacity states are not statistically different from one another. This provides an indication that executive willingness is particularly important for European Court deterrence. Following adverse European Court judgments, as long as the executive is willing as a result of mass public pressure, the likelihood of human rights policy change grows, regardless of the level of executive capacity.

7.1 Evidence of High Executive Capacity

The upper-right panel displays results from another test of Hypothesis 8b in the context of the European Court. More specifically, the upper-right panel shows the predicted level of respect for rights 3 years post–European Court judgment across values of executive willingness as a function of economic elite pressure (measured as logged FDI) when executive capacity (fiscal flexibility) is low (IIR value of 20) and when executive capacity is high (IIR value of 90). The results show that there is no statistically significant difference in the predicted level of respect for rights for low-capacity and high-capacity states at low levels of executive willingness (economic elite pressure). This suggests that when the executive is unwilling as a result of economic elite pressure, even highly capable executives are unlikely to adopt human rights policy. However, when an executive is willing (FDI inflows are high), executive capacity significantly amplifies the effect of executive willingness. That is, at high levels of executive willingness (6), the predicted level of respect for rights for states with low capacity (value of 20 on the IIR variable) is −0.350; however, for states with high capacity (value of 90 on the IIR variable), the predicted level of respect for rights rises to 3.40. Taken together, the results presented in the first row of Figure 7.2 show that European Court deterrence is more likely when the executive is highly willing to make human rights policy changes and the presence of a high capacity executive amplifies the effect of high executive willingness, but the amplified effect of capacity is greater when executive willingness is a function of economic elite pressure than when executive willingness is a function of mass public pressure.

Turning to the Inter-American Court, the bottom row of Figure 7.2 shows results from a test of Hypothesis 8b. More specifically, the bottom-left panel displays the predicted level of respect for rights following an adverse Inter-American Court judgment across executive willingness, conceptualized as mass public pressure (political stability) when executive capacity is low (IIR value of 10) and when executive capacity is high (IIR value of 70). Following an adverse Inter-American Court judgment, the predicted level of respect for rights is 2.65 when executive willingness is high (political stability value of 1.5) and when executive capacity is high (70 on IIR measure). However, despite high executive willingness, the predicted level of respect for rights declines to −0.83 when executive capacity is low (IIR value of 10), which means that capacity is particularly important for Inter-American Court deterrence. The results in the lower-left panel of Figure 7.2 also show that when executive willingness is low, there is no statistically significant difference across low- and high-capacity states. This suggests that even capable executives are unlikely to make human rights policy changes when executive willingness is low, likely because there are few political incentives to do so. The results indicate that executive willingness to make human rights policy changes in response to adverse Inter-American Court judgments is amplified by executive capacity.

As an additional test of Hypothesis 8b in the Inter-American Court context, the bottom-right panel of Figure 7.2 shows the influence of adverse Inter-American Court judgments on respect for rights across values of executive willingness as a function of political elite pressure (judicial power) 1 year postjudgment when executive capacity is low (IIR value of 10) and when executive capacity is high (IIR value of 70). The results in the lower-right panel show that at low levels of executive willingness (judicial power), there is no statistically significant difference in the predicted level of respect for rights for low- and high-capacity states. This means that absent executive willingness as a result of political elite pressure, the even high-capacity executives are unlikely to engage in human rights policy changes. On the other hand, when the executive is willing (judicial power is high), executive capacity significantly amplifies the effect of executive willingness. At high levels of executive willingness (0.9 on the judicial power measure), the predicted level of respect for rights for states with low capacity is −0.948; however, the predicted level of respect for rights increases to 2.30 when executive capacity is high. In the Americas, the results show that highly willing executives are most likely to make human rights policy change when the executive also has high capacity as a result of both mass public pressure and political elite pressure.

Taken together, the results show that regional human rights court deterrence is more likely when the executive is both capable and willing. In other words, following adverse European or Inter-American Court judgments, respect for rights is predicted to be at its highest level when the executive is both capable and willing. Generally, highly incapable executives are unlikely to make human rights policy changes following adverse regional court judgments, even when the executive is willing. Similarly, highly unwilling executives are unlikely to make human rights policy changes following adverse regional court judgments even when the executive is capable. However, in the European context, highly willing executives are likely to make human rights policy changes following adverse regional European Court judgments regardless of the level of executive capacity, an indication that executive willingness may be more important than executive capacity in the European context.

7.1.3 Robustness Tests: Examining Change in Respect for Rights

As robustness tests, I estimate additional models predicting the influence of adverse regional human rights court judgments, conditional on executive capacity and willingness, on the change in respect for physical integrity rights using changes in the Cingranelli, Richards, and Clay (2014) physical integrity rights index as the dependent variable. I use the same model as that used to generate the predictions in the upper-left panels of Figures 7.1 and 7.2, in which I interact adverse regional court judgments, executive capacity (fiscal flexibility), and executive willingness as a function of mass public pressure (political stability). Substantive results are reported in Table E.3 in the Appendix.

The results lend additional support to the hypothesis, particularly noting the importance of executive willingness (relative to executive capacity) in European Court deterrence. An adverse European Court judgment is associated with greater changes in respect for rights when executive capacity and willingness are high. More specifically, an adverse European Court judgment is associated with a 0.894 change in respect for physical integrity rights (on a scale ranging from −4 to +3) from the year of the judgment to 3 years postjudgment when the executive has high capacity (state is creditworthy − IIR of 90) and is highly willing (political stability is high − 2 on the political stability and absence of violence measure). However, the predicted change drops to 0.089 when executive capacity becomes low (10 on the IIR measure) and drops to −1.61 when executive willingness becomes low (−2 on the political stability and absence of violence measure). These results indicate the relative importance of executive willingness in the European Court context. High executive willingness and low capacity generate a positive, albeit small, change in respect for physical integrity rights following an adverse European Court judgment. However, even when an executive has high capacity, human rights practices are unlikely to positively change when executive willingness is low. Perhaps because executive capacity is higher, on average, in Europe than other parts of the world, capacity limitations are less problematic for regional court deterrence in Europe. The results also show that when both capacity and willingness are low, the change is also predicted to be negative, but the 90 percent confidence intervals around the estimate for states with incapable and unwilling executives is relatively wide, an indication that cases of low levels of executive capacity and willingness are less prevalent in the European context.

Turning to the Inter-American Court, as a robustness test, I estimate an additional model predicting the influence of adverse Inter-American Court judgments, conditional on executive capacity and willingness, on changes in respect for physical integrity rights, where the dependent variable represents changes in the Cingranelli, Richards, and Clay (2014) physical integrity rights index. I utilize the same model as that used to produce the results in the bottom-left panels of Figures 7.1 and 7.2. Table E.3 in the Appendix displays substantive results from this model, and the results lend support for Hypotheses 8a and 8b. An adverse Inter-American Court judgment is associated with a 3.69 change in respect for physical integrity rights (on a scale ranging from −4 to +6) from the year of the judgment to 3 years postjudgment when executive capacity is high (IIR value of 60) and when executive willingness is high (political stability value of 1.5). When executive capacity or willingness are low, the predicted change in respect for physical integrity rights declines. When executive willingness declines (political stability value of −2.5), the predicted change in respect for physical integrity rights is −2.59 3 years postjudgment, and when executive capacity declines (IIR value of 20), the predicted change in respect for physical integrity rights becomes −1.68. While in Europe, executive willingness is particularly important for regional court deterrence, in the Americas, both executive capacity and willingness play a key role in regional court deterrence. Notably, Table E.3 shows that when executive capacity and willingness are both low, the confidence intervals are fairly wide, indicating a high degree of uncertainty in the likelihood of regional court deterrence when an executive is neither capable nor willing to engage in human rights policy change.

7.2 CONCLUSION

In this chapter I show that executive capacity and willingness complement one another in generating executive human rights policy change following adverse regional court judgments. Following an adverse European Court judgment, in the face of mass public pressure, executive human rights policy change is likely regardless of the level of executive capacity. However, high-capacity European executives are more willing to engage in human rights policy change as a result of economic elite pressure. Moreover, incapable executives in Europe are unlikely to engage in human rights policy changes following adverse European Court judgments regardless of the level of executive willingness as a result of economic elite pressure. Perhaps incapable executives, with little access to outside resources, attract lower levels of FDI and therefore are less vulnerable to economic elite pressure.

Following adverse Inter-American Court judgments, greater executive capacity and willingness are likely to be associated with significantly higher levels of respect for rights. Executives in the Americas are significantly more likely to engage in human rights policy changes following an adverse Inter-American Court judgment when the executive is highly willing as a result of mass public pressure and political elite pressure, and this effect grows when the executive has high capacity. Similarly, following an adverse

Inter-American Court judgment, highly capable executives are more likely to make human rights policy changes when the executive is also highly willing. Also of note, highly incapable executives are unlikely to make human rights policy changes following adverse Inter-American Court judgments regardless of the level of executive willingness (generated by mass public pressure or political elite pressure). Similarly, highly unwilling executives (those experiencing little public or political elite pressure) are unlikely to make human rights policy changes following an adverse Inter-American Court judgment regardless of the level of executive capacity.

In this book, I assessed the extent to which adverse regional human rights court judgments deter future human rights abuses. I focused on the *capacity* and *willingness* of the executive to make comprehensive policy changes following an adverse regional human rights court judgment. In the following chapter, I conclude by summarizing the key findings of the book, drawing important inferences about the relative importance of capacity and willingness, making comparisons across Europe and the Americas, and discussing the influence of regional human rights courts in the context of the international human rights regime.

8

Conclusion

Deterrence is an essential component of regional human rights court effectiveness. Absent deterrence, regional human rights courts fail to fulfill a key mandate: preventing similar human rights abuses from occurring in the future. Improved respect for human rights following adverse regional human rights court judgments captures the broad effectiveness of the court and, arguably, a primary objective of regional courts. As a result, in this book, I focused on explaining regional court deterrence.

Regional human rights courts, like international law more generally, suffer from significant enforcement challenges. Although regional courts represent supranational judicial bodies, they do not have the authority to enforce legal commitments made by states. That is, despite being charged with a mandate to judge, regional courts cannot ensure that states engage in the policy changes necessary to give judgments meaning. As a result, significant variation exists in the extent to which regional human rights courts deter future human rights abuses, and explaining variation in regional court deterrence requires looking to domestic politics.

In this book, I argued that understanding regional court deterrence requires understanding executive capacity and willingness to make human rights policy changes postjudgment. Executive capacity, including the feasibility of making policy changes and access to outside resources, directly impacts the executive's ability to engage in policy change. Executive willingness, including pressure from the mass public and elites (economic and political), influences the executive's interest in engaging in human rights policy changes following adverse regional court judgments.

In this concluding chapter, I first provide a brief summary of my main argument and findings. I then suggest possible explanations for variation in the findings across Europe and the Americas. Next, I turn to the role of regional human rights courts in the international human rights regime. In doing so,

I consider questions like: How do regional human rights courts fit into the ever-expanding international human rights regime? Also, what implications do the findings of this book suggest for the design of international and regional human rights institutions? Finally, I turn to additional research questions raised by the findings of this book, and I suggest several paths for future research on regional courts.

8.1 MAIN ARGUMENT AND FINDINGS: SUMMARY

As a result of international enforcement challenges (e.g., Guzman, 2008; Hafner-Burton, 2013), regional human rights court deterrence is uneven across states. Outside of reputational concerns, international human rights law generally does not place significant costs on states, leading several scholars to conclude that international human rights law has little influence on state behavior (e.g., Posner, 2014). Yet, scholars have noted that international human rights law can be enforced domestically (e.g., Powell and Staton, 2009; Simmons, 2009; Conrad and Ritter, 2013; Hillebrecht, 2014; Lupu, 2015). In this book, I argue that following adverse regional human rights court judgments, the executive plays a key role in ensuring human rights policy changes, including the adoption, administration, monitoring, and enforcement of human rights policy. However, because human rights policy change is costly, both materially and politically, the executive may be reluctant to make such policy changes. Materially, the executive pays costs related to enforcing new policies, for example. Politically, adopting and enforcing human rights policy restricts the executive's ability to rely on repressive policies in the future, particularly during periods of time when executive political survival is threatened and the executive has an interest in repression. Given these costs, I claim that the executive is more likely to engage in human rights policy changes following an adverse judgment when the executive has the *capacity* and *willingness* to make such changes.

Beginning with executive capacity, I highlight two ways that capacity limitations can manifest following an adverse judgment. First, I argue that the executive has greater capacity to respond to some human rights abuses than others. Protecting civil and political rights is more feasible because civil and political rights are more directly within the executive's control than physical integrity rights abuses. The protection of civil and political rights often involves bureaucratic and administrative reforms undertaken directly by the executive. Protecting physical integrity rights, on the other hand, often involves delegation of policy to various state agents responsible for carrying out policy. As a result, the executive must consistently and comprehensively monitor state agents to ensure that physical integrity rights are protected, which often requires substantial resource expenditure. I show that adverse civil and political rights judgments are more strongly associated with human rights gains postjudgment than physical integrity rights judgments in both Europe and the Americas.

In addition to the feasibility of policy change, capacity limitations manifest in the executive's access to resources. Because responding to adverse judgments with human rights policy change requires often unexpected resource expenditure, the executive may need to reallocate resources from the provision of other public goods to ensuring rights protection. I maintain that states with greater access to outside resources, or those that are more fiscally flexible, have greater capacity to respond to adverse judgments with human rights policy change. I demonstrate that adverse judgments are positively related to respect for rights as the state's fiscal flexibility or creditworthiness grows. The findings show that access to outside resources allows executives to respond more promptly to adverse judgments with human rights policy change.

Turning to willingness, I contend that the executive has a greater interest in responding to adverse judgments with human rights policy change when the executive faces pressure to make such changes. Pressure to adopt and implement human rights policy to align with the regional court comes from two sets of actors, including the mass public and elites (foreign economic and domestic political). With respect to the former, the executive is more likely to experience mass public pressure when executive job security is threatened.

Executive job security is more likely to be threatened prior to an election, particularly a competitive election. I show that election timing plays a role in Inter-American Court deterrence. I also demonstrate that adverse European Court judgments are more likely to deter when they occur 2 years prior to a competitive election, as opposed to a noncompetitive election.

Although mass public pressure can generate pressure on the executive to adopt, administer, monitor, and enforce human rights policy following an adverse regional court judgment, the mass public can also generate competing pressure on the executive to not respond with human rights policy change. In the presence of threats to the political and social order, the mass public often prefers the executive utilize repressive policies in the name of national security and may even support human rights abuses of particular groups in society perceived as threatening. I establish that adverse judgments are associated with lower levels of respect for rights when political stability is relatively low and greater respect for rights when political stability is relatively high.

Elites also place pressure on the executive to engage in human rights policy change. I propose that there are two sets of elites that pressure the executive to adopt and implement human rights policy in response to adverse regional court judgments: foreign economic elites and domestic political elites. Foreign economic elites consist of foreign investors and lenders. Foreign investors have an interest in strong human rights protections as an indication of a stable investment climate. Foreign lenders, particularly international organizations with an interest in development, often condition foreign loans and aid on human rights practices, as strong human rights protections signal the presence of good governance practices, increasing the likelihood of sustainable development. The data indicate that adverse regional court judgments are associated with greater respect for rights in states that are more vulnerable to a loss of economic benefits, or those with larger foreign direct investment inflows.

In addition to foreign economic elites, domestic political elites also play an important role in placing pressure on the executive to adopt, administer, monitor, and enforce human rights policy following adverse regional court judgments. Regional courts often charge the national judiciary with tasks such as investigating human rights violations, identifying perpetrators, and imposing punishment for rights abuses. Regional courts also often require the national legislature to adopt, amend, or repeal legislation. I posit that when the executive expects national judicial or legislative implementation of regional court orders, the executive is more likely to adopt, administer, monitor, and enforce human rights policy because in the face of judicial and legislative action the executive seeks to avoid blame for persistent human rights policy failures. I maintain that the executive is more likely to expect national judicial implementation when the national judiciary is powerful because judicial decision making is free from external political influence, and national judicial decisions are more likely to be implemented by the government. I also expect that the executive is more likely to expect national legislative implementation when there is a relatively large legislative opposition with preferences that differ from the executive because the legislative opposition utilizes information contained in adverse regional court judgments as a means to pursue legislative changes.

I find evidence that national judicial power influences executive expectation of national judicial implementation and therefore the likelihood of executive adoption, administration, monitoring, and enforcement of human rights policy. Although national judicial power is important for judicial implementation in both Europe and the Americas, the importance of the national judiciary in regional court deterrence is particularly important in the Americas. With respect to the national legislature, I find limited support for the role of the legislative opposition in Europe. In the Americas, I find that the legislative opposition is significantly associated with respect for rights following an adverse

Inter-American Court judgment, but this finding is only significant in the presence of two or more adverse judgments in a given year.

Finally, in this book, I show that the combination of high executive capacity and high executive willingness is associated with the greatest predicted level of respect for human rights following adverse regional court judgments. I posit that in states with high-capacity executives, regional human rights court effectiveness is amplified when the executive is highly willing. Similarly, I posit that for states with highly willing executives, regional human rights court effectiveness is amplified when the executive is also highly capable. I find support for these expectations in the Americas. In Europe, I find that following an adverse European Court judgment, highly willing executives as a result of mass public pressure (political stability) are more willing to engage in human rights policy changes regardless of the level of executive capacity. However, I also find that highly willing executives as a result of economic elite pressure are more likely to engage in human rights policy changes when the executive is also highly capable. Generally, the results suggest that regional court deterrence is more likely when the executive is highly capable and willing. The results also suggest some differences across Europe and the Americas. In the following section, I discuss differences in the findings across the two regions and suggest some reasons for this variation.

8.2 COMPARING REGIONAL COURTS IN EUROPE AND THE AMERICAS

Adopting a comparative approach provides important insights for scholars and policymakers alike. The European and Inter-American Courts of Human Rights differ in several important ways, but the broad mandate and enforcement challenges of each court are similar. In Chapter 2, I generated similar expectations for the European and Inter-American Courts of Human Rights. That is, I expected both regional courts to deter future human rights abuses under the same conditions, and the results show that there are several conditions under which both regional human rights courts similarly deter future human rights abuses in Europe and the Americas. That said, the results also show that there are several differences across Europe and the Americas. Table 8.1 summarizes the findings from Chapters 4–7, noting the similarities and differences in findings across courts. The first column of Table 8.1 displays the hypotheses tested in Chapters 4–7. The second and fourth columns indicate whether the hypothesis was supported in the European and Inter-American contexts (with a ✓). The third and fifth columns indicate whether the hypothesis was partially or conditionally supported in

8.2 Comparing Courts in Europe and the Americas

TABLE 8.1. *Summary of findings in Europe and Americas*

Hypothesis	European Court		Inter-American Court	
	Support	Conditional support	Support	Conditional support
Capacity				
1: Feasibility of policy change	✓		✓	
2: Fiscal flexibility	✓		✓	
Willingness (mass public pressure)				
3: Executive job security		✓		✓
4: Threats to political and social order	✓		✓	
Willingness (elite pressure)				
5: Foreign economic elites		✓		✓
6: Political elites – judiciary		✓	✓	
7: Political elites – legislature		✓		✓
Capacity and willingness				
8a/8b: Fiscal flexibility*Political/social threats	–	–	✓	
8b/8b: Fiscal flexibility*Elites	✓		✓	

Notes: Table 8.1 displays a summary of results for each hypothesis. A check mark (✓) indicates support or conditional support for the hypothesis, while a dash (–) indicates no support for the hypothesis. A check mark in columns 2 and 4 indicates support for the hypothesis. A check mark in columns 3 and 5 indicates conditional support for the hypothesis. Conditional support for a hypothesis may indicate variation in the influence of adverse judgments on respect for rights at different periods in time postjudgment or support for only the disaggregated results (adverse judgment related to a specific type of human rights abuse [e.g., judgment finding violation of convention article related to torture] on respect for a specific type of rights abuse [e.g., torture]).

the European or Inter-American context (with a ✓). A dash (–) is used to indicate lack of support for a hypothesis in the European or Inter-American context.

Several hypotheses are consistently supported across Europe and the Americas. First, I argue and find that executives in both Europe and the Americas are more likely to make human rights policy changes that are more feasible following adverse regional human rights court judgments, such as civil and political rights changes, as opposed to physical integrity rights changes. Second, executives have greater capacity to make human rights policy changes following adverse judgments in both Europe and the Americas when the executive has greater fiscal flexibility, or when the state is more creditworthy. Finally, the results show that in Europe and the Americas, when executives face significant threats to the political and social order, they are less willing to make human rights policy changes following adverse regional court judgments.

However, for several other hypotheses, the results show variation across Europe and the Americas. I find variation in the influence of adverse judgments on respect for rights at different periods in time postjudgment. That is, executive capacity and willingness sometimes generate an executive response in the year following an adverse judgment, and sometimes executive human rights policy changes take several years to observe postjudgment. For several other hypotheses, I find that adverse judgments related to physical integrity rights are positively related to respect for physical integrity rights, but uncertainty in the estimates suggests that we should treat these results with some caution. Though, for several of these hypotheses, when I consider the influence of an adverse judgment related to a specific type of human rights abuse (e.g., judgment finding violation of convention article related to torture) on respect for a specific type of rights abuse (e.g., torture), there is stronger support for the hypothesis. That is, when I disaggregate adverse judgments and physical integrity rights, I observe stronger results.

I suggest that variation in findings across regions can be explained by either differences in domestic politics across Europe and the Americas and/or institutional design differences across the European and Inter-American Courts. Beginning with differences in domestic politics across Europe and the Americas, the European and Inter-American Courts emerged and developed under vastly different social and political contexts, as noted briefly in Chapter 3. Formed in 1950 following the atrocities and massive human rights violations of the Second World War, the European Court was an institution designed to ensure international human rights guarantees. The Western European countries responsible for the establishment of the Council of Europe (the constitutive body of the European Convention) included established liberal democracies with strong domestic institutional commitments to the rule of law (Helfer and Slaughter, 1997, 276). Strong and independent rule of law institutions were a favorable precondition for European state's receptiveness to European Court of Human Rights litigation (Helfer and Slaughter, 1997, 333–334).

The establishment of the Inter-American Court took place in a much different social and political environment. Formed in 1979, the Inter-American Court faced a region characterized by primarily authoritarian regimes enmeshed in systematic and violent human rights violations, including widespread extrajudicial killings, political imprisonment, torture, and forced disappearances committed by state agents with impunity. Military dictatorships governed most of Central and South America, leaving Costa Rica, Venezuela, Colombia, and Peru as the few states willing to support the Inter-American Commission on Human Rights (Buergenthal, 2005).

Most states in the Americas strongly opposed the establishment of a regional institution working for the protection of human rights. Throughout the 1980s, the political landscape in the Americas changed, as democratic states began to replace authoritarian regimes. Still, democratic consolidation in many states in the Americas generally lags behind that of states in Europe, and the persistence of nondemocratic legacies and large-scale poverty and economic inequality in the Americas means that democratic institutions and human rights norms are not fully entrenched in this region (Buergenthal, 1980, 156).

Turning to institutional design, there are several key differences in the practice and procedures of the European and Inter-American Courts of Human Rights that explain some of the variation in the findings across regions. One key difference involves each Court's mechanisms for monitoring the state postjudgment. The European Court relies on states to conceive of steps to remedy the human rights abuse, while the Inter-American Court gives the state a list of orders designed to remedy the abuse. Notably, the Committee of Ministers of the European Court will give states more specific steps if the Committee does not find state actions and efforts to be sufficient. Initially, though, European states have discretion to decide how to respond. The Inter-American Court, on the other hand, specifies the steps a state must take to comply immediately following an adverse judgment, and the Court follows up directly with the state periodically, publishing reports noting state compliance with specific orders.

Variation in domestic politics and institutional design of regional courts explains several of the divergent findings in Europe and the Americas. Beginning with the executive job security hypothesis (Hypothesis 3), the strength of domestic institutions in Europe and the Americas sheds some light on the different findings across regions. I find adverse Inter-American Court judgments are associated with higher respect for rights when the executive is insecure in office due to an upcoming election. However, executive job security as a result of the presence of an upcoming election has little influence on regional human rights court deterrence in Europe. Rather, adverse European Court judgments are associated with greater respect for rights when the executive is insecure in office due to an upcoming *competitive* election.

In the Americas, human rights norms are relatively less entrenched, and states in the region have a lengthy legacy of physical integrity abuses. Ending and preventing widespread physical integrity abuses in the future requires significant structural and systemic policy changes. As a result of the need for more extensive structural and systemic changes in the Americas than Europe, I suggest that adverse Inter-American Court judgments involving physical integrity abuses are likely more salient in the preelectoral period than adverse judgments in the preelectoral period in Europe. That is, voters in the Americas are more likely to look to candidate platforms and proposed policies related to improving human rights, particularly abuses that have remained prevalent since the judgment. For electoral challengers, publicizing human rights abuses of past regimes can be used as strategy on the campaign trail to secure more voter support. In the Americas, the election itself provides a mechanism to incorporate campaign promises related to human rights policy.

In Europe, however, the election itself may not provide a mechanism through which to expose incumbents for prior abuses of rights, particularly if such abuses were relatively minor compared to other policy blunders. When an election is competitive, though, challengers are likely to seek out and shed light on all incumbent policy failures. As a result, in expectation of a competitive election, incumbents have an interest in human rights policy changes consistent with international human rights law in an effort to avoid criticism for human rights policy failures in the run-up to the competitive election. Adverse judgments prior to competitive elections in Europe create the incentives necessary for executives to engage in human rights policy changes, as incumbents recognize the importance of leveraging large and important voting blocs, like those most susceptible to human rights abuses in the future.

With respect to the divergence in findings for foreign economic elite pressure (Hypothesis 5), I find variation in the influence of adverse judgments on respect for rights at different periods in time postjudgment. Executives in the Americas are more likely to respond to adverse judgments with human rights policy change 1 and 3 years postjudgment than 5 years postjudgment as foreign economic elite pressure (FDI inflows) grows. In Europe, foreign economic elite pressure is more strongly associated with better human rights practices 3 and 5 years postjudgment than 1 year postjudgment. I suggest that the divergence in findings can be explained by differences in domestic politics, specifically variation in the political economies of Europe and the Americas.

Generally, European states are less economically vulnerable than states in the Americas. As a result, the potential withdrawal of foreign direct investment or lending is likely less threatening to executives in Europe than it is to executives in the Americas. In the Americas, the threat of withdrawal of an investment as a result of human rights policy failures may represent a significant threat to economic stability. As a result, executives in the Americas likely find it beneficial to send prompt, strong signals of human rights policy changes to foreign economic elites. This finding is consistent with research showing that because developing democracies are more dependent on foreign aid and investment, they are more likely to adopt democratic norms, like gender quotas, in an effort to signal to outside actors such as foreign lenders that they are liberalizing (e.g., Kelley, 2008; Bush, 2011). Executives in Europe may be less likely to respond to foreign economic elite pressure to make human rights policy changes for several years postjudgment because European economies are relatively stable and likely to remain stable enough to attract investment regardless of human rights policies. The threat of withdrawal by foreign investors and lenders, then, may be less credible in the immediate aftermath of an adverse judgment. In the 3 and 5 years postjudgment, investors and lenders may be able to mobilize and more credibly threaten withdrawal in Europe. Differences in the political economies of Europe and the Americas offer a potential explanation for the difference in the timing of executive response to economic elite pressure in Europe and the Americas.

Turning to the divergence in findings for domestic political elites (Hypotheses 6 and 7), differences in domestic politics and institutional design of the European and Inter-American Courts both explain divergence in findings across regions. With respect to the domestic judiciary hypothesis (Hypothesis 6), I find that the executive is more likely to make physical integrity rights policy changes following adverse Inter-American Court judgments in expectation of domestic judicial implementation. The results are relatively weaker for the European Court. One explanation for the weaker results in Europe involves domestic political institutions. Europe represents a region characterized by high rule of law institutions that are particularly robust. Looking at the data on domestic judicial power shows the divergence in the strength of the judiciary across regions. The average judicial power score in the European sample (on a scale ranging from 0 to 1) is 0.80, while the average judicial power score among states in the Americas is 0.54 (Linzer and Staton, 2015). Given the relative strength of the judiciary in Europe, national judicial power may not represent an effective signal (to the executive) of the likelihood of national judicial implementation of adverse European Court judgments. Rather, executives in Europe may expect a relatively high likelihood of national judicial implementation of adverse European Court judgments, all else equal, because national judiciaries are relatively powerful.

With respect to institutional design, differences in regional court procedures also offer an explanation for the European Court findings related to the national judiciary hypothesis (Hypothesis 6) as well. As noted earlier, while the Inter-American Court gives adverse judgment recipients a specific list of orders to remedy a human rights abuse, the Committee of Ministers of the European Court only gives adverse judgment recipients specific recommendations if the Committee does not find state actions and efforts to be sufficient. Initially, though, European states have discretion to decide how to respond to an adverse judgment. In the European context, then, the national judiciary is often not specifically charged with implementation (at least not initially). As a result, national judges may not have a direct interest in the implementation of European Court judgments; after all, they were not specifically tasked with doing so by the regional court. The ambiguity over the necessity of judicial implementation, particularly if it conflicts with national law (e.g., double jeopardy laws) may send a relatively noisy signal to the executive about the likelihood of national judicial implementation in Europe. The results for the European Court show that adverse judgments related to violations of convention articles on torture are positively related with the right to be free from torture when the national judiciary is relatively powerful. Perhaps when it comes to a specific type of rights abuse, the national judiciary has a clearer understanding of national judicial responsibility. For example, in cases where an individual is at risk of torture or ill-treatment upon being deported, the national judiciary often plays a key role in overturning a prior ruling ordering the deportation of a an individual. As a result, finding a statistical relationship between physical integrity abuses broadly and respect for physical integrity rights is more difficult in Europe. However, evidence of the direct relationship between a judgment involving a specific convention article and a specific rights abuse across judicial power is stronger because the national judiciary more clearly understands the role of the judiciary in remedying a human rights abuse postjudgment.

Domestic politics and divergence in procedures may also explain the divergent findings for the role of national legislators in regional court deterrence (Hypothesis 7). I find that adverse European Court judgments are positively related to respect for rights as the size of the legislative opposition grows, though measures of uncertainty suggest these results should be treated with some caution. With respect to the Inter-American Court, the findings show that adverse Inter-American Court judgments are positively and significantly related to respect for rights as the legislative opposition grows, but only when a state is the recipient of two or more adverse judgments.

These findings are relatively weak, but point to a key domestic political issue related to legislative implementation. By design, legislatures are institutions of contestation and deliberation. Legislative change is inherently difficult as a result. The legislative opposition requires a clear signal of the necessity of legislative changes in order to have enough leverage to create and push legislation through the legislative process. For the Inter-American Court, a clear signal of the necessity of legislative change means at least two adverse judgments. Furthermore, the size of the legislative opposition may be one signal of the likelihood of legislative implementation, but the executive may rely on several,

8.2 Comparing Courts in Europe and the Americas

relatively noisy, signals from the legislature. For example, the executive may look to whether the legislative opposition agrees on the necessary legislative reforms. If the legislative opposition is not cohesive, the executive may not expect the legislative opposition to form enough backing to support human rights legislative changes. If the legislative opposition is relatively cohesive, the executive may look to the ideological leanings of the legislative opposition relative to the executive. The legislative opposition may have competing preferences with the executive generally, but executive and legislative *human rights* policy preferences may be similar. With respect to institutional design, a similar process may be at work in the European Court context as that described for the national judiciary. That is, because the European Court does not initially prescribe policy changes, the ambiguity of the necessity of legislative reform in the European context may send a nosier signal to the executive about the likelihood of legislative implementation than the clear order for legislative changes in the Inter-American context. Institutional design differences coupled with the challenges associated with national legislatures as domestic political institutions may explain the uncertainty in the findings for the role of the legislative opposition in European Court deterrence (H7).

Finally, Hypothesis 8a states that in the presence of high executive capacity, high executive willingness amplifies regional court deterrence. Similarly, I posit in Hypothesis 8b that in the presence of high executive willingness, high executive capacity amplifies regional court deterrence. Generally, I find support for these hypotheses in the European and Inter-American Court context. However, I find that when a European executive is highly willing as a result of mass public pressure, there is not a significant difference in respect for rights post-European Court judgment across high- and low-capacity executives. In other words, executive capacity does not significantly amplify the deterrent effect of the European Court when the executive is highly willing due to mass public pressure. One explanation for this finding is rooted in domestic politics. Executives in Europe have significantly greater capacity than executives in the Americas, meaning that capacity concerns likely play less of a role in executive behavior in Europe, particularly when the executive is highly willing.

Generally, variation in findings for the European and Inter-American Courts of Human Rights can be explained by looking at differences in domestic politics, including the domestic institutional context within which each court resides. Variation in findings can also be explained by considering the variation in institutional design among the European and Inter-American Courts of Human Rights, particularly their procedures for assessing implementation of the judgment. The findings from this book illuminate several differences in the effectiveness of international human rights law across different regions of the world and offer prescriptive suggestions for the adoption of effective regional human rights institutions in other regions of the world with similar domestic institutional structures.

8.3 POLICY IMPLICATIONS: AN EFFECTIVE INTERNATIONAL HUMAN RIGHTS REGIME

In addition to contributing to our understanding of the differences in regional human rights court effectiveness across Europe and the Americas, my research has broad implications for the effectiveness of the international human rights regime more generally. That is, this research suggests ways that international human rights institutions can be designed and reformed to enhance their effectiveness. First, this research has clear implications for the importance of coordination across institutions in the international human rights regime. The structure of international human rights treaties can limit their effectiveness, but when the priorities and objectives of regional courts and international treaties align, the potential to impact state human rights practices grows in magnitude. Second, beyond international human rights institutions, the findings of this book have implications for strengthening the current regional human rights arrangements and designing effective regional human rights arrangements in other parts of the world. Notably, because regional courts in Europe and the Americas have important conditional deterrent effects, continued financial support of regional legal bodies in Europe and the Americas as well as the development of regional legal bodies in other parts of the world represent important policy prescriptions.

8.3.1 Designing an Effective International Human Rights Regime

Regional human rights courts represent key features of the international human rights regime and as such, considering their role alongside other international human rights legal instruments is important for assessing the effectiveness of the international human rights legal regime more broadly. Regional human rights courts are unique legal bodies but represent part of the broader trend in international politics, a trend toward judicialization in international institutions (Sikkink, 2011). A growing number of international legal bodies seek to provide remedy for human rights abuses and understanding the effects (jointly and independently) of international judicial and quasi-judicial human rights institutions is important for securing better rights protections. In this section, I begin by discussing the structure of the international human

8.3 Policy Implications

rights regime and the role of regional human rights courts in the regime. Next, I discuss how the findings of this book speak to the potential deterrent effect of other international legal bodies and suggest international institutional reforms. Finally, given the structure of the current international human rights regime, I consider how regional human rights courts and international human rights treaties can work together to ensure greater rights protections.

Although my research focuses on regional human rights courts, the theory and findings presented in this book suggest mechanisms under which other international human rights institutions deter future human rights abuses as well, particularly the United Nations international human rights treaty bodies. On the surface, international human rights treaties appear to be significantly different from regional human rights courts, both in their processes and procedures. For example, international human rights treaties typically do not ensure enforcement through human rights courts.

That said, like courts, international human rights treaties also possess mechanisms to assess state behavior following state ratification, though scholarly work has generally not focused on such mechanisms. Instead, the influence of treaty *ratification* on state human rights practices has largely consumed scholarly attention (e.g., Simmons, 2009; Hill, 2010; Lupu, 2015). The extensive focus on ratification is unfortunate because much like regional human rights courts, international human rights treaties are extensively involved with states after the initial ratification of a treaty. Treaty bodies make recommendations to states every few years following the submission of reports by states and other nongovernmental actors detailing their efforts to implement and comply with treaty provisions. In addition, treaties with additional optional protocols typically establish an individual complaints mechanism, similar to the petition system in the European and Inter-American Human Rights Systems. Currently, eight human rights treaty bodies receive and consider individual complaints. Treaty bodies have the potential to deter future human rights abuses through their work in adjudicating individual complaints, particularly when the views that are adopted in jurisprudence find violations of rights. In fact, Alston and Crawford (2000) highlight the important deterrent effect of treaty bodies, stating,

> the protection of rights through adjudication is forward-looking ... Judicial arrangements make a better world more likely because of their effects in deterring potential violators, and encouraging them to modify behaviour to make it more consistent with the legal order. (36)

As a result, I expect treaty bodies to exert a deterrent effect similar to regional human rights courts, but only under certain conditions. For example, executive capacity to respond to international treaty bodies may be associated with a greater likelihood of deterrence of future human rights abuses. Or, the executive may be unwilling to adopt, administer, monitor, and enforce human rights policy following recommendations or jurisprudence from an international human rights treaty body as a result of political instability in the state.

However, treaty bodies face some limitations that presumably make them less effective than regional human rights courts. First, although treaty bodies issue many concluding observations, the small number of views adopted and issued by treaty bodies and the threat of mounting backlog make the threat of future jurisprudence relatively low (Alston and Crawford, 2000). In addition, while regional court judgments are well publicized (often by order of regional courts), many of the adopted views of treaty bodies receive little publicity (Alston and Crawford, 2000). Third, treaty bodies are fairly limited in their legalization by design. Unlike regional human rights courts, which primarily utilize an individual complaints mechanism, treaty bodies have some judicial functions, but they are not primarily judicial institutions. That is, treaty bodies engage in the monitoring and oversight of states' human rights practices through a variety of mechanisms, one of which involves an individual complaints procedure. Furthermore, regional human rights courts render adverse judgments, while treaty bodies rely on recommendations to member states.

Treaty bodies may also suffer from a legitimacy deficit in some states that do not view them as authoritative. But, when members of the government view treaty bodies as having greater legitimacy, treaty bodies' concluding observations are more likely to be effective (Krommendijk, 2015). Given the limitations of international human rights treaty bodies, regional human rights courts fulfill a unique role in the international human rights system. However, with some reform efforts, international human rights treaty bodies could imitate the successful design features of regional human rights courts. That is, by giving international human rights treaties a stronger judicial mandate, international human rights treaty bodies could overcome several of the aforementioned shortcomings. For one, a judgment from an international judicial body may carry more weight than a recommendation from an, at best, quasi-judicial body. Moreover, for the many states in the world not under the jurisdiction of a regional human rights court, or any type of supranational human rights court, international human rights treaty bodies represent the most authoritative institution in the international human rights regime for ensuring respect for rights.

8.3 Policy Implications

Still, designing international human rights institutions with greater legalization is likely not feasible due to high sovereignty costs states are unwilling to pay. Because greater legalization is unlikely, I suggest that reforms designed to ensure a more effective international human rights regime should come from greater integration. That is, regional human rights courts and international human rights treaty bodies have the potential to work together to ensure better rights protections. When both bodies work independently, the potential for overlap and inconsistency in the international human rights regime grows. For example, although regional human rights courts and UN human rights treaty bodies work on similar human rights issues, international treaty bodies may suggest different approaches than regional human rights courts to the same human rights problems. These inconsistent recommendations have the potential to overwhelm the state bureaucracy (e.g. foreign ministry) when processing human rights reports and judgments. In a report prepared by the Geneva Academy of International Humanitarian Law and Human Rights for an expert meeting in 2015, the problem of inconsistency (called the coherence challenge) is discussed at length. The report notes the fact that "there is no link between reporting to international monitoring bodies and the regional monitoring bodies. Even reporting to one treaty body bares no relation to reporting to another treaty body" (Geneva Academy, 2015, 3).

That said, the findings in this book point to the importance of regional human rights courts and international human rights treaties aligning their priorities and working together. The findings in Chapter 5, for example, suggest that regional human rights courts are more effective when the mass public places pressure on the executive to engage in human rights policy changes. For the mass public to place pressure on the executive, the mass public must have access to recommendations and judgments of international legal bodies. By coordinating their policy recommendations, regional human rights courts and international human rights treaty bodies send a stronger, more cohesive message to the public, thereby increasing the likelihood of mobilization by the mass public and subsequently, the executive's incentives to engage in human rights policy changes.

There is some evidence that regional and international bodies reinforce the work of one another. For example, the Committee Against Torture (the treaty body established by the Convention against Torture) has considered several cases related to nonrefoulment and torture prevention. That is, the Committee has evaluated individual complaints related to deportation of individuals at risk of torture. Complaints against Switzerland, Sweden, Denmark, and several other European states have been examined in the past several years. The

European Court of Human Rights has also been active in addressing this issue over the past several years as well, and has rendered several adverse judgments against states related to the deportation of individuals at risk of torture (e.g., *Saadi v. Italy*). Notably, in reports of the Committee Against Torture and the Committee of Ministers of the European Court, both bodies cite one another's decisions and recommendations. Further coordination among the legal bodies is likely to generate consistent and sustained public pressure on the executive to engage in human rights policy changes. Coordination of recommendations from international human rights treaty bodies and orders from regional human rights courts is also likely to increase the probability of national judicial and legislative implementation because national judges and legislators will receive a stronger and more cohesive signal from the international community of the judicial and legislative changes necessary to remedy future human rights abuses. By aligning priorities, recommendations, and objectives, international and regional human rights legal bodies present a unified front in their interactions with states, and such alignment is likely to lead to even greater deterrence of future human rights abuses.

8.3.2 *Designing Effective Regional Human Rights Arrangements*

The findings in this book also suggest that the continued support of the current regional human rights arrangements is important for deterring future human rights abuses, and the establishment and growth of other regional human rights systems presents an opportunity for deterring human rights abuses in other parts of the world. Beginning with continued support of the existing regional human rights arrangements, both the European and Inter-American Human Rights Systems have faced significant resource challenges over the past couple of decades. The 2018 budget of the European Court was 71,670,500 euros, and covers judges' remuneration, staff salaries, and operational expenditure.[1] Member states contribute to the budget based on population and economic development, yet the European Court has faced several financial hurdles. One report in 2011 noted that the financial situation of the European Court was untenable, and contributions from member states were not enough to fund their own judge at the court. Major financial challenges led to several important structural reforms in the European Court, including the move to a court-centered system (Protocol 9), the introduction of a filtering stage where applications could more easily be deemed inadmissible (Protocol 11), and the

---

[1] See www.echr.coe.int/Documents/Budget_ENG.pdf for more on the budget of the European Court.

8.3 Policy Implications

establishment of mechanisms to more easily handle repeat petitions (Protocol 14). In 2014, the European Court also started looking for alternative sources of funding, including funding from joint programs with the European Union and voluntary contributions. Alternative sources of funding jumped from 28 million in 2008 to 43 million in 2014 (Abdelgawad, 2016).

Similarly, the Inter-American Court has suffered major financial setbacks over the past decade. The Inter-American Court has a regular budget of 5 million USD from the Organization of American States (OAS). In 2016, the Inter-American Commission on Human Rights announced that it would have to let the contracts of 40 percent of its personnel expire and suspend its regular sessions, as well as the rest of its planned country visits. Later in 2016, several states agreed to donate funds, allowing the Commission to remain operational. Despite these donations, the financial sustainability of the Inter-American Human Rights System remains precarious. Executive Secretary of the Commission, Paulo Abrão, noted in reference to the donations, "This does not mean we have solved the severe structural issues of deficient funding, which still requires a determined action from the States" (IACHR, 2016). In 2017, the OAS approved to double the Regular Fund resources allocated to the Inter-American Human Rights System (Commission and Court). The research in this book suggests that continued and sustainable funding of both the European and Inter-American Human Rights Systems are vital to ensure rights protections in each region. Although regional court judgments may not directly impact states, they can have important deterrent effects under certain conditions and at least in the Inter-American Court context, adverse judgments can deter future human rights abuses even in states that are not direct recipients of adverse judgments.

Second, the findings in this book have important implications for the potential development and support of other regional human rights legal bodies. The African Commission on Human and People's Rights and the African Court on Human and People's Rights also hear rights-related cases. Neither the African Commission nor the African Court were designed with a level of legalization (obligation, delegation, and precision) similar to the regional legal bodies in Europe and the Americas. African Court activity has been limited, and the Court's progress has been slow. Entering into force in 2004, the African Court did not render its first judgment until 2009, ruling a case inadmissible. In 2013, the African Court rendered its first adverse judgment against Tanzania for violations of citizen rights to participate in government. In 2014, the African Court rendered an adverse judgment against Burkina Faso for failing to investigate the murder of a journalist. African Court and Commission activity lags far behind the activity of regional human rights courts in Europe and the Americas. Even so, the findings in this book suggest that the African Commission and Court can deter future human rights abuses under particular conditions. For example, given the similar results in Europe and the Americas regarding executive capacity, I expect that African Court judgments will be more effective in deterring future human rights abuses when judgments are more feasible to implement and the state has greater fiscal flexibility. Also, given the economic vulnerability of many African nations, the African Court may be more effective in states where economic elites generate pressure on the executive.

Although other parts of the world are moving in the direction of developing regional human rights systems, no region has yet created a regional treaty or court on par with those in Europe and the Americas. In 2009, the Association of Southeast Asian Nations (ASEAN) created the Intergovernmental Commission on Human Rights to hear rights-related cases. However, Commission decisions are made by consensus and are not legally binding. The subsequent adoption of the ASEAN Human Rights Declaration in 2012 faced criticism for noting that human rights were contingent on the performance of corresponding duties that every person has to individuals, the community, and society (United Nations News, 2012). Should the Southeast Asian regional human rights system grow in legalization, there is reason to expect deterrence based on the presence of several domestic conditions. More specifically, my research suggests that a regional human rights court in Southeast Asia has the potential to deter future human rights abuses when the executive is capable and willing. For example, given the consistent findings across Europe and the Americas, if Southeast Asia established a regional human rights court, there is reason to expect that fiscal flexibility would have a significant effect on human rights policy change postjudgment. Similarly, there is reason to expect that pressure from economic elites may generate executive willingness to make human rights policy changes following adverse regional court judgments. That is, because Southeast Asia is composed largely of developing countries, capacity limitations in some countries may significantly inhibit the executive's ability to adopt comprehensive human rights policy, and the executive's concern with attracting and maintaining foreign investment may produce pressure on the executive to respond to adverse regional court judgments with human rights policy change.

8.4 A PATH FORWARD: FUTURE RESEARCH

Although the findings presented in this book illuminate the importance of several conditions under which regional human rights courts deter future human rights abuses, there are a number of important questions still to be addressed in future research. First, my research shows that specific deterrence occurs under particular conditions, but we still know relatively little about general deterrence. To what extent do regional human rights courts generally deter? Does general deterrence only occur under certain conditions? Are the European and Inter-American Courts equally likely to generally deter? Second, in light of conditional deterrence, regional court judges have an opportunity to behave strategically, which begs the questions: How do regional court judges adjust their behavior in response to conditional regional court deterrence? Are they more likely to render judgments in some states than others? Do they adjust the content of their recommendations and rulings to account for the likelihood of successful deterrence? Third, given the size of the international human rights regime, do regional human rights courts complement the work of other international human rights institutions or do they compete for influence over states? Finally, what role will regional human rights courts play in the future? How does the public view international human rights institutions, and are their views evolving? In what follows, I briefly discuss each of these questions.

8.4.1 *General Deterrence and Regional Human Rights Courts*

In Chapter 2, I discussed the difference between general and specific deterrence. General deterrence focuses on the prevention of crime by making examples of specific violators, while specific deterrence focuses on deterring specific individuals who commit crimes. I argued that general regional human rights court deterrence occurs when the *presence* or the *activity* of the court in the region deters the commission of future human rights abuses. In Chapter 3, I find little evidence that the mere presence of the European or Inter-American Courts in the region deter future human rights abuses. However, I find some evidence that adverse Inter-American Court judgments in the region are associated with greater respect for human rights in the region, that is, there is some evidence that the Inter-American Court exhibits a general deterrent effect. The potential for regional human rights courts to deter across borders has not gone unrecognized by legal scholars and practitioners. In fact, in 2010, the Chairperson of the Committee on Legal Affairs and Human Rights of the Parliamentary Assembly of the Council of Europe noted in a report,

> We want State officials to understand the interpretive authority of European Court judgments, particularly those against *other* States, to strengthen

subsidiarity and reduce the need for applications to the Strasbourg Court (emphasis added). (Pourgourides, 2010)[2]

Regional human rights courts often set precedent in rulings that hold effect beyond the state where the regional court found a violation. Legal scholars refer to this effect as the *erga omnes* effect, which means "flowing to all," and highlights the influence of the court beyond the specific states involved in a regional court case. The intuition behind regional court deterrence across borders suggests that states under the jurisdiction of the court aim to avoid the costs of litigation, which include (1) international shaming and reputation costs, (2) adjudication costs (e.g., resources dedicated to investigations, hearings, and interactions with the regional court), (3) implementation costs (e.g., changes to legislation, criminal trials), and (4) costs associated with executive adoption, administration, monitoring, and enforcement of human rights policy. Should a state fail to deter litigation, the state faces all of the preceding costs. If states avoid litigation by making human rights policy change in expectation of future litigation, the state may avoid the international shaming and reputation costs and adjudication costs (the first two costs noted earlier).

Scholars argue that deterrence across borders takes place as a result of the threat of future litigation, the persuasive authority of judicial reasoning, and the agenda-setting effect of international court decisions (Helfer and Voeten, 2014). Looking specifically at LGBT rights in Europe, Helfer and Voeten (2014) find that European Court judgments "increase the likelihood that all European countries – even countries whose laws and policies the court has not explicitly found to violate the European Convention – will adopt pro-LGBT reforms" (29). Moreover, their research finds that the effect is strongest in countries where public support for sexual minorities is lowest.

Anecdotal evidence also supports this claim as shown the case of *Mubilanzila Mayeka and Kaniki Mitunga v. Belgium*. In this case, a young girl from the Democratic Republic of the Congo (DRC) was detained for 2 months in an immigration center for adults in Belgium before being deported back to the DRC. The mother and child filed an application with the European Court, and in 2006, the Court issued an adverse judgment against Belgium finding that the child's detention without her parents and deportation violated the prohibition of inhuman treatment and the right to liberty and security, among several other articles.[3] In 2010, the United Kingdom (UK) decided

---

[2] See the Committee on Legal Affairs and Human Rights, 2010 www.venice.coe.int/webforms/documents/?pdf=CDL-JU(2010)019-e.

[3] See *Mubilanzila Mayeka and Kanki Mitunga v. Belgium*, Judgment. European Ct. H.R. Oct. 6, 2006.

to end the detention of children. A reading of the European Court judgment against Belgium suggests that states that detain children are unlikely to be in compliance with the European Convention. Despite not being a recipient of an adverse judgment from the European Court, the United Kingdom abolished the detention of children and effectively implemented European Court case law, suggesting a role for general deterrence by the European Court.

Beyond anecdotal evidence, the systematic evidence of a broad general deterrent effect is mixed. Helfer and Voeten (2014) find a clear effect of regional court deterrence in Europe with respect to LGBT rights, but in Chapter 3, I find little support for general deterrence in Europe with respect to physical integrity rights. Though, I find that adverse Inter-American Court judgments related to physical integrity rights have the potential to deter across borders in the Americas. What explains these inconsistencies? Helfer and Voeten (2014) suggest that the general deterrent effect of the European Court is greatest in states that are lagging to adopt progressive policies that have been adopted by at least a majority of Council of Europe member states, suggesting that human rights norms have to cascade significantly before the regional court has an impact on states across borders. I suggest that like specific deterrence, general deterrence is likely conditional on domestic political factors as well. For example, deterrence across borders is more likely in the presence of high executive capacity and willingness to engage in human rights policy changes. Though, perhaps the general deterrent effect also depends on the similarity of a state's human rights practices with the judgment recipient or the likelihood of mobilization within a state. Nonetheless, general deterrence represents an important role for regional human rights courts, and future research should examine this role systematically.

8.4.2 *Strategic Regional Court Judges*

In this book, I focus on the conditional role of domestic politics in explaining regional human rights court deterrence. Arguably, though, regional human rights court judges have opportunities to behave strategically and can influence the likelihood of regional court deterrence as well. In this book, I do not discuss strategic behavior by regional court judges, largely because we know relatively little about regional judicial behavior. There are several ways that regional court judges can behave strategically, including tempering or elevating the level of regional court activity in particular states, engaging in more or less monitoring of state behavior postjudgment, and adjusting the content of rulings and recommendations. First, regional court judges may render adverse judgments in states where they are most likely to be effective in an effort to garner greater legitimacy for the court. Currently, there is no systematic evidence that judges are more likely to render adverse judgments where they expect deterrence to occur such as states with robust democratic institutions or strong rights protections. In fact, descriptive evidence suggests that adverse judgment recipients are often those with worse human rights practices and weaker democratic institutions than states that are not recipients of adverse judgments.

Another path for regional court judges to behave strategically involves their role in monitoring state implementation. For example, because the results in Chapter 6 show that national judicial implementation is associated with an increased probability of executive adoption, administration, monitoring, and enforcement of human rights policy in the Americas, Inter-American Court judges can direct their efforts at pressuring national judges to implement regional court orders. Or, because the executive is less willing to make human rights policy changes in states facing threats to the political and social order, in an effort to protect the legitimacy of the regional court, strategic regional court judges might grant politically unstable states more leeway in following through with court orders.

Finally, another promising avenue for future research currently being examined by several scholars involves the strategic behavior of regional court judges in terms of clarity in the text of judgments. A growing body of research suggests that national judges temper the level of clarity in judgments to manage uncertainty over policy outcomes and hide likely defiance from the public (Staton and Vanberg, 2008). Recently, these arguments have been extended to the Inter-American Court, and scholars find that vague Inter-American Court orders permit judges to take advantage of policy expertise in state bureaucracies by giving discretion to state bureaucrats (Staton and Romero, 2019). Also of note, Voeten (2012a) finds that characteristics of the judges themselves help explain the likelihood of implementation. That is, European Court judgments written by panels consisting of a relatively high number of career judges are implemented more promptly than judgments by panels with higher proportions of judges from other backgrounds. Questions related to the behavior of regional court judges, including the level of activity in particular states, the extent to which they monitor state responses, and the drafting of opinions and judgments, deserves further attention, as judges have the potential to profoundly impact regional court effectiveness.

8.4.3 Complementary or Competing: International and Regional Human Rights Bodies

The growth of the international human rights regime raises questions related to whether such institutions perform a complementary or competing role. To date, most scholarly work (including this book) has looked at the impact of one international human rights institution on state human rights practices. However, the international human rights regime represents an increasingly dense and complex set of institutions. States are now part of a large number of treaties designed to govern their human rights practices and receive an increasingly dense set of recommendations, decisions, and judgments (Carneiro and Wegmann, 2018). What are the implications for such growth in the international human rights regime?

We know relatively little about the overall effectiveness of the international human rights regime. Voeten (2017) claims that despite being dysfunctional in many ways, competition between regional and global human rights institutions does not represent a problem for the international human rights regime. Still, the increasing institutional density of the international human rights regime creates an environment ripe for competition. The sheer volume of recommendations and judgments processed by state foreign ministries overwhelms many state bureaucracies, causing them to prioritize or pick and choose among the various recommendations and judgments. The bureaucratic strain placed on states by an increasingly dense set of international human rights commitments opens up the door for human rights institutions to view their role and influence in a competitive light.

But there are many opportunities for various institutions in the international human rights regime to complement one another. International human rights treaty bodies, for example, may observe a regional court placing pressure on the state to engage in a specific legal change. The treaty body could either double down and focus on recommendations related to the specific legal change currently being emphasized by the court. Or, the treaty body could redirect its limited resources to other states committing rights violations but not under the jurisdiction of a regional court. In this way, various institutions can complement the work of one another in order to enhance their effectiveness. However, absent cross-institutional, cross-national data on recommendations and judgments from various institutions, assessing this complementary or competing role remains inherently difficult. Fortunately, Haglund and Hillebrecht (2019) have collected data on features of over 3,600 recommendations made to 46 European states on women's rights issues from three international and regional human rights legal bodies, including the Committee on the

Elimination of Discrimination against Women, the UN's Universal Periodic Review, and the European Court of Human Rights. These data represent an important advancement in the study of the international human rights regime and are the first to allow scholars to empirically assess competition and complementarity in the international human rights regime.

8.4.4 Backlash in the International Human Rights Regime

Despite the significant growth in the international human rights regime over the past several decades, evidence also suggests a growing state backlash against international human rights institutions. For example, the United Kingdom discussed and proposed withdrawal from the European Court of Human Rights in 2015, Venezuela denounced the Inter-American Court of Human Rights in 2012, and several African states began proceedings to withdraw from the International Criminal Court in the last couple of years, with Burundi officially leaving the court in 2017. Backlash occurs in several forms, including criticism of the decisions of international human rights institutions, criticism of the general authority of an institution, refusal to participate in an institution, threatening exit from the institution, and even withdrawing from an institution, among other forms (Voeten, 2019). Understanding when and why backlash occurs represents a question receiving increased attention by several scholars recently because backlash is particularly damaging to the legitimacy of international legal institutions.

Scholars argue that backlash against the European and Inter-American Courts of Human Rights and the International Criminal Court occurs when governments perceive the international court's actions to be too costly to implement. Governments may view the court's actions as a threat to the government's hold on power because court judgments and actions can reduce public support for the government generally, reduce support for the coalition in power, or empower the opposition (Sandholtz, Bei, and Caldwell, 2018). Or, backlash may be attributed to recent democratic reversals as illiberal governments lose interest in a strong commitment to international liberal institutions. Other scholars argue that backlash against human rights courts is more likely when human rights courts render judgments that support minorities (e.g., prisoners, immigrants), groups against whom there is pre-existing populist mobilization (Voeten, 2019). In fact, Voeten (2019) shows that international courts have become controversial in countries with strong populist movements.

More research assessing the conditions under which backlash occurs is vitally important for the effectiveness of the international human rights regime. In particular, the arguments in this book suggest that the public is less likely to support executive adoption, administration, monitoring, and enforcement of human rights policy in response to regional human rights court judgments when the state is politically unstable. Moreover, adverse judgments prior to an election in politically unstable states are associated with lower respect for rights than in the absence of an election, suggesting that the government responds to the public's commitment (or lack thereof) to international law and human rights. As a result, developing a greater understanding of backlash by the public and government is warranted.

8.5 CONCLUDING COMMENTS

This book suggests that regional human rights courts have the potential to deter future human rights abuses. That said, deterrence represents a highly domestic political process and requires that the executive has the capacity and willingness to engage in human rights policy changes. This finding suggests that regional human rights courts are more likely to be effective in some states rather than others. However, because capacity and willingness vary across states, strategies for ensuring deterrence vary as well. This book suggests various strategies that human rights advocates can rely on to ensure regional human rights court deterrence of future human rights abuses. For example, an executive in the Americas may expect a low likelihood of domestic judicial implementation of an adverse regional court judgment, decreasing executive willingness to engage in human rights policy changes in response to an adverse court judgment. Nonetheless, human rights advocates can adjust their strategies by looking to other mechanisms through which deterrence is likely. For example, advocates might appeal to executive willingness to engage in human rights policy changes prior to an election or might seek to bring the adverse judgment to the attention of foreign economic elites in an effort to pressure the government to engage in human rights policy change. Understanding regional court deterrence, then, represents a promising avenue to pursue greater protections of human rights in states with various domestic political environments and institutional arrangements.

Appendix A

Chapter 3 Appendix

A.1 CONTROL VARIABLES

I utilize several control variables in the analyses, and Table A.1 provides a list of all variables used in the analyses. First, in order to account for variation in executive willingness as a result of pressure from the mass public, I include a control variable for electoral institutions, specifically capturing competitiveness of executive recruitment *(Exec Recruit)* (Marshall, Jaggers, and Gurr, 2019). Second, I include a control variable for civil conflict, as human rights abuses are more common during violent conflict (e.g., Davenport, 1995). The public may also be less likely to pressure the executive to engage in human rights policy changes when the state is involved in conflict, as the public often gives the state leeway to use repression to maintain order. Data on the occurrence of civil conflict *(Civil War)* are obtained from the Uppsala armed conflict data project (Gleditsch et al., 2002; Harbom and Wallensteen, 2005). Third, because judicial independence has been found to be associated with respect for rights (e.g., Powell and Staton, 2009), and to account for executive willingness to make human rights policy change (examined in Chapter 6), I control for judicial power. A measure of judicial power *(Judicial Power)* created by Linzer and Staton (2015) is used in the analyses. Fourth, legislative institutions have also been found to be associated with respect for rights (e.g., Lupu, 2015), and as I argue in Chapter 6, executive willingness to make human rights policy changes also depends on legislative implementation, specifically the size of the legislative opposition. I include a variable capturing whether opposition parties are able to exercise oversight and investigatory functions against the wishes of the governing party *(Leg Opposition)* (Coppedge et al., 2019).[1] Finally, because economic elites can

---

[1] In Chapter 6, I utilize the Henisz (2002) *PolCon iii* measure of political constraints to capture the size of the legislative opposition. Models are robust to the inclusion of either variable.

TABLE A.1. *Control variables*

Variable	Source
Competitive executive recruitment	Marshall, Jaggers, and Gurr (2019)
Civil war	Gleditsch et al. (2002)
Judicial power	Linzer and Staton (2015)
Legislative opposition	Coppedge et al. (2019)
FDI inflows	World Bank (2017)
Multilateral aid	OECD (2018)
Freedom of speech	Cingranelli, Richards, and Clay (2014)
Civil society participation	Coppedge et al. (2019)
National human rights institution	Conrad et al. (2013)
GDP per capita	World Bank (2017)
Population	World Bank (2017)
Embeddedness	Fariss (2018)
Democracy	Coppedge et al. (2019)
Respect for physical integrity rights	Fariss (2014)

also influence executive incentives to make human rights policy changes, in each model I include a variable capturing economic incentives (*Economic Incentives*) (FDI inflows in Europe and multilateral aid in the Americas).

Civil society mobilization is also argued to be associated with respect for rights and is particularly likely in the presence of international legal guarantees (e.g., Simmons, 2009). The executive also behaves in expectation of the strength of civil society. Alter (2014) calls these actors *compliance supporters* because they can mobilize to induce governmental actors to adhere to a regional court ruling (21). A number of variables capturing the likelihood of civil society mobilization around an adverse regional court decision are included. First, freedom of *Speech* is particularly important because it allows individuals to identify and publicize regional court decisions. An ordinal variable capturing freedom of speech is included in the analysis (Cingranelli, Richards, and Clay, 2014). Second, including a measure of civil society participation (*Civil Society*) is important because greater civil society participation is likely associated with a higher likelihood of elected officials being held accountable and therefore, greater adherence to adverse regional court decisions. A variable measuring the size of involvement of people in civil society organizations, restrictions on participation, among other factors, retrieved from the VDEM dataset, is included. Third, the models include a binary variable capturing whether the state has adopted a national human rights institution (*NHRI*), including a classical ombudsman office, human rights commission, and human rights ombudsman office. This variable is taken from the Organizational NHRI Project Dataset for the year the NHRI was formally established (Conrad et al., 2013).

The models in this chapter focus on the influence of adverse judgments in the region on respect for rights (general deterrence), but states are also the direct recipients of adverse judgments (specific deterrence). As a result, I utilize a control variable capturing whether the state was a direct recipient of an adverse judgment (*Adverse Judgment (t-n)*). Another alternative explanation involves socialization, as states that are more socialized in the international human rights regime are more likely to respond to adverse regional court judgments with human rights policy change. I control for the extent to which the state is embedded in the international human rights regime (*Embeddedness*), taken from Fariss (2018).

In addition, I also include control variables commonly used in studies of state respect for human rights as well. Factors that improve human rights practices include democracy and economic development; factors that hinder good human rights practices include a large population and prior experience with repression (Davenport and Armstrong, 2004). Data on *Democracy* is taken from the VDEM dataset, in which democracy is conceptualized as the extent to which the electoral principle of democracy is achieved, including responsiveness and accountability between leaders and citizens through the mechanisms of competitive elections (the polyarchy index) (Coppedge et al., 2019). While several democratic institutions are included in the models, the measure of democracy I utilize only accounts for the electoral component of democracy rather than liberal democracy, and therefore, the measure of electoral democracy included in the models does not overlap conceptually with other democratic institutions included in the models (e.g., judicial power, freedom of speech). Notably, research shows mixed findings for the role of elections in human rights protections. Some research suggests that electoral institutions create opportunities for the voting public to remove leaders from office who violate rights, and elections are positively associated with rights (Davenport, 2007). However, other research shows that presidential elections are negatively associated with rights because presidential electoral systems lead to exclusion of the opposition for fixed periods of time, creating a lack of executive accountability mechanisms and an increased probability of dissent by opposition groups (Richards and Gelleny, 2007). Additional research shows that the electorate may not inherently value rights protection for the population at large and as such, leaders may not be willing to change repressive policies in the presence of electoral contestation unless "a sufficient number of voters are willing to cast their ballot on that issue" (Conrad, Hill, and Moore,

2017, 5). These conflicting findings suggest that electoral democracy may have a positive, negative, or null effect on respect for rights.

In order to account for economic development, the models include a measure of logged GDP per capita (*GDP*) taken from the World Bank's *World Development Indicators*. The logged total population, in millions, (*Population*) is also taken from the World Bank's *World Development Indicators*. While many studies explaining state respect for human rights include a lagged dependent variable in their models, the inclusion of such a variable is not necessary in the models in which the Fariss (2014) data is used as a dependent variable. The Fariss (2014) variable uses mean estimates generated from a dynamic item-response theory model, which allows for changing standards of accountability or more stringent standards on the part of monitoring agencies. In other words, the model accounts for the increase in the probability of observing and coding rights violations over time as monitoring agencies that produce reports used to generate repression variables have greater access to information. The estimates used in the empirical analysis in this book are generated from a model in which physical integrity rights scores for a country in a particular year are dependent on the value of the same country in the previous year (Fariss, 2014, 304).

A.2 FULL MODEL RESULTS

TABLE A.2. *The European Court of Human Rights and general deterrence*

	Europe (t-1)	Europe (t-3)	Europe (t-5)
Adverse judgments in Europe (lagged)	0.001 (0.000)	0.001 (0.001)	0.001 (0.001)
Adverse judgment (t-1)	0.005 (0.004)	0.004 (0.003)	0.003 (0.003)
Adverse judgment (t-2)		−0.001 (0.002)	−0.001 (0.002)
Adverse judgment (t-3)		−0.0002 (0.003)	0.001 (0.002)
Adverse judgment (t-4)			−0.003 (0.003)
Adverse judgment (t-5)			0.006** (0.003)
Judicial power (t-1)	0.217 (0.502)	−0.131 (0.414)	−0.093 (0.438)

(*Continued*)

TABLE A.2. (Continued)

	Europe (t-1)	Europe (t-3)	Europe (t-5)
Exec recruit (t-1)	0.145	0.119	0.183
	(0.135)	(0.148)	(0.214)
Economic incentives (t-1)	−0.000	−0.001	−0.001
	(0.003)	(0.003)	(0.004)
Embeddedness (t-1)	0.077	0.057	0.049
	(0.062)	(0.061)	(0.063)
Speech (t-1)	0.056	0.056	0.047
	(0.064)	(0.067)	(0.073)
Civil society (t-1)	0.395	0.620	0.510
	(0.555)	(0.597)	(0.643)
NHRI (t-1)	0.186**	0.220**	0.215**
	(0.086)	(0.092)	(0.092)
Leg opposition (t-1)	−0.040	−0.074	−0.025
	(0.078)	(0.076)	(0.077)
Population (logged) (t-1)	−0.255**	−0.228*	−0.240**
	(0.113)	(0.121)	(0.119)
GDP (logged) (t-1)	0.071	0.105	0.130
	(0.081)	(0.084)	(0.097)
Democracy (t-1)	1.63	1.31	0.700
	(1.32)	(1.24)	(1.03)
Civil War (t-1)	−0.060	−0.062	−0.015
	(0.126)	(0.111)	(0.101)
Constant	−1.38	−1.21	−1.04
	(1.23)	(1.24)	(1.25)
R^2	0.576	0.540	0.536
N	765	730	678

Notes: Table A.2 displays coefficient estimates and standard errors from a model examining the influence of adverse European Court judgments lagged 1 year (left column), lagged 3 years (center column), and lagged 5 years (right column) on respect for rights. The results in Table A.2 correspond with results reported in Figure 3.9. Statistical significance: ***$p < 0.01$, **$p < 0.05$, *$p < 0.10$. Models estimated with standard errors clustered on country. Two-tailed significance tests reported.

TABLE A.3. *The Inter-American Court of Human Rights and general deterrence*

	Americas (t-1)	Americas (t-3)	Americas (t-5)
Adverse judgments in Americas (lagged)	0.031***	0.018*	0.024**
	(0.010)	(0.01)	(0.012)
Adverse judgment (t-1)	0.052	0.045*	0.004
	(0.036)	(0.028)	(0.033)

TABLE A.3. (Continued)

	Americas (t-1)	Americas (t-3)	Americas (t-5)
Adverse judgment (t-2)		0.046	0.029
		(0.034)	(0.037)
Adverse judgment (t-3)		0.074**	0.027
		(0.028)	(0.035)
Adverse judgment (t-4)			0.043
			(0.029)
Adverse judgment (t-5)			0.030
			(0.031)
Judicial power (t-1)	2.49***	2.78***	1.97***
	(0.638)	(0.550)	(0.655)
Exec recruit (t-1)	0.021	−0.019	−0.110
	(0.067)	(0.065)	(0.102)
Economic incentives (t-1)	0.0004	0.001	0.001**
	(0.0003)	(0.0004)	(0.0004)
Embeddedness (t-1)	0.070	0.153**	0.200**
	(0.089)	(0.069)	(0.083)
Speech (t-1)	0.094***	0.086***	0.119***
	(0.030)	(0.031)	(0.045)
Civil Society (t-1)	−0.132	−0.064	−0.587
	(0.528)	(0.475)	(0.530)
NHRI (t-1)	0.368**	0.418***	0.207*
	(0.154)	(0.133)	(0.113)
Leg opposition (t-1)	−0.103	−0.131**	−0.087
	(0.073)	(0.051)	(0.086)
Population (logged) (t-1)	−0.399***	−0.392***	−0.440***
	(0.058)	(0.056)	(0.054)
GDP (logged) (t-1)	0.187*	0.138*	0.110
	(0.117)	(0.087)	(0.102)
Democracy (t-1)	1.12	1.08	2.27**
	(1.01)	(0.807)	(0.890)
Civil war (t-1)	−0.574***	−0.557***	−0.404*
	(0.159)	(0.154)	(0.236)
Constant	−3.02**	−2.79**	−2.52**
	(0.988)	(0.871)	(1.04)
R^2	0.790	0.781	0.810
N	436	400	368

Notes: Table A.3 displays coefficient estimates and standard errors from a model examining the influence of adverse Inter-American Court judgments lagged 1 year (left column), lagged 3 years (center column), and lagged 5 years (right column) on respect for rights. The results in Table A.3 correspond with results reported in Figure 3.9. Statistical significance: ***$p < 0.01$, **$p < 0.05$, *$p < 0.10$. Models estimated with standard errors clustered on country. Two-tailed significance tests reported.

Appendix B

Chapter 4 Appendix

B.1 CONTROL VARIABLES

I utilize several control variables in the analyses. Table B.1 provides a list of all variables used in the analyses. Because judicial independence has been found to be associated with respect for rights (e.g., Powell and Staton, 2009), and to account for executive willingness to adopt human rights policy (examined in Chapter 6), I control for judicial power. A measure of judicial power (*Judiciary*) created by Linzer and Staton (2015) is used in the analyses. Legislative institutions have also been found to be associated with respect for rights (e.g., Lupu, 2015), and as I show in Chapter 6, legislative implementation is positively associated with executive willingness to engage in human rights policy change. As a result, I control for the strength of the legislative opposition using a variable capturing whether opposition parties are able to exercise oversight and investigatory functions against the wishes of the governing party (*Leg Opposition*) (Coppedge et al., 2019). The legislative opposition variable is omitted from the model predicting freedom of association because the freedom of association measure includes the extent to which parties, including opposition parties, are allowed to form and to participate in elections, and the legislative opposition control variable overlaps conceptually with the dependent variable (freedom of association). The legislative opposition variable is also omitted from the model predicting civil and political rights because the civil and political rights index includes freedom of association.

Civil society mobilization is also argued to be associated with respect for rights and is particularly likely in the presence of international legal guarantees (e.g., Simmons, 2009). The executive also behaves in expectation of the strength of civil society. Alter (2014) calls these actors *compliance supporters* because they can mobilize to induce governmental actors to adhere to a regional court ruling (21). A number of variables capturing the likelihood

TABLE B.1. *Control variables*

Variable	Source
Judicial power	Linzer and Staton (2015)
Legislative opposition	Coppedge et al. (2019)
Freedom of speech	Cingranelli, Richards, and Clay (2014)
Civil society participation	Coppedge et al. (2019)
National human rights institution	Conrad et al. (2013)
Regional judgment	HUDOC database & Hawkins and Jacoby (2010)
GDP per capita	World Bank (2017)
Population	World Bank (2017)
Civil war	Gleditsch et al. (2002)
FDI inflows	World Bank (2017)
Embeddedness	Fariss (2018)
Competitive executive recruitment	Marshall, Jaggers, and Gurr (2019)
Civil and political rights/Democracy	Coppedge et al. (2019)
Physical integrity rights	Fariss (2014)
Institutional investor country credit rating	Clay and DiGiuseppe (2017)
Civil and political rights judgments	HUDOC database & Hawkins and Jacoby (2010)

of civil society mobilization around an adverse regional court decision are examined. First, freedom of *Speech* is particularly important because it allows individuals to identify and publicize regional court decisions. An ordinal variable capturing freedom of speech is included in the analysis (Cingranelli and Richards, 2010). Freedom of speech is omitted from the models predicting civil and political rights due to the conceptual overlap with the dependent variable. Second, including a measure of civil society participation (*Civil Society*) is important because greater civil society participation is arguably associated with a higher likelihood of elected officials being held accountable and, therefore, regional court deterrence. A variable measuring the size of involvement of people in civil society organizations, restrictions on participation, among other factors, retrieved from the VDEM dataset, is included in most of the models estimated for this chapter. The measure of civil society is omitted from the models predicting freedom of association and the civil and political rights index because the measure of freedom of association includes the extent to which civil society organizations are able to form and operate freely, and the civil and political rights index includes the measure of freedom of association. Third, the models include a binary variable capturing whether the state has adopted a national human rights institution (*NHRI*), including a classical ombudsman office, human rights commission, and human rights ombudsman office. This variable is taken from the Organizational NHRI Project Dataset for the year the NHRI was formally established (Conrad et al., 2013).

In addition to the role of the regional court in each state, rulings against other states in the region likely influence state behavior regarding respect for rights as well (Sikkink, 2011). Neighboring states, aiming to avoid shaming by the regional court and the subsequent costs associated with receiving an adverse decision (including systemic and institutional changes to remedy the violation) use regional court rulings in other states as a signal of future regional court activity. In Chapters 2 and 3, I call this the general deterrent effect of the regional court. As such, a variable representing the presence of adverse judgments found by the regional court within the region for every year is included (*Regional Judgment*).[1]

Control variables commonly used in studies of state respect for human rights are included as well. Factors that improve human rights practices include democracy and economic development; factors that hinder good human rights practices include a large population, internal conflict, and prior experience with repression (Davenport and Armstrong, 2004). Data on *Democracy* is taken from the VDEM dataset, in which democracy is conceptualized as the extent to which the electoral principle of democracy is achieved, including responsiveness and accountability between leaders and citizens through the mechanisms of competitive elections (the polyarchy index) (Coppedge et al., 2019). The democracy variable is omitted from the models predicting freedom of association and the civil and political rights index because the freedom of association measure is used to create the democracy measure, and the freedom of association measure is used to create the civil and political rights index.

To account for economic development, the models include a measure of logged GDP per capita (*GDP*) taken from the World Bank's *World Development Indicators*. GDP per capita is omitted from the models assessing fiscal flexibility (Hypothesis 2) because the institutional investor country credit rating is highly correlated with GDP per capita. The logged total population, in millions, (*Population*) is also taken from the World Bank's *World Development Indicators*. Data on the occurrence of civil conflict (*Civil War*) are obtained from the Uppsala armed conflict data project (Gleditsch et al., 2002; Harbom and Wallensteen, 2005).

---

[1] In order to examine the independent influence of the regional court in the region, this variable excludes any adverse regional court decisions against each individual state.

Although many studies explaining state respect for human rights include a lagged dependent variable in their models, the inclusion of such a variable is not necessary in the models in which the Fariss (2014) data are used as a dependent variable. The Fariss (2014) variable uses mean estimates generated from a dynamic item-response theory model, which allows for changing standards of accountability or more stringent standards on the part of monitoring agencies. In other words, the model accounts for the increase in the probability of observing and coding rights violations over time as monitoring agencies that produce reports used to generate repression variables have greater access to information. The estimates used in the empirical analysis in this book are generated from a model in which physical integrity rights scores for a country in a particular year are dependent on the value of the same country in the previous year (Fariss, 2014, 304). For the models estimated with a different dependent variable, I include a lagged dependent variable in the models. That is, for the models examining the influence of adverse regional court judgments associated with civil and political rights on respect for civil and political rights (Hypothesis 1), I include a lagged repression variable in the estimation. Also, for the models estimated as robustness checks, including the models utilizing the change in physical integrity rights from the Cingranelli, Richards, and Clay (2014) physical integrity rights index, I include a lagged dependent variable. I rely on changes in the Cingranelli, Richards, and Clay (2014) physical integrity rights index, rather than changes in the Fariss (2014) estimates because the Cingranelli, Richards, and Clay (2014) physical integrity rights index does not use human rights scores from prior years to generate current human rights scores. As a result, a change in the Cingranelli, Richards, and Clay (2014) physical integrity rights index captures substantive changes in respect for rights from year to year, not accounting for rights in prior years.

In addition, in each model I include the variables capturing economic incentives (FDI inflows or multilateral aid), embeddedness in the international human rights regime, and competitiveness of executive recruitment. *Economic incentives* are an indicator of executive willingness and are examined more fully in Chapter 6. *Embeddedness* in the international human rights regime captures the extent to which the state is socialized in the international human rights regime (Fariss, 2018). States that are more socialized are more likely to respond favorably to international human rights law. I also control for competitiveness of executive recruitment (*Exec Recruit*) to capture the extent to which there are electoral institutions in place that generate executive incentives to engage in human rights policy change. Executive elections are examined more fully as an indicator of executive willingness in Chapter 5.

B.2 FULL MODEL RESULTS

Tables B.2–B.4 display results from models estimated to test Hypothesis 1, and the results are presented graphically in Figures 4.2 and 4.3.

TABLE B.2. *Hypothesis 1: Effect of adverse European Court judgments on civil and political rights and physical integrity rights*

	Europe (Civ/Pol Rights)	Europe (Association)	Europe (Discussion)	Europe (Phyinst)
Adverse judgment (t-1)	0.002	0.012***	0.005**	0.005
	(0.007)	(0.004)	(0.002)	(0.004)
Adverse judgment (t-3)	0.013	0.008	0.011***	0.001
	(0.009)	(0.006)	(0.002)	(0.006)
Adverse judgment (t-5)	0.011**	0.009***	0.009***	0.001
	(0.005)	(0.002)	(0.002)	(0.006)
Economic incentives (t-1)	0.003	0.002	0.007**	−0.000
	(0.003)	(0.001)	(0.003)	(0.004)
Embeddedness (t-1)	0.015	0.007	0.013	0.007
	(0.009)	(0.005)	(0.008)	(0.010)
Judicial power (t-1)	0.171***	0.144***	0.028	0.009
	(0.063)	(0.053)	(0.065)	(0.067)
Speech (t-1)				0.006
				(0.011)
Civil society (t-1)			0.370***	0.104
			(0.110)	(0.107)
Leg opposition (t-1)			0.002	−0.007
			(0.015)	(0.011)
NHRI (t-1)	−0.022**	−0.013**	0.002	0.031**
	(0.010)	(0.006)	(0.013)	(0.014)
Exec recruitment (t-1)	0.078**	0.067***	0.006	0.024
	(0.030)	(0.019)	(0.030)	(0.034)
Respect for rights (t-1)	0.017**	0.006	−0.007	
	(0.009)	(0.005)	(0.009)	
Civil war (t-1)	0.027	0.015	−0.088	−0.003
	(0.026)	(0.020)	(0.058)	(0.017)
Democracy (t-1)			0.586***	0.112
			(0.185)	(0.160)
Population (logged) (t-1)	0.006	−0.002	0.013	−0.038**
	(0.011)	(0.014)	(0.012)	(0.018)
GDP (logged) (t-1)	0.001	0.002	−0.030***	0.018
	(0.012)	(0.007)	(0.007)	(0.013)

TABLE B.2. (Continued)

	Europe (Civ/Pol Rights)	Europe (Association)	Europe (Discussion)	Europe (Phyinst)
Regional judgments (t-1)	−0.000	0.000	0.000	0.000
	(0.000)	(0.000)	(0.000)	(0.000)
Constant	0.475***	0.513***	0.267	0.104
	(0.120)	(0.078)	(0.166)	(0.184)
R^2	0.516	0.451	0.650	0.541
N	814	682	672	669

Notes: Parameter estimates and standard errors reported. Statistical significance: ***$p < 0.01$, **$p < 0.05$, *$p < 0.10$. Models estimated with standard errors clustered on country. Two-tailed significance tests reported. Civil society, legislative opposition, and the democracy measures are omitted from the Civ/Pol Rights and Association models due to conceptual overlap (described in the preceding section on control variables). Freedom of speech is omitted from the Civ/Pol Rights, Association, and Discussion models due to conceptual overlap with the dependent variable. Respect for rights (t-1) omitted from Physint model due to the construction of the repression estimates (described in the preceding section).

TABLE B.3. *Hypothesis 1: Effect of adverse Inter-American Court judgments on civil and political rights and physical integrity rights*

	Americas (Civ/Pol Rights)	Americas (Association)	Americas (Discussion)	Americas (Physint)
Adverse judgment (t-1)	0.021*	0.016**	0.024***	0.011
	(0.011)	(0.008)	(0.007)	(0.010)
Adverse judgment (t-3)	0.024*	0.033**	0.012*	0.015
	(0.013)	(0.016)	(0.007)	(0.012)
Adverse judgment (t-5)	0.027*	0.026*	0.032**	0.017*
	(0.017)	(0.015)	(0.016)	(0.013)
Economic incentives (t-1)	−0.001	−0.000	−0.002	0.000
	(0.004)	(0.002)	(0.002)	(0.000)
Embeddedness (t-1)	−0.010	−0.000	−0.004	0.026*
	(0.012)	(0.007)	(0.008)	(0.014)
Judicial power (t-1)	0.382**	0.192**	0.154	0.567***
	(0.173)	(0.091)	(0.102)	(0.122)
Speech (t-1)				0.020**
				(0.007)
Civil society (t-1)			0.012	0.018
			(0.115)	(0.099)
Leg opposition (t-1)			0.015	−0.025**
			(0.013)	(0.013)

(Continued)

TABLE B.3. (Continued)

	Americas (Civ/Pol Rights)	Americas (Association)	Americas (Discussion)	Americas (Physint)
NHRI (t-1)	−0.038	−0.019	−0.015	0.085**
	(0.044)	(0.029)	(0.014)	(0.035)
Exec recruitment (t-1)	0.055***	0.037***	0.021	0.006
	(0.017)	(0.012)	(0.025)	(0.015)
Civil war (t-1)	−0.128***	−0.110***	0.007	−0.098***
	(0.045)	(0.032)	(0.048)	(0.029)
Respect for rights (t-1)	0.022	0.14	0.014	
	(0.025)	(.016)	(0.014)	
Population (logged) (t-1)	0.011	0.010	0.020	−0.081***
	(0.019)	(0.013)	(0.021)	(0.013)
GDP (logged) (t-1)	−0.020	−0.001	−0.006	0.023
	(0.019)	(0.010)	(0.11)	(0.018)
Regional judgments (t-1)	−0.002	−0.002*	−0.001	0.006***
	(0.002)	(0.001)	(0.001)	(0.002)
Constant	0.702***	0.664***	−0.062	−0.088
	(0.140)	(0.084)	(0.095)	(0.177)
R^2	0.595	0.652	0.499	0.768
N	375	375	375	364

Notes: Parameter estimates and standard errors reported. Statistical significance: ***$p < .01$, **$p < .05$, *$p < .10$. Models estimated with standard errors clustered on country. Two-tailed significance tests reported. Civil society, legislative opposition, and the democracy measures are omitted from the Civ/Pol Rights and Association models due to conceptual overlap (described in the preceeding section on control variables). Freedom of speech is omitted from the Civ/Pol Rights, Association, and Discussion models due to conceptual overlap with the dependent variable. Respect for rights (t-1) omitted from Physint model due to the construction of the repression estimates (described in the preceeding section).

TABLE B.4. *Hypothesis 1: Effect of adverse regional court judgments on change in respect for civil/political rights and physical integrity rights (3 years postjudgment)*

	Europe (Civ/Pol Rights)	Europe (Physint)	Americas (Civ/Pol Rights)	Americas (Physint)
Adverse judgment (t-3)	0.007*	−0.078	0.023**	0.010
	(0.004)	(0.075)	(0.011)	(0.140)
Adverse judgment (t-2)	0.004	−0.015	0.017	−0.083
	0.004	(0.077)	(0.012)	(0.225)
Adverse judgment (t-1)	0.003	−0.025	0.020*	−0.007
	(0.003)	(0.071)	(0.011)	(0.191)

TABLE B.4. (Continued)

	Europe (Civ/Pol Rights)	Europe (Physint)	Americas (Civ/Pol Rights)	Americas (Physint)
Economic incentives (t-1)	0.004	0.029	−0.004	0.001
	(0.003)	(0.029)	(0.002)	(0.001)
Embeddedness (t-1)	0.003	−0.061	−0.007	0.224*
	(0.007)	(0.060)	(0.014)	(0.120)
Judicial power (t-1)	0.143**	1.40**	0.207*	1.99**
	(0.071)	(0.610)	(0.110)	(0.963)
Speech (t-1)		0.082		0.331*
		(0.077)		(0.172)
Civil society (t-1)		2.97***		−1.86*
		(0.862)		(0.899)
Leg opposition (t-1)		0.076		−0.146
		(0.057)		(0.123)
NHRI (t-1)	−0.000	0.129	−0.019	0.241*
	(0.005)	(0.130)	(0.025)	(0.143)
Exec recruitment (t-1)	0.065**	−0.339	0.030*	0.282
	(0.033)	(0.313)	(0.019)	(0.185)
Respect for rights (t-1)	−0.493***	−0.621***	−0.631***	−0.767***
	(0.139)	(0.078)	(0.087)	(0.073)
Civil war (t-1)	0.009	−0.757**	−0.084**	−1.00**
	(0.020)	(0.292)	(0.034)	(0.453)
Democracy (t-1)		2.04		3.99**
		(1.50)		(1.43)
Population (logged) (t-1)	−0.008	−0.129**	−0.004	−0.629***
	(0.007)	(0.050)	(0.009)	(0.103)
GDP (logged) (t-1)	0.001	−0.139	−0.011	−0.131
	(0.008)	(0.091)	(0.017)	(0.136)
Regional judgments (t-1)	−0.0002	−0.000	−0.001	−0.007
	(0.0002)	(0.001)	(0.002)	(0.021)
Constant	0.147*	1.02	0.494***	1.59
	(0.078)	(1.01)	(0.109)	(1.38)
R^2	0.102	0.338	0.527	0.472
N	747	692	413	396

Notes: Parameter estimates and standard errors reported. Statistical significance: ***$p < 0.01$, **$p < 0.05$, *$p < 0.10$. Models estimated with standard errors clustered on country. Two-tailed significance tests reported. Coefficient estimates display the change in respect for rights 3 years following an adverse European or Inter-American Court judgment. Also included in these models is the lagged level of respect for rights. A negative estimate indicates that states with larger changes in respect for rights have lower levels of respect for rights.

Tables B.5–B.7 display results from models estimated to test Hypothesis 2. The results for Europe are presented graphically in Figure 4.4 (results from column 1 of Tables B.5–B.7). Results for the Americas are presented graphically in Figure 4.5 (column 3 of Tables B.5–B.7).

TABLE B.5. *Hypothesis 2: Effect of adverse regional court judgments and fiscal flexibility on respect for rights (1 year postjudgment)*

	Europe	Europe (Change DV)	Americas	Americas (Change DV)
Adverse judgment*Fiscal flexibility (t-1)	0.001 (0.001)	0.005* (0.003)	0.011*** (0.003)	0.029** (0.010)
Adverse judgment (t-1)	−0.011 (0.101)	−0.464* (0.258)	−0.331** (0.105)	−1.09** (0.391)
Fiscal flexibility (t-1)	0.005* (0.003)	−0.001 (0.004)	0.014** (0.006)	−0.003 (0.006)
Economic incentives (t-1)	0.001 (0.004)	0.009** (0.004)	0.001 (0.001)	0.001 (0.001)
Embeddedness (t-1)	0.081 (0.065)	−0.117** (0.045)	0.146* (0.090)	0.150 (0.123)
Judicial power (t-1)	0.274 (0.460)	1.16** (0.554)	2.06*** (0.642)	1.31** (0.522)
Speech (t-1)	0.024 (0.070)	0.018 (0.080)	0.072** (0.032)	0.183 (0.128)
Civil society (t-1)	0.783 (0.618)	2.60*** (0.723)	−0.307 (0.473)	−0.620 (0.522)
Leg opposition (t-1)	−0.015 (0.068)	0.043 (0.050)	−0.094 (0.067)	−0.081 (0.100)
NHRI (t-1)	0.220** (0.088)	0.205** (0.088)	0.281** (0.126)	0.225** (0.098)
Exec recruitment (t-1)	0.173 (0.145)	−0.094 (0.178)	0.033 (0.066)	0.228 (0.150)
Civil war (t-1)	−0.011 (0.124)	−0.716** (0.284)	−0.606*** (0.144)	−0.926*** (0.280)
Democracy (t-1)	0.806 (1.11)	0.458 (1.18)	1.21 (0.931)	2.17* (1.17)
Population (logged) (t-1)	−0.302*** (0.099)	−0.130** (0.050)	−0.475*** (0.082)	−0.482*** (0.104)
Regional judgments (t-1)	0.001 (0.001)	−0.002* (0.000)	0.159** (0.057)	−0.143 (0.105)
Physint (t-1)		−0.567*** (0.072)		−0.566*** (0.077)

TABLE B.5. *(Continued)*

	Europe	Europe (Change DV)	Americas	Americas (Change DV)
Constant	−0.657 (0.942)	0.964* (0.564)	−1.61*** (0.488)	0.800 (0.578)
R^2	0.613	0.288	0.783	0.302
N	683	683	391	389

Notes: Parameter estimates and standard errors reported. Statistical significance: ***$p < 0.01$, **$p < 0.05$, *$p < 0.10$. Models estimated with standard errors clustered on country. Two-tailed significance tests reported. Model results in the second and fourth columns report coefficient estimates and standard errors for models predicting the change in respect for rights 1 year following the judgment. I estimate a robustness check for the change in rights 1 year postjudgment because this is the most robust result of the models testing Hypothesis 2 reported in Chapter 4. Lagged physical integrity rights are included in the change models because they are estimated using the Cingranelli, Richards, and Clay (2014) physical integrity rights index, which does not take into account the level of respect for rights in the prior year like the Fariss (2014) latent repression estimates.

TABLE B.6. *Hypothesis 2: Effect of adverse regional court judgments and fiscal flexibility on respect for rights (3 years postjudgment)*

	Europe	Americas
Adverse judgment*Fiscal flexibility (t-3)	−0.002 (0.002)	−0.001 (0.004)
Adverse judgment (t-3)	0.123 (0.173)	0.073 (0.146)
Adverse judgment (t-2)	0.024 (0.026)	0.028 (0.062)
Adverse judgment (t-1)	0.012 (0.024)	0.075 (0.050)
Fiscal flexibility (t-1)	0.003 (0.003)	0.013** (0.006)
Economic incentives (t-1)	0.001 (0.004)	0.001 (0.0004)
Embeddedness (t-1)	0.082 (0.065)	0.207** (0.100)
Judicial power (t-1)	0.103 (0.429)	2.90*** (0.632)
Speech (t-1)	0.031 (0.072)	0.071** (0.035)
Civil society (t-1)	0.906 (0.628)	−0.027 (0.474)

(Continued)

TABLE B.6. *(Continued)*

	Europe	Americas
Leg opposition (*t*-1)	−0.070	−0.147***
	(0.065)	(0.055)
NHRI (*t*-1)	0.229**	0.314***
	(0.092)	(0.113)
Exec recruitment (*t*-1)	0.041	0.013
	(0.186)	(0.060)
Civil war (*t*-1)	−0.031	−0.557***
	(0.116)	(0.125)
Democracy (*t*-1)	1.03	0.679
	(1.21)	(0.796)
Population (logged) (*t*-1)	−0.272**	−0.398***
	(0.112)	(0.105)
Regional judgments (*t*-1)	0.0004	0.081
	(0.001)	(0.052)
Constant	−0.344	−1.95
	(1.12)	(0.499)
R^2	0.532	0.751
N	654	355

Notes: Parameter estimates and standard errors reported. Statistical significance: ***$p < 0.01$, **$p < 0.05$, *$p < 0.10$. Models estimated with standard errors clustered on country. Two-tailed significance tests reported.

TABLE B.7. *Hypothesis 2: Effect of adverse regional court judgments and fiscal flexibility on respect for rights (5 years postjudgment)*

	Europe	Americas
Adverse judgment*Fiscal flexibility (*t*-5)	−0.003	0.009
	(0.003)	(0.006)
Adverse judgment (*t*-5)	0.263	−0.300
	(0.252)	(0.239)
Adverse judgment (*t*-4)	−0.019	−0.024
	(0.027)	(0.057)
Adverse judgment (*t*-3)	−0.004	−0.104
	(0.029)	(0.069)
Adverse judgment (*t*-2)	0.025	−0.076
	(0.025)	(0.081)
Adverse Judgment (*t*-1)	0.008	−0.024
	(0.022)	(0.060)
Fiscal flexibility (*t*-1)	0.003	0.011*
	(0.004)	(0.006)

TABLE B.7. (Continued)

	Europe	Americas
Economic incentives (t-1)	0.001	0.001*
	(0.004)	(0.001)
Embeddedness (t-1)	0.076	0.300**
	(0.062)	(0.113)
Judicial power (t-1)	0.331	1.02
	(0.516)	(0.771)
Speech (t-1)	0.021	0.108
	(0.079)	(0.070)
Civil society (t-1)	1.08*	−0.291
	(0.635)	(0.356)
Leg opposition (t-1)	−0.017	−0.121
	(0.073)	(0.091)
NHRI (t-1)	0.227**	0.160
	(0.089)	(0.112)
Exec recruitment (t-1)	0.029	−0.230
	(0.245)	(0.144)
Civil war (t-1)	−0.014	−0.336
	(0.114)	(0.252)
Democracy (t-1)	0.568	3.48**
	(1.17)	(1.40)
Population (logged) (t-1)	−0.283***	−0.537***
	(0.102)	(0.082)
Regional judgments (t-1)	0.001	0.177**
	(0.001)	(0.090)
Constant	−0.221	−2.27**
	(1.14)	(0.859)
R^2	0.554	0.813
N	605	318

Notes: Parameter estimates and standard errors reported. Statistical significance: ***$p < 0.01$, **$p < 0.05$, *$p < 0.10$. Models estimated with standard errors clustered on country. Two-tailed significance tests reported.

Some of the key interaction terms of interest are not significant in the reported model results. However, as Brambor, Clark, and Golder (2006) indicate, for a model where two variables are interacted (e.g., X and Z), interaction terms may be insignificant because it is possible for the contribution of X on Y to be statistically significant for certain values of Z. As a result, one cannot infer whether X has a meaningful conditional effect on Y from the magnitude and significance of the coefficient on the interaction term. Instead, the conditional effect should be examined based on the marginal effect at every observed value of Z (Berry, Golder, and Milton, 2012). As a result, I utilize plots of the marginal linear effect of an adverse judgment across values of fiscal flexibility in the main text.

Some of the interaction terms are also negative, specifically in the European Court model 3 and 5 years postjudgment and the Inter-American Court model 3 years postjudgment. The interaction terms should be interpreted alongside the main effects (constituent terms). In this case, when the interaction term is negative, the constituent terms are positive. Fiscal flexibility is positively associated with rights in the absence of an adverse judgment. The interaction term indicates that when adverse judgments are present, the slope of fiscal flexibility decreases. However, the slope of fiscal flexibility is still positive, as shown when I plot the relationship. More specifically, the relationship between fiscal flexibility and respect for rights is positive in the absence of an adverse judgment, but in the presence of an adverse judgment, it is still positive, though weaker than in the absence of an adverse judgment. Also of note – in models where the adverse judgment is lagged 1 year, the interaction terms are positive, indicating that fiscally flexible states have greater capacity to deal with the policy changes required by the regional court more readily in the year following an adverse judgment. Executives with capacity may not find it necessary to delay policy changes needed for regional court deterrence.

Appendix C

Chapter 5 Appendix

C.1 CONTROL VARIABLES

I utilize several control variables in the analyses. Table C.1 lists all of the variables used in the analyses. Justification for each of the control variables is described in more detail in the Appendices to Chapters 3 and 4. Democracy and competitiveness of executive recruitment are omitted from the models testing Hypothesis 3 in which executive job security is conceptualized as election timing because of the conceptual overlap with the primary independent variable of interest (presence of executive elections). The democracy variable accounts for the extent to which the electoral principle of democracy is achieved and should predict whether elections are held, thereby overlapping conceptually with the presence of an executive election. The competitiveness of executive recruitment variable captures whether the chief executive is chosen through elections or in another manner and should also predict whether elections are held regularly, which overlaps conceptually with the presence of executive elections variable.

The democracy variable is included in the models testing Hypothesis 3 in which executive job security is conceptualized as executive electoral competitiveness because achievement of the electoral principle of democracy does not determine whether elections are competitive. The democracy variable captures whether suffrage is extensive, elections are clean and fair, among several other features of elections, and although these institutional features are highly associated with whether an election is held, they are unlikely to overlap conceptually with competitiveness of any particular executive election in practice. Competitiveness of executive recruitment is also included in the models in which executive job security is conceptualized as competitiveness of executive elections because competitive executive recruitment does not predict whether the election will be competitive, but whether electoral institutions in place to choose or select potential executives are competitive.

C.2 FULL MODEL RESULTS

TABLE C.1. *Control variables*

Variable	Source
Executive election	Coppedge et al. (2019)
Executive election vote share	Coppedge et al. (2019)
Political stability	World Bank (2014)
Competitive executive recruitment	Marshall, Jaggers, and Gurr (2019)
Civil war	Gleditsch et al. (2002)
Judicial power	Linzer and Staton (2015)
Legislative opposition	Coppedge et al. (2019)
FDI inflows	World Bank (2017)
Multilateral aid	OECD (2018)
Freedom of speech	Cingranelli, Richards, and Clay (2014)
Civil society participation	Coppedge et al. (2019)
National human rights institution	Conrad et al. (2013)
GDP per capita	World Bank (2017)
Population	World Bank (2017)
Embeddedness	Fariss (2018)
Democracy	Coppedge et al. (2019)
Level of respect for physical integrity rights	Fariss (2014)
Change in respect for physical integrity rights	Cingranelli, Richards, and Clay (2014)

TABLE C.2. *Hypothesis 3: Effect of adverse regional court judgments and electoral incentives on respect for rights (judgment 1 year before election)*

	Europe (election)	Europe (no election)	Americas (election)	Americas (no election)
Adverse judgment (t-1)	0.061	0.031	0.143	0.026
	(0.081)	(0.038)	(0.135)	(0.077)
Economic incentives (t-1)	0.006	0.0004	0.043	0.036
	(0.007)	(0.003)	(0.028)	(0.024)
Judicial power (t-1)	2.39***	0.116	2.09**	2.08**
	(0.707)	(0.482)	(0.852)	(0.689)
Embeddedness (t-1)	0.205**	0.099	0.204*	0.101
	(0.092)	(0.064)	(0.116)	(0.096)
Regional judgments (t-1)	−0.412**	0.016	0.140	0.201**
	(0.171)	(0.027)	(0.121)	(0.066)
Speech (t-1)	−0.066	0.031	0.020	0.084**
	(0.102)	(0.069)	(0.070)	(0.040)
Civil society (t-1)	0.402	0.595	0.758*	0.409
	(0.551)	(0.570)	(0.450)	(0.501)
NHRI (t-1)	0.170	0.155*	0.394**	0.313**
	(0.192)	(0.092)	(0.165)	(0.159)

TABLE C.2. *(Continued)*

	Europe (election)	Europe (no election)	Americas (election)	Americas (no election)
Leg opposition (t-1)	−0.086 (0.071)	−0.024 (0.078)	−0.045 (0.102)	−0.079 (0.075)
Population (logged) (t-1)	−0.349** (0.132)	−0.312*** (0.093)	−0.367*** (0.080)	−0.308*** (0.096)
GDP (logged) (t-1)	−0.049 (0.102)	0.140* (0.083)	0.040 (0.142)	0.177* (0.115)
Civil war (t-1)	−0.148 (0.335)	−0.049 (0.131)	−0.928*** (0.159)	−0.676*** (0.177)
Constant	−0.466 (0.848)	−1.73 (1.32)	−1.64 (1.07)	−2.47** (0.926)
R^2	0.698	0.665	0.779	0.751
N	73	734	103	344

Notes: Table C.2 displays coefficient estimates and standard errors from a model examining the influence of an adverse regional court judgment 1 year before an election on respect for rights. The results reported in Table C.2 correspond with the results reported in Figures 5.1 and 5.2. Democracy and competitiveness of executive recruitment are omitted from the models because of the conceptual overlap with the presence or absence of an election. The democracy variable accounts for the extent to which the electoral principle of democracy is achieved and should predict whether elections are held. The competitiveness of executive recruitment variable captures whether the chief executive is chosen through elections or in another manner and should also predict whether elections are held regularly. Statistical significance: ***$p < 0.01$, **$p < 0.05$, *$p < 0.10$. Models estimated with clustered standard errors on country. Two-tailed significance tests reported.

TABLE C.3. *Hypothesis 3: Effect of adverse regional court judgments and electoral incentives on respect for rights (judgment 2 years before election)*

	Europe (election)	Europe (no election)	Americas (election)	Americas (no election)
Adverse judgment (t-2)	0.095 (0.104)	0.019 (0.034)	0.337** (0.142)	0.054 (0.057)
Adverse judgment (t-1)	0.031 (0.085)	0.027 (0.032)	0.136 (0.109)	0.032 (0.063)
Economic incentives (t-1)	−0.002 (0.007)	0.0004 (0.003)	0.044 (0.030)	0.033 (0.025)
Judicial power (t-1)	2.39*** (0.758)	−0.026 (0.440)	2.42** (0.847)	2.38*** (0.623)
Embeddedness (t-1)	0.103 (0.094)	0.096 (0.064)	0.211** (0.096)	0.123 (0.084)

(Continued)

TABLE C.3. *(Continued)*

	Europe (election)	Europe (no election)	Americas (election)	Americas (no election)
Regional judgments (t-2)	−0.103	0.012	−0.017	0.154***
	(0.193)	(0.021)	(0.065)	(0.044)
Speech (t-1)	−0.061	0.038	0.047	0.078*
	(0.112)	(0.070)	(0.066)	(0.041)
Civil society (t-1)	0.613	0.640	0.648	0.628
	(0.691)	(0.588)	(0.454)	(0.502)
NHRI (t-1)	0.405**	0.165*	0.504***	0.369**
	(0.205)	(0.094)	(0.162)	(0.142)
Leg opposition (t-1)	−0.050	−0.047	−0.054*	−0.131**
	(0.075)	(0.076)	(0.085)	(0.057)
Population (logged) (t-1)	−0.318*	−0.304***	−0.373***	−0.290***
	(0.163)	(0.100)	(0.075)	(0.103)
GDP (logged) (t-1)	−0.027	0.137*	0.034	0.171*
	(0.119)	(0.088)	(0.118)	(0.103)
Civil war (t-1)	−0.875*	−0.048	−0.885***	−0.695***
	(0.494)	(0.126)	(0.184)	(0.157)
Constant	−0.756	−1.49	−1.75**	−2.73***
	(1.01)	(1.32)	(0.866)	(0.876)
R^2	0.714	0.645	0.771	0.733
N	70	719	100	330

Notes: Table C.3 displays coefficient estimates and standard errors from a model examining the influence of an adverse regional court judgment 2 years before an election on respect for rights. The results reported in Table C.3 correspond with the results reported in Figures 5.1 and 5.2. Democracy and competitiveness of executive recruitment are omitted from the models because of the conceptual overlap with the the presence or absence of an election. The democracy variable accounts for the extent to which the electoral principle of democracy is achieved and should predict whether elections are held. The competitiveness of executive recruitment variable captures whether the chief executive is chosen through elections or in another manner and should also predict whether elections are held regularly. Statistical significance: ***$p < 0.01$, **$p < 0.05$, *$p < 0.10$. Models estimated with standard errors clustered on country. Two-tailed significance tests reported.

TABLE C.4. *Hypothesis 3: Effect of adverse regional court judgments and electoral incentives on respect for rights (judgment 3 years before election)*

	Europe (election)	Europe (no election)	Americas (election)	Americas (no election)
Adverse judgment (t-3)	0.131	−0.017	−0.032	0.109*
	(0.116)	(0.035)	(0.126)	(0.058)
Adverse judgment (t-2)	0.020	0.018	0.373**	0.024
	(0.108)	(0.030)	(0.133)	(0.050)

TABLE C.4. (Continued)

	Europe (election)	Europe (no election)	Americas (election)	Americas (no election)
Adverse judgment (t-1)	0.049	0.025	0.102	0.020
	(0.092)	(0.031)	(0.141)	(0.055)
Economic incentives (t-1)	0.001	0.000	0.015	0.030
	(0.007)	(0.004)	(0.028)	(0.026)
Judicial power (t-1)	2.42**	−0.208	3.06***	2.53***
	(0.954)	(0.411)	(0.792)	(0.521)
Embeddedness (t-1)	0.103	0.088	0.182*	0.130*
	(0.108)	(0.065)	(0.110)	(0.072)
Regional judgments (t-3)	−0.102	0.013	0.110	0.159***
	(0.231)	(0.020)	(0.092)	(0.052)
Speech (t-1)	−0.076	0.037	0.031	0.090**
	(0.125)	(0.071)	(0.065)	(0.038)
Civil society (t-1)	0.644	0.651	0.105	0.612
	(1.13)	(0.579)	(0.477)	(0.455)
NHRI (t-1)	0.345*	0.167*	0.480***	0.379***
	(0.205)	(0.099)	(0.184)	(0.140)
Leg opposition (t-1)	−0.029	−0.079	−0.110*	−0.125**
	(0.124)	(0.076)	(0.066)	(0.055)
Population (logged) (t-1)	−0.334**	−0.292**	−0.370***	−0.282***
	(0.163)	(0.105)	(0.103)	(0.103)
GDP (logged) (t-1)	−0.044	0.155*	−0.006	0.154*
	(0.139)	(0.094)	(0.114)	(0.093)
Civil war (t-1)	−0.654	−0.053	−0.743***	−0.649***
	(0.544)	(0.118)	(0.191)	(0.149)
Constant	−0.545	−1.38	−1.17	−2.74***
	(1.19)	(1.32)	(0.801)	(0.746)
R^2	0.662	0.620	0.755	0.729
N	65	703	93	320

Notes: Table C.4 displays coefficient estimates and standard errors from a model examining the influence of an adverse regional court judgment 3 years before an election on respect for rights. The results reported in Table C.4 correspond with the results reported in Figures 5.1 and 5.2. Democracy and competitiveness of executive recruitment are omitted from the models because of the conceptual overlap with the presence or absence of an election. The democracy variable accounts for the extent to which the electoral principle of democracy is achieved and should predict whether elections are held. The competitiveness of executive recruitment variable captures whether the chief executive is chosen through elections or in another manner and should also predict whether elections are held regularly. Statistical significance: ***$p < 0.01$, **$p < 0.05$, *$p < 0.10$. Models estimated with standard errors clustered on country. Two-tailed significance tests reported.

TABLE C.5. *Hypothesis 3: Effect of adverse European Court judgments and electoral incentives on respect for rights (interaction term models)*

	Europe (t-1)	Europe (t-2)	Europe (t-3)
Adverse judgment (lagged)*Election	0.003	0.001	0.031**
	(0.011)	(0.010)	(0.010)
Adverse judgment (t-1)	0.005	0.036	0.027
	(0.004)	(0.034)	(0.030)
Adverse judgment (t-2)		0.003	0.027
		(0.004)	(0.030)
Adverse judgment (t-3)			0.0001
			(0.005)
Election (t)	−0.004	−0.020	−0.043**
	(0.021)	(0.017)	(0.019)
Economic incentives (t-1)	0.001	0.0003	0.0001
	(0.003)	(0.003)	(0.004)
Judicial power (t-1)	0.188	0.000	−0.194
	(0.504)	(0.459)	(0.422)
Embeddedness (t-1)	0.106*	0.100	0.101
	(0.064)	(0.065)	(0.066)
Regional judgments (lagged) (t-1)	−0.002	−0.001	0.003
	(0.026)	(0.027)	(0.028)
Speech (t-1)	0.023	0.028	0.027
	(0.067)	(0.068)	(0.069)
Civil society (t-1)	0.466	0.507	0.558
	(0.539)	(0.547)	(0.590)
NHRI (t-1)	0.163*	0.181*	0.181*
	(0.093)	(0.097)	(0.101)
Leg opposition (t-1)	−0.025	−0.046	−0.070
	(0.080)	(0.076)	(0.075)
Population (logged) (t-1)	−0.311**	−0.293**	−0.271**
	(0.102)	(0.109)	(0.115)
GDP (logged) (t-1)	0.124*	0.124	0.116
	(0.081)	(0.085)	(0.090)
Civil war (t-1)	−0.052	−0.053	−0.060
	(0.126)	(0.121)	(0.117)
Constant	−1.51	−1.24	−1.08
	(1.27)	(1.25)	(1.31)
R^2	0.654	0.631	0.598
N	807	789	768

Notes: Table C.5 displays coefficient estimates and standard errors from three models examining the influence of an adverse European Court judgment 1, 2, and 3 years before an election on respect for rights, utilizing interaction terms consisting of the presence of one or more adverse European Court judgments and the presence of an election. Democracy and competitiveness of executive recruitment are omitted from the models because of the conceptual overlap with the presence or absence of an election. The democracy variable accounts for the extent to which the electoral principle of democracy is achieved and should predict whether elections are held. The competitiveness of executive recruitment variable captures whether the chief executive is chosen through elections or in another manner and should also predict whether elections are held regularly. Statistical significance: ***$p < 0.01$, **$p < 0.05$, *$p < 0.10$. Models estimated with standard errors clustered on country. Two-tailed significance tests reported.

TABLE C.6. *Hypothesis 3: Effect of adverse Inter-American Court judgments and electoral incentives on respect for rights (interaction term models)*

	Americas (t-1)	Americas (t-2)	Americas (t-3)
Adverse judgment (lagged)*Election	−0.003 (0.056)	0.061** (0.029)	−0.102 (0.064)
Adverse judgment (t-1)	0.037 (0.037)	0.035 (0.052)	0.033 (0.053)
Adverse judgment (t-2)		0.035 (0.045)	0.031 (0.056)
Adverse judgment (t-3)			0.100** (0.034)
Election (t)	−0.012 (0.022)	−0.040 (0.027)	0.025 (0.028)
Economic incentives (t-1)	−0.0001 (0.0004)	−0.0002 (0.0004)	−0.0002 (0.0004)
Judicial power (t-1)	2.79*** (0.611)	2.73*** (0.626)	2.75*** (0.562)
Embeddedness (t-1)	−0.023 (0.140)	−0.026 (0.136)	0.014 (0.121)
Regional judgments (lagged) (t-1)	0.024* (0.012)	0.022* (0.013)	0.021 (0.013)
Speech (t-1)	0.105** (0.034)	0.101** (0.033)	0.090** (0.033)
Civil society (t-1)	0.392 (0.467)	0.256 (0.407)	0.471 (0.338)
NHRI (t-1)	0.270 (0.217)	0.275 (0.206)	0.290 (0.176)
Leg opposition (t-1)	−0.087 (0.083)	−0.087 (0.074)	−0.131** (0.053)
Population (logged) (t-1)	0.771 (1.10)	0.822 (1.09)	−0.661 (1.01)
GDP (logged) (t-1)	0.167 (0.129)	0.179 (0.119)	0.129 (0.100)
Civil war (t-1)	−0.604** (0.209)	−0.557** (0.195)	−0.620*** (0.162)
Constant	−4.98* (2.52)	−5.06* (2.47)	−4.45* (2.17)
R^2	0.654	0.651	0.667
N	440	426	408

Notes: Table C.6 displays coefficient estimates and standard errors from a model examining the influence of an adverse Inter-American Court judgment 1, 2, and 3 years before an election on respect for rights utilizing interaction terms consisting of the presence of one or more adverse Inter-American Court judgments and the presence or absence of an election. The results reported in the second column of Table C.6 correspond with the results reported in Figure 5.3. Democracy and competitiveness of executive recruitment are omitted from the models because of the conceptual overlap with the presence or absence of an election. The democracy variable accounts for the extent to which the electoral principle of democracy is achieved and should predict whether elections are held. The competitiveness of executive recruitment variable captures whether the chief executive is chosen through elections or in another manner and should also predict whether elections are held regularly. Statistical significance: ***$p < 0.01$, **$p < 0.05$, *$p < 0.10$. Models estimated with standard errors clustered on country. Two-tailed significance tests reported.

The following tables display full model results. Tables C.8, C.9, C.10, C.12, C.13, C.14, and C.16 all include models estimated utilizing interaction terms. Some of the key interaction terms of interest are not significant in the reported model results. However, as Brambor, Clark, and Golder (2006) indicate, for a model where two variables are interacted (e.g., X and Z), interaction terms may be insignificant because it is possible for the contribution of X on Y to be statistically significant for certain values of Z. As a result, one cannot infer whether X has a meaningful conditional effect on Y from the magnitude and significance of the coefficient on the interaction term. Instead, the conditional effect should be examined based on the marginal effect at every observed value of Z (Berry, Golder, and Milton, 2012). As a result, I utilize plots of the marginal linear effect of an adverse judgment in the presence or absence of an election, across values of executive vote share and political stability in the main text.

Tables C.7, C.11, and C.15 report results from robustness checks using changes in the Cingranelli, Richards, and Clay (2014) physical integrity rights index as the dependent variable. Table C.7 displays results from models predicting the influence of adverse Inter-American Court judgments on the change in respect for rights conditional on executive job security, operationalized as election timing. Table C.11 reports substantive results from models predicting the influence of adverse European and Inter-American Court judgments on the change in respect for rights conditional on executive job security, operationalized as electoral competitiveness. Table C.15 reports substantive results from models predicting the influence of adverse European and Inter-American Court judgments on the change in respect for rights conditional on political stability.

TABLE C.7. *Hypothesis 3: Effect of adverse Inter-American Court judgments and electoral incentives on respect for rights using change in respect for physical integrity rights dependent variable*

	Election Americas (*t-2*)	No election Americas (*t-2*)	Americas (*t-2*) interaction
Adverse judgment (*t-2*)	0.436*	−0.151	−0.021
	(0.277)	(0.224)	(0.111)
Adverse judgment (*t-1*)	0.169	−0.189	−0.099
	(0.323)	(0.174)	(0.153)
Adverse judgment (*t-2*)*Election			0.235*
			(0.137)
Election (*t*)			−0.044
			(0.174)

TABLE C.7. (Continued)

	Election Americas (t-2)	No election Americas (t-2)	Americas (t-2) interaction
Economic incentives (t-1)	0.045	−0.004	−0.0001
	(0.064)	(0.026)	(0.001)
Judicial power (t-1)	2.52	1.55**	4.92**
	(2.28)	(0.699)	(1.36)
Embeddedness (t-1)	0.323*	0.235**	−0.043
	(0.204)	(0.086)	(0.105)
Regional judgments (t-2)	−0.213	0.086	−0.011
	(0.296)	(0.142)	(0.022)
Speech (t-1)	0.112	0.245	0.091
	(0.241)	(0.162)	(0.117)
Civil society (t-1)	0.977	−0.589	−0.316
	(1.43)	(0.798)	(1.22)
NHRI (t-1)	0.606*	0.153	0.550
	(0.334)	(0.151)	(0.366)
Leg opposition (t-1)	0.225	0.023	−0.012
	(0.300)	(0.093)	(0.175)
Population (logged) (t-1)	0.416**	−0.404***	0.363
	(0.199)	(0.089)	(1.22)
GDP (logged) (t-1)	−0.584*	−0.153**	−0.096
	(0.355)	(0.078)	(0.199)
Civil war (t-1)	−1.39**	−1.16***	−1.64***
	(0.600)	(0.418)	(0.380)
Physical integrity (lagged)	−0.728***	−0.580***	−0.804***
	(0.106)	(0.056)	(0.051)
Constant	5.49*	3.70***	1.12
	(2.96)	(0.976)	(3.02)
R^2	0.350	0.353	0.447
N	99	325	418

Notes: Column 1 of Table C.7 displays coefficient estimates and standard errors from a model examining the influence of adverse Inter-American Court judgments 2 years before an election year on the change in respect rights (using changes in the Cingranelli, Richards, and Clay [2014] physical integrity rights index). Column 2 displays coefficient estimates and standard errors from a model examining the influence of adverse Inter-American Court judgments 2 years before a nonelection year on the change in respect for rights (using changes in the Cingranelli, Richards, and Clay [2014] physical integrity rights index). Column 3 displays coefficient estimates and standard errors from a model examining the influence of adverse Inter-American Court judgments and election presence (using an interaction term) on changes in respect for physical integrity rights (using changes in the Cingranelli, Richards, and Clay [2014] physical integrity rights index). Statistical significance: ***$p < 0.01$, **$p < 0.05$, *$p < 0.10$. Models estimated with standard errors clustered on country. Two-tailed significance tests reported.

TABLE C.8. *Hypothesis 3: Effect of adverse regional court judgments (1 year before election) and electoral incentives on respect for rights*

	Europe (vote share)	Americas (vote share)
Adverse judgment (t-1)*Vote share	−0.005	−0.011*
	(0.004)	(0.006)
Adverse judgment (t-1)	0.219	0.515**
	(0.208)	(0.230)
Vote share (t)	−0.007**	0.009
	(0.004)	(0.007)
Economic incentives (t-1)	0.013	0.0002
	(0.010)	(0.001)
Judicial power (t-1)	2.66***	1.78**
	(0.853)	(0.822)
Embeddedness (t-1)	0.046	0.210**
	(0.099)	(0.102)
Regional judgments (t-1)	−0.0003	0.020*
	(0.002)	(0.012)
Speech (t-1)	−0.175	0.079
	(0.115)	(0.073)
Civil society (t-1)	1.26	−0.421
	(0.861)	(0.590)
NHRI (t-1)	0.305*	0.397***
	(0.205)	(0.110)
Exec recruitment (t-1)	−0.345*	0.040
	(0.177)	(0.094)
Leg opposition (t-1)	−0.100	−0.044
	(0.098)	(0.118)
Population (logged) (t-1)	−0.189*	−0.420***
	(0.114)	(0.074)
GDP (logged) (t-1)	0.015	0.063
	(0.168)	(0.154)
Democracy (t-1)	0.338	1.92*
	(1.51)	(1.12)
Civil war (t-1)	−0.574*	−0.854***
	(0.348)	(0.237)
Constant	−0.380	−2.80*
	(1.13)	(1.50)
R^2	0.774	0.818
N	65	95

Notes: Table C.8 displays coefficient estimates and standard errors from a model examining the influence of an adverse regional court judgment (lagged 1 year) on respect for rights conditional on the competitiveness of an executive election. The results reported in Table C.8 correspond with the results reported in the left panel of Figures 5.4 and 5.5. The democracy variable is included in this model because achievement of the electoral principle of democracy does not determine whether elections are competitive. The democracy variable captures whether suffrage is extensive, elections are clean and fair, among several other components, and these institutional features do not overlap with the competitiveness of any particular executive election in practice. Competitiveness of executive recruitment is also included in this model because it does not predict whether the election will be competitive, but whether competitive electoral institutions are in place to recruit the executive. Statistical significance: ***$p < 0.01$, **$p < 0.05$, *$p < 0.10$. Models estimated with standard errors clustered on country. Two-tailed significance tests reported.

TABLE C.9. *Hypothesis 3: Effect of adverse regional court judgments (2 years before election) and electoral incentives on respect for rights*

	Europe (vote share)	Americas (vote share)
Adverse judgment (t-2)*Vote share	−0.011	−0.010*
	(0.009)	(0.006)
Adverse judgment (t-2)	0.459	0.526*
	(0.431)	(0.314)
Adverse judgment (t-1)	0.168	−0.060
	(0.140)	(0.183)
Vote Share (t)	−0.004	0.010
	(0.005)	(0.007)
Economic incentives (t-1)	0.009	0.0003
	(0.013)	(0.001)
Judicial power (t-1)	1.88**	1.64**
	(0.706)	(0.810)
Embeddedness (t-1)	−0.017	0.167
	(0.147)	(0.112)
Regional judgments (t-1)	−0.002	0.015
	(0.002)	(0.013)
Speech (t-1)	−0.177	0.060
	(0.172)	(0.075)
Civil society (t-1)	2.33	−0.457
	(1.58)	(0.556)
NHRI (t-1)	0.836**	0.362***
	(0.298)	(0.096)
Exec recruitment (t-1)	−0.390	0.050
	(0.258)	(0.103)
Leg opposition (t-1)	0.028	−0.015
	(0.171)	(0.122)
Population (logged) (t-1)	−0.231**	−0.452***
	(0.079)	(0.070)
GDP (logged) (t-1)	0.140	0.112
	(0.107)	(0.153)
Democracy (t-1)	0.040	2.14**
	(2.26)	(1.05)
Civil war (t-1)	−0.894***	−0.814***
	(0.255)	(0.249)
Constant	−1.93	−3.19**
	(1.46)	(1.50)
R^2	0.847	0.823
N	62	93

Notes: Table C.9 displays coefficient estimates and standard errors from a model examining the influence of an adverse regional court judgment (lagged 2 years) on respect for rights conditional on the competitiveness of an executive election. The results reported in Table C.9 correspond with the results reported in the center panels of Figures 5.4 and 5.5. The democracy variable is included in this model because achievement of the electoral principle of democracy does not determine whether elections are competitive. The democracy variable captures whether suffrage is extensive, elections are clean and fair, among several other components, and these institutional features do not overlap with the competitiveness of any particular executive election in practice. Competitiveness of executive recruitment is also included in this model because it does not predict whether the election will be competitive, but whether competitive electoral institutions are in place to recruit the executive. Statistical significance: ***$p < 0.01$, **$p < 0.05$, *$p < 0.10$. Models estimated with standard errors clustered on country. Two-tailed significance tests reported.

TABLE C.10. *Hypothesis 3: Effect of adverse regional court judgments (3 years before election) and electoral incentives on respect for rights*

	Europe (vote share)	Americas (vote share)
Adverse judgment (t-3)*Vote share	0.003	−0.006
	(0.009)	(0.006)
Adverse judgment (t-3)	−0.199	0.013
	(0.470)	(0.299)
Adverse judgment (t-2)	0.031	0.271
	(0.201)	(0.240)
Adverse judgment (t-1)	0.191	−0.069
	(0.140)	(0.227)
Vote share (t)	−0.009**	0.006
	(0.005)	(0.007)
Economic incentives (t-1)	0.014	0.0003
	(0.015)	(0.001)
Judicial power (t-1)	1.73**	1.60*
	(0.756)	(0.846)
Embeddedness (t-1)	−0.133	0.239*
	(0.123)	(0.122)
Regional judgments (t-1)	−0.002	0.017
	(0.002)	(0.012)
Speech (t-1)	−0.274	−0.010
	(0.203)	(0.095)
Civil society (t-1)	3.90**	−0.110
	(1.66)	(0.517)
NHRI (t-1)	0.871***	0.290**
	(0.298)	(0.114)
Exec recruitment	−1.03**	0.012
	(0.452)	(0.105)
Leg opposition (t-1)	0.148	0.007
	(0.178)	(0.129)
Population (logged) (t-1)	−0.276**	−0.464***
	(0.082)	(0.074)
GDP (logged) (t-1)	0.107	0.112
	(0.126)	(0.159)
Democracy (t-1)	0.089	0.969
	(2.31)	(1.53)
Civil war (t-1)	−0.645	−0.929**
	(0.482)	(0.310)
Constant	−0.524	−2.11
	(1.61)	(1.97)
R^2	0.834	0.826
N	57	86

Notes: Table C.10 displays coefficient estimates and standard errors from a model examining the influence of an adverse regional court judgment (lagged 3 years) on respect for rights conditional on the competitiveness of an executive election. The results reported in Table C.10 correspond with the results reported in the right panels of Figures 5.4 and 5.5. The democracy variable is included in this model because achievement of the electoral principle of democracy does not determine whether elections are competitive. The democracy variable captures whether suffrage is extensive, elections are clean and fair, among several other components, and these institutional features do not overlap with the competitiveness of any particular executive election in practice. Competitiveness of executive recruitment is also included in this model because it does not predict whether the election will be competitive, but whether competitive electoral institutions are in place to recruit the executive. Statistical significance: ***$p < 0.01$, **$p < 0.05$, *$p < 0.10$. Models estimated with standard errors clustered on country. Two-tailed significance tests reported.

TABLE C.11. *Hypothesis 3: Effect of adverse regional court judgments and electoral incentives on change in respect for rights*

Vote share	Europe (1-year change)	Americas (1-year change)
Low	0.282	1.05
	(−0.241, 0.805)	(−1.71, −0.384)
Medium	−0.017	0.302
	(−0.416, 0.383)	(−0.161, 0.764)
High	−0.415	1.31
	(−1.24, 0.411)	(0.394, 2.23)

Vote share	Europe (2-year change)	Americas (2-year change)
Low	0.180	1.10
	(−0.376, 0.736)	(−1.16, 3.36)
Medium	0.081	1.09
	(−0.232, 0.393)	(−0.342, 2.53)
High	−0.052	1.09
	(−0.808, 0.704)	(−2.20, 4.37)

Vote share	Europe (3-year change)	Americas (3-year change)
Low	0.683	−0.348
	(0.011, 1.35)	(−1.95, 1.25)
Medium	0.165	1.66
	(−0.220, 0.549)	(−0.381, 3.71)
High	−0.526	3.17
	(−1.09, 0.040)	(−1.16, 7.50)

Notes: Table C.11 displays the predicted change in respect for physical integrity rights across values of vote share and 90 percent confidence intervals in parentheses. In Europe, vote share is low (represents the largest vote-getter receiving 21 percent of the vote), medium (51 percent of the vote), or high (91 percent of the vote). In the Americas, vote share is low (represents the largest vote-getter receiving 20 percent of the vote), medium (60 percent of the vote), or high (90 percent of the vote). The predicted changes in respect for rights come from a model in which the primary independent variable of interest represents an interaction between an adverse judgment and vote share of the largest vote-getter in an executive election. The dependent variable represents a change in respect for physical integrity rights using changes in the Cingranelli, Richards, and Clay (2014) physical integrity rights index.

TABLE C.12. *Hypothesis 4: Effect of adverse regional court judgments and political stability on respect for rights (1 year postjudgment)*

	Europe	Americas
Adverse judgment*Political stability (t-1)	0.101*	−0.113*
	(0.056)	(0.068)
Adverse judgment (t-1)	−0.019	−0.066
	(0.031)	(0.056)
Political stability (t-1)	0.193**	0.219**
	(0.078)	(0.101)
Exec recruitment (t-1)	0.194**	0.007
	(0.080)	(0.083)
Economic incentives (t-1)	−0.0003	0.001*
	(0.002)	(0.001)
Judicial power (t-1)	0.751	1.77**
	(0.636)	(0.803)
Embeddedness (t-1)	0.171*	0.196**
	(0.114)	(0.093)
Regional judgments (t-1)	0.002*	0.071
	(0.001)	(0.055)
Speech (t-1)	0.099**	0.026
	(0.046)	(0.068)
Civil society (t-1)	0.639	0.714
	(0.424)	(0.726)
NHRI (t-1)	0.182*	0.405***
	(0.109)	(0.133)
Leg opposition (t-1)	−0.143**	−0.088
	(0.072)	(0.056)
Population (logged) (t-1)	−0.203***	−0.387***
	(0.078)	(0.067)
GDP (logged) (t-1)	−0.015	0.144*
	(0.063)	(0.085)
Democracy (t-1)	1.97*	1.24
	(1.22)	(1.36)
Constant	−1.98**	−3.13***
	(0.720)	(0.872)
R^2	0.671	0.786
N	417	231

Notes: Table C.12 displays coefficient estimates and standard errors from a model examining the influence of adverse regional court judgments (lagged 1 year) on respect for rights conditional on political stability. The results reported in Table C.12 correspond with the results reported in the left panels of Figures 5.6 and 5.7. Statistical significance: ***$p < 0.01$, **$p < 0.05$, *$p < 0.10$. Models estimated with standard errors clustered on country. Two-tailed significance tests reported.

TABLE C.13. *Hypothesis 4: Effect of adverse regional court judgments and political stability on respect for rights (3 years postjudgment)*

	Europe	Americas
Adverse judgment(t-3)*Political stability (t-1)	0.077	−0.170***
	(0.064)	(0.048)
Adverse judgment (t-3)	−0.001	−0.113**
	(0.041)	(0.052)
Adverse judgment (t-2)	0.070**	−0.001
	(0.024)	(0.040)
Adverse judgment (t-1)	0.053*	0.012
	(0.031)	(0.042)
Political stability (t-1)	0.168**	0.251**
	(0.082)	(0.097)
Exec recruitment (t-1)	0.163	−0.012
	(0.109)	(0.104)
Economic incentives (t-1)	−0.002	0.001*
	(0.002)	(0.001)
Judicial power (t-1)	0.784	1.76**
	(0.625)	(0.781)
Embeddedness (t-1)	0.197*	0.198**
	(0.116)	(0.095)
Regional judgments (t-1)	0.001	0.153**
	(0.001)	(0.047)
Speech (t-1)	0.074*	0.049
	(0.046)	(0.061)
Civil society (t-1)	0.827*	0.548
	(0.504)	(0.723)
NHRI (t-1)	0.232**	0.371**
	(0.117)	(0.118)
Leg opposition (t-1)	−0.158*	−0.088*
	(0.084)	(0.056)
Population (logged) (t-1)	−0.222***	−0.394***
	(0.084)	(0.062)
GDP (logged) (t-1)	−0.006	0.102
	(0.065)	(0.083)
Democracy (t-1)	1.59	1.40
	(1.31)	(1.39)
Constant	−1.81**	−2.79***
	(0.777)	(0.853)
R^2	0.643	0.800
N	404	230

Notes: Table C.13 displays coefficient estimates and standard errors from a model examining the influence of adverse regional court judgments (lagged 3 years) on respect for rights conditional on political stability. The results reported in Table C.13 correspond with the results reported in the center panels of Figures 5.6 and 5.7. Statistical significance: ***$p < 0.01$, **$p < 0.05$, *$p < 0.10$. Models estimated with standard errors clustered on country. Two-tailed significance tests reported.

TABLE C.14. *Hypothesis 4: Effect of adverse regional court judgments and political stability on respect for rights (5 years postjudgment)*

	Europe	Americas
Adverse judgment (t-5)*Political stability (t-1)	−0.016	−0.123*
	(0.075)	(0.071)
Adverse judgment (t-5)	0.022	0.020
	(0.049)	(0.110)
Adverse judgment (t-4)	0.017	0.047
	(0.033)	(0.057)
Adverse judgment (t-3)	0.043	0.078
	(0.028)	(0.058)
Adverse judgment (t-2)	0.068**	0.064
	(0.025)	(0.071)
Adverse judgment (t-1)	0.054*	0.071
	(0.030)	(0.069)
Political stability (t-1)	0.234**	0.638***
	(0.085)	(0.147)
Exec recruitment (t-1)	0.262*	−0.095
	(0.141)	(0.134)
Economic incentives (t-1)	−0.001	0.001*
	(0.002)	(0.001)
Judicial power (t-1)	0.509	1.00*
	(0.654)	(0.557)
Embeddedness (t-1)	0.180*	0.270**
	(0.110)	(0.111)
Regional judgments (t-1)	0.001	0.224***
	(0.001)	(0.071)
Speech (t-1)	0.075	0.073
	(0.047)	(0.072)
Civil Society (t-1)	0.609	−1.74**
	(0.566)	(0.744)
NHRI (t-1)	0.227*	0.257*
	(0.122)	(0.134)
Leg opposition (t-1)	−0.107	−0.048
	(0.090)	(0.082)
Population (logged) (t-1)	−0.227**	−0.345***
	(0.090)	(0.049)
GDP (logged) (t-1)	−0.003	−0.102
	(0.072)	(0.093)
Democracy (t-1)	0.938	4.12**
	(1.39)	(1.74)
Constant	−1.30	−1.26
	(0.871)	(1.03)
R^2	0.621	0.872
N	388	229

Notes: Table C.14 displays coefficient estimates and standard errors from a model examining the influence of adverse regional court judgments (lagged 5 years) on respect for rights conditional on political stability. The results reported in Table C.14 correspond with the results reported in the right panels of Figures 5.6 and 5.7. Statistical significance: ***p < 0.01, **p < 0.05, *p < 0.10. Models estimated with standard errors clustered on country. Two-tailed significance tests reported.

TABLE C.15. *Hypothesis 4: Effect of adverse regional court judgments and political stability on change in respect for rights*

Political stability	Europe (1-year change)	Americas (1-year change)
Low	−2.10 (−2.78, −1.42)	−0.359 (−1.39, 0.668)
Medium	−0.609 (−1.03, −0.185)	−0.123 (−0.528, 0.282)
High	0.885 (0.363, 1.41)	0.113 (−1.02, 1.24)
Political stability	Europe (3-year change)	Americas (3-year change)
Low	−0.719 (−1.53, 0.091)	−1.43 (−2.50, −0.358)
Medium	0.012 (−0.502, 0.527)	−0.032 (−0.395, 0.331)
High	0.743 (0.157, 1.33)	1.37 (0.023, 2.71)
Political stability	Europe (5-year change)	Americas (5-year change)
Low	−1.99 (−3.08, −0.911)	−1.32 (−2.67, 0.026)
Medium	−0.646 (−1.08, −0.211)	0.496 (0.028, 0.964)
High	0.704 (0.157, 1.25)	2.31 (0.470, 4.16)

Notes: Table C.15 displays the predicted change in respect for physical integrity rights across values of political stability and 90 percent confidence intervals in parentheses. In Europe, political stability is low (−2), medium (0), or high (2). In the Americas, political stability is low (−2.5), medium (−0.5), or high (1.5). The predicted changes in respect for rights come from a model in which the primary independent variable of interest represents an interaction between an adverse judgment and political stability. The dependent variable represents a change in respect for physical integrity rights using changes in the Cingranelli, Richards, and Clay (2014) physical integrity rights index.

The first column of Table C.16 displays coefficient estimates and standard errors from a model examining the influence of adverse European Court judgments on respect for rights conditional on vote share. The results reported in the first column correspond to results reported in Table 5.1. To produce the results reported in Table 5.1, political stability and electoral competitiveness are set to high and low values in postestimation analyses. The center column of Table C.16 displays coefficient estimates and standard errors from a model examining the influence of adverse Inter-American Court judgments on respect for rights before a nonelection year. The right column displays coefficient estimates and standard errors from a model examining the influence of adverse Inter-American Court judgments on respect for rights before an election year. The results from the second and third columns correspond with results reported in Table 5.2. To produce the results reported in Table 5.2, political stability is set to high and low values in postestimation analyses.

TABLE C.16. *Hypotheses 3 and 4: Effect of adverse regional court judgments, political stability, and electoral incentives on respect for rights (1 year postjudgment)*

	Europe	Americas (non-election)	Americas (election)
European Court (t-1)*Vote share	−0.004		
	(0.006)		
European Court (t-1)	0.453*		
	(0.284)		
Vote share (t)	−0.005		
	(0.005)		
Inter-American Court (t-1) *Political stability (t-1)		−0.185**	0.381**
		(0.069)	(0.170)
Inter-American Court (t-1)		−0.118*	0.324*
		(0.063)	(0.188)
Political stability (t-1)	0.378***	0.262**	0.633**
	(0.108)	(0.109)	(0.257)
Exec recruitment (t-1)	−0.603*		
	(0.331)		
Economic incentives (t-1)	0.0002	0.028	0.007
	(0.005)	(0.019)	(0.037)
Judicial power (t-1)	1.52**	1.16	0.662
	(1.16)	(0.845)	(1.03)

TABLE C.16. *(Continued)*

	Europe	Americas (non-election)	Americas (election)
Embeddedness (t-1)	−0.028	0.214**	0.414*
	(0.159)	(0.085)	(0.222)
Regional judgments (t-1)	0.003*	0.090*	0.318
	(0.002)	(0.053)	(0.250)
Speech (t-1)	0.163*	0.052	−0.055
	(0.104)	(0.061)	(0.174)
Civil society (t-1)	3.52**	1.18	−0.754
	(1.36)	(0.768)	(0.904)
NHRI (t-1)	0.276	0.574***	0.109
	(0.267)	(0.178)	(0.234)
Leg opposition (t-1)	−0.334***	−0.037	0.080
	(0.107)	(0.070)	(0.097)
Population (logged) (t-1)	−0.245**	−0.321***	−0.297**
	(0.109)	(0.077)	(0.114)
GDP (logged) (t-1)	−0.305	0.089	−0.311*
	(0.195)	(0.073)	(0.184)
Democracy (t-1)	0.542		
	(1.54)		
Civil war (t-1)	−0.014	−0.461**	0.121
	(0.281)	(0.207)	(0.387)
Constant	1.07	−2.05**	2.75*
	(1.61)	(0.902)	(1.68)
R^2	0.889	0.772	0.832
N	40	191	51

Notes: The results reported in the first column correspond to results reported in Table 5.1. The results from the second and third columns correspond with results reported in Table 5.2. Like the previous models, the democracy and competitiveness of executive recruitment variables are omitted from the models estimating the effectiveness of regional court judgments conditional on election timing. Parameter estimates and standard errors reported (in parentheses). Statistical significance: ***$p < 0.01$, **$p < 0.05$, *$p < 0.10$. Models estimated with standard errors clustered on country. Two-tailed significance tests reported.

Appendix D

Chapter 6 Appendix

D.1 CONTROL VARIABLES

I utilize several control variables in the analyses. Table D.1 lists all of the variables used in the analyses. Justification for each of the control variables is described in more detail in the Appendices to Chapters 3 (A) and 4 (B).

TABLE D.1. *Control variables*

Variable	Source
Competitive executive recruitment	Marshall, Jaggers, and Gurr (2019)
Civil war	Gleditsch et al. (2002)
Judicial power	Linzer and Staton (2015)
Legislative opposition	Coppedge et al. (2019), Henisz (2002)
FDI inflows	World Bank (2017)
Multilateral aid	OECD (2018)
Freedom of speech	Cingranelli, Richards, and Clay (2014)
Civil society participation	Coppedge et al. (2019)
National human rights institution	Conrad et al. (2013)
GDP per capita	World Bank (2017)
Population	World Bank (2017)
Embeddedness	Fariss (2018)
Democracy	Coppedge et al. (2019)
Regional judgment	HUDOC database & Hawkins and Jacoby (2010)
Respect for physical integrity rights	Fariss (2014)
Freedom from torture	Cingranelli, Richards, and Clay (2014)
Freedom from political imprisonment	Cingranelli, Richards, and Clay (2014)

D.2 FULL MODEL RESULTS

The following tables display full model results. Some of the key interaction terms of interest are not significant in the reported model results. However, as Brambor, Clark, and Golder (2006) indicate, for a model where two variables are interacted (e.g., X and Z) interaction terms may be insignificant because it is possible for the contribution of X on Y to be statistically significant for certain values of Z. As a result, one cannot infer whether X has a meaningful conditional effect on Y from the magnitude and significance of the coefficient on the interaction term. Instead, the conditional effect should be examined based on the marginal effect at every observed value of Z (Berry, Golder, and Milton, 2012). As a result, I utilize plots of the marginal linear effect of an adverse judgment across values of FDI, judicial power, and the legislative opposition in the main text.

TABLE D.2. *Hypothesis 5: Effect of adverse regional court judgments and foreign direct investment on respect for rights (1 year postjudgment)*

	Europe	Americas
Adverse judgment (t-1)*FDI (moving average)	0.002	0.014
	(0.021)	(0.022)
Adverse judgment (t-1)	0.029	0.035
	(0.033)	(0.078)
FDI (moving average)	0.009	0.039*
	(0.028)	(0.025)
Judicial power (t-1)	0.267	2.23***
	(0.501)	(0.662)
Exec recruitment (t-1)	0.132	−0.046
	(0.133)	(0.072)
Embeddedness (t-1)	0.073	0.113
	(0.060)	(0.093)
Regional judgments (t-1)	0.001*	0.153**
	(0.001)	(0.060)
Speech (t-1)	0.046	0.070**
	(0.062)	(0.035)
Civil society (t-1)	0.459	0.090
	(0.568)	(0.369)
NHRI (t-1)	0.175**	0.304**
	(0.083)	(0.137)
Leg opposition (t-1)	−0.052	−0.129*
	(0.070)	(0.067)
Population (logged)	−0.249**	−0.429***
	(0.109)	(0.048)
GDP (logged)	0.055	0.240**
	(0.076)	(0.118)
Democracy	1.63	1.24*
	(1.31)	(0.826)
Civil war	−0.069	−0.643***
	(0.126)	(0.166)
Constant	−1.27	−3.32**
	(1.18)	(1.08)
R^2	0.569	0.802
N	756	434

Notes: Table D.2 displays coefficient estimates and standard errors from a model examining the influence of adverse regional court judgments (lagged 1 year) on respect for rights conditional on FDI net inflows. The results reported in Table D.2 correspond with the results reported in the left panels of Figures 6.1 and 6.2. Statistical significance: ***$p < 0.01$, **$p < 0.05$, *$p < 0.10$. Models estimated with standard errors clustered on country. Two-tailed significance tests reported.

TABLE D.3. *Hypothesis 5: Effect of adverse regional court judgments and foreign direct investment on respect for rights (3 years postjudgment)*

	Europe	Americas
Adverse judgment (t-3)*FDI (moving average)	−0.039	−0.016
	(0.032)	(0.021)
Adverse judgment (t-3)	0.035	0.093
	(0.042)	(0.068)
Adverse judgment (t-2)	0.033	0.054
	(0.024)	(0.065)
Adverse judgment (t-1)	0.028	0.052
	(0.026)	(0.061)
FDI (moving average)	0.010	0.051**
	(0.024)	(0.022)
Judicial power (t-1)	−0.057	1.77**
	(0.400)	(0.643)
Exec recruitment (t-1)	0.096	−0.113
	(0.148)	(0.070)
Embeddedness (t-1)	0.045	0.158*
	(0.063)	(0.090)
Regional judgments (t-3)	0.001	0.195**
	(0.001)	(0.076)
Speech (t-1)	0.046	0.096**
	(0.064)	(0.038)
Civil society (t-1)	0.651	−0.042
	(0.605)	(0.403)
NHRI (t-1)	0.209**	0.303***
	(0.089)	(0.086)
Leg opposition (t-1)	−0.084	−0.106*
	(0.068)	(0.069)
Population (logged)	−0.233**	−0.445***
	(0.117)	(0.043)
GDP (logged)	0.100	0.136
	(0.081)	(0.098)
Democracy	1.34	1.93**
	(1.24)	(0.972)
Civil war	−0.076	−0.502**
	(0.114)	(0.219)
Constant	−1.16	−2.75**
	(1.21)	(0.912)
R^2	0.535	0.818
N	721	400

Notes: Table D.3 displays coefficient estimates and standard errors from a model examining the influence of adverse regional court judgments (lagged 3 years) on respect for rights conditional on FDI net inflows. The results reported in Table D.3 correspond with the results reported in the center panels of Figures 6.1 and 6.2. Statistical significance: ***$p < 0.01$, **$p < 0.05$, *$p < 0.10$. Models estimated with standard errors clustered on country. Two-tailed significance tests reported.

TABLE D.4. *Hypothesis 5: Effect of adverse regional court judgments and foreign direct investment on respect for rights (5 years postjudgment)*

	Europe	Americas
Adverse judgment(t-5)*FDI (moving average)	−0.077*	−0.012
	(0.041)	(0.333)
Adverse judgment (t-5)	0.090*	0.001
	(0.047)	(0.120)
Adverse judgment (t-4)	−0.005	0.004
	(0.029)	(0.053)
Adverse judgment (t-3)	−0.000	0.027
	(0.028)	(0.064)
Adverse judgment (t-2)	0.032	0.067
	(0.023)	(0.070)
Adverse judgment (t-1)	0.031	0.054
	(0.024)	(0.072)
FDI (moving average)	0.014	0.056***
	(0.026)	(0.019)
Judicial power (t-1)	0.048	1.20*
	(0.417)	(0.680)
Exec recruitment (t-1)	0.143	−0.255**
	(0.212)	(0.133)
Embeddedness (t-1)	0.034	0.260**
	(0.064)	(0.109)
Regional judgments (t-5)	0.001	0.160***
	(0.001)	(0.059)
Speech (t-1)	0.038	0.138**
	(0.068)	(0.065)
Civil society (t-1)	0.561	−0.369
	(0.645)	(0.458)
NHRI (t-1)	0.194**	0.213**
	(0.087)	(0.101)
Leg opposition (t-1)	−0.040	−0.117
	(0.071)	(0.081)
Population (logged)	−0.249**	−0.459***
	(0.115)	(0.039)
GDP (logged)	0.122	0.043
	(0.097)	(0.108)
Democracy	0.748	3.72***
	(1.04)	(1.18)
Civil war	−0.041	−0.401
	(0.100)	(0.261)
Constant	−0.975	−2.72***
	(1.25)	(1.03)
R^2	0.532	0.824
N	669	364

Notes: Table D.4 displays coefficient estimates and standard errors from a model examining the influence of adverse regional court judgments (lagged 5 years) on respect for rights conditional on FDI net inflows. The results reported in Table D.4 correspond with the results reported in the right panels of Figures 6.1 and 6.2. Statistical significance: ***$p < 0.01$, **$p < 0.05$, *$p < 0.10$. Models estimated with standard errors clustered on country. Two-tailed significance tests reported.

TABLE D.5. *Hypothesis 5: Effect of adverse regional court judgments and foreign direct investment on change in respect for rights*

FDI inflows	Europe (1-year change)	Americas (1-year change)
Low	−0.320	−1.93
	(−0.864, 0.224)	(−3.68, −0.177)
Medium	0.011	0.419
	(−0.279, 0.301)	(−0.156, 0.993)
High	0.508	1.59
	(0.041, 0.974)	(−0.034, 3.21)
FDI inflows	Europe (3-year change)	Americas (3-year change)
Low	−0.524	0.018
	(−1.05, 0.001)	(−1.82, 1.86)
Medium	−0.052	0.381
	(−0.340, 0.236)	(−0.009, 0.772)
High	0.658	0.563
	(0.120, 1.19)	(−0.651, 1.78)
FDI inflows	Europe (5-year change)	Americas (5-year change)
Low	−0.237	0.685
	(−0.944, 0.469)	(−2.51, 3.88)
Medium	−0.027	0.695
	(−0.343, 0.289)	(0.134, 1.26)
High	0.289	0.700
	(−0.475, 1.05)	(−1.33, 2.73)

Notes: Table D.5 displays the predicted change in respect for physical integrity rights across values of FDI net inflows as a percentage of GDP and 90 percent confidence intervals in parentheses. In Europe, FDI net inflows are low (logged value of −4), medium (logged value of 0), or high (logged value of 6). In the Americas, FDI net inflows as a percentage of GDP are low (−15 percent of GDP), medium (5 percent of GDP), or high (15 percent of GDP). The predicted changes in respect for rights come from a model in which the primary independent variable of interest represents an interaction between an adverse judgment and FDI net inflows as a percentage of GDP. The dependent variable represents a change in respect for physical integrity rights using changes in the Cingranelli, Richards, and Clay (2014) physical integrity rights index. Each model includes the standard set of control variables from the main models, as well as a lagged respect for physical integrity rights variable.

TABLE D.6. *Hypothesis 6: Effect of adverse regional court judgments and judicial power on respect for rights (1 year postjudgment)*

	Europe (Physint)	Europe (Torture)	Americas (Physint)
Adverse judgment*Judicial power (t-1)	0.134	2.86**	0.643***
	(0.152)	(1.14)	(0.236)
Adverse judgment (t-1)	−0.072	−2.19**	−0.260**
	(0.138)	(1.00)	(0.131)
Judicial power (t-1)	0.142	2.79**	2.28***
	(0.480)	(0.906)	(0.643)
Exec recruitment (t-1)	0.180	−0.418	0.008
	(0.135)	(0.328)	(0.076)
Economic incentives (t-1)	−.0004	−0.006	0.001*
	(0.003)	(0.015)	(0.0003)
Embeddedness (t-1)	0.079	−0.264*	0.092
	(0.060)	(0.137)	(0.095)
Regional judgments (t-1)	0.001	−0.635*	0.191**
	(0.001)	(0.337)	(0.063)
Speech (t-1)	0.053	0.070	0.086**
	(0.062)	(0.210)	(0.027)
Civil society (t-1)	0.596	2.86*	−0.428
	(0.542)	(1.55)	(0.523)
NHRI (t-1)	0.194**	0.040	0.395**
	(0.085)	(0.284)	(0.152)
Leg opposition (t-1)	−0.066	0.284	−0.509**
	(0.152)	(1.21)	(0.203)
Population (logged) (t-1)	−0.250**	−0.205**	−0.411***
	(0.108)	(0.103)	(0.054)
GDP (logged) (t-1)	0.077	0.235	0.237**
	(0.088)	(0.172)	(0.112)
Democracy (t-1)	0.720	0.270	0.919
	(0.897)	(3.53)	(0.971)
Civil war (t-1)	−0.068	−1.07**	−0.607***
	(0.126)	(0.411)	(0.172)
Torture (t-1)		1.89***	
		(0.216)	
Constant	−0.877		−2.83**
	(0.960)		(0.911)
R^2	0.584	0.406	0.799
N	766	766	436

Notes: Table D.6 displays coefficient estimates and standard errors from a model examining the influence of adverse regional court judgments (lagged 1 year) on respect for rights conditional on judicial power. The results reported in columns 1 and 3 of Table D.6 correspond with the results reported in the left panels of Figures 6.3 and 6.4. The results reported in column 2 of Table D.6 correspond with results reported in Table 6.1. Statistical significance: ***$p < 0.01$, **$p < 0.05$, *$p < 0.10$. Models estimated with standard errors clustered on country. Two-tailed significance tests reported.

TABLE D.7. *Hypothesis 6: Effect of adverse regional court judgments and judicial power on respect for rights (3 years postjudgment)*

	Europe	Americas
Adverse judgment (t-3)*Judicial power (t-1)	0.018	0.221
	(0.196)	(0.507)
Adverse judgment (t-3)	−0.014	−0.039
	(0.162)	(0.231)
Adverse judgment (t-2)	0.026	0.051
	(0.028)	(0.055)
Adverse judgment (t-1)	0.027	0.052
	(0.027)	(0.056)
Judicial power (t-1)	−0.125	2.53***
	(0.407)	(0.592)
Exec recruitment (t-1)	0.169	−0.026
	(0.159)	(0.084)
Economic incentives (t-1)	−0.001	0.001*
	(0.004)	(0.0004)
Embeddedness (t-1)	0.060	0.136*
	(0.061)	(0.079)
Regional judgments (t-3)	0.001	0.137**
	(0.001)	(0.061)
Speech (t-1)	0.052	0.091***
	(0.065)	(0.027)
Civil society (t-1)	0.752	−0.315
	(0.547)	(0.544)
NHRI (t-1)	0.230**	0.453***
	(0.090)	(0.125)
Leg opposition (t-1)	−0.069	−0.461**
	(0.157)	(0.222)
Population (logged) (t-1)	−0.227*	−0.404***
	(0.118)	(0.059)
GDP (logged) (t-1)	0.097	0.186*
	(0.093)	(0.086)
Democracy (t-1)	0.369	0.662
	(0.790)	(0.811)
Civil war (t-1)	−0.055	−0.576***
	(0.111)	(0.186)
Constant	−0.676	−2.47***
	(1.01)	(0.760)
R^2	0.543	0.788
N	731	400

Notes: Table D.7 displays coefficient estimates and standard errors from a model examining the influence of adverse regional court judgments (lagged 3 years) on respect for rights conditional on judicial power. The results reported in Table D.7 correspond with the results reported in the center panels of Figures 6.3 and 6.4. Statistical significance: ***$p < 0.01$, **$p < 0.05$, *$p < 0.10$. Models estimated with standard errors clustered on country. Two-tailed significance tests reported.

TABLE D.8. *Hypothesis 6: Effect of adverse regional court judgments and judicial power on respect for rights (5 years postjudgment)*

	Europe	Americas
Adverse (t-5)*Judicial power (t-1)	−0.078 (0.269)	1.58* (0.968)
Adverse judgment (t-5)	0.074 (0.223)	−0.803* (0.468)
Adverse judgment (t-4)	−0.008 (0.034)	0.021 (0.077)
Adverse judgment (t-3)	0.006 (0.030)	−0.019 (0.058)
Adverse judgment (t-2)	0.031 (0.027)	0.025 (0.080)
Adverse judgment (t-1)	0.031 (0.026)	0.039 (0.080)
Judicial power (t-1)	−0.038 (0.454)	1.37** (0.656)
Exec recruitment (t-1)	0.211 (0.215)	−0.179 (0.121)
Economic incentives (t-1)	−0.002 (0.004)	0.002** (0.001)
Embeddedness (t-1)	0.059 (0.061)	0.255*** (0.100)
Regional judgments (t-5)	0.001 (0.001)	0.081* (0.055)
Speech (t-1)	0.046 (0.071)	0.191*** (0.059)
Civil society (t-1)	0.514 (0.655)	−0.627 (0.490)
NHRI (t-1)	0.218** (0.089)	0.169 (0.112)
Leg opposition (t-1)	−0.115 (0.176)	−0.487** (0.244)
Population (logged) (t-1)	−0.226* (0.120)	−0.469*** (0.052)
GDP (logged) (t-1)	0.109 (0.110)	0.195* (0.109)
Democracy (t-1)	0.426 (1.01)	2.36** (0.970)
Civil war (t-1)	−0.001 (0.097)	−0.467* (0.294)
Constant	−0.796 (1.23)	−2.72** (1.00)
R^2	0.523	0.815
N	678	364

Notes: Table D.8 displays coefficient estimates and standard errors from a model examining the influence of adverse regional court judgments (lagged 5 years) on respect for rights conditional on judicial power. The results reported in Table D.8 correspond with the results reported in the right panels of Figures 6.3 and 6.4. Parameter estimates and standard errors reported in parentheses. Statistical significance: ***$p < 0.01$, **$p < 0.05$, *$p < 0.10$. Models estimated with standard errors clustered on country. Two-tailed significance tests reported.

TABLE D.9. *Hypothesis 6: Effect of adverse regional court judgments and judicial power on change in respect for rights*

Judicial power	Europe (1-year change)	Americas (1-year change)
Low	−0.569	−1.48
	(−0.969, −0.169)	(−2.05, −0.914)
Medium	−0.088	0.133
	(−0.366, 0.191)	(−0.257, 0.523)
High	0.394	1.75
	(0.062, 0.727)	(0.917, 2.57)
Judicial power	Europe (3-year change)	Americas (3-year change)
Low	−0.278	−1.94
	(−0.916, 0.360)	(−3.95, 0.058)
Medium	−0.007	0.346
	(−0.343, 0.329)	(−0.045, 0.737)
High	0.263	2.63
	(−0.040, 0.566)	(0.367, 4.91)
Judicial power	Europe (five-year change)	Americas (five-year change)
Low	−0.917	−2.57
	(−1.52, −0.312)	(−4.19, −0.963)
Medium	−0.469	0.690
	(−0.759, −0.179)	(0.210, 1.17)
High	−0.020	3.96
	(−0.342, 0.301)	(2.69, 5.22)

Notes: Table D.9 displays the predicted change in respect for physical integrity rights across judicial power and 90 percent confidence intervals in parentheses. In Europe, judicial power is low (0.4), medium (0.7), or high (1.0). In the Americas, judicial power is low (0.0), medium (0.5), or high (1.0). The predicted changes in respect for rights come from a model in which the primary independent variable of interest represents an interaction between an adverse judgment and judicial power. The dependent variable represents a change in respect for physical integrity rights using changes in the Cingranelli, Richards, and Clay (2014) physical integrity rights index. Each model includes the standard set of control variables from the main models, as well as the lagged respect for physical integrity rights.

TABLE D.10. *Hypothesis 7: Effect of adverse regional court judgments and legislative opposition on respect for rights (1 year postjudgment)*

	Europe (Physint)	Europe (Torture)	Americas (Physint)	Americas (Pol Imp)
Adverse judgment *Leg opposition (t-1)	0.173 (0.153)	3.84** (1.63)	0.210 (0.139)	2.39 (1.87)
Adverse judgment (t-1)	−0.045 (0.075)	−1.76** (0.899)	−0.014 (0.064)	−0.752 (0.711)
Leg opposition (t-1)	−0.113 (0.161)	−0.112 (1.21)	−0.517** (0.244)	−0.462 (0.566)
Exec recruitment (t-1)	0.171 (0.137)	−0.495 (0.397)	0.004 (0.074)	0.627** (0.270)
Economic incentives (t-1)	−0.001 (0.003)	−0.007 (0.016)	0.001* (0.001)	−0.002 (0.002)
Judicial power (t-1)	0.207 (0.479)	3.47*** (0.875)	2.41*** (0.612)	0.681 (0.590)
Embeddedness (t-1)	0.081 (0.063)	−0.252* (0.143)	0.064 (0.086)	−0.021 (0.215)
Regional judgments (t-1)	0.001 (0.001)	−0.569* (0.341)	0.027*** (0.010)	0.028 (0.348)
Speech (t-1)	0.053 (0.064)	0.070 (0.207)	0.103*** (0.028)	0.529** (0.233)
Civil society (t-1)	0.590 (0.548)	2.90* (1.54)	−0.384 (0.515)	0.287 (0.972)
NHRI (t-1)	0.189** (0.086)	−0.006 (0.289)	0.407*** (0.150)	0.473** (0.215)
Population (logged) (t-1)	−0.245** (0.109)	−0.187* (0.105)	−0.403*** (0.055)	−0.467*** (0.139)
GDP (logged) (t-1)	0.074 (0.083)	0.191 (0.179)	0.193* (0.106)	−0.245 (0.291)
Democracy (t-1)	0.730 (0.904)	0.189 (3.44)	0.960 (0.938)	3.52* (2.13)
Civil war (t-1)	−0.074 (0.124)	−1.06** (0.419)	−0.571*** (0.181)	−0.923** (0.383)
Torture (t-1)		1.88*** (0.217)		
Political imprisonment (t-1)				1.33*** (0.263)
Constant	−0.872 (0.929)		−2.62 (0.863)	
R^2	0.585	0.406	0.797	0.313
N	766	766	436	433

Notes: Table D.10 displays coefficient estimates and standard errors from a model examining the influence of adverse regional court judgments (lagged 1 year) on respect for rights conditional on the size of the legislative opposition. The results reported in columns 1 and 3 of Table D.10 correspond with the results reported in the left panels of Figures 6.5 and 6.6. The results reported in the second column correspond with results reported in Table 6.2 and the results reported in the fourth column correspond with the results reported in Table 6.3. Statistical significance: ***$p < 0.01$, **$p < 0.05$, *$p < 0.10$. Models estimated with standard errors clustered on country. Two-tailed significance tests reported.

TABLE D.11. *H7: Effect of adverse regional court judgments and legislative opposition on respect for rights (3 years postjudgment)*

	Europe	Americas
Adverse judgment (t-3)*Leg opposition (t-1)	−0.056	−0.185
	(0.218)	(0.119)
Adverse judgment (t-3)	0.027	0.141**
	(0.110)	(0.042)
Adverse judgment (t-2)	0.027	0.023
	(0.028)	(0.055)
Adverse judgment (t-1)	0.026	0.046
	(0.028)	(0.062)
Leg opposition (t-1)	−0.057	−0.372*
	(0.170)	(0.227)
Judicial power (t-1)	−0.128	2.49***
	(0.418)	(0.585)
Exec recruitment (t-1)	0.170	−0.018
	(0.158)	(0.075)
Economic incentives (t-1)	−0.001	0.0003
	(0.003)	(0.0003)
Embeddedness (t-1)	0.061	0.083
	(0.061)	(0.075)
Regional judgments (t-3)	0.001	0.024**
	(0.001)	(0.011)
Speech (t-1)	0.052	0.090***
	(0.065)	(0.026)
Civil society (t-1)	0.739	−0.338
	(0.552)	(0.529)
NHRI (t-1)	0.230**	0.426***
	(0.091)	(0.131)
Population (logged) (t-1)	−0.226*	−0.398***
	(0.119)	(0.058)
GDP (logged) (t-1)	0.094	0.178**
	(0.093)	(0.083)
Democracy (t-1)	0.359	0.549
	(0.785)	(0.811)
Civil war (t-1)	−0.053	−0.608***
	(0.110)	(0.182)
Constant	−0.643	−2.24***
	(0.995)	(0.748)
R^2	0.537	0.791
N	731	404

Notes: Table D.11 displays coefficient estimates and standard errors from a model examining the influence of an adverse regional court judgment (lagged 3 years) on respect for rights conditional on the size of the legislative opposition. The results reported in Table D.11 correspond with the results reported in the center panels of Figures 6.5 and 6.6. Statistical significance: ***$p < 0.01$, **$p < 0.05$, *$p < 0.10$. Models estimated with standard errors clustered on country. Two-tailed significance tests reported.

TABLE D.12. *Hypothesis 7: Effect of adverse regional court judgments and legislative opposition on respect for rights (5 years postjudgment)*

	Europe	Americas
Adverse judgment (t-5)*Leg opposition (t-1)	−0.242	−0.187
	(0.372)	(0.494)
Adverse judgment (t-5)	0.110	0.096
	(0.169)	(0.155)
Adverse judgment (t-4)	−0.010	0.007
	(0.034)	(0.079)
Adverse judgment (t-3)	0.001	−0.025
	(0.029)	(0.064)
Adverse judgment (t-2)	0.029	−0.034
	(0.027)	(0.082)
Adverse judgment (t-1)	0.028	0.006
	(0.026)	(0.082)
Leg opposition (t-1)	−0.104	−0.398*
	(0.202)	(0.228)
Judicial power (t-1)	0.130	1.47**
	(0.462)	(0.669)
Exec recruitment (t-1)	0.167	−0.157
	(0.220)	(0.121)
Economic incentives (t-1)	−0.001	0.001**
	(0.004)	(0.001)
Embeddedness (t-1)	0.041	0.234**
	(0.060)	(0.105)
Regional judgments (t-1)	0.001	0.021*
	(0.001)	(0.014)
Speech (t-1)	0.042	0.180***
	(0.072)	(0.058)
Civil society (t-1)	0.624	−0.726
	(0.688)	(0.517)
NHRI (t-1)	0.220**	0.146
	(0.089)	(0.111)
Population (logged) (t-1)	−0.254**	−0.457***
	(0.105)	(0.050)
GDP (logged) (t-1)	0.135	0.147
	(0.107)	(0.108)
Civil war (t-1)	−0.008	−0.424
	(0.108)	(0.310)
Constant	−1.23	−2.50***
	(1.20)	(1.08)
R^2	0.577	0.816
N	678	368

Notes: Table D.12 displays coefficient estimates and standard errors from a model examining the influence of adverse regional court judgments (lagged 5 years) on respect for rights conditional on the size of the legislative opposition. The results reported in Table D.12 correspond with the results reported in the right panels of Figures 6.5 and 6.6. Statistical significance: ***$p < 0.01$, **$p < 0.05$, *$p < 0.10$. Models estimated with standard errors clustered on country. Two-tailed significance tests reported.

TABLE D.13. *Hypothesis 7: Effect of adverse regional court judgments and legislative opposition on change in respect for rights*

Leg opposition	Europe (1-year change)	Americas (1-year change) (one judgment)	Americas (1-year change) (two judgments)
Low	−0.170 (−0.524, 0.184)	−0.243 (−0.946, 0.459)	−0.891 (−1.47, −0.311)
Medium	0.060 (−0.216, 0.335)	−0.086 (−0.641, 0.470)	−0.613 (−1.20, −0.027)
High	0.289 (−0.107, 0.686)	0.151 (−0.903, 1.20)	−0.197 (−1.14, 0.742)
Leg opposition	Europe (3-year change)	Americas (3-year change) (one judgment)	Americas (3-year change) (two judgments)
Low	−0.065 (−0.516, 0.386)	−0.249 (−0.886, 0.388)	−3.00 (−3.70, −2.31)
Medium	0.035 (−0.251, 0.322)	−0.231 (−0.783, 0.321)	−0.330 (−0.939, 0.279)
High	0.136 (−0.145, 0.417)	−0.205 (−0.885, 0.476)	3.68 (2.56, 4.81)
Leg opposition	Europe (5-year change)	Americas (5-year change) (one judgment)	Americas (5-year change) (two judgments)
Low	0.081 (−0.378, 0.540)	0.057 (−0.529, 0.643)	−0.358 (−1.04, 0.321)
Medium	0.263 (0.003, 0.522)	0.180 (−0.580, 0.940)	0.170 (−0.465, 0.804)
High	0.444 (0.256, 0.862)	0.364 (−1.38, 2.11)	0.961 (−0.576, 2.50)

Notes: Table D.13 displays the predicted change in respect for physical integrity rights across the legislative opposition and 90 percent confidence intervals in parentheses. In Europe, the legislative opposition is low (0.1), medium (0.4), or high (0.7). In the Americas, the legislative opposition is low (0.2), medium (0.4), or high (0.7). The predicted changes in respect for rights come from a model in which the primary independent variable of interest represents an interaction between adverse regional court judgments and the legislative opposition. The dependent variable represents a change in respect for physical integrity rights using changes in the Cingranelli, Richards, and Clay (2014) physical integrity rights index. Each model includes the standard set of control variables from the main models, as well as the lagged respect for physical integrity rights.

Appendix E

Chapter 7 Appendix

E.1 CONTROL VARIABLES

I utilize several control variables in the analyses. Table E.1 lists all of the variables used in the analyses. Justification for each of the control variables is described in more detail in the Appendices to Chapters 3 (A) and 4 (B).

TABLE E.1. *Control variables*

Variable	Source
Competitive executive recruitment	Marshall, Jaggers, and Gurr (2019)
Civil war	Gleditsch et al. (2002)
Judicial power	Linzer and Staton (2015)
Legislative opposition	Coppedge et al. (2019), Henisz (2002)
FDI inflows	World Bank (2017)
Multilateral aid	OECD (2018)
Freedom of speech	Cingranelli, Richards, and Clay (2014)
Civil society participation	Coppedge et al. (2019)
National human rights institution	Conrad et al. (2013)
Population	World Bank (2017)
Embeddedness	Fariss (2018)
Democracy	Coppedge et al. (2019)
Regional judgment	HUDOC database & Hawkins and Jacoby (2010)
Respect for physical integrity rights	Fariss (2014)

E.2 FULL MODEL RESULTS

The following tables display full model results. Some of the key triple interaction terms of interest are not significant in the reported model results. However, as Brambor, Clark, and Golder (2006) indicate, for a model where two variables are interacted (e.g., X and Z) interaction terms may be insignificant because it is possible for the contribution of X on Y to be statistically significant for certain values of Z. As a result, one cannot infer whether X has a meaningful conditional effect on Y from the magnitude and significance of the coefficient on the interaction term. Furthermore, in a triple interaction, it becomes increasingly difficult to determine the effect of X on Y at various values of W and Z. Instead, the conditional effect should be examined based on the marginal effect at every observed value of Z (Berry, Golder, and Milton, 2012). As a result, I utilize plots of the marginal linear effect of an adverse judgment across values executive capacity and willingness.

TABLE E.2. *Triple interaction model results (1 year postjudgment)*

	Europe (stability)	Europe (FDI)	Americas (stability)	Americas (judiciary)
Triple interaction (lagged)	−0.001	−0.0001	0.003	0.061
	(0.002)	(0.0005)	(0.004)	(0.042)
Adverse judgment *Capacity (lagged)	0.002	−0.002	0.003	−0.020
	(0.002)	(0.002)	(0.003)	(0.021)
Adverse judgment *Willingness (lagged)	0.159	−0.005	−0.180	−2.37
	(0.141)	(0.004)	(0.220)	(1.69)
Capacity*Willingness (t-1)	−0.001	0.002*	0.0004	0.027
	(0.003)	(0.001)	(0.002)	(0.024)
Adverse judgment (lagged)	−0.124	0.223	−0.155	0.728
	(0.093)	(0.173)	(0.138)	(0.784)
Capacity (t-1)	0.004	0.003	0.009**	−0.007
	(0.003)	(0.003)	(0.004)	(0.017)
Willingness (t-1)	0.290**	−0.137	0.449**	0.363
	(0.130)	(0.095)	(0.155)	(1.24)
Economic incentives (t-1)	0.001		0.001	0.0005
	(0.003)		(0.001)	(0.001)
Judicial power (t-1)	0.682	−0.013	1.25	
	(0.639)	(0.431)	(1.02)	
Exec recruitment (t-1)	0.223**	0.063	0.230	−0.037
	(0.107)	(0.188)	(0.148)	(0.084)

(*Continued*)

TABLE E.2. *(Continued)*

	Europe (stability)	Europe (FDI)	Americas (stability)	Americas (judiciary)
Embeddedness (t-1)	0.089	0.064	0.051	0.218*
	(0.103)	(0.058)	(0.154)	(0.117)
Regional judgments (t-1)	0.001	0.0002		0.176**
	(0.001)	(0.001)		(0.069)
Speech (t-1)	0.035	0.019	0.006	0.138**
	(0.041)	(0.064)	(0.047)	(0.055)
Civil society (t-1)	0.972*	1.13*	0.920	−0.324
	(0.543)	(0.638)	(0.686)	(0.432)
NHRI (t-1)	0.192**	0.217**	0.446*	0.250**
	(0.075)	(0.091)	(0.282)	(0.092)
Leg opposition (t-1)	−0.112*	−0.078	−0.051	−0.534**
	(0.064)	(0.064)	(0.077)	(0.216)
Population (logged) (t-1)	−0.269***	−0.300***	−0.461***	−0.463***
	(0.074)	(0.110)	(0.129)	(0.071)
Democracy (t-1)	1.19	1.06	0.056	1.87**
	(0.998)	(1.09)	(2.82)	(0.904)
Civil war (t-1)		−0.012		−0.757***
		(0.100)		(0.247)
Constant	−1.56**	−0.332	−1.06	−1.04**
	(0.603)	(0.977)	(1.55)	(0.437)
R^2	0.697	0.558	0.806	0.814
N	340	649	131	393

Notes: Parameter estimates and standard error reported (two-tailed significance tests). Statistical significance: ***$p < 0.01$, **$p < 0.05$, *$p < 0.10$. Standard errors clustered on country. The triple interaction is Adverse judgment*Capacity*Willingness. GDP is omitted because of its high correlation with fiscal flexibility. Civil war is omitted from the models using political stability as an indicator of executive willingness as the presence of internal threats is captured by the political stability variable. Economic incentives are omitted from the European Court model using FDI to capture executive willingness because FDI directly captures economic incentives. Number of judgments in the region are omitted from the Inter-American Court model using political stability to capture executive willingness due to multicollinearity with the interaction of adverse judgment and political stability. Judicial power is omitted as a standard control variable from the Inter-American Court model using judicial power as an indicator of executive willingness.

TABLE E.3. *Predicted influence of adverse regional court judgments across capacity and willingness on three-year change in respect for physical integrity rights*

	High capacity (Europe)	Low capacity (Europe)
High willingness (Europe)	0.894 (0.293, 1.49)	0.089 (−0.887, 1.07)
Low willingness (Europe)	−1.61 (−3.39, 0.166)	−0.100 (−1.66, 1.46)
	High capacity (Americas)	Low capacity (Americas)
High willingness (Americas)	3.69 (1.78, 5.59)	−1.68 (−3.64, 0.288)
Low willingness (Americas)	−2.59 (−4.43, −0.758)	0.891 (−1.05, 2.83)

Notes: Table E.3 displays the predicted change in respect for physical integrity rights across executive capacity, conceptualized as the institutional investor credit rating, and executive willingness, conceptualized as political stability and absence of violence. The numbers in parentheses represent 90 percent confidence intervals. In Europe, capacity is high (IIR of 90) or low (IIR of 20). Executive willingness in Europe is high (political stability value of 2), and executive willingness is low (political stability value of −2). In the Americas, executive capacity is high (IIR of 60), and executive capacity is low (IIR of 20). Executive willingness in the Americas is high (political stability value of 1.5) and low (political stability value of −2.5). The predicted changes in respect for rights come from a model in which the primary independent variable of interest represents an interaction between an adverse judgment, fiscal flexibility (IIR), and political stability. The dependent variable represents a change in respect for physical integrity rights from the year of the judgment to three years postjudgment using changes in the Cingranelli, Richards, and Clay (2014) physical integrity rights index. Each model includes the standard set of control variables from the main models, as well as the lagged respect for physical integrity rights.

References

Abdelgawad, Elisabeth Lambert. 2016. "The Economic Crisis and the Evolution of the System Based on the ECHR: Is There Any Correlation?" *European Law Journal* 22(1):74–91.

Alchian, Armen A. and Harold Demsetz. 1972. "Production, Information Costs, and Economic Organization." *American Economic Review* 62(5):777–795.

Alesina, Alberto and David Dollar. 2000. "Who Gives Foreign Aid to Whom and Why?" *Journal of Economic Growth* 5(1):33–63.

Alston, Philip and James Crawford. 2000. *The Future of UN Human Rights Treaty Monitoring*. Cambridge: Cambridge University Press.

Alter, Karen J. 2014. *The New Terrain of International Law: Courts, Politics, Rights*. Princeton, NJ: Princeton University Press.

Amnesty International. 2009. *Spain: Adding Insult to Injury: Police Impunity Two Years On*. London: Amnesty International. Available at: https://bit.ly/2BbYdR1.

2014. *Do Not Erase Me from the Story, Truth, Justice and Reparation in Bolivia (1964–1982)*. London: Amnesty International.

2017. *Turkey 2017/2018 Annual Report*. London: Amnesty International. Available at: https://bit.ly/1GWxwJZ.

Anagnostou, Dia and Alina Mangui-Pippidi. 2014. "Domestic Implementation of Human Rights Judgments in Europe: Legal Infrastructure and Government Effectiveness Matter." *The European Journal of International Law* 25(1):205–227.

Ausderan, Jacob. 2014. "How Naming and Shaming Affects Human Rights Perceptions in the Shamed Country." *Journal of Peace Research* 51(1):81–95.

Baluarte, David C. and Christian M. DeVos. 2010. *From Judgment to Justice: Implementing International and Regional Human Rights Decisions*. New York: Open Society Justice Initiative.

Bargent, James. 2014. "2014 a Record Year for Disappearances in Mexico." Available at: https://bit.ly/2rww42A.

Belousov, Yury, Oleksandr Bondarenko, Valentyna Obolensteva, Kostiantyn Tarasenko, Victor Chuprov, and Zlata Shvets. 2017. "Ill-Treatment in the Activities of the National Police of Ukraine: Types, Scale, Reasons." Available at: https://rm.coe.int/ill-treatment-in-police-in-final-eng/16808b17ef.

Bendinelli, Shauna. 2015. "Hilaire, Constantine and Benjamin et al. v. Trinidad and Tobago." *Loyola of Los Angeles International and Comparative Law Review* 37(4):1091–1124.

Benson, Kathrynn. 2015. "Blanco Romero et al. v. Venezuela." *Loyola of Los Angeles International and Comparative Law Review* 37(4):1175–1202.

Bernath, Barbara. 2010. *Preventing Torture: An Operational Guide for National Human Rights Institutions*. Geneva, Switzerland: Office of the United Nations High Commissioner for Human Rights, Association for the Prevention of Torture, and Asia Pacific Forum of National Human Rights Institutions. Available at: www.ohchr.org/Documents/Publications/PreventingTorture.pdf.

Berry, William D., Matt Golder, and Daniel Milton. 2012. "Improving Tests of Theories Positing Interaction." *Journal of Politics* 74(3):653–671.

Blanton, Robert G. and Clair Apodaca. 2007. "Economic Globalization and Violent Civil Conflict: Is Openness a Pathway to Peace?" *The Social Science Journal* 44(4):599–619.

Blanton, Shannon Lindsey and Robert G. Blanton. 2007. "What Attracts Foreign Investors? An Examination of Human Rights and Foreign Direct Investment." *Journal of Politics* 69(1):143–155.

Brambor, Thomas, William Roberts Clark, and Matt Golder. 2006. "Understanding Interaction Models: Improving Empirical Analyses." *Political Analysis* 14(1):63–82.

Bueno de Mesquita, Bruce, George W. Downs, Alastair Smith, and Feryal Marie Cherif. 2005. "Thinking Inside the Box: A Closer Look at Democracy and Human Rights." *International Studies Quarterly* 49(3):439–457.

Buergenthal, Thomas. 1980. "The American and European Conventions on Human Rights: Similarities and Differences." *American University Law Review* 30(1):155–166.

  2005. "New Upload – Remembering the Early Years of the Inter-American Court of Human Rights." *N.Y.U. Journal of International Law and Politics* 37:259–280.

Burgorgue-Larsen, Laurence and Amaya Úbeda de Torres. 2011. *The Inter-American Court of Human Rights: Case-Law and Commentary*. New York: Oxford University Press.

Bush, Sarah Sunn. 2011. "International Politics and the Spread of Quotas for Women in Legislatures." *International Organization* 65(1):103–137.

Carey, John M. 2000. "Parchment, Equilibria, and Institutions." *Comparative Political Studies* 33(6):735–761.

Carey, Sabine C. 2007. "European Aid: Human Rights versus Bureaucratic Inertia?" *Journal of Peace Research* 44(4):447–464.

Carnegie, Allison and Nikolay Marinov. 2017. "Foreign Aid, Human Rights, and Democracy Promotion: Evidence from a Natural Experiment." *American Journal of Political Science*. 61(3): 671–683.

Carneiro, Cristiane Lucena and Simone Wegmann. 2018. "Institutional Complexity in the Inter-American Human Rights System: An Investigation of the Prohibition of Torture." *The International Journal of Human Rights* 22(9):1–20.

Carrubba, Clifford J. 2005. "Courts and Compliance in International Regulatory Regimes." *Journal of Politics* 67(3):669–689.

  2009. "A Model of the Endogenous Development of Judicial Institutions in Federal and International Systems." *Journal of Politics* 71(1):55–69.

Cavallaro, James L. and Stephanie Erin Brewer. 2008. "Reevaluating Regional Human Rights Litigation in the Twenty-First Century: The Case of the Inter-American Court." *American Journal of International Law* 102(4):768–827.

CEJIL. 2017. *Inter-American Court Condemns Brazil for Favela Killings Case.* Washington DC: Center for Justice and International Law. Available at: https://bit.ly/2UASSvx.

Chang, Diane. 2016. "Bulacio v. Argentina." *Loyola of Los Angeles International and Comparative Law Review* 38:1084–1103.

Christou, Theodora and Juan Pablo Raymond. 2005. *European Court of Human Rights: Remedies and Execution of Judgments.* London: British Institute of International and Comparative Law.

Cichowski, Rachel A. 2007. *The European Court and Civil Society: Litigation, Mobilization and Governance.* Cambridge, UK: Cambridge University Press.

Cichowski, Rachel and Elizabeth Chrun. 2017. "European Court of Human Rights Database, Version 1.0." Available at: http://depts.washington.edu/echrdb/.

Cingranelli, David, David L. Richards, and Chad Clay. 2014. "The CIRI Human Rights Dataset." Available at: www.humanrightsdata.com.

Clay, K. Chad and Matthew R. DiGiuseppe. 2017. "The Physical Consequences of Fiscal Flexibility: Sovereign Credit and Physical Integrity Rights." *British Journal of Political Science* 47(4):783–807.

Cohen, Jacob. 1988. *Statistical Power Analysis for the Behavioral Sciences.* New York: Erlbaum.

Cole, Wade M. 2015. "Mind the Gap: State Capacity and the Implementation of Human Rights Treaties." *International Organization* 69(2):405–441.

Committee of Ministers. 1999. "Interim Resolutions: DH (99) 434." Strasbourg, France: Council of Europe.

Conrad, Courtenay R., Sarah E. Croco, Brad T. Gomez, and Will H. Moore. 2017. "Threat Perception and American Support for Torture." *Political Behavior* 40(4): 989–1009

Conrad, Courtenay R., Jacqueline H. R. DeMeritt, Will H. Moore, and Ryan Welch. 2013. *National Human Rights Institutions (NHRI) Institutional Data Project: (Beta) Coding Rules.* Charlotte, Denton, and Tallahassee: National Human Rights Institutions Data Project. Available at: https://nhridata.weebly.com/.

Conrad, Courtenay, Jillienne Haglund, and Will H. Moore. 2013. "Disaggregating Torture Allegations: Introducing the Ill-Treatment and Torture (ITT) Country-Year Data." *International Studies Perspectives* 14(2):199–220.

Conrad, Courtenay R., Daniel W. Hill, Jr., and Will H. Moore. 2017. "Torture and the Limits of Democratic Institutions." *Journal of Peace Research.* 55(1): 3–17.

Conrad, Courtenay and Will H. Moore. 2010. "What Stops the Torture?" *American Journal of Political Science* 54(2):459–476.

Conrad, Courtenay and Emily Ritter. 2013. "Treaties, Tenure, and Torture: The Conflicting Domestic Effects of International Law." *Journal of Politics* 75(2):397–409.

Coppedge, Michael, John Gerring, Carl Henrick, Staffan I. Linberg, Jan Teorell, David Altman, Michael Bernhard, M. Steven Fish, Adam Glynn, Allen Hicken, Kyle L. Marquardt, Kelly McMann, Pamela Paxton, Daniel Pemstein, Brigitte

Seim, Rachel Sigman, Svend-Erik Skaaning, Jeffrey Staton, Steven Wilson, Agnes Cornell, Lisa Gastaldi, Haakon GjerlÃ„w, Nina Ilchenko, Joshua Krusell, Laura Maxwell, Valeriya Eitan Tzelgov, Yi-ting Wang, Tore Wig, and Daniel Ziblatt. 2019. *V-Dem Codebook v9*. V-Dem Project V-Dem Institute: Department of Political Science, University of Gothenburg. Available at: //www.v-dem.net/en/data/data-version-9/.

Council of Europe. 2004. *Protocol No. 14 to the Convention for the Protection of Human Rights and Fundamental Freedoms, Amending the Control System of the Convention*. Strasbourg, France: Council of Europe.

Coveney, Crystal. 2014. "Boyce et al. v Barbados." *Loyola of Los Angeles International and Comparative Law Review* 36(1):1029–1047.

Dai, Xinyuan. 2005. "Why Comply? The Domestic Constituency Mechanism." *International Organization* 59(2):363–398.

Davenport, Christian. 1995. "Multi-Dimensional Threat Perception and State Repression: An Inquiry into Why States Apply Negative Sanctions." *American Journal of Political Science* 39(3):683–713.

2007. *State Repression and the Domestic Democratic Peace*. New York: Cambridge University Press.

Davenport, Christian and David A. Armstrong II. 2004. "Democracy and the Violation of Human Rights: A Statistical Analysis from 1976 to 1996." *American Journal of Political Science* 48(3):538–554.

Davenport, Christian, Will H. Moore and David Armstrong. 2007. "The Puzzle of Abu Ghraib: Are Democratic Institutions a Palliative or Panacea?" Available at: SSRN: https://papers.ssrn.com/sol3/papers.cfm?abstract_id=1022367.

Delaplace, Edouad and Matt Pollard. 2006. "Torture Prevention in Practice." *Torture* 16(2):220–246.

DeMeritt, Jacqueline H. R. and Courtenay Conrad. 2019. "Repression Substitution: Shifting Human Rights Violations in Response to UN Naming and Shaming." *Civil Wars* 21(1): 128–152.

Dilorenzo, Sarah. 2018. "Rio Could Be 'Laboratory' for Solving Brazil's Crime Crisis." *Washington Post*. Available at: https://wapo.st/2DNY88W.

Downs, George W., David M. Rocke, and Peter N. Barsoom. 1996. "Is the Good News about Compliance Good News about Cooperation?" *International Organization* 50(3):379–406.

ECtHR. 2017. *The European Court of Human Rights in Facts and Figures 2016*. Strasbourg, France: European Court of Human Rights. Available at: www.echr.coe.int/Documents/Facts_Figures_2016_ENG.pdf.

Englehart, Neil A. 2009. "State Capacity, State Failure, and Human Rights." *Journal of Peace Research* 46(2):163–180.

Fariss, Christopher J. 2014. "Respect for Human Rights Has Improved over Time: Modeling the Changing Standard of Accountability." *American Political Science Review* 108(2):297–318.

2018. "The Changing Standard of Accountability and the Positive Relationship between Human Rights Treaty Ratification and Compliance." *British Journal of Political Science* 48(1):239–271.

Frost, Sarah. 2014. "Lysias Fleury et al. v. Haiti." *Loyola of Los Angeles International and Comparative Law Review* 36:1095–1112.

Garriga, Ana Carolina. 2016. "Human Rights Regimes, Reputation, and Foreign Direct Investment." *International Studies Quarterly* 60(1):160–172.

Gauri, Varun and Daniel M. Brinks. 2008. "Introduction: The Elements of Legalization and the Triangular Shape of Social and Economic Rights." In *Courting Social Justice: Judicial Enforcement of Social and Economic Rights in the Developing World*, eds. Varun Gauri and Daniel M. Brinks. Cambridge, UK: Cambridge University Press pp. 1–37.

Gelman, Andrew and Jennifer Hill. 2007. *Data Analysis Using Regression and Multilevel/Hierarchical Models*. New York: Cambridge University Press.

Geneva Academy. 2015. "Fundamental Challenges of the UN Human Rights Treaty Body System." Available at: https://tinyurl.com/rpvf4db.

Gibbs, Jack P. 1975. *Crime, Punishment, and Deterrence*. New York: Elsevier.

Gibney, Mark, Linda Cornett, Reed Wood, Peter Haschke, and Daniel Arnon. 2016. "Political Terror Scale." Available at: http://www.politicalterrorscale.org/.

Gleditsch, Nils Petter, Peter Wallensteen, Mikael Eriksson Margareta Sollenberg, and Havard Strand. 2002. "Armed Conflict 1946–2001: A New Dataset." *Journal of Peace Research* 39(5):615–637.

Gourevitch, Peter. 1978. "The Second Image Reversed: The International Sources of Domestic Politics." *International Organization* 32(4):881–912.

GOV.UK. 2015. "Mexico and Impunity: A Case Study from the 2014 Human Rights and Democracy Report." Available at: https://www.gov.uk/government/case-studies/mexico-and-impunity.

Grasmick, Harold G. and George J. Bryjak. 1980. "The Deterrent Effect of the Perceived Severity of Punishment." *Social Forces* 59(2):471–491.

Guzman, Andrew T. 2008. *How International Law Works: A Rational Choice Theory*. New York: Oxford University Press.

Hacaoglu, Selcan. 2007. *Turkey Says Attack Was Suicide Bombing*. Washington DC: Washington Post. Available at: https://wapo.st/2BzIfld.

Hafner-Burton, Emilie M. 2005. "Trading Human Rights: How Preferential Trade Agreements Influence Government Repression." *International Organization* 59(3):593–629.

2008. "Sticks and Stones: Naming and Shaming and the Human Rights Enforcement Problem." *International Organization* 62(4):689–716.

2013. *Making Human Rights a Reality*. Princeton, NJ: Princeton University Press.

Hafner-Burton, Emilie M., Brad L. LeVeck, and David G. Victor. 2016. "How Activists Perceive the Utility of International Law." *Journal of Politics* 78(1):167–180.

Hafner-Burton, Emilie M. and Kiyoteru Tsutsui. 2005. "Human Rights in a Globalizing World: The Paradox of Empty Promises." *American Journal of Sociology* 110(5):1373–1411.

Hafner-Burton, Emilie M., Kiyoteru Tsutsui, and John W. Meyer. 2008. "International Human Rights Law and the Politics of Legitimation: Repressive States and Human Rights Treaties." *International Sociology* 23(1):115–141.

Haglund, Jillienne and Courtney Hillebrecht. 2019. "Overlapping International Human Rights Institutions: Introducing the Women's Rights Recommendations Digital Database (WR2D2)." Forthcoming at *Journal of Peace Research*.

Harbom, Lotta and Peter Wallensteen. 2005. "Armed Conflict and Its International Dimensions, 1946–2004." *Journal of Peace Research* 42(5):623–635.

Hassan, Heather. 2014. "Bámaca Velásquez v. Guatemala." *Loyola of Los Angeles International and Comparative Law Review* 36(5):1563–1596.

Hathaway, Oona A. 2002. "Do Human Rights Treaties Make a Difference?" *Yale Law Journal* 111(8):1935–2042.

Hawkins, Darren and Wade Jacoby. 2010. "Partial Compliance: A Comparison of the European and Inter-American American Courts of Human Rights." *Journal of International Law and International Relations* 6(1):35–85.

Helfer, Laurence R. and Anne-Marie Slaughter. 1997. "Toward a Theory of Effective Supranational Adjudication." *Yale Law Journal* 107(2):273–392.

Helfer, Laurence R. and Erik Voeten. 2014. "International Courts as Agents of Legal Change: Evidence from LGBT Rights in Europe." *International Organization* 68(1):77–110.

Henisz, Witold J. 2002. "The Institutional Environment for Infrastructure Investment." *Industrial and Corporate Change* 11(2):355–389.

Hill, Daniel W. Jr. 2010. "Estimating the Effects of Human Rights Treaties on State Behavior." *Journal of Politics* 72(4):1161–1174.

Hillebrecht, Courtney. 2012. "The Domestic Mechanisms of Compliance with International Human Rights Law: Case Studies from the Inter-American Human Rights System." *Human Rights Quarterly* 34(4):959–985.

2014. *Domestic Politics and International Human Rights Tribunals: The Problem of Compliance*. Cambridge, UK: Cambridge University Press.

Hillebrecht, Courtney, Dona-Gene Mitchell, and Sergio C. Wals. 2015. "Perceived Human Rights and Support for New Democracies: Lessons from Mexico." *Democratization* 22(7):1230–1249.

Hood, Roger and Florence Seemungal. 2010. *Public Opinion on the Mandatory Death Penalty in Trinidad: A Summary of the Main Findings of a Survey*. London: The Death Penalty Project. Available at: https://tinyurl.com/sob7hqd.

Human Rights Watch. 2004. *Rigging the Rule of Law: Judicial Independence Under Siege in Venezuela*. New York: Human Rights Watch. Available at: https://bit.ly/2Qodjxa.

Huneeus, Alexandra. 2012. "Courts Resisting Courts: Lessons from the Inter-American Court's Struggle to Enforce Human Rights." *Cornell International Law Journal* 44(3):494–533.

IACHR. 2016. "IACHR Overcomes Its Severe Financial Crisis of 2016 and Thanks Countries and Donors Who Made It Possible." Washington, DC: Author.

International Justice Resource Center. 2014. *New IACtHR Judgments Address Length of Criminal Proceedings and Forced Disappearances*. San Francisco, CA: International Justice Resource Center. Available at: https://bit.ly/2C6jopy.

Jo, Hyeran and Beth A. Simmons. 2016. "Can the International Criminal Court Deter Atrocity?" *International Organization* 70(3):443–475.

Kahan, Dan M. 1997. "Social Influence, Social Meaning, and Deterrence." *Virginia Law Review* 83(2):349–395.

Keller, Helen and Alec Stone-Sweet. 2008. *A Europe of Rights: The Impact of the ECHR on National Legal Systems*. New York: Oxford University Press.

Kelley, Judith. 2008. "Assessing the Complex Evolution of Norms: The Rise of International Election Monitoring." *International Organization* 62(2):221–255.

Khananashvili, Meri. 2014. "Radilla Pacheco v. Mexico" *Loyola of Los Angeles International and Comparative Law Review* 36:1789–1815.

Kieiman, Mark A. R. 2009. *When Brute Force Fails: How to Have Less Crime and Less Punishment*. Princeton, NJ: Princeton University Press.

Kornhauser, Lewis A. 2002. "Is Judicial Independence a Useful Concept?" In *Judicial Independence at the Crossroads: An Interdisciplinary Approach*, eds. Steven B. Burbank and Barry Friedman. New York: Sage Publications, pp. 45–55.

Kristicevic, Viviana. 2007. "Reflections on the Enforcement of the Decisions of the Inter-American Human Rights System." In *Implementation of the Decisions of the Inter-American Human Rights System: Jurisprudence, Regulations and National Experiences*, eds. Viviana Kristicevic and Lilliana Tojo. Buenos Aires: Center for Justice and International Law, pp. 15–112.

Krommendijk, Jasper. 2015. "The Domestic Effectiveness of International Human Rights Monitoring in Established Democracies. The Case of the UN Human Rights Treaty Bodies." *Review of International Organizations* 10(4):489–512.

Lebovic, James H. and Erik Voeten. 2009. "The Cost of Shame: International Organizations and Foreign Aid in the Punishing of Human Rights Violators." *Journal of Peace Research* 46(1):79–97.

Linzer, Drew A. and Jeffrey K. Staton. 2015. "A Global Measure of Judicial Independence: 1948–2012." *Journal of Law and Courts* 3(2):223–256.

Lupu, Yonatan. 2013a. "Best Evidence: The Role of Information in Domestic Judicial Enforcement of International Human Rights Agreements." *International Organization* 67(3):469–503.

    2013b. "The Informative Power of Treaty Commitment: Using the Spatial Model to Address Selection Effects." *American Journal of Political Science* 57(4):912–925.

    2015. "Legislative Veto Players and the Effects of International Human Rights Agreements." *American Journal of Political Science* 59(3):578–594.

Marinova, Raya. 2015. "Heliodoro Portugal v. Panama." *Loyola of Los Angeles International and Comparative Law Review* 37:1565–1589.

Marshall, Monty, Keith Jaggers, and Ted Gurr. 2019. *Polity IV Project: Political Regime Characteristics and Transitions, 1800–2018. Data Users' Manual*. Center for Systemic Peace. Available at: www.systemicpeace.org/inscr/p4manualv2018.pdf.

Meisel, Sascha and Zach Tripodes. 2015. "Gelman v. Uruguay." *Loyola of Los Angeles International and Comparative Law Review* 37:1861–1885.

Mitchell, Neil J. 2004. *Agents of Atrocity: Leaders, Followers, and the Violation of Human Rights in Civil War*. New York: Palgrave Macmillan.

Moe, Terry M. 1984. "The New Economics of Organization." *American Journal of Political Science* 28(4):739–777.

Nagin, Daniel S. and Greg Pogarsky. 2001. "Integrating Celerity, Impulsivity, and Extralegal Sanction Threats into a Model of General Deterrence: Theory and Evidence." *Criminology* 39(4):865–892.

Neyer, Jürgen and Dieter Wolf. 2005. "The Analysis of Compliance with International Rules: Definitions, Variables, and Methodology." In *Law and Governance in Postnational Europe: Compliance Beyond the Nation-State*, eds. Michael Zürn and Christian Joerges. Cambridge, UK: Cambridge University Press, pp. 40–64.

OECD. 2018. *International Development Statistics (IDS) Online Databases*. Paris, France: Organization for Economic Co-operation and Development. Available at: http://www.oecd.org/development/financing-sustainable-development/development-finance-data/idsonline.htm.

Office of the United Nations High Commissioner for Human Rights. 2002. *Human Rights and Law Enforcement: A Trainer's Guide on Human Rights for the Police*. Geneva, Switzerland: OHCHR. Available at: www.ohchr.org/Documents/Publications/training5Add2en.pdf.

Páez, Ángel. 2008. "Peru: El Fronton Massacre Case Heads Back to Inter-American Court." *Inter-Press Service News Agency*. Available at: https://bit.ly/2BzKyol.

Pasqualucci, Jo M. 2003. *The Practice and Procedure of the Inter-American Court of Human Rights*. Cambridge, UK: Cambridge University Press.

Peace Brigades International. 2010. "The Radilla Case before the Inter-American Court of Human Rights: Interview with Humberto Guerrero, Legal Director of the Mexican Commission for the Defence and Promotion of Human Rights." Available at: www.pbi-mexico.org/fileadmin/user_files/projects/mexico/files/Entrevista_16_CMDPDH_RadillaCoIDH_EN.pdf.

Posner, Eric A. 2014. *The Twilight of Human Rights Law*. New York: Oxford University Press.

Posner, Eric A. and Miguel F. P. de Figueiredo. 2005. "Is the International Court of Justice Biased?" *Journal of Legal Studies* 34(2):599–630.

Posner, Eric A and John C. Yoo. 2005. "Judicial Independence in International Tribunals." *California Law Review* 93(1):1–74.

Pourgourides, Christos. 2010. "Strengthening Subsidiarity: Integrating the Court's Case-Law into National Law and Judicial Practice." Prepared for the Conference on Subsidiarity, Skopje, October 1–2, 2010.

Powell, Emilia J. and Jeffrey K. Staton. 2009. "Domestic Judicial Institutions and Human Rights Treaty Violation." *International Studies Quarterly* 53(1):149–174.

Raustiala, Kal. 2000. "Compliance and Effectiveness in International Regulatory Cooperation." *Case Western Reserve Journal of International Law* 32(3):387–440.

Rejali, Darius. 2007. *Torture and Democracy*. Princeton, NJ: Princeton University Press.

Richards, David L. and Ronald D. Gelleny. 2007. "Good Things to Those Who Wait? National Elections and Government Respect for Human Rights." *Journal of Peace Research* 44(4):505–523.

Richards, David L., Ronald D. Gelleny, and David H. Sacko. 2001. "Money with a Mean Streak? Foreign Economic Penetration and Government Respect for Human Rights in Developing Countries." *International Studies Quarterly* 45(2):219–239.

Ross, Stephen A. 1973. "The Economic Theory of Agency: The Principal's Problem." *American Economic Review* 63(2):134–139.

Saenz, Rodolfo D. 2010. "Confronting Mexico's Enforced Disappearance Monsters: How the ICC Can Contribute to the Process of Realizing Criminal Justice Reform in Mexico." *Vanderbilt Journal of Transnational Law* 50:45–112.

Samyan, Emma. 2017. "Zambrano Vélez et al. v. Ecuador." *Loyola of Los Angeles International and Comparative Law Review* 30(3):1743–1760.

Sandholtz, Wayne, Yining Bei and Kayla Caldwell. 2018. "Backlash and International Human Rights Courts." In *Contracting Human Rights: Crisis, Accountability, and Opportunity*, eds. Alison Brysk and Michael Stohl. Cheltenham, UK: Edward Elgar, pp. 159–178.

Savarese, Mauricio. 2018. *President Calls in Army as Murderous Gang Crime Threatens to Overwhelm Rio de Janeiro*. London: Independent. Available at: https://tinyurl.com/tmum4ap.

Scharrer, Olivia. 2014a. "Ticona Estrada v. Bolivia." *Loyola of Los Angeles International and Comparative Law Review* 36:1237–1255.

2014b. "Trujillo Oroza v Bolivia." *Loyola of Los Angeles International and Comparative Law Review* 36:1257–1279.

Sikkink, Kathryn. 2011. *The Justice Cascade: How Human Rights Prosecutions are Changing World Politics*. New York: W.W. Norton & Company.

Simmons, Beth A. 1998. "Compliance with International Agreements." *Annual Review of Political Science* 1(1):75–93.

2009. *Mobilizing for Human Rights: International Law in Domestic Politics*. New York: Cambridge University Press.

Soltman, Daniel. 2013. "Applauding Uruguay's Quest for Justice: Dictatorship, Amnesty, and Repeal of Uruguay Law No. 15.848." *Washington University Global Studies Law Review* 12(4):829–848.

Sorens, Jason and William Ruger. 2012. "Does Foreign Investment Really Reduce Repression?" *International Studies Quarterly* 56(2):427–436.

Stafford, Mark C. and Mark Warr. 1993. "A Reconceptualization of General and Specific Deterrence." *Journal of Research in Crime and Delinquency* 30(2):123–135.

Stargardter, Gabriel. 2018. *Murders, Killings by Cops Rise in Rio de Janeiro, Six Months into Intervention*. London: Reuters. Available at: https://reut.rs/2PW8tHd.

Staton, Jeffrey K. 2006. "Constitutional Review and the Selective Promotion of Case Results." *American Journal of Political Science* 50(1):98–112.

Staton, Jeffrey K. and Will H. Moore. 2011. "Judicial Power in Domestic and International Politics." *International Organization* 65(3):553–587.

Staton, Jeffrey K. and Alexia Romero. 2019. "Rational Remedies: The Role of Opinion Clarity in the Inter-American Human Rights System." *International Studies Quarterly* 63(3): 477–491

Staton, Jeffrey K. and Georg Vanberg. 2008. "The Value of Vagueness: Delegation, Defiance, and Judicial Opinions." *American Journal of Political Science* 52(3):504–519.

Telesur. 2017. "Morales Declares 'Total Independence' from World Bank and IMF." Available at: www.telesurenglish.net/news/Morales-Declares-Total-Independence-from-World-Bank-and-IMF--20170722-0020.html.

Tello, Sandra Acosta. 2016. "Perozo et al. v. Venezuela." *Loyola of Los Angeles International and Comparative Law Review* 38(4):1035–1066.

Terenzani, Michaela. 2010. "Slovakia Ignores Court, Deports Labsi to Algeria." *The Slovak Spectator*. Available at: https://bit.ly/2QK1L74.

Thompson, Rhonda. 2010. "Hang Them!" *Nation News*. Available at: www.nationnews.com/nationnews/news/2155/hang.

Tsebelis, George. 2002. *Veto Players: How Political Institutions Work*. Princeton NJ: Princeton University Press.

United Nations Committee Against Torture. 2015. "Concluding Observations on the Third Periodic Report of Slovakia." Available at: https://digitallibrary.un.org/record/815798.

United Nations News. 2012. "UN Official Welcomes ASEAN Commitment to Human Rights, but Concerned over Declaration Wording." Available at: https://news.un.org/en/story/2012/11/426012.

US State Department. 2001. *Guatemala 2000 Country Report on Human Rights Practices*. Washington, DC: Bureau of Democracy, Human Rights, and Labor. Available at: https://2009-2017.state.gov/j/drl/rls/hrrpt/2000/wha/775.htm.

——— 2006. *Bolivia 2006 Country Report on Human Rights Practices*. Washington DC, United States: Bureau of Labor, Democracy, and Human Rights. Available at: https://2009-2017.state.gov/j/drl/rls/hrrpt/2005/61717.htm.

——— 2009. *Turkey 2008 Country Report on Human Rights Practices*. Washington, DC: Bureau of Democracy, Human Rights, and Labor. Available at: https://2009-2017.state.gov/j/drl/rls/hrrpt/2008/eur/119109.htm.

Vanberg, Georg. 2005. *The Politics of Constitutional Review in Germany*. New York: Cambridge University Press.

Voeten, Erik. 2007. "The Politics of International Judicial Appointments: Evidence from the European Court of Human Rights." *International Organization* 61(4):669–701.

——— 2008. "The Impartiality of International Judges: Evidence from the European Court of Human Rights." *American Political Science Review* 102(4):417–433.

——— 2012a. "Does a Professional Judiciary Induce More Compliance? Evidence from the European Court of Human Rights." Available at: Paper presented at the International Studies Association Annual Conference, San Diego, April 2012. Available at: https://tinyurl.com/yyfw55zt

——— 2012b. "International Judicial Independence.: In *Interdisciplinary Perspectives on International Law and International Relations*, eds. Jeffrey L. Dunoff and Mark A. Pollack. Cambridge, UK: Cambridge University Press, pp. 421–444.

——— 2014. "Domestic Implementation of European Court of Human Rights Judgments: Legal Infrastructure and Government Effectiveness Matter: A Reply to Dia Anagnostou and Alina Mungiu-Pippidi." *The European Journal of International Law* 25(1):229–238.

——— 2017. "Competition and Complementarity between Global and Regional Human Rights Institutions." *Global Policy* 8(1):119–123.

——— 2019. "Populism and Backlashes against International Courts." *Perspectives on Politics*. Forthcoming.

von Hirsch, Andrew, Anthony E. Bottoms, Elizabeth Burney, and P.-O. Wilkstrom. 1999. *Criminal Deterrence and Sentence Severity: An Analysis of Recent Research*. Portland, Oregon: Hart Publishing.

Von Stein, Jana. 2005. "Do Treaties Constrain or Screen? Selection Bias and Treaty Compliance." *American Political Science Review* 99(4):611–622.
Wallace, Geoffrey P. R. 2013. "International Law and Public Attitudes toward Torture: An Experimental Study." *International Organization* 67(1):105–140.
Weingast, Barry R. 1997. "The Political Foundations of Democracy and the Rule of Law." *American Political Science Review* 91(2):245–263.
Wickham, Peter. 2010. "To Hang or Not to Hang." Available at: www.nationnews.com/nationnews/news/31568/hang-hang.
Williams, Emily. 2016. "Gomes Lund et al. ("Guerrilha do Araguaia") v. Brazil." *Loyola of Los Angeles International and Comparative Law Review* 38:1645–1669.
Woody, Christopher. 2018. "Brazil took an 'Extreme Measure' to Fight Crime in One of Its Biggest Cities, but It's Only Made Things Worse." *Business Insider*. Available at: https://tinyurl.com/v4htwuv.
World Bank. 2014. *Worldwide Governance Indicators*. Washington, DC: World Bank. Available at: https://info.worldbank.org/governance/wgi/.
    2017. *World Bank Development Indicators*. Washington, DC: World Bank. Available at: https://datacatalog.worldbank.org/dataset/world-development-indicators.
Wright, Valerie. 2010. *Deterrence in Criminal Justice: Evaluating Certainty vs. Severity of Punishment*. Washington, DC: The Sentencing Project.
Yeung, Rachel. 2016. "Montero Aranguren et al. v. Venezuela." *Loyola of Los Angeles International and Comparative Law Review* 38:1713–1732.
Zimring, Franklin E. and Gordon J. Hawkins. 1973. *Deterrence: The Legal Threat in Crime Control*. Chicago: University of Chicago Press.

Index

accountability, 9, 36, 89
adverse judgment, 1–4, 13, 24, 33, 46–47, 117, 207, 209, 211, 213
   data, 94, 117
African Court on Human and People's Rights, 245
Aksoy v. Turkey, 114
American Convention on Human Rights, 1, 3, 34, 51, 58–59, 81, 93–94, 96, 100, 113, 117, 119, 134, 139, 152–153, 167–168, 173, 182–183, 191, 200–201, 209, 213
amnesty, 133–135, 167, 171
Amnesty International, 1–2, 25, 86, 169
Argentina, 33, 64, 101, 183, 184
Association of Southeast Asian Nations, 246
asylum, 136, 169, 170
Aydin v. Turkey, 111–112

Bámaca Velásquez v. Guatemala, 213
Barbados, 17, 97, 101, 153–155
Belgium, 99–101, 136, 248
Ben Khemais v. Italy, 136, 170
Blanco Romero et al. v. Venezuela, 181
Bolivia, 1–2, 4, 101, 173–175
Boyce et al. v. Barbados, 153
Brazil, 25–26, 57, 101, 170
Bulacio v. Argentina, 64, 183

capacity
   fiscal flexibility, 53, 112–113, 126–129, 215, 230, 233
   policy change feasibility, 50–52, 110, 112, 114–115, 122–124, 229, 233
CEJIL, 26
Chile, 51, 97, 101
civil and political rights, 6, 52, 112, 115–120, 229–230
   Americas, 117, 124–126
   Europe, 117, 122–123

Cingranelli, Richards, and Clay human rights dataset, 4, 24, 78, 86, 104, 121, 124–125, 129, 131, 138, 143, 145, 150–151, 158, 160, 178–179, 182, 186–187, 190, 196–197, 199, 200, 214, 225
civil society, 11, 33, 40, 55, 255, 260–261
Claude Reyes v. Chile, 51
Colombia, 17, 63, 97, 101
Committee Against Torture, 212, 243–244
Committee of Ministers, 34, 80, 111–112, 115, 126, 235, 237, 244
comparing regional courts, 13–14, 17–20, 82–83, 85, 102, 106–107, 151, 163–164, 180, 190, 202, 232–240
compliance, 38–39, 41–42, 79, 88–90, 107
   checklist, 82
   delegative, 80
control variables, 254–257, 260–263, 273–274, 292, 306
Council of Europe, 12, 15, 79–81, 87, 97, 105, 120–121

data, 115, 137, 172
   adverse judgments, 13, 92, 94–97, 116–118, 138, 172
   civil and political rights, 116
   compliance, 88–89
   electoral timing, 140
   electoral competitiveness, 147
   foreign direct investment, 175
   institutional investor country credit rating, 127
   judicial power, 184
   legislative opposition, 193–194
   physical integrity rights, 2, 4, 86–87, 103–104, 115–116, 137–138, 172
   political imprisonment, 200
   political stability, 156
   torture, 187, 196

democracy, 34, 54, 100, 256
deterrence, 5, 28, 42
  general, 5, 29, 31, 76, 79, 91, 97, 102, 106, 108, 247–248
  prosecutorial, 30, 35
  social, 30, 35, 36
  specific, 5, 29, 33, 78
disappearance, 1–3, 25, 33, 104, 134, 139, 166–167, 170–171, 174, 181, 191–193, 214, 234
domestic politics, 13, 26, 38, 234

Ecuador, 17, 97, 100–101, 139–140
economic elites, 7, 22, 27, 60, 166, 168, 173, 175, 177–178, 180–181, 231, 236, 246
effectiveness, 40, 79, 85, 88, 90, 107
El Salvador, 101–102, 166–168
elections, 56, 140–142, 147
enforcement, 5–6, 8–9, 37, 42, 228
Erdogan, Recep Tayyip, 24–25
European Convention on Human Rights, 76, 79, 94, 95, 100, 111, 117, 119–120, 124, 126, 137, 169–170, 187–188, 196–197, 211, 249
European Court of Human Rights, 12–16, 24–25, 34, 38, 41, 79, 82, 92–93, 96–98, 106, 108, 110–111, 114, 122–123, 126, 128, 135–136, 142, 149, 156–157, 161, 169, 170, 176, 185, 194, 207, 211, 218, 221, 225, 248
  Committee of Ministers, 34, 80, 111–112, 115, 126, 235, 237, 244
  exhaustion of domestic remedies, 82
  practice and procedure, 80
  procedural violations, 92–94
  repeat cases, 37, 81, 245
  resource challenge, 244
  substantive violations, 92–93
executive, 4, 6
  capacity, 6, 27, 49, 110
  capacity and willingness, 69, 207, 215, 218, 232, 239
  decision making, 47
  implementation, 38
  policy change, 41–42, 44, 45, 52, 229
  trade-off, 44, 46
  willingness, 7, 27, 54, 230
extrajudicial executions, 2, 24, 46, 104, 167, 234

Fariss latent variable estimates, 86–88, 103, 115, 137, 263
Favela Nova Brasília v. Brazil, 25
feasibility of policy change, 6, 48, 50, 110, 112, 114–115, 122, 229–230
fiscal flexibility, 7, 53, 112, 114, 126–132, 230
foreign aid, 60, 62, 74, 168, 174–175
foreign direct investment, 60–61, 74, 175, 231

Gelman v. Uruguay, 133–134
Germany, 99–100, 207–208

Gomes Lund et al. ("Guerrilha do Araguaia") v. Brazil, 170
Greece, 99–100, 114
Guatemala, 17, 97, 100–101, 213–214

Haiti, 17, 100–101, 112–113
Heliodoro Portugal v. Panama, 138
Hilaire, Constantine, and Benjamin et al. v. Trinidad and Tobago, 58, 152
human rights monitoring, 9, 34, 41–42, 44–45, 49, 51–53
human rights training programs, 38, 41–44, 52, 86, 111, 115, 127, 134, 140, 167, 174, 212
hypothesis, 52, 53, 57, 59, 62, 66, 68–70

institutional design, 10, 12, 235, 242
  membership, 10
  mechanism of influence, 10
  independence, 11–12
  Inter-American Commission on Human Rights, 15, 17, 32, 81–82, 84–85, 113, 245
  Inter-American Court of Human Rights, 14, 17–18, 25, 32, 34, 38, 41, 51–52, 57–58, 64, 82, 85, 94, 97, 98, 100, 106, 108, 112–113, 124, 129, 133, 138–139, 143, 150, 152–153, 158, 162, 166–167, 169–170, 173, 178, 181, 183, 189, 191, 199, 209, 213, 220, 223, 225
  exhaustion of domestic remedies, 82
  practice and procedure, 81–82
  resource challenge, 245
International Criminal Court, 9, 29–31, 35, 252
international human rights law, 8, 36–37, 46, 55–56, 241, 251
  backlash, 252
international treaties, 8, 10, 241–242, 251
investigations, 2, 29, 93–94, 111, 113, 127, 166–167, 169, 181, 191, 209–212, 248
Iribarren Pinillos v. Spain, 169
Italy, 15, 81, 99–100, 136, 169–170
Iwańczuk v. Poland, 78

Jalloh v. Germany, 207
judicial power, 7, 22, 64–66, 84, 182, 184–190, 214, 231, 237–238
jurisdiction, 9, 31, 58, 76, 91, 97, 100, 102, 105, 120–122, 152, 242

Kaverzin v. Ukraine, 126
Koky and Others v. Slovakia, 211

Labsi v. Slovakia, 136
legislative opposition, 27, 67–68, 172, 191–203, 205–206, 231, 238–239
legitimacy, 11, 14, 63, 242, 250
Lysias Fleury et al. v. Haiti, 112

Manoussakis and Others v. Greece, 114
mass public, 7, 19, 54, 57, 60, 74, 133, 135, 137–138, 160
measurement, 86, 91, 103, 115–116, 119, 127–128, 137, 156, 175, 184, 193–194
Mexico, 2, 54, 101, 170, 191
Miguel Castro-Castro Prison v. Peru, 51
military, 1–3, 25, 33, 35, 41–42, 138, 191–192, 213, 234
Montero Aranguren et al. v Venezuela, 167
Mubilanzila Mayeka and Kaniki Mitunga v. Belgium, 136, 248

national human rights institutions, 44–45, 255, 261
national judiciary, 62–65
national legislature, 62, 66, 67

Organization of American States, 10, 81, 102, 121, 245

Panama, 100–101, 138–139
Perozo et al. v. Venezuela, 209
Peru, 17, 51–52, 63–65, 97, 100–101, 234
physical integrity rights, 84–86, 103–104, 115, 138, 172
  Americas, 87, 124, 129
  Europe, 87, 123, 128
Poland, 76–78, 99, 129
police, 6, 25–26, 35, 41–42, 44, 49, 112–115, 126, 167–169, 183, 207, 209, 211–212
policy change, 6–7, 27, 44–48
policy implications, 19, 240
political elites, 7, 47, 62–63, 168, 172, 181, 231, 237
political imprisonment, 2, 104, 201–202
political stability, 7, 74, 154–160
principal-agent theory, 44, 49, 52, 53, 187

Radilla Pacheco v. Mexico, 3, 170, 191
recommendations, 10–11, 212, 241–244, 251
regional court judges, 249
repeat cases, 37, 81, 245
research design, 19, 85, 91, 115–116, 118–120, 127, 138, 156, 172, 184, 194, 215
Rohac Hernández and Others v. El Salvador, 166
Russia, 15, 81, 97, 99–100, 109

Saadi v. Italy, 169
selection, 120
  Americas, 121
  Europe, 120
Slovakia, 99, 136, 211–212
socialization, 31
Spain, 99, 169
subsidiarity, 248

Temer, Michel, 25
terrorism, 7, 24, 57–58, 137, 156, 158
Ticona Estrada v. Bolivia, 1
torture, 2–3, 24–25, 55–56, 58, 67, 126–127, 133, 138, 169–170, 174, 182, 187–188, 191, 196–198, 212
Trinidad and Tobago, 58–59, 152–153
Trujillo Oroza v. Bolivia, 173
Turkey, 15, 24–25, 99–100, 109–112, 114, 115

Ukraine, 15, 97, 99, 126–127
United Communist Party of Turkey and Others v. Turkey, 110
United Kingdom, 99–100, 248–249
United Nations, 9, 97, 102, 191, 212, 241
Uruguay, 17, 97, 100–101, 133–135
US State Department, 2, 24, 86, 174, 213–214

Venezuela, 100–101, 167–168, 181–183, 208–210, 234, 252

World Bank, 53, 62, 154
willingness
  domestic political elite pressure, 62–66, 168, 171, 181, 184, 191, 193, 217, 231, 237, 238
  foreign economic elite pressure, 60, 61, 166, 168, 173, 175, 216, 231, 236
  job security, 56, 133, 138, 140, 142–143, 147, 149–151, 230, 235
  mass public pressure, 54, 55, 57, 133, 151, 154, 157, 160, 216, 230
  national judiciary, 181, 184
  national legislature, 191, 193
  political and social threats, 57, 59, 135, 152, 154–155, 157, 160, 230, 233

Ximenes Lopes v. Brazil, 57

Zambrano Vélez et al. v. Ecuador, 139

Lightning Source UK Ltd.
Milton Keynes UK
UKHW022323020920
369267UK00005B/38